𝒟.

PRINCIPLES
OF
ENVIRONMENTAL MANAGEMENT:
THE GREENING OF BUSINESS

PRINCIPLES
OF
ENVIRONMENTAL MANAGEMENT:
THE GREENING OF BUSINESS

~

Rogene A. Buchholz

College of Business Administration
Loyola University of New Orleans

PRENTICE HALL, *Englewood Cliffs, New Jersey 07632*

Library of Congress Cataloging-in-Publication Data

Buchholz, Rogene A.
    Principles of environmental management / Rogene A. Buchholz.
      p.   cm.
    Includes bibliographical references and index.
    ISBN 0-13-720541-4 (paper)
    1. Environmental policy. 2. Environmental protection.
    3. Industrial management--Environmental aspects. 4. Social
    responsibility of business.   I. Title.
    HC79.E5B83   1993
    363.7--dc20   92-247
                                                          CIP

Acquisition Editor: *Alison Reeves*
Production Editor: *Edith Pullman*
Copy Editor: *Anne Lesser*
Cover Design: *JoAnne Cournoyer*
Prepress Buyer: *Trudy Pisciotti*
Manufacturing Buyer: *Bob Anderson*
Supplements Editor: *Lisamarie Brassini*
Editorial Assistant: *Diane Pierano*

Cover Art: Vincent van Gogh, *The Starry Night,* (1889). Oil on canvas, 29 × 36¼".
  Collection, The Museum of Modern Art, New York. Acquired through the Lillie
  P. Bliss Bequest. Photograph © 1992 The Museum of Modern Art, New York.

Printed in the United States of America

10 9 8 7 6 5 4 3 2 1

ISBN 0-13-720541-4

Prentice-Hall International (UK) Limited, *London*
Prentice-Hall of Australia Pty. Limited, *Sydney*
Prentice-Hall Canada Inc., *Toronto*
Prentice-Hall Hispanoamericana, S.A., *Mexico*
Prentice-Hall of India Private Limited, *New Delhi*
Prentice-Hall of Japan, Inc., *Tokyo*
Simon & Schuster Asia Pte. Ltd., *Singapore*
Editora Prentice-Hall do Brasil, Ltda., *Rio de Janeiro*

To my teenage daughter,

Heidi Buchholz,

whose generation will have to cope
with the environmental problems we have left them.
Hopefully this book will make a contribution
to the solution of these problems
and help us understand the urgency of the situation.

CONTENTS

PART III RESPONSES TO ENVIRONMENTAL PROBLEMS

PREFACE

Several years ago, the National Wildlife Federation (NWF) conducted an informal telephone survey of several instructors at schools of business and management around the country. These instructors, for the most part, taught courses in business and society, business and public policy, or strategic management. The purpose of the survey was to determine if anything of substance regarding the physical environment and resource management was being taught at these schools.

The general conclusion was that not much environmental material was being taught in the business curriculum. None of the courses dealt very thoroughly with environmental concepts and issues, and there was no course, either required or elective, that dealt exclusively with environmental concerns.

The NWF then decided to do something to promote the teaching of the environment in schools of business and management. It formed an outreach committee composed of half a dozen members of the Corporate Conservation Council (CCC). The CCC is composed of 15 senior-level executives who are responsible for environmental affairs at some of the country's major corporations. The outreach committee was thus a subset of the CCC and included executives from 3M, Dow Chemical, and Du Pont.

The purpose of the committee was to develop a plan promoting the inclusion of environmental materials in courses and programs where future corporate managers are trained. It was believed that students of business and management should be sensitized to environmental issues and be made aware of the environmental consequences of managerial actions. The outreach committee decided to develop environmental materials such as case studies for business faculty and to promote the development of pilot courses in the environment at a few key schools around the country.

To accomplish this task, the committee asked three faculty members from different schools to work on putting together the actual material — writing cases about environmental issues and evaluating bibliographic and conceptual materials. The corporations represented on the committee supported these efforts and made resources available to promote the development of the materials. I was one of the three professors, and thus *Principles of Environmental Management* is an outgrowth of my involvement in this project.

It is difficult to think of a more timely book. Environmental issues such as the greenhouse effect, ozone depletion, deforestation, and acid rain have been in the news constantly. Traditional problems such as air pollution, water pollution, pesticide use, and cleanup of hazardous waste dumps are also of continuing concern. Other issues such as wetlands protection and protection of endangered species have led to a great deal of controversy in certain areas of the country. Millions of dollars have been devoted to the solution of these problems by the federal government and by corporations.

Despite the importance of environmental issues, schools of business and management have not devoted much time and effort to the physical environment. Part of the reason may be that there has been no comprehensive textbook that could be used for a separate course in environmental issues or as a supplementary text for a course in strategic management or business and society. This book fills that void and provides a comprehensive coverage of the physical environment that will be useful to students of business and management.

The text is organized into three major sections. Part I deals with the development of the environment as a major concern, and provides some background theoretical material related to ecology, environmental ethics, and environmental management from the standpoint of regulation and public policy. It provides a theoretical framework for the analysis of environmental issues and deals with some fundamental concepts that may help in understanding more concrete problems. Chapters 1 through 4 strike a balance between theory and practice by making a conscious attempt to link theoretical concepts and issues to managerial practice.

Part II discusses specific environmental problems, starting with such macro issues as global warming and ozone depletion. Chapters 6 through 11 then move into more traditional environmental issues: air pollution, water pollution, pesticide use, control of toxic substances, solid and hazardous waste disposal, deforestation and other land use problems, and coastal erosion and wetlands protection. Each chapter discusses the nature of the problem, presents a history of legislation, current legislation and regulations that are pertinent to business, and analyzes the problems with current efforts.

Finally, Part III deals with strategic approaches to environmental problems from the standpoint of business and society. Chapter 12 discusses strategies for business such as waste minimization and recycling, and what is happening in the marketing area with respect to the environment. The last chapter talks about strategies for the society as a whole related to the concept of sustainable development.

Principles of Environmental Management can serve as a primary text for a stand-alone environmental course. As stated earlier, the NWF wants to promote the teaching of such courses and intends to work with the American Assembly of Collegiate Schools of Business (AACSB) and other groups to implement this objective. The faculty on the CCC project have received numerous requests for materials from other faculty who are starting courses on the environment. Because of these requests, a casebook has already been published in conjunction with the project. This textbook complements the casebook and provides a very useful package of materials for faculty who are teaching courses in the environment. The accompanying instructor's manual contains suggestions on how to use the cases.

There have been an increasing number of conferences and workshops held over the past few years on environmental problems and the teaching of environmental issues in schools of business and management. For example, the theme of the annual meeting of the Strategic Management Society in its 1991 fall meeting was the greening of strategy. A conference was held in the fall of 1990 in Fontainebleau, France, sponsored by INSEAD (European Institute of Business Administration) and Tufts University, among others, that dealt with the teaching of environmental issues in schools of business and management. Many other conferences have been held on green marketing and other such topics of current interest. All of these activities should help to promote the teaching of environmental concepts and issues.

Besides this market, the book could serve as a supplementary text in business and society and business policy and strategy courses where instructors want to go into some depth regarding environmental issues and their significance for management and corporations. The book should also have a market in the trade for corporations that have an emphasis on environmental concerns in their management training programs. There are many activities of this sort going on in corporations, especially those that have a major impact on the environment and are seriously affected by environmental regulations.

There are many people who were extremely helpful in the writing of this book. First of all, I want to thank Alison Reeves, senior editor at Prentice Hall, for her immediate interest in this book and continuing support during the time it was being developed.

Equally important are the people I have worked with on the NWF project. My academic colleagues, Jim Post at Boston University and Alfred Marcus at the University of Minnesota, have been fun to work with and have provided a great deal of motivation and knowledge with respect to environmental interests. All the members of the CCC deserve credit for their support of this project, but a few must be singled out because of their direct and sustained contact. Dr. Robert P. Bringer, Staff Vice President, Environmental Engineering and Pollution Control of 3M Corporation, Robert L. Dostal, Director of Safety, Environmental Affairs, Security and Loss Prevention of Dow Chemical, and Dr. J. R. Cooper, Director, Environmental Affairs Division of Du Pont have been particularly helpful and supportive of the NWF project. And finally, the NWF staff, in particular Barbara Haas, Director of the CCC, and Mark Haveman, Project Coordinator on the staff of the CCC, have devoted a great deal of time and effort to the project.

Many other colleagues in the Social Issues in Management Division of the Academy of Management could also be mentioned, as we have had many interesting discussions about environmental issues over the years and I have learned a lot from them. In particular, I would like to thank Charles Schrader of Iowa State University, Sandra Waddock from Boston College Carroll School of Management, and Craig P. Dunn from San Diego State University for reviewing the first draft of this book and making many suggestions for improvement. The support I received from the dean and faculty at Loyola University was essential in developing a pilot course in environmental management that enabled me to write teaching materials which found their way into this textbook. The response of the students to the course was extremely gratifying, and their interest in the material provided me with a great deal of motivation. And finally, my daughter, to whom this book is dedicated, and I have enjoyed nature together on numerous hikes in the mountains and have had some interesting discussions about environmental problems.

To all of these people and many others, I owe a debt of gratitude for providing me with many interesting opportunities to learn more about our world and the environment in which we live. If the human race is to have any chance of survival, and I sincerely believe we are talking about a survival issue here, we must become scholars of the environment and adopt an interest in ecology and nature. Rather than just walk through nature as if it weren't there, we must become attuned to our natural environment and come to appreciate it for itself, not just for the services it provides for human beings. Some kind of environmental consciousness is essential if we are to cope successfully with the environmental problems we have created. Hopefully, this book may make a small contribution to their solution.

CHAPTER 1

DEVELOPMENT OF
ENVIRONMENTAL CONCERNS

~

Events of the past few years have accelerated an already growing concern for the environment. Substantial attention has been given to the discovery of the ozone hole over the Antarctic and the link between depletion of the ozone layer and chlorofluorocarbons (CFCs), which are now believed to be the major culprit in destroying the layer. The hot and dry summer of 1988 was confirmation enough for some scientists and policymakers to conclude, as did James Hansen, a NASA climatologist, that the greenhouse effect is real, and changing our climate in ways that are only beginning to be understood. Medical waste washed up on the shore of some eastern seaboard states contaminating the water and closing the beaches. And the dramatic oil spill from the Exxon Valdez in the pristine environment of Prince William Sound reverberated in the U.S. Congress and throughout the country and the world.

The twentieth anniversary of Earth Day celebrated in the spring of 1990 brought with it a new awareness of environmental problems and a new sense of urgency that mobilized people all over the world. Public opinion polls in the United States revealed a steady and widespread growth in public concern for environmental quality, even throughout the 1980s when a conservative administration tried its best to cut back on environmental expenditures. Data from a variety of polls indicated that the American public is increasingly aware of the gravity of environmental problems and wants the federal government to become more actively involved in their solution. Many people think tougher laws and regulations are needed and feel more money should be spent on environmental protection. They also say they are

1

more willing than ever before to pay for environmental cleanup and believe economic growth must be sacrificed in order to protect the environment.[1]

Some writers suggest that environmental consciousness has trickled down from its core of relatively affluent and well-educated supporters to the American population in general because of four factors: (1) the less well off are being visibly affected by environmental problems far more than they are suffering because of environmental protection measures, (2) environmentalists have become more equity conscious, and through their adoption of the sustainable growth logic of the appropriate technology movement, they have largely cast off charges of antigrowth obstructionism, (3) the environmental movement managed to mobilize informational and political resources successfully and avoided displacement of its goals even during the Reagan years, and (4) the youthful core of supporters of the early 1970s has matured, largely retaining its environmental ideals, and has resolved claims of conflict between environment and equity by arguing that the two goals are in many cases consistent.[2]

Growing recognition exists among corporate leaders that environmental issues are here to stay, and that environmental protection must be considered a normal part of doing business. It is becoming increasingly clear that positive corporate environmental performance cannot be adequately addressed through either the enunciation of environmental policies by top management or the efforts of environmental staff specialists, but must be institutionalized by being incorporated into the fundamental responsibilities of line management. This task will require increased environmental awareness and sophistication on the part of managers throughout the organization and the development of new skills and strategies.

Although environmental concerns have been on the public agenda for over two decades during which a good deal of environmental legislation has been passed and implemented, what is different about today's world is that the issue of the environment is rapidly overshadowing all other social issues, and has become a survival rather than a quality-of-life issue. More and more business executives have identified the environment as the issue that will most affect their companies in the 1990s. And more and more scientists are suggesting that if we don't come to grips with environmental problems in this decade, irreversible processes will have been set in motion that will lead inevitably to serious environmental degradation all over the globe and widespread human suffering.

THE WORLD AT RISK

What are some of the major environmental problems, and how serious are they? The latter question is the subject of much debate. But at least we have a fairly good knowledge of what the problems are even if we are not sure of their exact causes in all instances or what to do about them. First are the so-called global problems that affect everyone in the world to some degree. The two problems that are generally considered to be in this category are global warming and ozone depletion. No one can escape their effects and they have an impact on every country in the world. Thus they are international in nature and require a global solution.

The more controversial of the two is the global warming phenomenon. It in a fact that the buildup of infrared absorbing trace gases such as carbon dioxide, methane, CFCs, and nitrous oxide has mounted dramatically over the past few decades, primarily, but not solely, from industrial processes and products. Carbon dioxide is produced during the burning of fossil fuels in electric-generating plants, automobiles, and other such sources. Methane comes from cattle, and the huge feedlots that have sprung up around the country to serve our needs for beef are a major contributor to the problem. CFCs are released into the air when old automobiles or refrigerators are scrapped. At the same time this buildup has occurred, carbon dioxide absorbing resources, such as the world's rain forests, are being cut down at an alarming rate. So the buildup of trace gases continues.

The 1980s also appeared to be the warmest years on record, with 1988, 1987, and 1981 being the warmest in that order.[3] New data indicate that 1990 was the warmest year in more than a century of record keeping. Thus the 7 warmest years since 1880 have all occurred in the past 11 years.[4] While there is a dispute about this warming with evidence to suggest that certain areas of the world are actually cooler, most scientists agree that some warming has taken place. The controversy surrounds the question of linkage: Is there a connection between climate change and the buildup of greenhouse gases, or is the warming we have experienced due to other causes? The consequences of global warming, should it continue and result in several degrees of additional warming as some scientists are predicting, are severe. Many coastal cities would be flooded if the polar ice caps melted and the sea level rose significantly, and people would either have to build seawalls to keep out the water or move to another location.[5]

The critical policy question is, What steps do we take at present? Do we limit carbon dioxide emissions based on what we know now and accept the limitations of our computer models, or do we wait for additional evidence and develop more sophisticated models that take cloud cover into effect, for example? If we wait, the risk is that things may rapidly deteriorate and be more costly to try and correct somewhere down the road, and may even become irreversible. But if we act now and limit emissions of carbon dioxide by requiring utilities to install expensive scrubbers, we may find that money was wasted if carbon dioxide should prove not to have been a major culprit.

The situation with ozone depletion is more certain. The ozone layer in the stratosphere protects us from exposure to excessive ultraviolet radiation, which can cause skin cancer and cataracts, reduce crop yields, deplete marine fisheries, and interfere with the process of photosynthesis, which is essential to all life on the planet. Two scientists at the University of California at Irvine had already theorized in 1974 that CFCs were the culprit. While the various CFC compounds proved to be a remarkable product useful in air conditioning, insulation, and as a solvent in chip making, as well as in a host of other products because of their chemical inertness, this very stability meant that they did not break down in the lower reaches of the atmosphere, but drifted up to the ozone layer where they finally reacted with the ozone molecules to break them apart.

The use of CFCs in aerosol spray cans was banned in the United States on the basis of this theory, but no other action was taken, and the use of CFCs continued to grow worldwide. There was a great deal of debate about whether CFCs were the real culprit and how serious a problem ozone depletion really was in the larger scheme of things. This debate ended for all practical purposes in the spring of 1987 when scientists discovered that ozone concentration was down 50 percent over the South Pole and had actually disappeared entirely in some places. Subsequently, scientists began to gather evidence that the ozone layer around the globe may be eroding much faster than predicted.[6]

These findings galvanized the industrial nations of the world to take action and put aside the debate. They signed the Montreal Treaty in 1987 agreeing to phase out CFC production over a period of years, allowing Third World countries a reprieve from these restrictions in order to improve their economies. Du Pont, the world's largest producer of CFCs, agreed to eliminate their production ahead of schedule. Based on new findings about the rapid deterioration of the ozone layer, many scientists believed the treaty was outdated and needed to be strengthened, which it was a few years later. But even if all companies were to stop production of CFCs today, there are six or seven years' worth of CFCs already in the atmosphere that will eventually drift up to the ozone layer to do their damage and expose us to more ultraviolet radiation.

There are other problems that are more regional in nature but have global implications. Destruction of the tropical rain forests is one such problem. The tropical rain forests are scattered in an uneven green belt that lies roughly between the Tropic of Cancer and the Tropic of Capricorn. Rain forests grow in regions where at least 4 inches of rain fall monthly, where the mean monthly temperature exceeds 75°F, and where frost never occurs. Not all the rain forests in the world are tropical, for example, consider the Olympic Peninsula of Washington and the Tongass National Forest in Alaska. But these forests are much less diverse and contain far fewer species of trees and other forms of life than the tropical rain forests.[7]

The tropical rain forests cover less than 5 percent of the earth's surface, but are home to perhaps half of all the earth's species. Some scientists estimate that the actual number of species of insects in tropical forests might be between 30 and 80 million. Fewer than half a million tropical species of any kind have been cataloged. There may be as many as 200 species of trees in a single acre of tropical rain forest. There are only about 400 species of trees in all of temperate North America. A single square mile of Amazonian Ecuador or Brazil may be home to more than 1,500 kinds of butterflies; only about 750 occur in all of the United States and Canada.[8]

Every year, an area roughly the size of Illinois is slashed and burned, logged, or otherwise destroyed, and at least an equal amount is disturbed. About half of the original rain forest is already gone, with the remainder covering an area about the size of the 48 contiguous states. During the next 20 to 30 years, this area will be reduced to scattered remnants except for major patches in the Amazon region and the interior of Africa. Clearing these forests for settlement is counterproductive because the soil is not rich enough to support long-term farming or cattle ranching. The nutrients in the soil are exhausted after a few years, and thus new land must be cleared. Because of this destruction, biological extinction is occurring at a more rapid rate than at any time since the demise of the dinosaurs 66 million years ago.[9]

Saving respectable pieces of these forests depends on addressing problems of overpopulation and economic inequities. Although family planning is slowing birthrates in the tropics, the population there—estimated at 2.8 billion in 1990—will grow by another billion in this decade. Sustainable forestry and agricultural practices could advance the welfare of these people while taking pressure off the tropical forests. Biological wealth needs to be taken as seriously as material or cultural wealth because biota is part of a country's heritage, the product of millions of years of evolution centered on that place and hence as much a reason for national concern as the particularities of language and culture.[10]

Acid rain is a phenomenon that affects some regions of the world much more than others. It is believed to place severe stress on many ecosystems in reducing the size and diversity of fish populations and to play a role in forest damage. Recently, however, the National Acid Precipitation Assessment Program questioned the linkage between SO_2 emissions and the severity of the problem. The program noted that SO_2 emissions are down 23 percent from 1973–1988 levels, with no apparent trend in the acidity of rainfall. Perhaps it is too early to see the effects of SO_2 reductions, but nonetheless, the study does raise some interesting questions.[11]

More traditional problems such as air pollution have seemingly become more serious despite the best efforts of government and industry to deal with them. Some 60 American cities still violate one or more of the existing air pollution standards. Although lead emissions are down about 87 percent over the past few years, smog seems to be an intractable problem. Cities like Los Angeles are proposing drastic measures such as eliminating all backyard barbecuing and requiring cars to burn alternative fuels like methanol. The new Clean Air Bill that was passed by Congress and signed by the president requires new controls on industrial installations releasing smog-forming chemicals and may cost as much as $25 billion a year when all its requirements go into effect toward the end of the decade.[12]

Regarding water pollution, many coastal towns along the Atlantic and Gulf of Mexico have had to close their beaches during the summer months because of pollution. Groundwater is being contaminated by underground storage tanks, fertilizers, and pesticides, hazardous waste sites, and other sources threatening 50 percent of the nation's drinking water for half the population. Wetlands are being destroyed at the rate of between 350,000 and 500,000 acres per year, much of that destruction taking place in the state of Louisiana, which has more wetlands than any other state. Because of this destruction of wetlands along the Gulf Coast, the state is experiencing coastal erosion at an alarming rate that is a cause of grave concern.[13]

Approximately 158 million tons of municipal solid waste is generated each year in the United States, but many municipal landfills are close to overflowing and almost 70 percent are expected to reach capacity in 15 years. Municipalities are having trouble opening new landfills, however, because of the Not In My Backyard (NIMBY) effect. With respect to hazardous waste, approximately 30,000 potentially contaminated sites that may pose a threat to human health or the environment have been identified nationwide. But cleanup of these sites is proceeding slowly because of the problem of identifying what is in these sites and because of legal conflict over who is responsible.[14]

And finally, airborne toxic substances are a relatively new problem of significant proportions. Under Title III of the Superfund Amendments and Reauthorization Act (SARA) of 1986, also known as the Emergency Planning and Community Right-to-Know Act, facilities that manufacture, process, or use any of 309 designated chemicals in greater than specified amounts must report routine releases of those chemicals. The EPA is required to make information from these reports available to the public. This Toxics Releases Inventory, as it is called, is designed to assist citizen groups, local health officials, state environmental managers, and the EPA to identify and control toxic chemical problems.[15]

The nation's first inventory of toxic releases showed that in 1987, industry released 2.4 billion pounds of toxic substances into the air we breathe. The chemical industry headed the list with 886.6 million pounds of toxic releases. Emissions in eight states exceeded 100 million pounds. These emissions included 235 million pounds of carcinogens such as benzene and formaldehyde, and 527 million pounds of such neurotoxins as toluene and trichloroethylene. The EPA estimated that air toxins cause more than 2,000 cases of cancer each year based on only 20 chemicals, not the 239 that were included in the survey of toxic releases. Industry argues that these chemicals become so diluted in the air that they are innocuous. But the EPA says that living near chemical plants poses a cancer risk greater than the national average.[16]

Information now coming out of Eastern Europe and the Soviet republics as these countries have opened up to the outside world show that traditional environmental problems are even worse than in the Western world. In the Soviet commonwealth, the air in 103 cities, which are home to more than 50 million people, exceeds the toxicity of the Soviet health-based standard by 10 times. In 1988, 16 cities periodically experienced pollution levels 50 times the standard. In former East Germany, the average annual SO_2 levels are 5 times the U.S. standard, and average annual particulate levels are 13 times the U.S. standard.[17]

Seventy percent of the rivers in Czechoslovakia are badly polluted. One-third of the rivers and 9,000 lakes in former East Germany are biologically dead. Eighty percent of Romania's river water is unpotable. In Hungary, some 1.3 billion cubic meters of untreated sewage is discharged into the country's surface waters each year. Half of Poland's cities and 35 percent of its industries do not treat their waste. In 1988, the Soviet Union could adequately treat only 30 percent of its sewage.[18]

Though data are scarce, hazardous wastes appear to have been indiscriminately dumped on land throughout the region. Some 15,000 hazardous dumpsites are said to be awaiting evaluation in former East German territory. In the former Soviet Union, more than half of nearly 6,000 official landfills do not meet sanitary regulations.[19] Similar conditions are believed to exist in other Eastern European nations.

Because these environmental factors are superimposed on a more general health-care crisis, sorting out the precise causes and consequences of health problems is impossible. Yet in the dirtiest areas of Czechoslovakia life expectancy is as much as five years less than in relatively clean parts of the country. In industrialized Poland, people die three to four years earlier than in the rest of the country. In Halle, Germany, a center of the industrial chemistry industry, people can expect to live five years less than other Germans. Shortened life expectancies, soaring cancer rates, and a host of other maladies have been recorded in highly polluted regions of Eastern Europe.[20]

THE DEVELOPMENT OF ENVIRONMENTALISM

These problems pose serious challenges to our planet and our way of life, particularly for those of us who live in advanced industrial societies. Such dilemmas have made many of us step back and take a look at traditional ways we have thought about the environment and at how we have understood human beings in relation to our surrounding environment. The physical environment includes, air, water, and land, without which life as we know it would be impossible. This environment provides a number of services that human beings cannot do without. Chief among them is provision of a habitat in which plant and animal life can survive. If this habitat is seriously degraded, plant and animal life will be adversely affected. The physical environment is also called on to provide resources that are used in the production process, whatever form that process might take to produce goods and services for the members of society.

Some of these resources are nonrenewable and may become completely exhausted. Others, such as timber, are renewable, but conscious effort is generally needed to replace them. This replacement usually does not happen automatically, at least not fast enough to support a growing population. The physical environment is also used as a dumping ground for waste material that results from the production of goods and services as well as from their consumption. Problems arise when this waste material overwhelms the absorption capacity of the environment, and serious degradation is the result.

Pollution of the physical environment interferes with its ability to provide a habitat in which life can survive and flourish. The ability of the physical environment to serve as a gigantic waste disposal facility depends on its dilutive capacity. Pollution occurs when the waste discharged into the environment exceeds its dilutive capacity — when air can no longer dilute the wastes dumped into it without air quality being adversely affected; water can no longer absorb the wastes dumped into it without some fundamental change taking place in the quality of the water; and land cannot absorb any more waste material without producing harmful effects that relate to land usage itself or drinking water supplies.

The amount of damage that results to a particular medium (air, water, land) varies by the type of pollutant, the amount of pollutant disposed of, and the distance from the source of pollution. These damages, however, alter the quality of the environment and render it, to some degree, unfit to provide its normal services. Thus the air can become harmful for human beings to breathe, water unfit to drink, and land unfit to live on because of toxic wastes that begin seeping to the surface and pose a threat to human health.

Before the advent of pollution control legislation, air, water, and land were treated as free goods available to anyone for dumping wastes. This behavior caused no problem when the population was sparse, factories small, and products few in number compared to today. The environment's dilutive capacity was rarely exceeded and was perceived as infinite in its ability to absorb waste. Changes in society, however, began to cause serious pollution problems. The following factors were critical in this transformation:

Population growth and concentration: More people means more manufactured goods and services to provide for their needs, which in turn means more waste material to be discharged into the environment. The concentration of people in urban areas compounds the problem. Eventually the dilutive capacity of the air, water, and land in major industrial centers becomes greatly exceeded and a serious pollution problem results.

Rising affluence: As real income increases, people are able to buy and consume more goods and services, throw them away more quickly to buy something better, travel more miles per year using various forms of transportation, and expand their use of energy. In the process, much more waste material is generated for the society as a whole.

Technological change: Changes in technology have expanded the variety of products available for consumption, increased their quantity through increases in productivity, made products and packaging more complex, and raised the rate of obsolescence through rapid innovation. All of this has added to the waste disposal problem. In addition, the toxicity of many materials was initially unknown or not a matter of concern, with the result that procedures for the abatement of these pollution problems have lagged far behind the technology of manufacture.

Increased expectations and awareness: As society became more affluent, it could give attention to higher order needs. Thus expectations for a higher quality of life have increased, and the physical environment is viewed as an important component of the overall quality of life. We cannot fully enjoy the goods and services that are available in a hostile or unsafe environment. In addition, our awareness of the harmful effects of pollution increased due to mounting scientific evidence, journalistic exposé, and the attention given environmental problems by the media.

These forces combined about the mid-1960s to give birth to an environmental movement that developed very quickly. Many of the energies that had gone into the civil rights movement were channeled into the environmental movement as the former matured. The result was a major public policy effort to control pollution and correct for the deficiencies of the market system in controlling the amount and types of waste being discharged into the environment. These efforts have had a major impact on business and consumers alike and have caused attitudinal and behavioral changes throughout society.

CHANGING CONSCIOUSNESS

The problems we face with respect to the environment and the implications of these problems for the survival of our planet and the human race can perhaps be seen as providing yet another impetus for a major change in human consciousness regarding the place of human beings in the larger scale of the universe. There have been several such shifts in thinking throughout history as people have had to come to grips with new scientific realities. Adoption of these new realities has never come easily because people are reluctant to change perceptions unless forced to do so by overwhelming evidence or by the magnitude of the problems. (See Exhibit 1.1).

The first such change in human consciousness was stimulated by the development of science and the scientific method as it was applied to the physical reality in which we exist, particularly to the nature and composition of the universe. Prior to that time it was accepted as an article of faith that the sun and the other planets revolved around the earth and that human beings were the center of the universe. When observations began to be made regarding movement of the planets and the sun, early scientists developed elaborate theories to explain the irregularities of their rotation based on this earth-centered assumption. But none of their explanations proved satisfactory.

Finally, the only thing that made sense was to abandon old views and recognize that the earth and the other planets revolved around the sun instead. The earth was not the center of the universe or even of our own solar system. But the early scientists who developed these new theories did so at considerable personal cost because they received formidable opposition from the Church. As we noted, changes in our intellectual perceptions of reality do not come easily. The result of this change was a humbling experience for humans. We now know we live on this rather small inconspicuous planet that is only one of millions of such bodies in the vast surrounding universe.

The second change in human consciousness was provoked by the theory of evolution, which has not been accepted by some religions even today. The theory of evolution challenged the notion of creationism, the idea that human beings were created directly by God after the world had been created, and that they have a special status with respect to the rest of creation. The theory of evolution is again a humbling experience because it places human beings

Exhibit 1.1

Changes in Human Consciousness

Theories About the Universe	The earth is not at the center of the solar system, let alone the universe.
Theories of Evolution	Human life is the result of an evolutionary process that incorporates the principle of natural selection.
Theories of the Unconsious	Human freedom is circumscribed by unconscious wishes and desires.
Theories About Nature	Humans are a part of nature and must see themselves as but one part of a vast and interdependent ecosystem.

in an evolutionary process, where the creation of plant and animal life is the result of a lengthy process of natural selection that has gone on for centuries before humans existed and will continue to go on as long as the world exists. Many people have not accepted this perception of reality because they believe it degrades humans to mere animals in a long chain of evolution. Battles between creationists and evolutionists continue.

The third such intellectual challenge was posed by psychology and the discovery of the unconscious. Human freedom has been of particular importance in American culture and in the Protestant religion, which emphasizes free will and the importance of choice. Yet psychology presents a different perception of choice and places limits on free will with its notion of the unconscious. Many of our so-called choices are not really choices at all, in the sense in which we usually think about them. We are told many of our decisions are based on unconscious wishes or desires, and are not really free at all. It is only as these unconscious wishes or desires are brought to consciousness in psychotherapy or psychoanalysis that we can expand our choices and free ourselves from these unconscious motives and fears.

Environmentalism has posed yet another challenge to human self-understanding and provides another humbling experience. The traditional view of humans and their relationship to nature is dualistic: Humans stand over against nature and are somehow apart from nature, and they exist separate from their environment. The task of humans is to conquer nature, to take dominion over the animals and the natural world as some Christian doctrine has emphasized. This view led to an objectification of nature and allowed us to manipulate nature to our advantage and exploit it for our own purposes. But challengers to this perspective advocate that humans must instead see themselves as a part of nature, and through education about ecology must come to see themselves as but one link in the great chain of being. Only by adopting this perspective, it is argued, can humans see nature properly and understand what must be done to promote survival of the planet and the human race.

Stages of Ecological Consciousness

There have been changes in our perspectives on nature itself as reflected in the policies we have adopted as a nation. (See Exhibit 1.2). The first approach we took was exemplified in the conservation movement that began in the early years of this century. During the frontier days, we recklessly exploited our resources by cutting down trees as fast as possible, plowing up grassland on a vast scale, and destroying our wildlife, including bringing the buffalo to near extinction. It was finally recognized that such wanton exploitation could not continue, and that we must take steps to conserve our resources for future use and not deplete them needlessly.

Exhibit 1.2

Stages of Ecological Consciousness

Stage	Principle or Focus	Ethic
Conservation	Use resources wisely and do not deplete them needlessly. Emphasize efficient development and use of natural resources.	Instrumental view of nature: Nature has utility only as it serves human purposes.
Preservation	Preserve certain areas of the country in their natural state and close them to development.	Nature has intrinsic value in its own right apart from the services it provides for human beings.
Protection	Focus on pollution control and dangers to human health.	Human-centered.
Survival	Be concerned with global problems and sustainable growth.	Eco-centered.

The conservation movement developed as an attempt to restrain the reckless exploitation of forests and wildlife that characterized the pioneer state of social development. This movement curbed the destructive environmental impacts of individuals and corporations who exploited nature for profit without regard for the larger social good or the welfare of future generations. It emphasized that resources should be used wisely and that consideration should be given to a sustainable society. This movement began to get a glimpse of natural limits to resource exploitation that would require different norms of conduct for the society to become sustainable on a long-term basis.[21]

The conservation movement thus promoted the wise and efficient use of resources. During this era, the national park ideal began where we set aside areas of the country for human enjoyment. The essence of the conservation approach was rational planning to promote efficient development and the use of natural resources. Resource management was at the heart of the conservation movement.[22] The ethic behind this movement was still, however, the idea that nature is instrumental, that nature has value only for human purposes, whether it is used to provide resources for human use or whether certain beautiful areas of the country are set aside for human enjoyment.

The Wilderness Act of 1964 ushered in a new stage where nature was recognized as having value in its own right independent of its potential use for human purposes. Certain areas of the country were set aside to be preserved in their natural state and closed to resource development through a permanent wilderness designation. It came to be believed that land and wildlife could only be conserved by leaving them in their natural state and eliminating human presence as much as possible. The Wilderness Act recognizes a wilderness "as an area where the earth and community of life are untrammeled by man, where man himself is a visitor who does not remain."[23]

This kind of thinking is also found in the Endangered Species Act where certain animals are protected for their own sakes, regardless of the effect on human beings. This act has had an impact in Louisiana and Texas with the controversy over the use of TEDs (Turtle Excluder Devices) to protect the Kemp-Riddley turtle from being drowned in shrimp nets, and in the Pacific Northwest in the controversy over the northern spotted owl and the continued logging of old-growth forests. The important values in this movement are ecological, which means that natural systems should be allowed to operate as freely from human interference as possible.

Designating an area as wilderness has become a way to stop economic activity and prevent development in some areas of the country. Human activity is considered to be bad in these areas and natural conditions are believed to be good. Some supporters of this approach treat wilderness as a semisacred place that should be preserved and placed beyond humanity's intrusion. They believe that human beings can only be truly free in wilderness. Society enslaves people, and only in a state of nature does humanity live in a state of fulfillment. Wilderness areas must be preserved so that people can seek a temporary release from civilization. Others consider such a view to be romantic and out of touch with changing world conditions.

> The rebirth of the wilderness ethic has come at a particularly inopportune time in our national history. It has begun promoting a myth of isolation and "self-sufficiency" at exactly the moment when, for the first time in our history, we are being firmly drawn into an economic interdependence with the rest of the world. We now rely on foreign countries for energy and raw materials to a degree that is unprecedented in our history. All indications are that this trend is irrevocable. In this context, romantic images of wilderness isolation and self-sufficiency really seem nothing more than an attempt to avoid acknowledging our growing interconnections with the world.[24]

These two approaches present fundamental differences in their assumptions about nature and the relationship of human beings to natural objects. Treating nature as instrumental implies that nature only has utility as it is used to provide something for human use, whether that use be the extraction of materials to make something useful or the preservation of mountain beauty for human enjoyment. The timber or mineral executive reduces nature to a commodity, something to be taken out and made into something useful. The tourist seeking scenic beauty reduces nature to pleasing images, enjoyed and then taken home on film or preserved in mental images.

This approach does not recognize nature as a living system of which our human lives are part, on which our lives and all lives depend, and which places strict limits on us even as it sustains our lives. The alternative approach, however, sees nature as having intrinsic value in its own right apart from the services it can provide for human beings. Treating nature as having intrinsic value results in more respect for animal rights in testing procedures, food production, and the use of animal pelts for fur coats and other clothing. It could even mean giving trees standing so that they can be protected explicitly by environmental groups rather than having to use the Endangered Species Act to stop logging.

The Environmental Movement

Modern-day concerns about the environment began in the 1960s, when there was a social revolution taking place in the United States. Concern about the environment took its place alongside civil rights, consumer protection, safety and health, and a host of other social issues that were on the public agenda at the time. From society's point of view, concern about the environment stemmed from a desire to improve the quality of life and protect human health. Many scholars linked the environment and consumerism, for example, arguing that people could not enjoy the products they were buying in the marketplace in an environment that was deteriorating, where the air was unfit to breathe and the water risky to drink. This concern for the quality of life and health was reflected in all of the major social issues of those days, but was particularly evident in concern about the environment.

> Fifteen or so years ago, pollution and ecology were two terms rarely found in the lexicon of business. Today environmental survival and pollution abatement are major topics of the times and receive prominent exposure in the literature of business and economics. If any one issue provided the initial sustenance for social responsibility proponents, that issue was the effect of business operations and practices on the physical environment. Probably more words have been written on this subject than on most others of a business and social problems context.[25]

The environmental movement that began in the 1960s was initially concerned about air and water pollution, and was sparked by Rachel Carson's book *Silent Spring,* which pointed out the problems of increasing and unrestricted pesticide usage. Carson brought together the findings of toxicology, ecology, and epidemiology in a form accessible to politicians and the general public. She discussed the bioaccumulation of fat-soluble insecticides in the fatty tissues of fish and the birds that eat fish, the natural resistance of surviving insects to these toxins, the natural dispersion of the toxins far from the source of the substance, and the biochemical interaction of toxins in the human body without human permission or awareness. Weaving together scientific, moral, and political arguments, she combined knowledge about the environment with the need for political action.[26]

As a result of Carson's writing and other concerns expressed in society, people began to be educated about the environment and what services it provides for human beings. The central value of environmentalism is respect for the laws of nature. Ecology is believed to be more fundamental than human wants and needs. The love of nature and recognition of natural limits leads to humility about the place of the human species in the ecosystem. Environmentalists see that the earth is a commons and the solutions to many environmental problems must be undertaken on a global scale. Many environmentalists also argue that solutions to our environmental problems must involve greater decentralization. But however much they might prefer a decentralized, self-managed future, the environmental effect in advanced industrial economies has been to broaden and strengthen the powers of central government.[27]

The results of this movement increased awareness about environmental problems throughout society and institutionalized environmental concerns in business and government through a host of legislation and regulation. Indeed, the primary result of this concern in the 1960s and 1970s was many new laws at the federal, state, and local levels to deal with environmental problems and the establishment of new agencies such as the Environmental Protection Agency (EPA) to administer the laws and make sure the business community in particular was in compliance. The focus of this agency, and indeed of the movement itself, was on protection of the environment from serious degradation and harm from human and industrial activities and protection of human health.

Several new metaphors were developed in these early days of concern about the environment. Garrett Hardin, for example, introduced the notion about the tragedy of the commons in getting at the root of environmental problems. Imagine a pasture that was common land and open to all herdsmen who wanted to use it for grazing. As rational beings, each herdsman would try to keep as many cattle as possible on the commons and maximize their gain. Since each herdsman receives all the proceeds from the sale of an additional animal, there is an incentive to keep adding animals. The additional overgrazing created by one more animal is shared by all the herdsmen and thus there is a net positive reason for each herdsman to add additional animals.[28]

The problem is that each herdsman sharing the commons reaches this same conclusion and continues to add animals to his herd. Each is locked into a system that compels him to increase his herd without limit in a world that is limited. Eventually, the carrying capacity of the commons is exceeded, and the commons is unable to support any more animals because of overgrazing and is ruined. The pursuit of self-interest in a society that believes in freedom of the commons brings eventual ruin to all who want to use the commons. Decisions that are reached individually do not, in fact, work out to be the best decisions for the entire society.

This analysis has application to the pollution problem our society has experienced. The rational executive finds that his share of the costs of the wastes discharged into the commons, in this case air and water, is less than the cost of purifying the wastes before releasing them. There is no incentive for a manufacturer to reduce wastes when the commons is treated as a free good available to all for the dumping of wastes. But the commons is eventually ruined when its carrying capacity is exceeded and air and water pollution become so bad as to threaten human health and the existence of many species of fish and other wildlife. Thus society has to take steps to regulate use of the commons in the interests of society as a whole.

Other writers developed the notion of the earth as a spaceship, and used this metaphor to argue for policies that were frugal instead of wasteful in order to ensure survival in the limited world in which we live. We were encouraged to think of the earth as a spaceship floating in a vast universe where everything we needed to survive was more or less self-contained. There were no external inputs or outputs that we could depend on to help solve our problems. Just as on a spaceship, we needed to think about conserving our use of resources and recycle our waste as much as possible because eventually we would run out of room. The spaceship earth concept was used to get people to think holistically and accept the idea of limitations on human activity.[29]

Barry Commoner offered a somewhat more optimistic assessment. He believed the economy could continue to grow, and that the standard of living and jobs could increase while environmental quality could be improved. In the United States, he argued, neither the increase in population nor in affluence could account for the very large increase in environmental pollution. The real culprit, he argued, was changes in the technology of production that had been introduced over the past several decades. Natural products were replaced by synthetic products such as detergents, synthetic fibers, and plastics. These products are the real problem as far as pollution is concerned. And these changes in the technology of production have also brought about a serious decline in the efficiency with which resources and capital have been used in our society.[30]

The production system is governed almost exclusively by economic considerations. Profit maximization governs the design of the system of production and therefore the fate of ecosystems. Technology is a social institution that reflects to a large degree the governing aims of the society in which it develops. In the United States, technology is used to enhance what capitalists want, namely, profit maximization and domination of the market rather than the welfare of the people. The solution, according to Commoner, is some form of democratic socialism where technology is used for society's benefit rather than private gain. Society must develop an investment policy that is under social rather than private control. The key to any solution to our environmental problems is social governance of the choice of production technologies through democratic control of investment decisions.

Finally, Paul Ehrlich argued that the root cause of most environmental damage was excessive growth in human population. Either humanity must change its ways of reproducing or mass starvation was inevitable. Neither technological breakthroughs nor social adjustments, other than an end to population increase, were adequate. In *The Population Bomb,* he was absolutely explicit about the cause of the coming tragedy, recommended luxury taxes on cribs, diapers, and other children's goods, and proposed other economic disincentives to reproduction. Population control for developing countries must involve even more drastic measures than for advanced countries. Food aid should be given only to those countries that have an aggressive population control policy and clear hope of obtaining food self-sufficiency.[31]

Taken as a whole, these writings pointed out the complexity of the environmental problem. Technology, affluence, overpopulation, and use of the commons all contribute to the problem. But no single cause is dominant, and it would be unduly optimistic to suggest that stabilization or correction of only one of these factors might be sufficient. In the final analysis, there is probably not a single principal cause of ecological damage. Solutions to environmental problems require a multifaceted, global approach. No single nation can solve environmental problems all by itself, and focusing on only one facet of the problem does not recognize the interrelatedness of natural and social phenomena.

Current Environmentalism

The current worldwide environmental movement, sometimes called the *new environmentalism,* views all environmental issues as in some sense global, rather than as simply regional and local problems. All environmental problems are interrelated, reflecting the nature of ecology itself. As we mentioned before, problems such as global warming and the depletion of the ozone layer threaten the entire planet and require international cooperation for their solution. But all environmental problems are in some sense global. It is difficult to talk about air pollution in one country and efforts being made to reduce air pollution without talking about other countries' problems. The same is true of water pollution and waste disposal problems. Although public policy measures can be implemented by individual countries, these problems really do not respect the boundaries of nations or localities and are fundamentally global in nature and in many cases require global solutions.

The new environmentalism transcends the old ideologies and has become something of a new ideology itself, cutting across liberal-conservative lines, and affecting both socialist and capitalist systems. People of different political persuasions all over the world have been able to unite behind environmental causes because all countries of whatever ideology have their share of environmental problems. The new environmentalism challenges old ways of thinking and of organizing reality and calls for new paradigms and intellectual constructs that are more comprehensive and less reductionist in nature. Instead of age-old battles between capitalism and socialism and conservative and liberal ideologies, we are now challenged to transcend these ways of thinking and focus on a more comprehensive and inclusive view of reality, where humans are a part of nature and have to take environmental effects into account in all their activities.

The new environmentalism may provide a useful base from which to make individual life choices, take collective political action, and decide a surprisingly broad range of public policy issues. Some believe that environmentalism now has the potential to become the first original ideological perspective to develop since the middle of the nineteenth century. Such an ideology could help to halt or slow the expansionism inherent in both capitalist and socialist systems, which tend to seek ever bigger economies well past the point where greater economic activity is either sustainable or desirable. This ideology questions whether expansion beyond a reasonable level is a net benefit at all, regardless of the manner in which those benefits are distributed.[32]

The new environmentalism recognizes resource limitations, and questions the wisdom of a continued emphasis on economic growth. Instead of harping about limits to growth, however, the banner of the new environmental movement is sustainable growth or sustainable development. Only a few short years ago, there was intense debate about the limits to economic growth in the world in general, and in the advanced industrial nations in particular. The first Club of Rome's study emphasized resource shortages, pollution problems, and populations pressures in the industrialized nations and the world.[33] With an impressive array of computer graphs and statistics, the study proceeded to show that even under the best of assumptions, the limits to growth on this planet would be reached sometime within the next 100 years. The most probable result would be a rather sudden and uncontrollable decline in both population and industrial capacity. If this danger were recognized, it would be possible to alter these growth trends and establish a condition of ecological and economic stability that could be sustained far into the future.

The second Club of Rome study made many of the same points and recommendations.[34] Then came the Global 2000 Report with equally pessimistic conclusions. These predictions became all too real with the oil embargo in the mid-1970s that caused long gasoline lines in the United States and brought home to every American our vulnerability regarding energy resources. There was a great deal of emphasis placed on the search for alternative sources of energy in the hopes of reducing our dependence on foreign sources of oil and gaining some degree of energy independence. The

U.S. government proposed an $88 billion Synfuels Corporation to promote the research and development of new sources and forms of energy.

These efforts came to naught, however, with the election of the Reagan administration. Talk about limits to growth came to an end except perhaps in some isolated corners of academia. Instead the emphasis was on opportunity and the unlimited potential of technology and the human spirit. The debate about supply-side economics shifted concern from the redistribution of an existing out of resources in a more num type of situation, to expanding the size of the pie and lifting the boats of everyone, rich and poor alike, through uninterrupted economic growth. Investment, growth, creativity, and entrepreneurship were hallmarks of the Reagan administration, which harbored an unbounded optimism in the future of America and the spirit of the American people.

It is no mystery that young people in the United States supported Reagan in record numbers. Common sense would indicate that young people just starting their careers and families want to hear about opportunity and don't want to hear about limits to growth and shrinking opportunities, particularly from middle-aged people who have made their mark in life and accumulated their share of the world's goods. Limits to growth only appeals to those who already have enough wealth to live comfortably and want to prevent further growth from threatening their lifestyle. The limits-to-growth movement was something of an elitist concern, and did a great deal of harm to the environmental movement of earlier years in labeling it as antigrowth and obstructionist to those on the lower rungs of the economic ladder.

Sustainable growth, however, has a much better chance of being accepted and implemented in public and corporate policy. This concept is concerned with finding paths of social, economic, and political progress that meet the needs of the present without compromising the ability of future generations to meet their own needs. This concept reflects a change of values in regard to managing our resources in such a way that equity matters, equity among peoples around the world and equity between parents and their children and grandchildren.[35] It thus has an appeal to people at all levels of development, and in particular has appeal to people and nations at early stages of economic development. They obviously don't want to see resources depleted before they have had their share, and must be concerned about growth that is sustainable for many years to come.

THE END OF NATURE

Recent developments have provided us with new perspectives on the environment. Space travel has given us the ability to look at planet earth from space and pictures of earth from space, which allow us to adopt a holistic perspective and understand in a real way what earlier writers meant when they developed the concept of spaceship earth. Because life has not been discovered thus far on any other planet, many are coming to understand that the earth is a unique place where human life exists, and that this life is dependent on maintenance of appropriate environmental conditions. The earth has finite resources and a fragile environment, so we have a responsibility to manage the human use of planet earth.

Environmentalists are concerned, however, that nature will be crowded out by human interference, and oppose the idea that humans should exercise their dominion over nature for the sake of material progress. They have a sense of loss because nature's independence is being destroyed. Humility toward nature is what they prefer, and human beings should neither control nor dictate to nature. For much of history, humans beings have not experienced nature as kind and gentle, but as harsh and dangerous, and therefore humans have felt compelled to subordinate nature in order to protect themselves. But the greenhouse effect and ozone depletion are the first environmental problems that can't be escaped by moving to the woods. There are no ways to avoid these problems, and global solutions entail infringements on individual rights which are far different from anything that has gone before.

The *End of Nature* is a book by Bill McKibben that captures these concerns and provides a new way of viewing the present situation. McKibben's basic thesis is that nature as we have known it in the past in its pure form no longer exists. Human beings have conquered nature because the entire natural world now bears the stamp of humanity. We have left our imprint on nature everywhere and have altered it beyond recognition in some cases. We have made nature a creation of our own, and have lost the otherness that once belonged to the natural world. The natural world is so affected by human technology that it is more and more becoming one of our own creations and thus is no longer the autonomous nature in which we sought refuge from human civilization.[36]

Human activities alter natural processes far greater than anyone can imagine, and these processes have been subjugated and altered according to human needs. What this means is that nature no longer can take care of itself. We simply cannot proceed as we have in the past to exploit nature and not worry about the environmental consequences of our activities. The leaders of business and industry, as well as government and educational institutions, need to think in terms of managing nature, managing planet earth, and taking responsibility for nature to assure the survival of the world.

We have learned to manage a great many things. Sometimes we do a good job of managing; oftentimes we do something less than acceptable. But we cannot afford to make mistakes with nature. The cost is too great. Managing nature involves making value judgments regarding the kind of planet we want. Although science can tell what kind of planet we can get, what we want is a value judgment. Value judgments include the answer to questions like, How much species diversity should be maintained? Should the size or growth rate of the human population be curtailed to protect the global environment? How much climate change is acceptable? How much poverty is acceptable throughout the world? Science can tell us something about the broad patterns of global transformation taking place, but value questions about the pace and direction of those patterns have to be answered through political systems.

In order to answer those value questions, we need better education about ecology in order to understand nature and the impacts we have on nature. We need new measurement systems to quantify these impacts and clarify the nature of the decisions we face relative to resource usage and environmental degradation. This way of thinking provides quite a challenge to all of us, those of us in the educational world as well as those in the business world. But we simply must think in terms of taking responsibility for our actions and managing nature in the interests of the world and in the interests of future generations. We have to make conscious choices about the kind of world we want for ourselves and for our children.

The system of national accounting we use in the United States to measure economic progress incorporates the depreciation of plant and equipment but not the depletion of natural capital. The principal measure of economic progress is the gross national product, but this measure does not take into account the depletion of nonrenewable and renewable resources and thus produces a misleading sense of national economic health. If all the environmental consequences of economic activity from resource depletion to numerous forms of environmental damage were included in this measure, real economic progress would be much less than conventional economic measures indicate. Nations must apply some kind of an ecological deflator if they are to measure real progress in human and social welfare.[37]

We have no choice in these matters, because our science and technology have taken us across a threshold that cannot be recrossed. We cannot go back to a simpler age where small is beautiful and everyone grows their own food organically. Such notions of a return to a pristine past where nature was more respected are romantic and unrealistic. We must go forward to develop new strategies that are environmentally sensitive, and we must be more responsible in our use of resources. Not to take these kinds of steps and to change our way of thinking will most assuredly lead to environmental degradation on a scale that far surpasses anything we have experienced in our lifetime.

Individuals have begun to respond to an increased awareness of global environmental change by altering their values, beliefs, and actions. Many steps have been taken to respond to environmental problems and begin to manage our relations with the environment in a more responsible manner. However, we must respond as a global species, pooling knowledge, coordinating our actions, and sharing what the planet has to offer. Only in adopting a global perspective do we have any realistic prospect for managing the planet's transformation along pathways of sustainable development.[38]

Efforts to manage the sustainable development of the earth must have three specific objectives according to one author: (1) to disseminate the knowledge and the means necessary to control human population growth, (2) to facilitate sufficiently vigorous economic growth and equitable distribution of its benefits to meet the basic needs of the human population in this and subsequent generations, and (3) to structure the growth in ways that keep its enormous potential for environmental transformation within safe limits yet to be determined.[39] The greatest responsibility and immediate potential for the design of sustainable-development strategies may be in the high-income and high-density regions of the industrialized world.[40]

Through a gradual awakening, people are beginning to develop a new perception of humanity's relationship to the earth's natural systems. People are crossing perceptual thresholds, which is necessary to respond to environmental problems and support an effective political response. There is a growing sense of the world's interdependence and connectedness, and an understanding that progress is an illusion if it destroys the conditions for life to thrive on earth. The leaders of industrial and Third World countries alike recognize their common interest in and responsibility for participating in sustainable development. Looming threats to the world's climate and undermining of other global commons may soon make the transition to stronger international solutions inevitable.

~

Questions for Discussion

1. Do you agree that the world is at risk? In what ways? How would you categorize the risks mentioned in the chapter? Which are most severe and need immediate attention?

2. Is the distinction between global problems and more traditional environmental problems valid in your opinion? What would be a more meaningful distinction? What, if any, significant difference exists between these two groups of environmental problems?

3. Is socialism any better than capitalism in terms of its environmental record? Why or why not? What implications does your answer have for the future of socialist systems?

4. What is pollution? Why does it occur? What factors were critical in making pollution a serious problem in the 1960s, and getting pollution on the national agenda?

5. What are the changes in human consciousness mentioned in the chapter? What does human consciousness mean in this context? How do such changes come about? Is a change in environmental awareness of the same significance as the other changes? Why or why not?

6. What is conservation? What ethic is behind this movement? What major conservation efforts have been attained? Is conservation important today? In what ways?

7. What is an intrinsic value? How does this ethical approach manifest itself in the preservation movement? Would you advocate this approach be extended? In what ways?

8. What was Rachel Carson's book about? What does the title *Silent Spring* mean? What effects did her book have on society? What has been the result of the environmental movement that began in the 1960s?

9. Describe the tragedy of the commons. List all the commons you can think of in our society. Does Hardin's metaphor apply to these commons? Does his analysis help you to understand what happens to these commons?

10. What was Commoner's assessment of the environmental problem? Do you agree or disagree with his analysis? Would his solution work given what we know about the world today?

11. In what ways does new-age environmentalism differ from earlier environmental movements? What does it mean to say that the new environmentalism has become something of an ideology in itself? Will this kind of environmental concern continue for very long, or is it something of a fad in your opinion?

12. What is sustainable growth? How does this concept differ from limits to growth? Why did the latter fade from public consciousness? Is sustainable growth possible?

13. What does Bill McKibben mean by the end of nature? Do you agree or disagree with his thesis? What are the implications of his thesis for the future of the planet?

14. What does it mean to manage planet earth? How can science help us in this regard? What kind of value judgments have to be made? What kind of institutional changes are necessary to make this kind of approach a reality?

~

NOTES

1. David Kirkpatrick, "Environmentalism: The New Crusade," *Fortune,* February 12, 1990, pp. 44–55.

2. Denton E. Morrison and Riley E. Dunlap, "Environmentalism and Elitism: A Conceptual and Empirical Analysis," *Environmental Management,* Vol. 10, No. 5 (1986), pp. 581–589.

3. Stephen H. Schneider, "The Changing Climate," *Scientific American,* Vol. 261, No. 3 (September 1989), p. 72.

4. "Hot Times," *Time,* January 21, 1991, p. 65.

5. See Jodi Jacobson, "Holding Back the Sea," in *State of the World 1990,* Linda Starke, ed. (New York: Norton, 1990), pp. 79–97.

6. See Cynthia Pollock Shea, "Protecting the Ozone Layer," in *State of the World 1989,* Linda Starke, ed. (New York: Norton, 1989), pp. 77–96.

7. Peter H. Raven, "Endangered Realm," in *The Emerald Realm: Earth's Precious Rain Forests,* Martha E. Christian, ed. (Washington, DC: National Geographic Society, 1990), p. 10.

8. Ibid.

9. Ibid., p. 24.

10. Ibid., pp. 190–191.

11. S. Fred Singer, "The Answers on Acid Rain Fall on Deaf Ears," *Wall Street Journal,* March 6, 1990, p. A-20.

12. See Michael D. Lemonick, "Forecast: Clearer Skies," *Time,* November 5, 1990, p. 33.

13. U.S. Environmental Protection Agency, *Environmental Progress and Challenges: EPA's Update* (Washington, DC: U.S. Government Printing Office, 1988), p. 44.

14. Ibid., pp. 78–109.

15. Ibid., p. 124.

16. Sharon Begley, "Is Breathing Hazardous to Your Health?" *Newsweek,* April 3, 1989, p. 25.

17. Hillary E. French, *Green Revolutions: Environmental Reconstruction in Eastern Europe and the Soviet Union* (Washington, DC: Worldwatch Institute, 1990), p. 11.

18. Ibid., p. 17.

19. Ibid., pp. 19–20.

20. Ibid., pp. 21–22.

21. John Rodman, "Four Forms of Ecological Consciousness," in *Ethics and the Environment,* Donald Scherer and Thomas Atteg, eds. (Englewood Cliffs, NJ: Prentice-Hall, 1983), p. 84.

22. William Tucker, *Progress and Privilege: America in the Age of Environmentalism* (Garden City, NY: Anchor Press, 1982), pp. 42–45.

23. Ibid., p. 129.

24. Ibid., p. 138.

25. Arthur Elkins and Dennis W. Callaghan, *A Managerial Odyssey: Problems in Business and Its Environment,* 2nd ed. (Reading, MA: Addison-Wesley, 1978), p. 173.

26. Robert C. Pahlke, *Environmentalism and the Future of Progressive Politics* (New Haven: Yale University Press, 1989), pp. 28–32.

27. Ibid., pp. 149–156.

28. Garrett Hardin, "The Tragedy of the Commons," *Science,* Vol. 162, No. 1 (December 13, 1968), pp. 1243–1248.

29. Kenneth E. Boulding, "The Economics of the Coming Spaceship Earth," in *Environmental Quality in a Growing Economy,* H. Jarrett, ed. (Baltimore, MD: Johns Hopkins Press, 1966).

30. Barry Commoner, "Economic Growth and Environmental Quality: How to Have Both," *Social Policy,* Summer 1985, pp. 18–26.

31. Paul Erlich, *The Population Bomb* (New York: Ballantine Books, 1971)

32. Pahlke, *Environmentalism,* pp. 3–7.

33. Donella H. Meadows, Dennis L. Meadows, Jorgen Randers, and William W. Behrens III, *The Limits to Growth: A Report for the Club of Rome's Project on the Predicament of Mankind* (New York: Universe Books, 1972).

34. Mihajlo D. Mesarovic, *Mankind at the Turning Point: The Second Report to the Club of Rome* (New York: Dutton, 1974).

35. William C. Clark, "Managing Planet Earth," *Scientific American,* Vol. 261, No. 3 (September 1989), p. 48.

36. Bill McKibben, *The End of Nature* (New York: Random House, 1989).

37. Lester R. Brown, "The Illusion of Progress," in *State of the World 1990,* Linda Starke, ed. (New York: Norton, 1990), pp. 7–9.

38. Clark, "Managing Planet Earth," p. 47.

39. Ibid., p. 49.

40. Ibid., p. 53.

SUGGESTED READINGS

Boulding, Kenneth E. "The Economics of the Coming Spaceship Earth," in *Environmental Quality in a Growing Economy,* H. Jarrett, ed. Baltimore, MD: Johns Hopkins Press, 1966.

Brundtland, G. H. *Our Common Future: World Commission on Environment and Development.* New York: Oxford University Press, 1987.

Conservation Foundation. *State of the Environment: A View Toward the Nineties.* Washington, DC: Conservation Foundation, 1987.

Erlich, Paul. *The Population Bomb* New York: Ballantine Books, 1971.

Fox, Stephen. *John Muir and His Legacy: The American Conservation Movement.* Boston: Little, Brown, 1981.

French, Hillary E. *Green Revolutions: Environmental Reconstruction in Eastern Europe and the Soviet Union.* Washington, DC: Worldwatch Institute, 1990.

Hartzog, George B., Jr. *Battling for the National Parks.* Mt Kisco, NY: Moyer Bell, 1988.

Hays, Samuel P. *Beauty, Health, and Permanence: Environmental Politics in the United States, 1955–1985*. Cambridge, MA: Cambridge University Press, 1987.

Leopold, Aldo. *A Sand County Almanac*. New York: Oxford University Press, 1949.

McCormick, John. *Reclaiming Paradise: The Global Environmental Movement*. Bloomington: Indiana University Press, 1989.

McKibben, Bill. *The End of Nature*. New York: Random House, 1989.

Meadows, Donella H., Dennis L. Meadows, Jorgen Randers, and William W. Behrens III. *The Limits to Growth: A Report for the Club of Rome's Project on the Predicament of Mankind*. New York: Universe Books, 1972.

Mesarovic, Mihajlo D. *Mankind at the Turning Point: The Second Report to the Club of Rome*. New York: Dutton, 1974.

Nash, Roderick. *Wilderness and the American Mind*, 3rd ed. New Haven, CT: Yale University Press, 1982.

Nicholson, Max. *The New Environmental Age*. New York: Cambridge University Press, 1987.

Pahlke, Robert C. *Environmentalism and the Future of Progressive Politics*. New Haven: Yale University Press, 1989.

Petulla, Joseph M. *American Environmental History*, 2nd ed. Columbus, OH: Merrill, 1988.

Rodman, John. "Four Forms of Ecological Consciousness," in *Ethics and the Environment*, Donald Scherer and Thomas Atteg, eds. Englewood Cliffs, NJ: Prentice-Hall, 1983.

Roth, Dennis M. *The Wilderness Movement and the National Forests*. Washington, DC: Forest Service, 1984.

Speth, James Gustave. *Environmental Pollution: A Long-Term Perspective*. Washington, DC: World Resources Institute, 1988.

Tucker, William. *Progress and Privilege: America in the Age of Environmentalism*. Garden City, NY: Anchor Press, 1982.

World Resources Institute. *The Crucial Decade: The 1990s and the Global Environmental Challenge*. Washington, DC: World Resources Institute, 1989.

Worthington, E. B. *The Ecological Century*. New York: Oxford University Press, 1983.

CHAPTER 2

CONCEPTS AND PRINCIPLES OF ECOLOGY

~

Just as it is important for you as students in business and management to have some knowledge of economics so you can understand how the economy works and the role business plays in the economy, so it is vital for you to have some understanding of the way in which ecological systems work in order to understand the impact of business activities on the environment. This chapter provides a rudimentary understanding of nature and acquaints you with some basic concepts and principles of ecology that will help you understand the nature of environmental problems and what can be done about them.

Their lack of basic ecological knowledge and understanding means that some policymakers and business executives are really unfit to make rational judgments on many environmental issues. They simply don't understand the ecological impact of their decisions or the more environmentally responsible alternatives. Ecological education is sadly lacking in our educational system, perhaps reflecting our perception that nature will take care of itself, and we can go about our business of pursuing more and more economic growth irrespective of the impact on the environment. The concept of sustainable development is saying that such a course can lead to environmental and economic disaster, if economic growth is undermining the very environmental conditions which make that growth possible.

> With better ecological understanding, media and the public would have known that the spotted owl, though the legal focus of the fracas, is but a single species that scientists use as an indicator of the health and diversity of old-growth forests. Once the system is damaged so much that owls can't survive, other species—and ultimately the entire forest as a living system—may be affected beyond repair. Reporters and readers could pick up on the fact that a tree farm, though it might have

as many trees as a forest, is radically different, and cannot be considered an adequate replacement for the complex old-growth ecosystem. Lacking both this specific information and the long-term perspective of biological science, decision-makers often favor economists' and business managers' short-term, bottom-line-for-the-current-quarter judgments.[1]

The science of ecology has become more important as industrial societies have matured and as our knowledge of the world has become more complex. Even in primitive societies, ecology was important because human beings needed to have some knowledge of the environment, the forces of nature, and the plants and animals around them in order to survive. But as population increased and as human beings expanded their power to alter the environment, it became more important than ever for people to have a better knowledge of the environment and of what they are doing to themselves and the planet on which they depend for survival. Ecology is the science which provides that knowledge.

As a distinct field of biology, ecology dates from about 1900, but only in past decades has the term become part of our general vocabulary. During the 1960s when social problems were brought to the nation's attention, ecology was introduced to the general public as more and more attention was given to the physical environment and to the pressing pollution problems that were appearing all over the world. People gradually became aware of the importance of the environmental sciences in providing an understanding of the environment and giving us tools to maintain the quality of human civilization. Ecology rapidly became extremely relevant to every person on earth.

Plants, microorganisms, and animals are not isolated entities. They are parts of a vast complex of natural machinery that ecology seeks to understand. They are related elements in a system that can be examined scientifically and described in a way that enlarges our knowledge of ourselves and the world in which we live.[2] Increasing our understanding of how nature is assembled and maintains itself is one of the most difficult and exciting challenges for ecologists. Comprehending how natural communities are organized and how their diversity is maintained is essential for their preservation. Animal and plant communities all over the world are under assault from ever-expanding human populations and activities.[3]

Ecology is historical and comparative in its approach as well as holistic in its outlook. Most scientists are reductionist in their approach: They reduce nature to its components and seek to understand the structure and function of each of these components. Consequently, knowledge has become fragmented as different fields of science have developed and have become more and more specialized. Most scientists do not have to be holistic and understand the relationship of the parts to the whole, but can concentrate on the parts without dealing with interrelationships or the relation of the parts to the whole.

Ecologists, on the other hand, seek to understand the rationale for the present makeup of nature and the operation of the entire mechanism, as well as the history of its construction.[4] Ecologists seek a comprehensive understanding of the environment and how all of its components relate to one another. These interrelationships are just as important as the individual components. Ecology is thus a synthetic science where the whole is greater than the sum of the parts. When the whole is reduced to its parts, the quality of the whole is likely to disappear. The interrelationships between the parts can be studied separately from the breakdown and analysis of the parts themselves.

THE REALM OF ECOLOGY

The word ecology comes from the Greek *oikos,* and means "house" or "place to live." Taken literally, ecology refers to the study of organisms at home in their natural habitat.[5] Ecology is concerned with the biology of groups of organisms and with functional processes on the land, in the oceans and fresh water, and in the air. Ecology can also be defined as the study of the structure and function of nature. Ecologists seek to explain or understand nature, a search for knowledge in the pure scientific tradition. They also try to predict what will happen to organisms, populations, or communities under a particular set of circumstances.[6]

For more practical purposes, we can consider ecology as the study of organisms and their environment. It is the science of the interrelations between living organisms and their environment and deals with the interactions of plants and animals in natural systems.[7] Ecology is a science that proceeds at three levels: (1) the individual organism, (2) the population (consisting of individuals of the same species), and (3) the community (consisting of a greater or lesser number of populations).

At the level of the *organism,* ecology deals with how individuals are affected by (and how they affect) their environment. Is acid rain killing spruce trees, and if so, what is the mechanism of damage? Is the greenhouse effect a real danger, and what are the implications for human life as the earth heats up further? At the level of *population,* ecology deals with the presence or absence of particular species and with trends and fluctuations in their numbers. To understand population fluctuations, the changes happening to individuals making up the population must be analyzed. *Community* ecology deals with the composition or structure of communities, and with the pathways followed by energy, nutrients, and other chemicals as they pass through communities.[8] Communities are not constant but are continually changing because of interactions among the populations and because of disturbances caused by climactic and geological events as well as by human activities.

Exhibit 2.1

The Realm of Ecology

Ecosystem	The community of organisms and populations interacting with one another and with the chemical and physical factors making up their environment.
Community	Populations of different plants and animals living and interacting in an area at a particular time.
Population	Group of individual organisms of the same species living within a particular area.
Organism	Any form of life including all plants and animals.

The idea of the *ecosystem* is the most fundamental concept in the field of ecology. The ecosystem is the basic functional unit in ecology, and includes organisms, populations, and communities, each influencing the properties of the other. (See Exhibit 2.1). The ecosystem emphasizes obligatory relationships, interdependence, and causal relationships. The parts of an ecosystem are operationally inseparable from the whole, and thus systems analysis techniques are especially appropriate for understanding how an ecosystem works. A pond, lake, or a tract of forest, for example, are convenient units of analysis for such purposes. An entity may be considered an ecosystem as long as the major components of the system are present and operate together to achieve some sort of functional stability, if only for a short period of time.[9]

All human beings and human activities are imbedded in and dependent upon the ecosystems of our planet. Ecosystems are the machinery of nature, the machinery that supports our lives. Without the services provided by natural ecosystems, civilization would collapse and human life would not be possible. . . . An ecosystem consists of the physical environment and all the organisms in a given area, together with the network of interactions of these organisms with that physical environment and with each other.[10]

Ecosystems are capable of self-maintenance and self-regulation, as are their component populations and organisms. There is a natural tendency for ecosystems to resist change and to remain in a state of equilibrium. Thus cybernetics, or the science of controls has an important application in terms of understanding how ecosystems maintain themselves. Since human activities tend to disrupt the natural functioning of control mechanisms or substitute artificial mechanisms for natural ones, it is important to have some understanding of how an ecosystem works and how the balance or forces in a ecosystem is likely to be upset by human projects.

An ecosystem is not a static concept, however, even in the absence of human intervention. Ecosystems do develop and succeed each other; in other words, they are in a constant state of evolution. According to one ecologist, ecological succession may be defined in terms of three parameters: (1) ecological succession is an orderly process of community development that involves changes of species and community structures and processes over time, but these changes are reasonably directional and predictable; (2) such succession results from modification of the physical environment by the community and is thus community-controlled even though the physical environment determines the pattern, rate of change, and often sets limits on how far development can proceed; and (3) succession culminates in another stabilized ecosystem where some kind of equilibrium can be maintained over a period of time.[11]

When human intervention is introduced, changes can be produced that are unnatural and life threatening. Since the industrial revolution, humans in so-called advanced societies have generally been preoccupied with obtaining as much production from the land mass available to them as possible. Intensive farming and forestry, for example, have been practiced to achieve high rates of production of readily harvestable products with little standing crop left to accumulate on the landscape. This goal of maximum production often conflicts with nature's strategy of maximum protection (trying to achieve maximum support of complex ecological structures) that often characterizes ecological development. Thus there is a conflict between humans and nature that must be recognized if rational land use and resource extraction policies are to be established.[12]

> Many essential life-cycle resources, not to mention recreational and esthetic needs, are best provided for man by the less "productive" landscapes. In other words, the landscape is not just a supply depot but is also the oikos—the home—in which we must live. Until recently mankind has more or less taken for granted the gas-exchange, water-purification, nutrient-cycling, and other protective functions of self-maintaining ecosystems, that is, until his numbers and his environmental manipulations became great enough to affect regional and global balances.[13]

This dynamic element of ecosystem development must be taken into account when human projects are planned. Oftentimes these projects have unintended consequences when they alter the ecosystem in a manner that not only affects future productivity of the environment, but also affects the ability of the ecosystem to sustain human as well as animal life. The ecosystem has multiple functions that land use policies as well as industrial development must recognize. The productive orientation of industrial societies must be balanced with the protective orientation of many natural processes in order to promote the welfare of the entire biological community.

IMPORTANT CONCEPTS*

The concept of *cycles* is important in ecology because the chemical elements, including those that are essential to human life, circulate in the biosphere in characteristic paths from the environment to organisms and back to the

*For a summary see Exhibit 2.2.

environment. Of the 90 odd elements that are known to occur in nature, some 30 to 40 are required by human organisms. The movement of these elements is called nutrient cycling. Some of these elements, such as carbon, hydrogen, oxygen, and nitrogen, are needed in large quantities; others are needed in small, or even in some cases, minute quantities.[14]

The global cycling of carbon dioxide (CO_2) illustrates the concept of nutrient cycling. Carbon dioxide is released into the atmosphere by humans as they take in oxygen that is essential to life and release carbon dioxide as a waste product. Carbon dioxide is also released from the soil because of agricultural activities, especially frequent plowing of large land areas. This carbon dioxide is used by plants in the process of photosynthesis, which releases oxygen into the atmosphere. Carbon dioxide is also absorbed by the carbonate system of seawater. Human activities on a global scale can upset this balance and interfere with the recycling process. Release of carbon dioxide into the air through the increased burning of fossil fuels and a subsequent decrease in the removal capacity of the green belt through the destruction of the rain forests in South and Central America can have an effect on the atmosphere and on world climate.

Corporate managers must understand the nature of these cyclical processes in order to evaluate the effect of major industrial processes on the ecosystem on which we depend for our very existence. All of the major macro environmental problems such as the greenhouse effect, acid rain, and depletion of the ozone layer of the atmosphere have cyclical components. There is another aspect to this notion of a cycle in ecology that relates to conservation of natural resources. As some nonrenewable resources become more and more scarce, recycling must become a major goal for society. This concept is especially important in relation to those resources that are essential for human life and for which no effective and readily available substitutes can be found.

The concept of the *food chain* is also important to understand. The transfer of food energy from its source in plants through a series of organisms where eating and being eaten is repeated a number of times is referred to as the food chain. Since at each transfer point a large proportion of the available energy is lost, the number of steps or links in a sequence is limited. The concept of a food chain is familiar to most people, since human beings occupy a position at or near the end of most food chains. For example, people eat big fish that eat little fish, that eat zooplankton that eat phytoplankton that fixes the energy of the sun.[15]

The concept of a food chain is important for another reason beyond simply understanding how energy gets transferred from one organism to another. Pollutants also are transferred in this process, and rather than lose their effect, they generally become more concentrated as they progress through the food chain. Thus pesticide residues that wash off soil into a stream or lake can come to reside in fish, and as smaller fish are eaten by larger fish, these residues tend to become more concentrated. By the time humans eat these fish, the concentrations of some pollutants can already have reached harmful levels to human health.

The concept of a *community* mentioned previously deserves to be highlighted because corporate managers work in a society that emphasizes individualism as a key component of its ideology. A community can be defined as any assemblage of populations living in a prescribed area or physical habitat that has characteristics in addition to its individual and population components. Major communities are those of sufficient size and organizational completeness that they are relatively independent of inputs and outputs from adjacent communities. Minor communities are relatively dependent on neighboring aggregations.[16]

The community concept emphasizes the fact that diverse organisms usually live together in an orderly manner and are not just haphazardly strewn over the earth as independent beings. There is an interdependence factor built into the notion of community. Communities just don't happen because of ecological accidents, but they evolve out of mutual needs and patterns of dependence where an ecological balance can be maintained and organisms can be provided for their needs and interests. Abrupt changes in the physical environment can disrupt communities and cause organisms to become extinct if they can't adapt to the changes.

Organisms are thus not self-contained units that are independent of their surroundings. Remember the statement, As the community goes, so goes the organism. Often the best way to control a particular organism, whether you want to encourage or discourage its development, is to modify the community in which it exists, rather than mount a direct attack on the organism itself. For example, mosquitoes can often be controlled more efficiently by modifying the entire aquatic community in which they develop, such as lowering water levels in marshes and swamps, than by attempting to poison the organisms directly.[17]

Human welfare, like that of the mosquito, depends on the nature of the communities and ecosystems in which humans live and work out their existence. Industrial processes and products that alter essential elements of the community or create communities where the balance of ecological factors are changed, are ultimately going to affect humans for good or ill in some fashion. We need to have some idea of how humans are going to be affected before these changes are introduced and have irreversible effects or at least cause problems that are going to be very expensive to reverse.

Carrying capacity is another important concept. Every ecosystem does have limits in terms of the size of various populations that it can support, whether we are talking about human beings or animal populations. Every species or organism has certain needs that the community must provide in order for it to survive and continue to exist. But if any population gets too large in relation to its community, the ecosystem is overloaded and cannot provide the basic needs to every organism. Human beings need space, clean air, water, food, and other essentials in order to survive and maintain a quality existence, but if the human population gets too large relative to its environment, the carrying capacity of that ecosystem may be overtaxed, and human welfare may be affected adversely.

The same concept applies to essential elements of the environment such as air and water. Every medium has a certain ability to absorb waste material without serious harm done to the quality of that medium. Thus air, for example, can absorb a certain amount of waste material without serious harm done to its quality. But if the air's carrying capacity is exceeded, it becomes fouled by certain pollutants and the quality of the air is affected. Its natural dilutive capacity is violated, and human health is affected as a result because of exposure to harmful pollutants.

A related concept is that of *limiting factors*. Organisms depend for their success, and indeed their very existence, on a complex set of conditions. Any one condition that approaches or exceeds the limits of tolerance is said to be a limiting condition or a limiting factor. Under steady state conditions, an organism can be said to be no stronger than the weakest link in its chain of requirements. But under dynamic conditions, organisms may substitute a closely related substance for one that is required but is deficient in the environment. Or they may be able to alter the conditions in which they are living so as to reduce their requirements.[18]

Something that is in short supply may thus be a limiting factor, but something that is in oversupply may also provide limits. Factors such as heat, light, and water in greater amounts than required also inhibit an organism's development. Organisms thus have an ecological minimum and maximum. The range in between this minimum and maximum represents the limits of tolerance. Organisms with a wide range of tolerance for all factors are likely to be most widely distributed, but some organisms may have a wide range of tolerance for one factor and a narrow range for another. Thus their habitats are more restricted.[19]

Primary attention should be given to those factors that are believed to be "operationally significant" to the organism at some time during its life cycle. If policymakers are concerned about the environmental impact of a particular project, they should focus on those environmental conditions most likely to be critical or limiting to the organism that will be affected by the project. The purpose of an environmental analysis, such as preparation of an environmental impact statement, should be (1) to discover by observation, analysis, and experiment which factors are "operationally significant" to the organisms under consideration, and (2) to determine how these factors affect the individual, population, or community. Focusing on these objectives gives a decision maker a better chance of predicting with reasonable accuracy the environmental effects of disturbances or proposed environmental alterations.[20]

The *habitat* of an organism is simply the place where an organism lives. Some organisms need specialized habitats and thus finding them means searching out their characteristic habitats. The Endangered Species Act, for example, does not just address the organism and its right to exist, but also has implications for the habitat in which that organisms lives and moves. Thus environmentalists hope to preserve old-growth forests in the western part of the United States by using the act to preserve the habitat for a certain kind of owl that is on the endangered species list. The owl cannot be preserved without preserving its habitat. The term habitat may also refer to the place occupied by an entire community.[21]

There are four major habitats: the biosphere and the marine and estuarine, freshwater, and terrestrial habitats. The biosphere refers to the atmosphere surrounding the earth, a habitat that is under threat from modern industrial processes. The ozone layer that protects humans from ultraviolet rays of the sun is being depleted, and some industrial nations have taken steps to limit the production and use of certain compounds that are causing the depletion. The greenhouse effect has to do with the increased amounts of carbon dioxide dumped into the air and the apparent warming of the earth that results. Using the biosphere as a place in which to dispose of waste material is now causing some serious global environmental problems that need to be addressed. Pollutants dumped into the air prevent the biosphere from providing the kind of habitat plant and animal life need in order to survive.

The oceans of the world have been a source of food for centuries, and provide a rich habitat for many thousands of species of fish and other marine animals and plants. The role the oceans play in controlling the earth's atmosphere and climates is better understood than in the past as science discovers more about the importance of this habitat. The oceans are also a source of minerals as more and more deposits of minerals are found that are useful in industrial processes. They also became a source of oil as offshore drilling technology was developed to tap vast pools of oil underneath the ocean bottom. And they may even provide living space for future generations who want to live under the sea to escape the crowded conditions on earth. Humans must consider the oceans an integral part of their total life support system, and not as an inert supply depot that provides resources for the taking or as a vast waste disposal system that is impossible to pollute.[22]

An estuary is a semienclosed coastal body of water that has a free connection with the open sea. It is thus strongly affected by tidal action, and consists of a mixture of seawater and fresh water from land drainage. The mouths of rivers, coastal bays, tidal marshes, and bodies of water behind offshore beaches are examples of estuaries. Many different kinds of seafood are found in estuaries and many commercial and sport fisheries are dependent on the preservation of these habitats. When they become fouled with pollutants, these fisheries are threatened with extinction. Estuaries also function as permanent habitats for waterfowl and other birds or as resting places during their migration.[23]

Freshwater habitats include standing water such as lakes and ponds and running water such as streams or rivers. Although freshwater habitats occupy a relatively small portion of the earth's surface as compared to other habitats, their importance is far greater because they are the cheapest and most convenient sources of water for domestic and industrial needs, and freshwater ecosystems provide the least expensive and most convenient waste disposal systems for the majority of human communities. Because of abuses of this resource, the scarcity of fresh water often becomes the limiting factor to the growth of human communities.[24]

Finally, land masses are where the majority of human beings live, along with a rich diversity of plant and animal life. Humans derive most of the resources necessary for the production of goods from the land and depend on the land for most of their food. The terrestrial habitat is thus of utmost importance in the survival and growth of the human species, and yet land usage often follows destructive patterns because of the prevailing productive orientation toward land. The destruction of the Amazon rain forest is a good example of destroying an essential resource that to some has more value in the short run when it is cleared for farming because it is not seen as productive in its natural state. To an ecologist, nothing could make less sense and be further from the truth.

The concept of *ecological niche* is different from that of habitat. Niche is more inclusive and refers to the organism's functional role in the community or its status in terms of its activities, its rate of metabolism and growth, its effect on other organisms with which it comes into contact, and the extent it modifies or is capable of modifying important operations in the ecosystem. By way of analogy, it could be said that the habitat is the organism's address and the niche is its profession or role in the community. If we wish to become acquainted with some individual in our human community, we would first need to know his or her address in order to find them. But to really know the person, we would want to know something about his or her occupation, interests, associates, and the part he or she plays in community life in general.[25]

So it is with all organisms. They have an address where they can be found. But we also need to know about the particular niche or role they play in the larger scheme of things. They may perform some essential role in the ecosystem that cannot be replaced, and thus if the organism is destroyed, the ecosystem may be altered in some fundamental way. This concept is important in relation to the Amazon rain forest, where the habitat of certain plants and animals that are a form of unique species is rapidly being destroyed even before scientists have had a chance to study them and determine the unique niche they play in nature and the important role they may play with respect to the welfare of human beings.

The concept of a *biological clock* refers to natural rhythms or cycles that are in the nature of physiological mechanisms for measuring time in some fashion. There are two theories regarding the biological clock: (1) the endogenous timer hypothesis where the organism has some internal mechanism that can measure time without environmental clues, and (2) the external timing hypothesis where the internal clock is triggered by external signals from the environment, such as seasonal changes, or changes in light, temperature, tides, and similar factors. With regard to human beings, for example, many depend on an alarm clock to wake them up in the morning, but others seem to have an internal clock that wakes them up without an external source. This internal clock seems to work even in instances where there is a need to rise earlier than normal in order to catch an early flight, for example.[26]

These persistent rhythms have been found in a wide variety of organisms. The migratory habits of birds, for example, depends on some kind of biological clock that tells them when it is time to head north or south. Other organisms know when it is time to shed their skin or make other adjustments in regard to changing seasons. From the point of view of human activities, particularly in regard to the prevalence of external cues, if the environment is altered and these cues are no longer present or are changed in some fashion, the organism will have to adapt or may be made extinct if it can't adapt to these changes. Thus the total ecosystem may be affected by a change in some element that alters the biological rhythms of organisms in that ecosystem.

Exhibit 2.2

Important Concepts of Ecology

Cycles	The circulation of the chemical elements in the biosphere from the environment to organisms and back to the environment.
Food Chain	The transfer of food energy from its source in plants through a series of organisms where eating and being eaten is repeated a number of times.
Community	Any assemblege of populations living in a prescribed area or physical habitat that has characteristics in addition to its individual and population components.
Carrying Capacity	Maximum population of a particular species that a given habitat can support over a given period of time.
Limiting Factors	Single factor that limits the growth, abundance, and distribution of the population of a particular organism in an ecosystem.
Habitat	The place where an organism lives. The four major habitats are the biosphere, and marine and estuarine, freshwater, and terrestrial habitats.
Ecological Niche	An organism's functional role in the community or its status. Habitat is the organism's address; niche refers to its role in the community.
Biological Clock	Natural rhythms or cycles that are in the nature of physiological mechanisms for measuring time in some fashion.

PRINCIPLES OF ECOLOGY

The science of ecology deals with principles as does any other science, and part of the scientific process consists of the discovery of new principles that describe how nature works so we can have a better understanding of the ecological world in which we live. There are many such principles that can be found in the ecological literature, but only a few such principles that form the chapters of a recent book in ecology entitled the *Message of Ecology* are presented here. The purpose is to acquaint you with some important principles of ecology that have application to the practice of management. (See Exhibit 2.3).

    1. *The distribution of species is limited by barriers and unfavorable environments.* Every plant and animal seems to have a restricted distribution on earth. Barriers to dispersal of species — land, water, and mountains — have set the broad limits to distribution of species on a global scale. The movement of species by humans from one continent to another in the last 200 years has produced pest problems of one sort or another which provide evidence that ecological ignorance of natural dispersal can cause long-range problems.

    Some ecologists recommend that no one should be allowed to introduce any exotic animal or plant from one continent to another unless rigorous research has been done to show that the organism will not do damage to the environment or other native organisms. It is recommended that we stop the ecologically naive practice of assuming that newly introduced species are harmless additions. While there may be some short-run commercial benefits to be gained from the introduction of new species, the long-run consequences can be disastrous.[23]

    2. *No population increases without limit.* A population is a group or interbreeding organisms belonging to the same species. There are two processes that add plants or animals to a population: the addition of new organisms

Exhibit 2.3

Principles of Ecology

    1. The distribution of species is limited by barriers and unfavorable environments.
    2. No population increases without limit.
    3. Good and poor places exist for every species.
    4. Overexploited populations can collapse.
    5. Communities can rebound from disturbances.
    6. Communities can exist in several stable configurations.
    7. Keystone species may be essential to a community.
    8. Natural systems recycle essential materials.
    9. Climates change — communities change.
    10. Natural systems are products of evolution.

through births or seed production and the addition through movement into a population called immigration. There are also two processes that remove organisms from a population: deaths and emigration or movement out of a population. If we want to find out why a population either increased or decreased, we must determine which of these four processes changed to allow the increase or decrease.[24]

There are four components of the environment that act to change births, deaths, immigration, and emigration: (1) weather, (2) food, (3) other organisms, and (4) a place in which to live.[25] A change in any of these components will have an effect on the population. These components must be considered when human projects alter the environment in some significant manner. Predictions must be made as to what populations will be affected and whether they will increase or decrease because of these changes. Ignorance of these effects can cause some serious long-range problems.

This principle also holds true for human beings. For most of human history, the human population rose and fell because of the combined effect of starvation, disease, climactic catastrophes, and self-inflicted losses because of wars and other human events. But over the last several centuries, the human population has been on a growth spiral because of improvements in agriculture, public health, housing, and a reduction of warfare. This growth has been extremely rapid during the last century.

Improvements in science and technology have enabled humans to push back some of the natural limits to growth that previously held population growth in check. But the human population cannot continue to increase without limit according to most ecologists, as the carrying capacity of the earth will and has been exceeded. Science and technology cannot be depended on to extend the limits indefinitely, but humans must take steps to limit their growth through some forms of population control. Humans differ from other organisms in that we have the capability to impose our own controls rather than relying on the natural mechanisms of famine, plagues, or aggression to provide limits to growth.[26]

3. *Good and poor places exist for every species.* Every species is dependent on a good habitat in order for it to survive and grow. This is the reason some species are found in some habitats and not in others. Human beings, for example, can't survive in extremely cold or hot climates without altering the environment in some fashion. In order to protect a species, we need to know what kind of a habitat it needs in order to survive. And if we want to eliminate a species like unwanted pests, we can make habitats poor in order to get rid of them. Every species is affected by the weather, nutrients, other species, and shelter. Manipulation of these factors in the habitat of a species can affect its ability to thrive and develop. By proper management of habitats, we can assist the growth and development of those species we want to preserve, and hasten the demise of those pests and other predators we want to get rid of for one reason or another.[27]

4. *Overexploited populations can collapse.* If any population is overexploited for human or other purposes, the population may not be able to maintain itself under the current conditions. The buffalo were overexploited and almost became an extinct species. The same thing has happened to other plants and animals that were used beyond the level at which they could sustain themselves. Ecologists mention three factors that are important in this regard: (1) below a certain level of exploitation populations are resilient and increase survival, growth, or recruitment to compensate for loss, (2) exploitation may be raised to a point at which they cause extinction of the resource, and (3) somewhere between no exploitation and excessive exploitation there is a level of maximum sustainable yield.[28]

Extinctions of plants and animals have occurred throughout history, and many of these extinctions have been the result of natural causes. However, the role humans have played in the extinction of species is being recognized as more important than previously expected. Even in prehistoric times, it is suspected that humans played an important role in the demise of some species of animals because of overkill. And certainly in modern times where technology has given humans greater powers of destruction and the means to alter habitats on a scale not known before, the role that humans play in the extinction of species because of overexploitation is terribly important. The exploitation of populations can be managed if we know the conditions that are necessary for continuance of the population and take steps to maintain a balance between human needs and the needs of the population itself.

5. *Communities can rebound from disturbances.* Populations of plants and animals exist in a matrix of other plants and animals that is called a community. When these communities are disturbed by an incident like an oil spill, the community can rebound and reach a new level of stability, but it most likely will not return to its original configuration, especially if the disturbance is large enough. One of the tasks of ecologists who study communities is to find the limits of stability of natural communities and see how they rebound from disturbances of one kind or another.

Oil spills like the one in Prince William Sound have many far-reaching and long-lasting effects on biological communities. Crude oil contains substances that are toxic to marine animals and plants and may stay in the water for some length of time posing a long-term danger. A more immediate disturbance is that birds and sea animals become coated with the oil and die as a result. Organisms accumulate hydrocarbons from oil in their tissues, and if these hydrocarbons are not broken down, they may reach high concentrations. If the species is edible, it eventually may pose a cancer threat to humans. Thus oil spills have multiple effects on marine organisms and the community in which they exist. (See Figure 2.1.)

The recovery time varies depending on the climactic zone and other factors, but eventually the community will recover from an oil spill or other

Figure 2.1

Effects of Oil Pollution on Marine Organisms

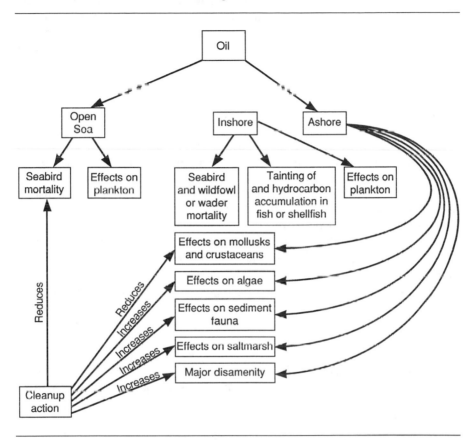

Source: Charles J. Krebs, *The Message of Ecology* (New York: Harper & Row, 1988), p. 77.

disturbance. However, this ability of communities to recover from major disturbances must not be translated into a license to disturb natural communities or allow us to be complacent and not take the proper precautions to prevent oil spills from occurring or being ready to contain them if they should happen. It is recommended that we treat natural communities the same way we treat our bodies. We have all recovered from various diseases, but we do not go about needlessly exposing ourselves to these diseases. We try to avoid them if possible, and so should we try to avoid disturbances to natural communities.[29]

6. *Communities can exist in several stable configurations.* Sometimes a biological community can rebound from a disturbance and return to its original configuration, but if the disturbance is large enough or is permanent in

nature, the community may shift to a new configuration. The fish community of Lake Erie, for example, has moved to a new configuration because of uncontrolled overfishing, erosion and nutrient pollution, introduced species, stream destruction, dams and shoreline changes, and toxic chemicals and pesticides.[30] While these communities can thus exist in several stable configurations, humans will typically find some of these configurations more desirable than others.

The simple belief that biological communities will return to their pristine configuration once a disturbance is removed is a myth, as they may not revert to their original condition when the stress is removed. The promise of Exxon to return Prince William Sound to its original condition is a bit of ecological nonsense as well as arrogant public relations material. We need to find out more about what forces can move communities from one configuration to another. At the present time, we introduce major disturbances into biological communities and then act surprised by the results of our disturbances. If we can discover the rule by which communities change, we would be in a better position to restore them when they are damaged. Biological communities are resilient, but it is not easy and cheap to return them to a desirable state, and they will not necessarily return to their original state naturally.[31]

7. *Keystone species may be essential to a community.* This principle is important when it comes to determining what species belong on rare and endangered species lists. Biological communities contain hundreds of plants and animals and the important question to ask is whether they are of equal importance in a community. Species are important if their removal causes the community to change in some significant manner either by gaining or losing some additional species. The questions to be asked concern how replaceable a species is and how much its loss reverberates to other species in a community.[32]

Every community has one or two dominant species at various levels that are the most abundant or contain the most biomass. But these dominant species, according to some ecologists, are not necessarily essential to a community. The essential species are called keystone species. Their activities determine the structure of the entire community, and those species often turn out to be unexpected. If communities are controlled by competition, the removal of one or a few species may not be noticed. But if a community is controlled by a keystone species, the removal of this species can have dramatic consequences.[33]

8. *Natural systems recycle essential materials.* Nature consists of various kinds of recycling mechanisms that conserve essential resources. Gaseous elements such as nitrogen, oxygen, and hydrogen all circulate in global cycles and long-distance transfers are common. The oxygen we breathe is part of a large pool or reservoir that has had many different sources. Solid elements circulate in local cycles where there are no mechanisms for long-distance

transfers. Nutrient cycles have been studied in many biological systems, particularly those that can and have been exploited by human activities.[34]

Human activities can disrupt these nutrient cycles and enough nutrients can be lost to cause a downgrading of a particular ecological system. But ecosystems can also be affected by nutrient additions as is the case in the eutrophication of lakes and the problem that acid rain causes for large bodies of water as well as for trees and other plants. Ecologically sound management practices can be used to allow ecosystems to recover nutrients that are lost because of human activities such as tree cutting so that ecosystems are not destroyed. Humans must help nature recycle essential materials because our fate is linked to the nutrient cycles needed for human existence.

9. *Climates change—communities change.* Climates change on all time scales, and these changes have dramatic implications for all populations, including human populations, that exist on earth. Not all the changes that occur in biological communities are due to changes in climate, but an examination of the changes in human communities that have taken place throughout history shows that climate plays a major role in these changes. While climates change because of natural causes, human activities have come to play a larger role as their scale and extent has increased. The greenhouse effect is one such example, and if indeed, humans are changing the climate in various parts of the world because of increased industrial activity, communities have no choice but to change accordingly. This principle must be recognized as these global environmental problems become more important.

10. *Natural systems are products of evolution.* According to some ecologists, one of the greatest and most persistent errors of biological thought is to regard each species as a constant and fixed type in which all organisms are genetically equal. Supposedly, Charles Darwin was one of the first scientists to deal with this mistake and recognize cumulative change in the characteristics of organisms over many generations. While the principle of evolution had been discovered before Darwin, his contribution was to recognize that the mechanism for evolution is natural selection.[35]

Natural selection operates over time to produce organisms that are adapted to their environment. Favorable attributes give higher reproductive rates or better survival rates. Thus individuals with these favorable attributes are selected because they live and survive longer, and these attributes thus become more common in the population over several generations. As humans change environments, they are also thus going to change the evolutionary patterns in ways they do not understand. Organisms are going to adapt to the new environment and the process of natural selection is going to favor some attributes over others because of changes in the environment.

The evolutionary process is the net result of ecology in action where change is inevitable. Since Darwin discovered the principle of natural selection, biologists have continually discovered how much natural selection has changed organisms to the local physical and biological environment. But there is still much to learn about the evolutionary process and how human activities affect this process. "We are one species in a world whose biological heritage is as irreplaceable as our own cultural heritage. We are the custodians of this biological heritage and our goals must be to study it, to understand it, to enjoy it, and to pass it to our children undiminished."[36]

These and other concepts and principles of ecology are important for business managers to know something about. A narrow lookout on the part of business managers with respect to business activities is likely to lead to environmental disaster. By focusing on economic concerns and ignoring environmental impacts, the environment is left to fend for itself, and under the pressure of more and more demands from human activities, it is becoming seriously degraded throughout the world. Education about important ecological concepts and principles is one important component of a strategy to counter this narrow outlook. By taking these concepts and principles into account, business managers can develop policies that are consistent with environmental preservation and learn to live in harmony with nature instead of perpetuating the dualistic conception of humans against nature.

Questions for Discussion

1. What is the science or study of ecology? How does ecology differ from other sciences? What is the focus of its concern? When did the science of ecology begin?

2. Distinguish between an ecosystem, community, population, and organism. How do these four components of ecology relate to each other and to the whole of ecology?

3. What is an ecosystem? Why is it important for business executives to have some knowledge about the ways in which an ecosystem functions? Describe a major impact that a business activity has had on an ecosystem. What was done to mitigate the impact?

4. Describe the concept of cycles and their importance to the study of ecology. What relevance does the concept of cycles have to environmental problems that concern business?

5. Why is the concept of a food chain important? Describe how pesticide residues, for example, can be concentrated as they move up the food chain. What implications does this concentration have for human beings?

6. Distinguish between carrying capacity and limiting factors. What are the implications of both these concepts for economic and population growth? How do they relate to a concept such as sustainable growth?

7. What is a habitat? Describe the four major habitats. How do habitats relate to the Endangered Species Act and the controversy over old-growth forests? What are the important habitats in your area, and how are they being protected?

8. What is the importance of an ecological niche? How does this concept differ from a habitat? What is the importance of this concept to economic development, particularly in countries that have vast rain forests that are being cut down?

9. What is the notion of a biological clock? Do humans have a biological clock inside them? Give evidence for your opinion. How can economic development activities interfere with the functioning of this internal mechanism?

10. Review the ten ecological principles described in the chapter. Think of their relevance to business activities. Which are most important, in your opinion, for business to consider? Are there other ecological principles that you are aware of that should be considered?

NOTES

1. Joseph S. Levine, "Your Child Can Learn Science," *World Monitor*, Vol. 4, No. 2 (February 1991), p. 44.

2. Paul R. Ehrlich, *The Machinery of Nature* (New York: Simon & Schuster, 1986), p. 13.

3. Ibid., p. 236.

4. Ibid., p. 226.

5. Eugene P. Odum, *Fundamentals of Ecology*, 3rd ed. (Philadelphia: Saunders, 1971), p. 3.

6. Michael Begon, John L. Harper, and Colin R. Townsend, *Ecology: Individuals, Populations, and Communities* (Sunderland, MA: Sinauer, 1986), p. xi.

7. Odum, *Fundamentals*, p. 3.

8. Begon, Harper, and Townsend, *Ecology*, p. x.

9. Odum, *Fundamentals*, p. 9.

10. Ehrlich, *Machinery*, p. 239.

11. Odum, *Fundamentals*, p. 251.

12. Ibid., p. 267.

13. Ibid.

14. Ibid., p. 86.

15. Ibid., p. 63.

16. Ibid., p. 140.

17. Ibid., pp. 140–141.
18. Eugene P. Odum, *Basic Ecology* (New York: Saunders, 1983), pp. 221–222.
19. Ibid., p. 223.
20. Ibid., p. 225.
21. Odum, *Fundamentals,* pp. 234–235.
22. Ibid., p. 324.
23. Ibid., p. 352.
24. Ibid., p. 295.
25. Ibid., pp. 234–235.
26. Ibid., p. 245.
27. Charles J. Krebs, *The Message of Ecology* (New York: Harper & Row, 1988), pp. 15–16.
28. Ibid., pp. 17–18.
29. Ibid., p. 18.
30. Ibid., p. 29.
31. Ibid., pp. 31–43.
32. Ibid., p. 48.
33. Ibid., pp. 76–77.
34. Ibid., p. 89.
35. Ibid., p. 97.
36. Ibid.
37. Ibid., p. 106.
38. Ibid., pp. 113–114.
39. Ibid., p. 147.
40. Ibid., p. 167.

～

Suggested Readings

Abrahamson, Warren G. (ed) *Plant-Animal Interactions.* New York: McGraw-Hill, 1989.

Andresartha, H. G., and L. C. Birch. *The Ecological Web.* Chicago: University of Chicago Press, 1984.

Attenborough, David. *The Living Planet.* Boston: Little, Brown, 1984.

Begon, Michael, John L. Harper, and Colin R. Townsend. *Ecology: Individuals, Populations, and Communities.* Sunderland, MA: Sinauer, 1986.

Deshmukh, Ian. *Ecology and Tropical Biology.* Palo Alto, CA: Blackwell Scientific Publications, 1986.

Ehrlich, Paul R. *The Machinery of Nature.* New York: Simon & Schuster, 1986.

Krebs, Charles J. *The Message of Ecology.* New York: Harper & Row, 1988.

Miller, G. Tyler. *Living in the Environment,* 6th ed. Belmont, CA: Wadsworth, 1990.

Odum, Eugene P. *Basic Ecology.* New York: Saunders, 1983.

Odum, Eugene P. *Fundamentals of Ecology,* 3rd ed. Philadelphia: Saunders, 1971.

Smith, Robert L. *Elements of Ecology,* 2nd ed. New York: Harper & Row, 1985.

Watt, Kenneth E. F. *Understanding the Environment.* New York: Cambridge University Press, 1985.

CHAPTER 3

ENVIRONMENTAL ETHICS AND ECOLOGY

~

Environmental ethics, as a form of applied normative ethics, deals with the approach to the environment that *ought* to be taken as well as the approach that *is* taken. It demands critical thinking about the policies of the private and public sectors that have been developed in response to environmental issues. It also questions the assumptions upon which those policies are based. The ethical approach examines traditional solutions and advocates new ways of thinking about the environment. Questions are asked about our responsibilities toward the environment and how these responsibilities ought to be reflected in the policies adopted by the government and private companies as well as in the habits of the population as a whole.

The traditional approach of Western societies has been to objectify nature and see it as there to be manipulated to serve human interests with no interests of its own that deserve respect. Trees have no value in and of themselves; they are only valuable when they are cut down and processed into lumber that can then be used to build houses. Scenic areas of the country have been set aside as national parks for human enjoyment, but they have no particular value in and of themselves. The desert is considered a wasteland waiting to be developed rather than a particular kind of ecosystem with its own value and beauty that deserves protection from developers.

This approach to nature is anthropocentric: Right and wrong are determined by human interests, and the promotion of human welfare is the ultimate objective. This view has sometimes been called humanistic because concern for the environment is of a lower priority than concern for humans, who are helped or hurt by the conditions of their environment.[1] Nature has

48

value only because people value it, and environmental preservation is good only because it is good for human beings.

It has been argued that only humans are moral agents, and thus only they have moral status and can pursue moral claims. Something that has no consciousness and so can experience no pleasure or pain, joy or suffering, does not deserve moral respect.[2] Why shouldn't a tree be cut down if no harm comes to any human being from its destruction? Why do certain species need to be preserved if they have no use for human beings? Nothing can have intrinsic value except the activities, experiences, and lives of sentient beings. The ecological community has no intrinsic value over and above that contained in the lives of its human members.[3]

Ethics has been defined as a concern with actions and practices whose aim is to improve the welfare of people. Ethicists explore the concepts and language that are used to direct such practices, and are concerned with clarifying what constitutes human welfare and the kind of conduct necessary to promote such welfare.[4] Ethics attempts to understand what makes a good life.[5] It studies what goals people ought to pursue and what actions they ought to perform. Ethics concerns itself with human conduct, meaning human activity that is done knowingly and, to a large extent, willingly.[6]

All of these definitions are profoundly anthropocentric, in that they say nothing about the welfare of nature and the rights of nature or animals that may interfere with the human quest for the good life. It may be convenient for humans to use animals extensively in testing substances for toxic effects, but what about the rights of animals to be protected from such abuse? Human beings knowingly cut down the rain forest in their quest for a better life without thinking about the ecological function of that forest in the larger scheme of things. By limiting ethical concerns to human beings, nature is shut out and is subject to exploitation and abuse in the interests of promoting human welfare.

The traditional approach to nature and ethics serves the interests of economics and the ethical concerns that are at the heart of a materialistic approach to human welfare. Nature is there to be exploited and used for human purposes and is viewed as more or less self-sufficient. The corporation is seen as an economic institution with economic responsibilities to produce goods and services as efficiently as possible. Its ethical responsibilities are largely tied up with using resources efficiently to promote economic growth, which enhances human welfare, at least in a materialistic sense. Concern for nature, if it exists at all, is limited to conserving resources coupled with a concern to minimize pollution. But there has been little respect shown for the rights of nature or a concern to view nature from an ecological rather than an economic perspective. An economic ethic is at the base of our view of the corporation and poses a problem when we try to incorporate environmental concerns into corporate behavior.

THE TRADITIONAL VIEW:
AN ECONOMIC ETHIC

The so-called traditional view of the corporation assumes that good ethics and good business is all part of the same approach. There is and can be no divergence between the operation of a successful business organization and ethical behavior on the part of the organization because ethical responsibilities are defined in terms of marketplace performance. What is considered to be ethical is precisely what is considered to be good business. The ethical notion that forms the basis of this view is the principle of economizing. A business organization is formed to provide goods and services that people in a society are willing to buy at prices they can afford. In order to accomplish this goal successfully, business must economize in the use of resources — combine resources efficiently — so that it can earn profits to continue in business and perhaps even expand into new markets.

The ethical performance of business is thus tied up with marketplace performance. If a business organization is successful and earns a satisfactory level of profits, it means that the business has economized in the use of resources, assuming that competition exists in the markets it is serving. The business has produced something people want to buy, and has done so in such a way that it has met the competition. Successful performance in the marketplace is ethical behavior, and there is no divergence between being ethical and being successful in the marketplace. Successful business performance and acceptable ethical behavior are believed to be one and the same thing.

The traditional view was stated some years ago by Oliver Sheldon, a management theorist who in a classic 1923 book strongly advocated the development of a professional creed for management.[7] Sheldon believed that the managerial function was a constant factor in any industrial organization no matter what external forces exist or the nature of the economic system in which the organization operates. The function of management remains much the same under any set of external conditions and is that element charged with guiding the organization through periods of change. Management is the one stable element in the process of evolution. There is no structure or system where management does not fulfill approximately the same functions under the present system.

Because management was such an important factor in modern societies all over the world, Sheldon thought it was important to develop a managerial creed, to devise a philosophy of management or a code of principles that is "scientifically determined and generally accepted," to act as a guide for the daily practice of the profession.[8] Without such a creed, says Sheldon, there can be "no guarantee of efficiency, no hope of concerted effort, and no assurance of stability."⁹ Such a creed, in other words, can help to establish the legitimacy of the managerial function and assure its continuity.

Sheldon's creed links the managerial function to the well-being of the community of which it is a part, and encourages management to take the initiative in raising the general ethical standards and conception of social justice in the community. The goods and services produced by a company "must be furnished at the lowest prices compatible with an adequate standard of quality, and distributed in such a way as directly or indirectly to promote the highest ends of the community."¹⁰ Such a statement calls for management to be responsible and ethical in relation to broader community interests. Management is encouraged to look beyond the bottom line and the interests of stockholders and be concerned about the public interest. The creed recognizes that management serves at the discretion of society and derives its legitimacy from maintaining a useful social function, a theme found in the literature on modern social responsibility.

But what are the interests of the community, at least as Sheldon sees them? The creed is based on the ethic of economizing. The primary concern of management, according to Sheldon, is to promote the efficient use of resources, both personal, or human resources, and capital, or material resources. The primary focus of the creed is on economic utilization of the factors of production, which can be determined by the scientific method. Thus the community is presumably interested in an efficient use of resources in order to increase its standard of living. Management thus derives its legitimacy from applying scientific principles to the running of corporate organizations.

> Industry exists to provide the commodities and services which are necessary for the good life of the community, in whatever volume they are requested. . . . It is for Management, while maintaining industry upon an economic basis, to achieve the object for which it exists by the development of efficiency — both personal or human efficiency, in the workers, in the managerial staff, and in the relations between the two, and impersonal efficiency, in the methods and material conditions of the factory.¹¹

There is no mention in the creed about what is now called the social responsibilities of management. Although Sheldon recognizes the importance of certain aspects of the external environment, such as government, public attitudes, foreign trade, and so on, social issues are not mentioned. Perhaps it is not fair to criticize Sheldon for this omission because his creed only reflects the times in which he wrote. Problems such as pollution, equal opportunity, occupational safety and health, and other social issues were not generally recognized as serious problems that needed attention in the twenties. However, a more modern statement of the same view by Milton Friedman, who engages in the debate about social responsibility, argues that the social responsibility of business is to increase its profits.[12] In other words, the social and ethical responsibilities of business are exhausted in terms of marketplace performance. As long as business performs its economizing function well, it has fulfilled its social and ethical responsibilities and nothing more need be said.

Another characteristic of this view exists in the method Sheldon advocates to make the creed specific and develop a set of standards to guide managerial practice. These standards, according to Sheldon, can be determined by the analytical and synthetical methods of science. The aim of those who are practicing the management profession should be to develop a "science of industrial management," which is distinct from the science it employs and the technique of any particular industry.[13] Yet if management is truly a science, and the practice of management can be circumscribed by a set of scientific principles, what need is there for a philosophy or professional creed for management? If management is a science, it becomes nothing more than the application of scientific principles to concrete situations. It involves no consideration of responsibilities to the larger community outside of marketplace behavior or any conscious ethical reflection that is a part of a true professional activity.

Thus the traditional view of ethics and business subsumes ethics under marketplace performance and does not necessitate any conscious ethical considerations of business's responsibilities to society or to the environment other than successful economic performance. Ethics is totally captured by the notion of economizing, which can be promoted by the development of scientific principles related to an efficient combination of resources. One advantage of this view is that it does at least place ethics at the core of managerial behavior and makes ethics central to the performance of the management function. The disadvantage of this approach is that it removes any need for conscious ethical reflection on the part of management, but leaves it for the management scientists and economists to develop guidelines and principles that promote efficiency.

CHANGING VIEWS: SOCIAL RESPONSIBILITY

While not everyone accepted the notion that business was solely an economic institution with only economic responsibilities, it does seem that this view of ethics and business has been the prevailing view in our society since its inception. As long as the system worked well enough for most people, there were not any serious questions raised about the ethical behavior of businesspeople outside of the marketplace context. But a concern with social responsibilities began to raise serious questions about this view of ethics and business. The problems that social responsibility advocates addressed, such as pollution and unsafe workplaces, were in large part created by the drive for efficiency in the marketplace. Thus it began to be argued that there was a divergence between the performance of business in the marketplace and its performance as far as the social aspects of its behavior were concerned.

People began to believe that cleaning up pollution, providing safer workplaces, producing products that were safe to use, promoting equal opportunity, and attempting to eliminate poverty in our society had something to do with promoting human welfare and creating the good life in our society. Yet business was causing some of these problems and perpetuating others in its quest for an efficient allocation of resources. For example, by economizing in the use of resources and disposing of its waste material as cheaply as possible by dumping it into the air or disposing of toxic material by simply dumping barrels of chemicals in some out-of-the-way place, business was causing some serious pollution problems. By always hiring the best qualified person for a job opening and not having some kind of an affirmative action program, business was helping to perpetuate the effects of discrimination against minorities and women.

It was at these points of intersection between the economic performance of business and changing social values of society that ethical questions began to surface. Business increasingly came to be viewed as a social as well as an economic institution. Social responsibility advocates strongly argued that management needed to take the social impacts of business into account when developing policies and strategies, and much effort was devoted to convincing management to take its social responsibilities seriously. A great deal of research was done to help management redesign corporate organizations and develop policies and practices that would enable corporations to respond to the social expectations of society and measure their social performance.

The deficiencies of the traditional view of ethics and business began to be exposed. It became clear that there were many points of divergence between good business performance and what society expected of its business organizations in terms of ethical behavior. An ethical creed based on this traditional view, such as the one proposed by Sheldon, doesn't include these social aspects of corporate activities or encourage management to pay attention to the social impacts of corporate operations. Thus it provides no means or rationale for management to internalize the social costs of production and leaves this task to government regulation, a social control mechanism that is generally unacceptable to management as well as inefficient.

Although Sheldon wanted to see management in a broader social and ethical context, he ended up being a victim of his own scientific outlook. Science is descriptive in nature, and cannot prescribe for management or society the objectives that are worth pursuing. While the scientific method is crucially important to management, it is not sufficient by itself to provide an ethical or moral philosophy for management. Such a philosophy can no longer be built solely on the notion of economizing, but must include the broader purposes of the community and its welfare, an ethical vision that Sheldon so eloquently stated but then failed to develop.

The problem facing modern management theorists who accept the fact that a divergence often exists between ethical behavior and marketplace behavior is how to connect ethics with management in such a way that it is not peripheral to mainstream business concerns. One way is simply to argue that good ethics is good business, that being ethical will lead to success in the marketplace. Ethical behavior will be rewarded by increased profits, improved performance on the stock market, and other relevant measures of business success. Ethical considerations are not exhausted by economizing in the use of resources and deserve conscious reflection and attention. But by choosing to be ethical in all aspects of business operations and following separate ethical principles, management will be economically successful as well as ethical in its behavior.

The social responsibility advocates tried to make this argument in convincing management to take the notion seriously. They made various arguments based on the notion of long-run self-interest, that by being socially responsible business was taking care of its long-range health and survival. Business could not remain a healthy and viable organization in a society that was deteriorating. Thus it made sense for business to devote some of its resources to helping solve some of the most serious social problems of society, whether they be education, discrimination, or poverty, because business could function better in a society where most of its members shared in a high standard of living and enjoyed an improved quality of life.

Other arguments had to do with gaining a better public image, that is, by being socially responsible business organizations could gain more customers and provide more of an incentive for investors to put their money in the company. There are several contemporary examples of companies that have tried to appear concerned about public health and the environment through their advertising program. Finally, other arguments had to do with the avoidance of government regulation. By being socially responsible and responding to changing social expectations effectively, business might be able to eliminate the need for onerous government regulations that would affect its profits and other aspects of its performance.

These arguments were never very convincing because they were not based on a solid moral philosophy about the nature of the corporation and its management but were more in the nature of moralizing about certain aspects of business behavior. It now seems that social responsibility was more of a doctrine than a serious theory for business. Scholars and executives who advocated social responsibility seemed to do so more as an article of faith than as a theoretical paradigm that could bid for serious attention and begin to compete with the economic theory as an alternative description of ethical responsibilities. By and large, the economic theory of the firm has survived intact from attacks mounted by social responsibility advocates and has not been replaced by any new theories or ways of thinking about the corporation and its responsibilities. The bottom line of corporate organizations as well as for the whole nation is still economic in nature.

There are several reasons for this development, not the least of which is the difficulty of implementing social responsibility in a competitive context. Being socially responsible costs money. Pollution control equipment is expensive to buy and operate. Ventilation equipment to take toxic fumes out of the workplace is expensive. Proper disposal of toxic wastes in landfills can be very costly and time consuming. These efforts cut into profits, and in a competitive system, companies that go very far in this direction will simply price themselves out of the market. This is a fact of life for companies operating in a free enterprise system that the social responsibility advocates never took seriously.

> [E]very business . . . is, in effect, "trapped" in the business system it has helped to create. It is incapable, as an individual unit, of transcending that system. . . . the dream of the socially responsible corporation that, replicated over and over again can transform our society is illusory. . . . Because their aggregate power is not unified, not truly collective, not organized, they [corporations] have no way, even if they wished, of redirecting that power to meet the most pressing needs of society. . . . Such redirection could only occur through the intermediate agency of government rewriting the rules under which all corporations operate.[14]

Management has to be concerned about the economic performance of the organization. It cannot set aside these requirements to pursue social objectives that conflict with economic performance and expect to remain in business for very long. When there is a choice to be made between an ethical "ought" and a technical "must," something business must do to remain a viable organization within the system, it seems clear which path most managements will follow. Technical business matters are the ultimate values — a technical business necessity is a must that always takes precedence over an ethical ought that would be nice to implement but is simply not practical under most business conditions.[15]

It could be argued that social responsibility theory and principles cannot provide answers to the problems of finance, personnel, production, and general management decision making. The businessperson's role is defined largely, though not exclusively, in terms of private gain and profit, and to suggest that this can be set aside for adherence to a set of social responsibilities, however well intentioned, is startlingly naive and romantic. The businessperson is locked into a going system of values and ethics that largely determine the actions that can be taken. There is little question that at any given time individuals who are active within an institution are subject in large measure to its prevailing characteristics.

The power of the traditional view of the corporation, whether evoked by Oliver Sheldon or Milton Friedman, is that it is relatively precise and makes sense in a mechanistic way. Most people can immediately grasp the essential elements of economic theory and understand how all the pieces fit together. The traditional view of the corporation legitimizes self-interest, prescribes the responsibilities of corporations in ways that can be measured, and provides relatively clear guidelines for managerial decision making. It rests on an ethic that is acceptable to society at large where a utilitarian perspective is used to justify an instrumental approach to nature. Competition assures that resources will be used efficiently to promote human welfare by producing more goods and services to increase economic wealth.

Social responsibility doctrines, on the other hand, are amorphous, fuzzy, and provide no clear guidelines for managerial behavior. The critics of social responsibility were right when they anticipated the difficulty of providing a legitimate basis for social action on the part of corporate managers. Social responsibility advocates provided no sound moral basis for managerial social action other than some impossible-to-measure notions of enlightened self-interest or creation of a better corporate image. Worthy goals perhaps, but certainly difficult to implement in a competitive context.

PUBLIC POLICY AND SOCIAL RESPONSIVENESS

Some scholars turned to public policy as an alternative to social responsibility because of these frustrations. It was difficult to teach students anything substantive about social responsibility that might be useful in their careers as managers of corporate organizations. And during the 1970s, most, if not all, social issues became public policy matters as legislation was passed and regulations were issued dealing with environmental protection, workplace safety and health, equal opportunity, consumer protection, and other social concerns. Events seemed to be overtaking corporate managers, even those who made their best efforts to be socially responsible. These efforts did not stem the tide of government involvement in more and more aspects of corporate behavior.

The public policy approach seemed to offer several advantages over the notion of social responsibility as a theoretical framework for an expanded notion of corporate responsibilities. When regulations were issued, these effectively operationalized the social responsibilities of management in great detail. These regulations sometimes specified what kind of wood could be used in ladders, what standards had to be met with regard to specific pollutants, what kind of advertising content would pass muster with federal agencies, and similar concerns. The public policy approach took the institutional context of business into account and provided a legitimacy for socially responsible actions on the part of management, as government, acting on behalf of its citizens, had a legitimate right grounded in democratic theory, to provide guidelines for managers and shape corporate behavior to correspond more closely with societal expectations.

There did not seem, at least on the surface, a need for a theoretical underpinning for public policy at least as it affected corporations, because business has a moral obligation to obey the law as a good citizen. Failure to do so subjects the corporation to all sorts of penalties and other problems in society. Thus the social responsibility of business is not only to perform well in the marketplace and meet its economic objectives, but also to follow the directives of society at large as expressed in and through the public policy process. The public policy process and marketplace are both sources or guidelines for managerial behavior.[16]

> Society can choose to allocate its resources any way it wants and on the basis of any criteria it deems relevant. If society wants to enhance the quality of air and water, it can choose to allocate resources for the production of these goods and put constraints on business in the form of standards. . . . These nonmarket decisions are made by those who participate in the public policy process and represent their views of what is best for themselves and society as a whole. . . . It is up to the body politic to determine which market outcomes are and are not appropriate. If market outcomes are not to be taken as normative, a form of regulation which requires public participation is the only alternative. The social responsibility of business is not operational and certainly not to be trusted. When business acts contrary to the normal pressures of the marketplace, only public policy can replace the dictates of the market.[17]

Other scholars turned to corporate social responsiveness as an alternative, and avoided the frustration of dealing with social responsibility by focusing on the manner in which corporations were responding to societal expectations. This effort was more pragmatic and management oriented and less philosophical in its approach. The attempt of scholars proceeding in this direction was to discover patterns of responsiveness that will help in understanding how corporations have coped with a changing social environment, and to try and explain differences in responses between corporations. This research was largely directed to help corporations respond more effectively to social problems by identifying key variables within the organization that were determinative of the response pattern.

> Corporate social responsiveness refers to the capacity of a corporation to respond to social pressures. The literal act of responding, or of achieving a generally responsive posture, to society is the focus of corporate social responsiveness. . . . One searches the organization for mechanisms, procedures, arrangements, and behavioral patterns, that, taken collectively, would mark the organization as more or less capable of responding to social pressures. It then becomes evident that organizational design and managerial competence play important roles in how extensively and how well a company responds to social demands and needs.[18]

Many scholars dealing with social responsiveness have utilized the stakeholder concept to describe the various constituencies to which corporations have to respond and prescribe corporate responsibilities. The stakeholder model is a useful tool to analyze and describe the various relationships of a corporation to its main constituents in society, but it is by no means a serious theoretical attempt that could even begin to replace the economic paradigm. Stakeholder relations can be analyzed in economic terms, and often are, and while a manager might have to balance the interests of various stakeholder groups in order to resolve a problem, he or she does so in an economic context. In order to stay in business and continue to make a profit, business may have to respond to certain stakeholder interests.

Both of these approaches, public policy and social responsiveness, have been criticized on the basis of ignoring the deeper value issues involved in corporate responsibility. The criticism is made that scholars in both camps have tried to ignore deeper value issues by focusing on non-normative concerns. The advocates of social responsiveness urged corporations to avoid philosophic questions of social responsibility and concentrate on more pragmatic matters related to responding effectively to social pressures. They shunned normative questions by attempting to conduct value-free inquiry into the corporate response processes and developing various techniques such as social forecasting and issues management that could improve the ability of corporations to respond to social concerns.[19]

The same is true for advocates of the public policy approach, as they have been criticized for failing to acknowledge how thoroughly saturated the public process is with value-laden phenomena. There was a hope that by using the public policy approach, scholars could escape the subjectivity and vagueness of corporate social responsibility philosophizing and substitute a more objective and value-neutral basis for measuring and judging business social performance. If business adhered to the standards of performance expressed in the law and existing public policy, then it could be judged as being socially responsive to the changing expectations of society. But when we dig beneath the surface of the public policy approach, we find it is plagued by the same kinds of ethical dilemmas that bogged down earlier attempts to deal with the social responsibilities of business. Public policy is, in the final analysis, all about values and value conflicts, and public policy solutions to social problems are built on some conception of the good life that has to do with the promotion of human welfare by corporate activities.[20]

Neither of these approaches advanced an understanding of the normative dimension related to corporate behavior, and they contributed little, if anything, to the development of an alternative theory for supporting the notion of social or environmental responsibility. The economic theory of the corporation stayed largely intact as social responsiveness and public policy concerned themselves with mostly peripheral matters. Responses to social concerns are made within the established framework of the traditional enterprise where economizing is dominant over social values. And public policy responses are shaped to correspond with the dominant economic value system that determines corporate behavior. All of the normative questions about corporate social responsibilities are still on the table and largely unanswered.[21]

Toward an Environmental Ethic

The normative question that is unanswered has to do with the nature of the attempts to broaden the ethical responsibilities of business. All of the previously described attempts to develop broader notions of the good society and prescribe a corresponding set of social responsibilities for corporations suffer from the same problem. They are profoundly anthropocentric, that is to say, human centered. This characteristic leaves them lacking in a world besieged by environmental problems that just a few years ago were seen only as quality-of-life issues, not survival issues. All of these efforts to deal with corporate responsibility and redefine the good life reflect the arrogance of Western culture with respect to its approach to nature.

Although the social responsibility issues that developed in the 1960s did include environmental concerns, these concerns were also largely human centered. The public policy measures passed in the 1960s and 1970s were based on the protection of human health, not on a concern for the protection of the environment for its own sake. The typical stakeholder map includes stockholders, creditors, employees, consumers, government, and so forth, but it never includes plants and animals or nature in general, all of which have a significant stake in corporate activities. The social contract model, which is often used to support ethical responsibilities, is a contract between human beings. The natural world is never included in the bargain.

Scholars simply must take a broader ecological view and abandon an anthropological perspective. Human beings are not the center of the universe, nor are they at the center of the earth. They are but one species, albeit an important one, in a world populated by thousands of species. Human beings could not survive without the existence of these species, whereas other plant and animal species could survive quite well without human interference. Humans are positioned at the end of the food chain and thus stand to suffer the most from poisons introduced into the chain. They will be without sustenance if any part of the food chain is broken. Humans are very vulnerable and dependent on the environment for survival, and cannot exist without the services and resources the environment provides.

Economic growth cannot take place without the appropriate environmental conditions to support it. The notion that policymakers have to accept a trade-off between economic growth and environmental protection in decisions about public and corporate policy no longer makes sense. The two goals are consistent with each other. The environment must be protected and enhanced for economic growth to take place. If the environment is destroyed, as is taking place in the Amazon rain forest, for example, economic growth will eventually come to a halt as resources are exhausted. All we will be left with is a ravaged earth that cannot support human life, and perhaps not any form of life at all. Economic growth that undermines the conditions for that growth is not sustainable. This awareness must sink into Western consciousness and become a part of ethical thinking for any kind of reasonable theories to be developed that would offer a significant challenge to the dominant economic paradigm. Such a task is no longer merely an interesting intellectual exercise; it is necessary to the survival of planet earth and all the life-forms that exist on earth.

Since the corporation now has additional responsibilities largely because of government regulation, it may be fruitful to uncover an environmental ethic that may be embedded in this process. Despite several years of discussion about social responsibilities, environmental concerns have become matters of public policy in the sense that laws have been passed and regulations issued to make business respond to environmental problems. Voluntary responses out of a sense of social responsibility have not been relied on to get the job done. What kind of an ethic informs this regulation and how does this ethic work in practice? What are the implications of an environmental ethic for business and government in terms of institutional responsibilities and rights? What responsibilities do consumers have from this point of view?

A new nonhuman-centered approach to the environment is sometimes called the *naturalistic ethic*. This approach holds that some natural objects and ecosystems have intrinsic value and are morally considerable in their own right apart from human interests. Nature is not simply a function of human interests, but has intrinsic value. The naturalistic ethic respects each life-form and sees it as part of a larger whole. All life is sacred, and we must not be careless about species that are irreplaceable. Particular individuals come and go, but nature continues indefinitely, and humans must come to understand their place in nature. Each life-form is constrained to flourish in a larger community, and moral concern for the whole biological community is the only kind of an environmental ethic that makes sense and preserves the integrity of the entire ecosystem.[22]

Nature itself is a source of values, it is argued, including the value we have as humans, since we are a part of nature. The concept of value includes far more than a simplistic human-interest satisfaction. Value is a multi-faceted idea with structures that are rooted in natural sources.[23] Value is not just a human product. When humans recognize values outside themselves, this does not result in dehumanizing of the self or a reversion to beastly levels of existence. On the contrary, human consciousness is increased when we praise and respect the values found in the natural world. This recognition results in a further spiritualizing of humans.[24]

The beauty of a sunset is not only in the eye of the beholder. That beauty has some objective value apart from the specific emotions it evokes in an onlooker. That particular part of nature is a carrier of value, in some sense, that elicits a certain response from human beings. Humans do not necessarily bring their own sense of values to that situation and apply them to the sunset. The same could be said for all other natural objects or phenomena. Thus this school of thought holds that there are natural values intrinsic to the natural object itself apart from humans and their particular valuing activities. Values are found in nature as well as humans. Humans do not simply bestow value on nature, but nature also conveys value to humans. Thus there is an interrelational aspect to values between humans and nature.[25]

Such an ethic was advocated several years ago by Aldo Leopold, a wildlife management expert in Wisconsin, who in 1948 talked about a land ethic as a different approach to the natural world. Such a land ethic changes the role of humans from conquerors of nature to plain members and citizens of nature. We abuse land, said Leopold, because we regard it as a commodity belonging to us. When we see land as a community to which we belong, we may begin to use it with love and respect. His most widely quoted precept with regard to land usage is that "A land-use decision is right when it tends to preserve the integrity, stability, and beauty of the biotic community. It is wrong when it tends otherwise."[26]

This approach calls us to a new kind of relationship with the earth, as it does not involve simply measuring water pollution, for example, and taking steps to reverse this pollution. It is a matter of coming to know water in a new way, as a fellow citizen of our earth community. This approach involves the notions that (1) other members of the earth community deserve respect or moral consideration in their own right and not simply because they are useful to humans, and (2) a consciously developed relationship with these fellow natural beings is essential to understanding what the ethics of respect demands.[27]

The world of nature should not be defined in terms of commodities that are capable of producing wealth for humans who manage them in their own interests. All things in the biosphere are believed to have an equal right to live and reach their own individual forms of self-realization. Instead of a hierarchal ordering of entities in descending order from God through humans to animals, plants, and rocks, where the lower creatures are under the higher ones and are ruled by them, nature is seen as a web of interactive and interdependent life that is ruled by its own natural processes. These processes must be understood if we are to work in harmony with nature and preserve the conditions for our own continued existence. Protecting the rain forest is not just a matter of someone from the outside trying to preserve it as something apart from human existence. It is a matter of seeing oneself as part of the rain forest and acting to protect oneself from extinction.[28]

As stated by Thomas Berry, "any diminishment of the natural world diminishes our imagination, our emotions, our sensitivities, and our intellectual perception, as well as our spirituality."[29] Human beings are integral with the entire earth and even with the universe as the larger community we belong to by the very nature of our existence. But most of us do not live within this perspective and are not in intimate communion with the natural world. We have become autistic and do not hear the voices of nature. We have been blindly pursuing more and more economic growth and all the while replacing nature with our own view of reality, and in the process we have destroyed much that is good and beautiful.

> The mountains and valleys, the rivers and the sea, the birds and other animals, this multitude of beings that compose the natural world no longer share in our lives and we have ceased to share in their lives except as natural resources to be plundered for their economic value. . . . We might wonder how it was that we let this fascinating world be taken from us to be replaced with the grime of our cities disintegrating the very stones of our buildings, as well as increasing the physical and emotional stress under which we live. It was, of course, the illusion of a better life, foisted on us largely through hypnotic advertising and the promise of economic enrichment.[30]

Treating nature as instrumental places the natural world in a utilitarian position in relation to human beings. The material world has value only to the extent it can serve humans. Such an approach promotes an unhealthy separation between people and the rest of nature. Humans must also ask how they can serve nature and recognize a mutual interdependence between human life and life in the natural world. Human life, in fact, is part of the natural world, and the dualism and individualism that is characteristic of Western thought is no longer functional. Such thinking leads to policies and practices that undermine the conditions for supporting human life and activities by destroying the natural world on which we all depend.

This view, sometimes called *biocentrism,* or *deep ecology,* accords nature ethical status that is at least equal to that of human beings. The difference between this viewpoint and the older anthropocentric viewpoint is the difference between believing that cruelty to animals is bad for humans, or the more recent belief that cruelty violates animals' rights. From the perspective of the ecosystem, the difference is between thinking that people have a right to a healthy ecosystem or thinking that the ecosystem itself possesses certain rights, not the least of which is the right to exist.[31]

The deep ecologists argue for a biocentric perspective and a holistic environmental ethic regarding nature. Human beings are to step back into the natural community as a member and not the master. The philosophy of conservation for Holmes Ralston, for example, was comparable to arguing for better care for slaves on plantations. The whole system was unethical, not just how people operated within the system. In his view, nothing mattered except the liberation of nature from the system of human dominance and exploitation. This process involved a reconstruction of the entire human relationship with the natural world.[32]

The heart of deep ecology is the idea that identity of the individual is indistinguishable from the identity of the whole. The sense of self-realization in deep ecology goes beyond the modern Western sense of the self as a isolated ego striving for hedonistic gratification. Self in a new sense is experienced as integrated with the whole of nature. Human self-interest and interest of the ecosystem are one and the same. There is a fundamental interrelatedness of all things and all events. But few humans could attain this state of final enlightenment. Thus environmental ethics was necessary to restrain ordinary selfishness.[33]

MORAL EXTENSIONISM AND ELIGIBILITY

The particular philosophical position we hold with respect to the environment in general influences our position vis-à-vis specific environmental issues. If nature is only a resource for human needs, natural things thus have only instrumental value, and this belief determines the way we treat animals and other natural objects. If, however, we believe that intrinsic values reside in ecosystems and natural objects apart from human interests, then determinations have to be made regarding how these values are carried by natural things and how they are to be traded against other human values and the demands of industry and business for economic growth. There are questions related to the way we treat animals and plants, and what we owe to future generations, and other such interesting questions.

The concept of rights has become standard when extending moral considerations to a host of business practices. The civil rights movement extended the notion of rights to blacks and other minorities, and had as a goal the extension and implementation of basic rights afforded to Americans of any race or color. Equal rights dealt with the same problems with regard to equal treatment for women in all aspects of society. The rights to a safe and hazard-free workplace found their way into legislation and regulation regarding safety and health in the workplace. A consumer bill of rights dealt with product safety and other aspects of the marketplace that needed attention.

Another right that has been enunciated is the right to a clean environment: People have a right to breathe clean air and to drink water that is not contaminated with health-threatening chemicals; consumers ought to be confident that the food they buy in grocery stores is not contaminated with pesticide residues. The concept of human rights has been extended into many aspects of life in our society and has been used as the basis of much legislation and regulation that has changed the nature of business behavior to respect those rights.

The question is whether this notion of rights can also be extended to the natural world, or at least some of its components, and whether this extension can help us to deal effectively with environmental problems. Where does the ethical cutoff fall with regard to moral eligibility? Many philosophers extend ethics only as far as domestic animals on the grounds that animals are sentient beings and able to suffer and feel pain. More radical thinkers widen the circle to include all life such as plants. Still others see no reason to draw a moral boundary at the edge of life and argue for ethical considerations for rocks, soil, water, air, and biophysical processes that constitute ecosystems. Some are led to the conclusion that even the universe has rights superior to those of its most precocious life form.[34]

Peter Singer, for example, argues that the view holding that the effects of our actions on nonhuman animals have no intrinsic moral significance is arbitrary and morally indefensible. He makes an analogy between the way we now treat animals with the way whites used to treat black slaves. The white slaveowners limited their moral concern to the white race and did not regard the suffering of a black slave as having the same moral significance as that of a white person. Thus the black could be treated inhumanly with no moral compulsion. This way of thinking and treating blacks is now called racism, but we could just as well substitute the word speciesism in regard to the manner in which animals are treated. The logic of racism and the logic of speciesism are the same.[35]

Just as our concern about equal treatment of blacks through legislation and regulation moved us to a different level of moral consciousness, so too will treating of animals as beings who have interests and can suffer and therefore deserve moral consideration move us to a different level of moral consciousness. (See Figure 3.1). This level may involve the stopping of certain practices such as using animals for testing purposes and subjecting them to slow and agonizing deaths. It may also involve stopping the practice of raising animals in crowded conditions solely for the purpose of human consumption. The decision to avoid speciesism of this kind will be difficult, but no more difficult, states Singer, than it would have been for a white southerner to go against the traditions of his society and free his slaves.[36]

The creatures in Singer's moral community had to possess nervous systems of sufficient sophistication to feel pain, that is, they had to be sentient beings. Ethics ended at the boundary of sentience. A tree or a mountain or a rock being kicked did not feel anything and therefore did not possess any interests or rights. Since these objects could not be harmed by human action they had no place in ethical discourse. There is nothing we can do that matters to them and thus they are not deserving of moral consideration.[37]

While many philosophers now find this requirement too limiting, Singer at least deserves credit for helping liberate moral philosophy from its fixation on human beings. Other philosophers, such as Joel Fineberg, also limited their moral concerns to animals. Fineberg excluded plants from the rights community on the grounds that they had insufficient "cognitive equipment" to be aware of their wants, needs, and interests. He also denied rights to incurable "human vegetables," and using the same logic disqualified species from moral consideration. Protection of rare and endangered species became protection of humans to enjoy and benefit from them. Even less deserving of rights were mere things.[38]

Some philosophers, such as Christopher Stone, pushed the boundaries of moral eligibility even further, however, to include other aspects of the natural world. Stone saw no logical or legal reason to draw any ethical boundaries whatsoever. Why should the moral community end with humans or even animals? While this idea may seem absurd to many people, so did the extension of certain rights to women and blacks at one point in our history.

Figure 3.1

The Expanding Concept of Rights

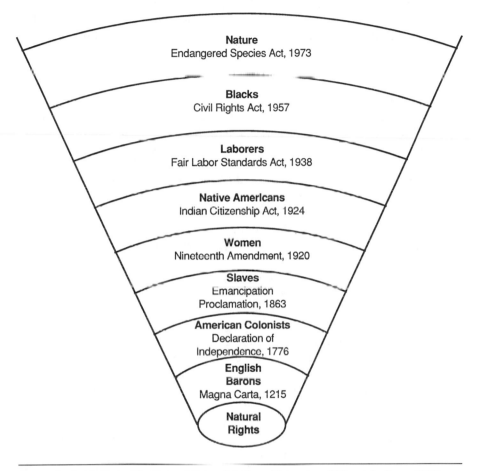

Source: Roderick Nash, *The Rights of Nature* (Madison: University of Wisconsin Press, 1989), p. 7.

The extension of rights in this manner would help environmentalists better protect the environment and also reflects the view that nature needs to be preserved for its own sake and not just for the interests of human beings.[39]

Stone's experience with the Mineral King case in the late 1960s stimulated him to write his landmark essay "Should Trees Have Standing," which made a case for the extension of moral concern to the plant community. Mineral King was a beautiful valley in the southern Sierras that was the subject of a proposal by Walt Disney Enterprises for development into a massive ski resort. The Sierra Club saw itself as a longtime guardian of this region, and tried to stop the development. But the U.S. Court of Appeals of California ruled that since the club was not itself injured it had no standing or legal reason to sue against the development. But something was going to be injured, Stone reasoned, and the courts should be receptive to its need for protection. Thus he argued in his essay that society should extend legal rights to forests, oceans, rivers, and other so-called natural objects in the environment, and indeed, to the natural environment as a whole.[40]

John Rodman, a political theorist at California's Claremont Graduate School, protested the whole notion of extending human-type rights to nonhumans because this action categorizes them as "inferior human beings" and "legal incompetents" who need human guardianship. This was the same kind of mistake that some white liberals made in the 1960s with regard to blacks. Instead we should respect animals and everything else in nature "for having their own existence, their own character and potentialities, their own forms of excellence, their own integrity, their own grandeur." Instead of giving nature rights or legal standing within the present political and economic order, Rodman urged environmentalists to become more radical and change the order. All forms of domestication must end along with the entire institutional framework associated with owning land and using it in one's own interests.[41]

Another philosopher from the University of Wisconsin, J. Baird Callicott, an admirer of Aldo Leopold's land ethic, declared that the animal liberation movement was not even allied with environmental ethics, as it emphasized the rights of individual organisms. The land ethic, on the other hand, was holistic and had as its highest objective the good of the community as a whole. The animal rights advocates simply added individual animals to the category of rights holders, whereas "ethical holism" calculated right and wrong in reference not to individuals but to the whole biotic community. The whole, in other words, carried more ethical weight than any of its component parts. Oceans and lakes, mountains, forests, and wetlands are assigned a greater value than individual animals who might happen to reside there.[42]

Thus biocentric ethics, or deep ecology led the more radical philosophers to devalue individual life relative to the integrity, diversity, and continuation of the ecosystem as a whole. This approach offended many proponents of animal rights, and presumably those who advocated rights for plants and other aspects of the natural community, to say nothing of those whose moral community ended with human society. According to Roderick Nash, this perspective on environmental ethics created entirely new definitions of what liberty and justice meant on planet earth and an evolution of ethics to be ever more inclusive. (See Figure 3.2). This approach recognized that there can be no individual welfare or liberty apart from the ecological matrix in which individual life must exist. "A biocentric ethical philosophy could be interpreted as extending the esteem in which individual lives were traditionally held to the biophysical matrix that created and sustained those lives."[43]

Figure 3.2

The Evolution of Ethics

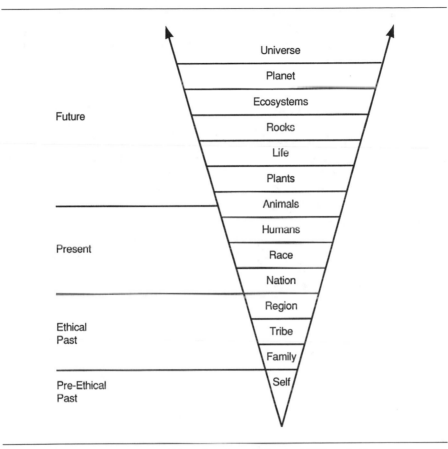

Source: Roderick Nash, *The Rights of Nature* (Madison: University of Wisconsin Press, 1989), p. 6.

The question of moral extensionism and eligibility also comes into play when we talk about our obligations to future generations. There is probably general agreement that it would be wrong to use all of the earth's resources and to contaminate the environment that we pass on to our children. But at what point do we draw the line? How many resources do we leave to future generations and in what condition will we leave the environment? Do future generations in any sense have any rights to the resources we are presently using, and do they have a right to a clean environment? Since they are not yet alive, they cannot lay claim to a livable environment and do not seem, at least on the surface, to have any interests in our present activities.

Yet Joel Feinberg argues that whatever future human beings turn out to be like, they will have interests that we can affect, for good or ill, in the present. The interests of these future generations do need to be protected from irresponsible invasions of those interests by present generations. Present generations have a responsibility to save something for the future, so their offspring can enjoy some of the amenities that we presently enjoy. Rather than focus on the rights and interests of individuals, others have argued that we have an obligation to consider the good of the continuing human community.[44]

Richard DeGeorge, on the other hand, believes that future persons, either individually or as a class, do not presently have the right to existing resources. Future generations or individuals have rights only to what is available when they come into existence — when their future rights become actual and present. It is only when a being actually exists that it has needs and wants and interests. It then has a right only to the kind of treatment or to the goods available to it at the time of its conception. It cannot have a reasonable claim to what is not available. But to argue that future generations do not have present rights does not mean that present generations do not have some obligation to try and provide certain kinds of environments and leave open as many possibilities as feasible for future generations. But the needs of the present and already existing people take precedence over consideration of the needs of future generations.[45]

Kenneth Goodpaster argues that the extension of rights beyond certain limits is not necessarily the best way to deal with moral growth and social change with respect to the environment. The last thing we need, he states, is a liberation movement with respect to trees, animals, rivers, and other objects in nature. The mere enlargement of the class of morally considerable beings is an inadequate substitute for a genuine environmental ethic. The extension of rights to other objects or to future generations does not deal with deeper philosophical questions about human interests and environmental concerns. Moral considerations should be extended to systems as well as individuals. Societies need to be understood in an ecological context, and it is this larger whole which is the bearer of value. An environmental ethic, while paying its respects to individualism and humanism, must break free of them and deal with the way the universe is operating. Looking at an environmental ethic in this manner may lead us to conclude that recent industrial history is an episode in a drama that will lead to a destruction of the system by one of its own participants.[46]

> The upshot is that the dominant ethical systems of our times, those clustered as the Western ethic and other kindred human chauvinistic systems, are far less defensible, and less satisfactory, then has been commonly assumed, and lack an adequate and nonarbitrary basis. Furthermore, alternative theories are far less incoherent than is commonly claimed, especially by philosophers. Yet although there are viable alternatives to the Dominion thesis, the natural world is rapidly being preempted in favor of human chauvinism — and of what it ideologically underwrites, the modern economic-industrial superstructure — by the elimination or overexploitation of those things that are not considered of sufficient instrumental

value for human beings. Witness the impoverishment of the nonhuman world, the assaults being made on tropical rain forests, surviving temperate wildernesses, wild animals, the oceans, to list only a few of the victims of man's assault on the natural world. Observe also the associated measures to bring primitive or recalcitrant peoples into the Western consumer society and the spread of human-chauvinistic value systems. The time is fast approaching when questions raised by an environmental ethic will cease to involve live options. As things stand at present, however, the ethical issues generated by the preemptions — especially given the weakness and inadequacy of the ideological and value-theoretical basis on which the damaging chauvinistic transformation of the world is premised and the viability of alternative environmental ethics — are not merely of theoretical interest but are among the most important and urgent questions of our times, and perhaps the most important questions that human beings, whose individual or group self-interest is the source of most environmental problems, have ever asked themselves.[47]

These comments suggest that a radical change in our thinking and values systems is called for if the human race is to survive, let alone flourish and grow. Perhaps no less than a reversal of values is necessary and the economic values that have been dominant since the beginnings of industrial society will have to become subservient to environmental values related to preservation of the environment and the creation of truly sustainable human communities. Social responsibility and even government regulation are only temporary measures that at best deal at the periphery by trying to introduce environmental values into management decision making. But as long as economic values are the primary determinant of corporate behavior, environmental values will always be subservient. This situation may no longer be tolerable or workable as environmental problems become more severe in the last decade of the twentieth century.

CULTURE AS THE ROOT CAUSE OF ENVIRONMENTAL PROBLEMS

In the final analysis, the cause of our environmental problems is probably the culture in which we live, a culture based on certain ethical perspectives with regard to economics and the environment and central values that guide decision making in both the public and private sectors. Economic values are dominant in our culture and provide the basis for decisions about the uses and abuses of the environment. We do not have an ecological perspective that informs our decisions and guides our actions. Our approach to nature is dualistic, our vision of reality is fragmented, and we view resources and technology as infinite in some sense. According to Kenneth Watt, there are five basic beliefs at the heart of our culture that inform our thinking and practice.[48]

   1. *The fixation on money.* We believe that money is the measure of all things, and things that have no monetary value in their natural state are not worth anything. Thus nature must be changed and made into something

useful that can be exchanged on the marketplace so a monetary value can be determined. The old-growth forests, for example, have no value in their natural state, and preservation of that particular ecosystem has no monetary or economic value. The only value these forests have is their lumber that can be used for construction. Money determines whether these forests have any worth in our society.

2. *The belief in omnipotent technology.* We believe that technology can be used to solve all our problems. If we run up against limits, we look for a technological solution that will extend those limits beyond the present. We do not have to plan for the future, as the future will take care of itself through more technological developments. If oil begins to run out, technology will save us through more effective drilling techniques, such as horizontal drilling, which will allow us to extract more oil from old wells, or we will discover new sources of supply that are as yet untapped. We believe that on the whole technology is good, and we exploit new technologies as quickly as possible before their environmental effects have been thoroughly researched.

3. *The belief in management through fragmentation.* The way to approach and manage reality is through fragmenting a large task into many small ones that can then be controlled and managed. We do not want to worry about the whole, but concentrate on doing manageable tasks that do not require holistic thinking. We believe that the whole is nothing more than the sum of the parts. Thus if we pay attention to the parts, the whole will take care of itself. We do not think of communities and interdependencies, but are individualistic in our approach to reality and attach more value to private property than we do to public property. We know how to manage private property quite well, but we do not know how to manage the commons in the interests of society as a whole.

4. *The belief in force.* If something doesn't work, perhaps it is because we haven't tried hard enough or applied enough force to the situation. Thus we tend to build bigger and more concentrated approaches to problems, or pour more money at them in an attempt to overwhelm reality and make it serve our interests. We will to master nature rather than work in harmony with nature, and we are drawn in the direction of the big activity rather than the little activity. Our energy-generating systems, for example, release massive amounts of energy at a point source rather than lots of little systems producing energy where it is needed.

5. *Growth is good.* Economic growth is the bottom line of our society, as is the measure of all progress, both economic and social. Our measure of success as a society is growth of gross national product (GNP), and we do not bother to factor out the environmental damage this growth may have caused or take account of the natural capital that was depleted to attain this growth. We do not particularly care about maintaining a diversity in nature that would lead to a more stable world, but promote uniformity with our emphasis on economic growth and the promotion of an economic lifestyle that is based on the accumulation of more and more material goods and services.

THE NATURE OF THE CULTURAL REVOLUTION IN OUR SOCIETY

The Central Beliefs of the Old Civilization

Technology is not limited by human ingenuity, thermodynamic constraints (the net energy problem), or limitations of the resource base. Therefore, we should plan on using technological innovations ("technological fixes") to recover more and more of the stock of nonrenewable resources on the planet. The basic driving force behind civilization will be the consumption of fixed stocks (that is, the principal accumulated through past energy production by the sun: coal, oil, and gas).

The appropriate way to manage systems problems is by fragmenting problems into components (the "reductionist" approach). Humanity and nature are separate (the "dualistic" belief system).

Humans can and should use their own will and force to master nature and triumph over competitors: this is the essence of life. The way to achieve mastery is to be the competitor exploiting the largest share of the available material and energy resource base. Since other competitors will have the same strategy, this means that being the winning competitor will require using a constantly increasing volume of resources.

Since the essence of life is maximizing production, the way to do this is through use of the largest possible systems. This implies very large refineries, coal-mining operations, ocean-going tankships, liquid natural gas port facilities, and the like. In general, that in turn implies great centralization of energy, economic, and political systems so as to maximize economics of scale.

Since humans can and do manage the system, then it follows that they, not natural forces, are the dominant factor in determining system behavior. Therefore, in trying to manage the economy, we overlook the role of natural forces as causes of inflation or recession (such as crop-growing weather fluctuations, or real increases in the cost of obtaining fossil energy), but instead try to manage economic cycles by "fine-tuning" the rate of increase in the money supply, and adjusting interest rates on borrowed capital.

The Central Beliefs of the New Culture

Technology is limited by thermodynamic constraints; human ingenuity can only function at a limited speed; and the resource base is limited. Therefore, we must switch from a society run off a dwindling stock of nonrenewable resources to a society run off constant flows of renewable resources (that is, the interest resulting each day from the energy production by the sun: solar, wind, biomass, waves, and ocean thermal gradients).

The appropriate way to manage systems problems is by using methods based on a holistic perspective of the entire system. Humanity and nature are interacting components of an integrated system (the "monistic" belief system).

The way to be a winning competitor and a survivor in the struggle to succeed within environmental limits is to maximize efficiency in the use of resources, not production. Further, this implies that the efficient processing of information will be used as a substitute for the production of matter and energy (the "information society").

Since the essence of life is maximizing efficiency, the way to do this is through small, decentralized systems that produce energy where it is to be used, and therefore avoid the hidden overhead energy cost of transmission and distribution, and also are dispersed efficiently enough to capture energy from dispersed sources as the sun, wind, and waves, with a resultant savings in fossil fuel.

Since natural forces and flows and available stocks of resources are important determinants of economic fluctuations, we try to maintain a stable economy by adjusting to changes in those forces, flows, and stocks. Thus, we would try to adjust to increased real cost of extracting U.S. crude oil by changing our social patterns so as to use energy more efficiently, rather than by importing more and trying to compensate for the consequences by printing money faster (inflating the currency).

Source: Kenneth E. F. Watt, *Understanding the Environment,* © 1982, p. 205. Reprinted by permission of Prentice Hall, Englewood Cliffs, New Jersey.

In order to deal adequately with our environmental problems a cultural revolution may have to take place. (See box.) Our culture needs a new kind of belief system that is holistic and has a systems-oriented worldview. Perhaps the radical ecologists are correct: We need a new order that is based on different cultural values and a new kind of environmental ethic that guides our policies. The economic system must be made to serve environmental values so that sustainable growth becomes a possibility. Otherwise the conditions for further economic growth of any kind will be destroyed, and all cultures will be worse off as a result. This kind of change will not be easy because cultures such as ours that have been relatively successful tend to do things the same way as in the past. But change must come because of environmental pressures that can no longer be ignored.

Questions for Discussion

1. Describe an anthropocentric approach to nature. Do you agree that this approach is characteristic of Western industrial societies? Why or why not? What does it mean to say that this approach treats nature as having only instrumental value?

2. What is an economic ethic? Is this ethic consistent with an instrumental approach to nature? What role does nature play in such an economic outlook? What is the goal of a business organization in this view?

3. Are ethics and marketplace performance consistent with each other? Where do ethics and the marketplace performance begin to diverge from each other? What problems was society addressing through the concept of social responsibility?

4. What are the difficulties of using the social responsibility concept to support a broader notion of corporate responsibility to society? Why is it difficult to implement social responsibility on a scale large enough to solve pollution problems effectively?

5. What is public policy? What advantages does this concept have over the social responsibility approach? Can we avoid ethical considerations by using the public policy approach?

6. What is the difference between social responsibility and social responsiveness? With what aspects of the organization is social responsibility concerned? What are the advantages and disadvantages of this approach? Where does ethics become of concern?

7. What is the relation between economic growth and environmental problems? Is a trade-off necessary between these two goals? Or is further economic growth dependent on a certain level of environmental protection?

8. What is a naturalistic ethic? How does this approach differ from the anthropocentric approach? What does it mean to say nature has intrinsic value? What are the policy implications of this approach?

9. What are rights and how have they been used in our society? Should rights be extended to nature or at least some of its aspects? What examples of such rights currently exist in our society?

10. Where does the ethical cutoff fall with respect to moral eligibility? Should animals have rights? What about plants? What about rocks, soil, water, air, and ecosystems? Where do we draw the line, or is it even possible to draw a line as far as moral eligibility is concerned?

11. What is deep ecology? What are some of its major tenets? What is biocentric ethics and how does this differ from other ethical approaches to the environment?

12. What rights do future generations have, if any? Do you agree with Fineberg's or DeGeorge's position on this issue? Is there a third possibility that you like better?

13. What are the dominant values in our culture? How have these values related to the environmental problems we are currently facing? Is culture the major problem with respect to the environment?

14. What new values would have to emerge, in your opinion, so our society could adequately address environmental problems? Would these values constitute a new culture or merely a minor change in existing culture? Are we moving toward a new culture based on an environmental ethic?

Notes

1. Holmes Ralston III, "Just Environmental Business," in *Just Business: New Introductory Essays in Business Ethics,* Tom Regan, ed. (New York: Random House, 1984), p. 325–343.

2. W. K. Frankena, "Ethics and the Environment," in *Ethics and Problems of the 21st Century,* K. E. Goodpaster and K. M. Sayre, eds. (Notre Dame, IN: University of Notre Dame Press, 1979), p. 11.

3. Ibid., p. 17.

4. Charles W. Powers and David Vogel, *Ethics in the Education of Business Managers* (Hastings-on-Hudson, NY: Hastings Center, 1980), p. 1.

5. Robert C. Solomon and Kristine R. Hanson, *Above the Bottom Line: An Introduction to Business Ethics* (New York: Harcourt Brace Jovanovich, 1983), p. 9.

6. Richard T. DeGeorge, *Business Ethics,* 2nd ed. (New York: Macmillan, 1986), p. 15.

7. Oliver Sheldon, *The Philosophy of Management* (London: Sir Isaac Pitman & Sons, 1923), pp. 280–291.

8. Ibid., p. 284.

9. Ibid.

10. Ibid., p. 285.

11. Ibid., pp. 285, 286. Quoted by permission of Pitman Publishing, London.

12. See Milton Friedman, "The Social Responsibility of Business Is to Increase Its Profits," *New York Times Magazine,* September 13, 1970, pp. 122–126.

13. Sheldon, *The Philosophy of Management,* p. 290.

14. Neil W. Chamberlain, *The Limits of Corporate Responsibility* (New York: Basic Books, 1973), pp. 4, 6. Copyright © 1973 by Basic Books, Inc., Publisher. Reprinted by permission of the publisher.

15. See Benjamin and Sylvia Selekman, *Power and Morality in a Business Society* (New York: McGraw-Hill, 1956).

16. See Lee E. Preston and James E. Post, *Private Management and Public Policy* (Englewood Cliffs, NJ: Prentice-Hall, 1975), pp. 12–13.

17. Rogene A. Buchholz, "An Alternative to Social Responsibility," *MSU Business Topics* (Summer 1977), pp. 12–16.

18. William C. Frederick, "From CSR1 to CSR2: The Maturing of Business and Society Thought," Graduate School of Business, University of Pittsburgh, 1978, Working Paper No. 279, p. 1.

19. William C. Frederick, "Toward CSR3: Why Ethical Analysis Is Indispensable and Unavoidable in Corporate Affairs," *California Management Review,* Vol. XXVII, No. 2 (Winter 1986), p. 131.

20. Ibid., p. 133.

21. Ibid.

22. Ralston, "Just Environmental Business," pp. 325–343.

23. Holmes Ralston III, *Philosophy Gone Wild: Essays in Environmental Ethics* (Buffalo, NY: Prometheus Books, 1987), p. 121.

24. Ibid., p. 141.

25. Ibid., pp. 103–104.

26. Roderick Frazier Nash, *The Rights of Nature: A History of Environmental Ethics* (Madison: University of Wisconsin Press, 1989), p. 71.

27. Sara Ebenreck, "An Earth Care Ethics," *The Catholic World: Caring for The Endangered Earth,* Vol. 233, No. 1396 (July/August 1990), p. 156.

28. Ibid., p. 157.

29. Thomas Berry, "Spirituality and Ecology," *The Catholic World: Caring for the Endangered Earth,* Vol. 233, No. 1396 (July/August 1990), p. 159.

30. Ibid., p. 161.

31. Nash, *The Rights of Nature,* p. 10.

32. Ibid., p. 150.

33. Ibid., p. 151.

34. Ibid., p. 125.

35. Peter Singer, "The Place of Nonhumans in Environmental Issues," in *Moral Issues in Business,* 4th ed., William Shaw and Vincent Barry, eds. (Belmont, CA: Wadsworth, 1989), p. 471.

36. Ibid., p. 474.

37. Nash, *The Rights of Nature,* p. 140–141.

38. Ibid., p. 126.

39. Christopher D. Stone, "Should Trees Have Standing? — Toward Legal Rights for Natural Objects," in *Moral Issues in Business,* 4th ed., William Shaw and Vincent Barry, eds. (Belmont, CA: Wadsworth, 1989), pp. 475–479.

40. Nash, *The Rights of Nature,* pp. 128–129.

41. Ibid., p. 152.

42. Ibid., p. 153.

43. Ibid., p. 160.

44. "The Environment," in *Moral Issues in Business,* 4th ed., William Shaw and Vincent Barry, eds. (Belmont, CA: Wadsworth, 1989), pp. 452–453.

45. Richard T. DeGeorge, "The Environment, Rights, and Future Generations," in *Ethics and Problems of the 21st Century,* K. E. Goodpaster and K. M. Sayre, eds. (Notre Dame, IN: University of Notre Dame Press, 1979), pp. 93–105.

46. K. E. Goodpaster, "From Egoism to Environmentalism," in *Ethics and Problems of the 21st Century,* K. E. Goodpaster and K. M. Sayre, eds. (Notre Dame, IN: University of Notre Dame Press, 1979), pp. 21–33.

47. R. and V. Routley, "Against the Inevitability of Human Chauvinism," in *Ethics and Problems of the 21st Century,* K. E. Goodpaster and K. M. Sayre, eds. (Notre Dame, IN: University of Notre Dame Press, 1979), p. 57.

48. Kenneth E. F. Watt, *Understanding the Environment* (Boston: Allyn & Bacon, 1982), pp. 193–205.

SUGGESTED READINGS

Attfield, Robin. *The Ethics of Environmental Concern.* New York: Cambridge University Press, 1983.

Brennan, Andrew. *Thinking About Nature: An Investigation of Nature, Value, and Ecology.* Athens: University of Georgia Press, 1988.

Cahn, Robert. *Footprints on the Planet: A Search for an Environmental Ethic.* New York: Universe Books, 1978.

Callicott, J. Baird. *In Defense of the Land Ethic: Essays in Environmental Philosophy.* Albany, NY: SUNY Press, 1988.

Chamberlain, Neil W. *The Limits of Corporate Responsibility.* New York: Basic Books, 1973.

Clark, Stephen R. L. *The Moral Status of Animals.* New York: Oxford University Press, 1984.

Daly, Herman E., ed. *Economics, Ecology, and Ethics.* San Francisco: W. H. Freeman, 1980.

DeGeorge, Richard T. *Business Ethics,* 2nd ed. New York: Macmillan, 1986.

Devall, Bill, and George Sessions. *Deep Ecology: Living as If Nature Mattered.* Salt Lake City: Gibbs M. Smith, 1985.

Goodpaster, K. E., and K. M. Sayre, eds. *Ethics and Problems of the 21st Century.* Notre Dame, IN: University of Notre Dame Press, 1979.

Hardin, Garret. *Exploring New Ethics for Survival,* 2nd ed. New York: Viking Press, 1978.

Hargrove, Eugene C. *Foundations of Environmental Ethics.* Englewood Cliffs, NJ: Prentice Hall, 1989.

Leopold, Aldo. *A Sand County Almanac.* New York: Oxford University Press, 1949.

McCloskey, H. J. *Ecological Ethics and Politics.* Totowa, NJ: Bowman & Littlefield, 1983.

Midgley, Mary. *Animals and Why They Matter.* Athens: University of Georgia Press, 1984.

Nash, Roderick Frazier. *The Rights of Nature: A History of Environmental Ethics.* Madison: University of Wisconsin Press, 1989.

Partridge, Ernest, ed. *Responsibilities for Future Generations: Environmental Ethics.* Buffalo, NY: Prometheus Books, 1981.

Passmore, John. *Man's Responsibility for Nature: Ecological Problems and Western Traditions.* New York: Scribner, 1980.

Preston, Lee E., and James E. Post. *Private Management and Public Policy.* Englewood Cliffs, NJ: Prentice-Hall, 1975.

Regan, Tom, ed. *Just Business: New Introductory Essays in Business Ethics.* New York: Random House, 1984.

Regan, Tom. *The Case for Animal Rights.* Berkeley: University of California Press, 1983.

Rolston, Holmes, III. *Environmental Ethics: Duties to and Values in the Natural World.* Philadelphia: Temple University Press, 1988.

Rolston, Holmes, III. *Philosophy Gone Wild: Essays in Environmental Ethics.* Buffalo, NY: Prometheus Books, 1987.

Selekman, Benjamin, and Sylvia Selekman. *Power and Morality in a Business Society.* New York: McGraw-Hill, 1956.

Shaw, William, and Vincent Barry, eds. *Moral Issues in Business,* 4th ed. Belmont, CA: Wadsworth, 1989.

Singer, Peter. *Animal Liberation*. New York: New York Review of Books, 1975.

Solomon, Robert C., and Kristine R. Hanson. *Above the Bottom Line: An Introduction to Business Ethics*. New York: Harcourt Brace Jovanovich, 1983.

Taylor, Paul W. *Respect for Nature: A Theory of Environmental Ethics*. Lawrenceville, NJ: Princeton University Press, 1986.

Tobias, Michael, ed. *Deep Ecology*. San Diego, CA: Avant Books, 1985.

CHAPTER 4

PUBLIC POLICY
AND THE ENVIRONMENT

~

As we discussed earlier, the environment can be considered a commons that provides services and a habitat for everyone on earth. Although the concept of private property does apply to land and in some cases to water, with respect to controlling pollution, the concept does not work very well. Pollution does not respect the boundaries of private property and affects many people who do not own property. Thus the air we breathe, the water we drink and use for recreation, and the land we enjoy are in some sense common to humankind. The question is how this commons is going to be managed and to what ends and purposes. Who will determine environmental policy and what institution will implement the policy?

The belief that markets alone will bring about a utopian social order has been abandoned as far as environmental policy is concerned. Concepts of resource and welfare economics are largely obsolete and irrelevant for environmental purposes. Other concepts and processes must be considered to solve environmental and social problems. The concept of public policy may be useful to understand how the commons is managed in our society and how the society decides on environmental policy with respect to corporations. The general goals of public policy are determined through a political process in which citizens participate.[1]

The business institution has been reshaped and the managerial role affected by many public policy measures designed to accomplish both the economic and noneconomic goals of the larger society. Over the last two decades, public policy has become an important determinant of corporate behavior as market outcomes have been increasingly altered through the public policy process. These changes are making it clear that business functions via two major social processes through which decisions are made about the allocation of corporate resources: the market system and the public policy process. Both the market mechanism and public policy are sources of guidelines and criteria for managerial behavior. But as far as environmental policy is concerned, public policy is more important.

THE NATURE OF PUBLIC POLICY

Anderson, Brady, and Bullock define public policy as purposeful, goal-oriented behavior that is formulated and implemented to deal with a public problem. Public policy consists of courses of action, according to these authors, rather than separate, discrete decisions or actions performed by government officials. Furthermore, public policy refers to what governments actually do, not what they say they will do or intend to do with respect to some public problem.[2] With these criteria in mind, the authors offer the following as their definition of public policy.

> A goal directed or purposeful course of action followed by an actor or set of actors in an attempt to deal with a public problem. This definition focuses on what is done, as distinct from what is intended, and it distinguishes policy from decisions. Public policies are developed by governmental institutions and officials through the political process (or politics). They are distinct from other kinds of policies because they result from the actions of legitimate authorities in a political system.[3]

Theodore J. Lowi defines public policy as a government's expressed intention, which is sometimes called purpose or mission. Lowi points out that a public policy is usually backed by a sanction, which is a reward or punishment to encourage obedience to the policy. Governments have many different sanctions or techniques of control to assure that their policies are followed.[4] Thomas R. Dye defines public policy as whatever governments choose to do or not to do. Dye argues that public policy must include all actions of government and not just stated intentions of either government or government officials. He also points out that public policy must include what government chooses not to do because government inaction with respect to particular issues can have as great an impact on society as government action.[5]

Preston and Post offer a much different definition of public policy. They refer to policy, first of all, as principles guiding action, and they emphasize that this definition stresses the idea of generality, by referring to principles rather than specific rules, programs, practices, or the actions themselves. Preston and Post also stress activity or behavior as opposed to passive adherence.[6] Public policy, then, refers to the principles that guide action relating to society as a whole. These principles may be made explicit in law and other formal acts of governmental bodies, but Preston and Post are quick to point out that a narrow and legalistic interpretation of the term public policy should be avoided. Policies can be implemented without formal articulation of individual actions and decisions. They call these implicit policies.[7]

The first few definitions we described are unnecessarily restrictive. Government need not engage in a formal action for public policies to be put into effect. A good example is the debate about South Africa. Before the U.S. government took any specific actions regarding economic sanctions, various religious and secular groups in society brought pressure to bear by divesting themselves of stock in companies that were doing business in South Africa and did their best to persuade companies with facilities in the country to leave. Many companies responded to these pressures and changed their policies without the sanctions of formal public policy to motivate them.

The Preston and Post definition confuses principles and action. Principles can guide action, but the principles themselves are not necessarily the policy. Policy does more appropriately refer to a specific course of action with respect to a problem, but not to the principles that guide the action. Current monetary policy is a specific course of action taken by the Federal Reserve Board to either tighten or loosen the money supply. The principles that guide this action are derived from monetary or economic theories, but these principles do not constitute the policy itself. Public policy involves choices related to the allocation of scarce resources to achieve goals and objectives. But public policymakers cannot ride off in all directions at once, and must make choices among contending allocations of scarce resources. These choices represent courses of action taken with respect to particular problems.

Thus *public policy* is a specific course of action taken collectively by society or by a legitimate representative of society, addressing a specific problem of public concern that reflects the interests of society or particular segments of society. Our definition emphasizes a course of action rather than principles. It does not restrict such action to government, it refers to the collective nature of such action, and it does not claim that each and every public policy represents the interests of society as a whole. Enough interests have to be represented, however, so that the policy is supported and can be implemented effectively.

The public policy agenda is that collection of topics and issues with respect to which public policy may be formulated.[8] There are many problems and concerns that various people in society would like to see acted on, but only those that are important enough to receive serious attention from policymakers comprise the public policy agenda. Such an agenda does not exist in concrete form, but is found in the collective judgment of society, actions and concerns of interest groups, legislation introduced in Congress, cases being considered by the Supreme Court, and similar activities. The manner in which problems in American society get on the public policy agenda is complex and involves many sets of actors.

THE PUBLIC POLICY PROCESS

There is no one single process by which public policy is made in our country.[9] It is formulated by means of a complex, subtle, and not always formal process. Many agents who do not show up on any formal organization chart of government nevertheless influence the outcome of the public policy process.[10] The public policy process refers to all the various methods by which public policy is made in our society. Formulation of public policy is not limited to formal acts of government, but can be achieved by interest groups that bring issues to public attention and attempt to influence public opinion as well as government.

The policy of our country with respect to South Africa, for example, was formed through a process involving public opinion, interest groups, institutions, demonstrations, the media, and a host of other actors. When public policy is formalized by government, there still is no single process. Public policy can be made through legislation passed by Congress, regulations issued in the Federal Register, executive orders issued by the president, or decisions handed down by the Supreme Court. The process of making public policy begins in the society as problems and issues are defined. These issues may find their way into formal institutions for some policy decisions, and then are returned to the society again for implementation.[11]

Most public policy that affects business and the environment, however, is the result of formal government action, particularly at the federal level. Interest group pressure and public opinion eventually translate into legislation and/or regulation on most environmental issues that prescribe a specific form of business behavior. The public policy process allows citizens to express their shared values regarding health, well-being, safety, and respect and reverence for nature, and to translate these values into specific policies with regard to some aspect of the environment.

People have different values and different objectives with respect to their roles as consumer and citizens. As consumers, people are out to satisfy self-interested preferences in markets, and they are not concerned about the larger good of the community. The interests, goals, or preferences we entertain as citizens differ logically from those we seek to satisfy as individual consumers.[12] The public policy process allows people to express what they believe, what they are, and what they stand for, not simply what they wish to buy as individuals. The public policy process reflects values people choose collectively, which may conflict with the wants and interests they pursue individually.[13] People may love their cars and hate buses, and yet vote for candidates who promise to tax gasoline to pay for public transportation. People may also support the Endangered Species Act even though they have no earthly use for the Kemp Riddley turtle or the northern spotted owl.[14]

Environmental goals such as clean air and water are not to be construed as simply personal wants and preferences; they are not interests to be priced by markets. Rather, they are views or beliefs that may find their way as public values into legislation and regulation. These goals stem from our character as a people, and a person who makes a value judgment or a policy recommendation claims to know what is right and not just what is preferred. People who participate in the public policy process regard themselves as thinking beings capable of discussing issues on their merits rather than as bundles of preferences capable primarily of revealing their wants.[15] Consumer preferences reveal a person's interests with regard to his or her own consumption opportunities, whereas value judgments made through public policy are concerned about the distribution of resources in society generally.[16] Ideas or convictions that can be supported by reasons in the political process are different from wants and interests satisfied in markets.[17]

> Goals such as a cleaner environment are goals we determine for ourselves as a community, goals we could not conceive, much less achieve, as individuals trading in markets. People in communities are not an aggregate of individuals or set of preferences to be satisfied. People in communities know purposes and aspirations together they could not know alone.[18]

Values are assigned to particular entities in the public policy process, and decisions are made about the allocation of resources through a political process. The business of the political process is to pursue the common or public interest of the community, which is separate from the aggregate private interests of individuals as defined by efficient markets. The political process is a complex amalgam of power and influence that involves many actors pursuing different interests who try to persuade and influence others in order to achieve their objectives.

Politics has often been called the art of the possible, meaning that balancing interests is necessary to resolve conflicts and arrive at a common course of action. People usually have to be willing to compromise in order to reach agreement among all the members of a group. The usual outcome of the political process reflects the principle that no one gets everything of what they want and yet everyone has to get something in order to satisfy themselves that the objective is worth pursuing. Thus compromise and negotiation are necessary skills to participate effectively in the political process.

The function of the political process is to organize individual effort to achieve a collective goal or objective that individuals or private groups would find difficult, if not impossible, to achieve by themselves. People participate in the market because they believe they can achieve their individual objectives better by making some kind of trade, but the parties to the exchange do not have to share objectives or agree on a course of action. But let's say some people in a community want to build a road, which no one person in the community can or would want to build by themselves. To get the road built, enough people in the community have to agree they want a road and would contribute the necessary resources. But even after this decision is made, these people are going to have different ideas about what kind of road should be built, where it should be located, and other related matters. These differences have to be resolved through the political process in order for the road to be constructed.

The task of the political system is to manage such conflicts by (1) establishing rules of the game for participants in the system, (2) arranging compromises and balancing interests of the various participants, (3) enacting compromises in the form of public policy measures, and (4) enforcing these public policies.[19] The outcome of the political process is not usually under the control of a single individual or group like the outcome of an exchange process. The outcome of the political process depends on how much power and influence you have, how skillful you are at compromising and negotiating, and the variety and strength of other interests involved. Decisions can be made by vote where the majority rule, by building a consensus, or by exercising raw power and coercing other members of a group to agree with your course of action.

Outcomes in the political process are highly uncertain, in most instances, and contain many surprises. In the political process, especially if it involves a representative democracy, people are not always sure what they are getting. They may vote for a candidate they believe will support the issues they favor and who seems to share similar values. But elected public officials are a very poor store of value in this sense. They may not carry out their campaign promises, and even if they do, their vote might count for nothing in the final outcome if few others voted the same way on an issue.

People pursue their own interests through the political process based on the values they hold relative to the objectives being sought collectively. But these values cannot be expressed directly or precisely, particularly in a representative democracy. Individual preferences are rarely matched because of the need for compromise, and the outcome is highly uncertain because of the complex interactions that take place between all the parties to a transaction. Yet resources for the attainment of public policy objectives are allocated through the political process that combines individual preferences into common objectives and courses of action.

The reason public policy decisions have to be made through a political process is the nature of the goods and services that are provided through the public policy process. These public goods and services can be distinguished from the private goods and services pursued in the market system. Just as in the market system, these public goods and services are provided to meet the demands of people for them as expressed through the political system.

Public goods and services are indivisible in the sense that the quantity produced cannot be divided into individual units to be purchased by people according to their individual preferences. For all practical purposes, we cannot, for example, buy a piece of clean air to carry around and breathe wherever we go. Nor can we buy a share of national defense over which we would have control. This indivisibility gives these goods their public character because if people are to have public goods and services at all, they must enjoy roughly the same amount.[20] No one owns these goods and services individually—they are collectively owned, and private property rights do not apply. Thus there is nothing to be exchanged, and the values people hold in regard to these goods and services and decisions about them cannot be made through the exchange process.

We might argue, however, that even though public goods and services have these characteristics, they could still be provided through the market system rather than the public policy process. Suppose, for example, the market offered a consumer the following choice: Two automobiles in a dealer's showroom are identical in all respects, even their gas mileage. The only difference is that one car has pollution control equipment to reduce emissions of pollutants from the exhaust while the other car has no such equipment. The car with the pollution control equipment sells for $500 more than the other.

If the prospective buyer values clean air, it could be argued that he or she would choose the more expensive car to reduce air pollution. However, such a decision would be totally irrational from a strictly self-interest point of view. The impact that one car out of all the millions on the road will have on air pollution is infinitesimal—it cannot even be measured. Thus there is no relationship in this kind of a decision between costs and benefits—we would, in effect, be getting nothing for our money unless we could assume that many other people would make the same decision. Such actions, however, assume a common value for clean air that doesn't exist. Thus the market never offers consumers this kind of choice. Automobile manufacturers know that pollution control equipment won't sell in the absence of federally mandated standards.

There is another side to the coin, however. If enough people in a given area did buy the more expensive car so that the air was significantly cleaner, there would be a powerful incentive for others to be free riders. Again, the impact of any one car would not alter the character of the air over a region. We would be tempted to buy the polluting car for a cheaper price and be a free rider by enjoying the same amount of clean air as everyone else and not paying a cent for its provision.

Because of these characteristics of human behavior and the nature of public goods and services, the market system will not work to provide them for a society that wants them. When goods are indivisible among large numbers of people, the individual consumer's actions as expressed in the market will not lead to the provision of these goods.[21] Society must register its desire for public goods and services through the political process because the bilateral exchanges facilitated by the market are insufficiently inclusive.[22] Only through the political process can compromises be reached that will resolve the value conflicts which are inevitable in relation to public goods and services.

Value conflicts are more pronounced in the public policy process because of the existence of a diverse value system. There is no underlying value system into which other values can be translated, no common denominator by which to assess trade-offs and make decisions about resource allocation to attain some common economic objective such as improving one's material standard of living or increasing the nation's gross national product.

What is the overall objective, for example, of clean air and water, equal opportunity, occupational safety and health, and similar public goods and services? We could say that all these goods and services are meant to improve the quality of life for all members of society. But if this is the objective, what kind of common value measure underlies all these goods and services so that benefits can be assessed in relation to costs, and trade-offs analyzed in view of this common objective of improving the quality of life?

The costs of pollution control equipment, for example, can be determined in economic terms. The benefits this equipment provides should be positive in improving health by reducing the amount of harmful pollutants people have to breathe and improving the aesthetic dimension by making the air smell better. Safety may also be enhanced through an improvement of visibility for aircraft. The difficulty lies in translating all these diverse benefits into economic terms so that a direct comparison with costs can be made.

What is the price tag for the lives saved by avoiding future diseases that may be caused by pollution? What is the economic value of having three more years added on to one's life span because of living in a cleaner environment? What is the value of reducing the probability that children will be born with abnormalities because of toxic substances in the environment? What is the value of preserving one's hearing because money has been spent to reduce the noise emitted by machinery in the workplace? What is the appropriate value of being able to see the mountains from one's house in Los Angeles and enjoy whatever benefits this view provides?[23]

The difficulty of expressing all these intangibles in economic terms so that people's preferences are matched should be apparent. But in spite of these difficulties, insurance agents, legal experts, scientists, and agency administrators routinely assign values to human life ranging from a few dollars to many millions of dollars, depending on the methods used to calculate these values. One of the most precise ways of calculating the value of a human life is to break down the body into its chemical elements. Some experts have determined that the value of a human life on this basis is about $8.37, which has increased $1.09 in six years because of inflation.[24] Obviously, such a method is not acceptable for public policy purposes.

There are at least five ways of determining the value of a human life: (1) calculating the present value of estimated future earnings that are foregone due to premature death, (2) calculating the present value of the losses others experience because of a person's death, (3) examining the value placed on an individual life by presently established social policies and practices, (4) using the "willingness to pay" method where people are asked how much they would be willing to pay to reduce the probability of their death by a certain amount, and (5) looking at the compensation people accept as wage premiums for dangerous jobs or hazardous occupations.[25]

The diversity of economic valuation that results from these techniques is not surprising. People are going to value their lives in ways vastly different from each other. Some people may believe they are worth any economic expenditure no matter how great. Others may feel their lives are relatively worthless. People's valuation of their lives also change with age and other circumstances. Such diversity renders the use of analytical techniques such as those just described highly questionable.

When people are making individual choices about private goods and services, a diverse value system presents no problems. They are forced to translate these diverse values into economic terms and make choices accordingly. But making choices about public goods and services is another matter. There seems to be no way to force a translation of the diversity into a common value system that is acceptable, realistic, and appropriate. Should more money be spent on reducing the emissions from coke ovens than on improving highway safety? How much money should be spent on cleaning up existing dumpsites for hazardous wastes? For these kinds of public policy questions, the political process seems to be a reasonable way to aggregate the diversity of people's values to make a decision about a course of action when there is no common value system to use for more rational calculations.

GENERAL MODELS OF THE PUBLIC POLICY PROCESS

There are various ways to describe the larger public policy process in order to understand its operation. Anderson, Brady, and Bullock, for example, describe six stages of the public policy process. (See Exhibit 4.1.) The first stage, problem formation, involves a situation where a human need exists that must be addressed or deprivation and dissatisfaction appear relative to some particular problem for which relief is sought. If enough people believe the nature of the problem is such that government should respond, it then becomes a public rather than a private problem. Public problems are distinguished from private problems by the number of people involved and the fact that public problems have broad-ranging effects, including consequences for people not directly involved, such as a strike by railroad workers that affects the entire society.[26]

Not all problems get the attention of government, however, and reach the policy agenda stage. Those that do, get there by a variety of routes. If

Exhibit 4.1

The Policy Process

Policy Terminology	1st stage Problem Formation	2nd Stage Policy Agenda	3rd Stage Policy Formulation	4th Stage Policy Adoption	5th Stage Policy Implementation	6th Stage Policy Evaluation
Definition	Relief is sought from a situation that produces a human need, deprivation, or dissatisfaction	Those problems, among many, which receive the government's serious attention	Development of pertinent and acceptable proposed courses of action for dealing with public problems	Development of support for a specific proposal such that the policy is legitimized or authorized	Application of the policy by the government's bureaucratic machinery to the problem	Attempt by the government to determine whether or not the policy has been effective
Common Sense	Getting the government to see the problem	Getting the government to begin to act on the problem	The government's proposed solution to the problem	Getting the government to accept a particular solution to the problem	Applying the government's policy to the problem	Did the policy work?

Source: From *Public Policy and Politics in America, 2nd Edition*, by J.E. Anderson, D.W. Brady, C.S. Bullock III, and J. Stewart, Jr. Copyright © 1984, 1978 by Wadsworth, Inc. Reprinted by permission of Brooks/Cole Publishing Company: Pacific Grove, CA 93950.

group interests are affected by the problem, whether the problem gets on the public policy agenda or not depends on the power, status, and number of people in the group. Political leadership is another factor in agenda setting, with the president of the United States as the most important actor. Crises, such as wars and depressions, as well as protests and demonstrations, also put problems on the policy agenda.[27]

The stage of policy formation and adoption involves the development of proposed courses of action for dealing with public problems. Policy formulation does not automatically mean adoption, of course, as many policy proposals are never formally adopted by the government. Public policies to address particular problems are formulated by the president and his immediate advisers, other members of the executive branch, career and appointed administrative officials, specially appointed committees and commissions, and legislators who introduce bills for consideration by the Congress. Whether these policies are adopted, of course, depends on winning enough support from everyone whose approval is necessary. While the most formal adoption strategy is one of proposal, congressional approval, and presidential signature, there are other adoption strategies that exist in government.[28]

Policy implementation involves the actual application of an adopted policy. The administrative agencies are the primary implementers of public policy, but the courts and Congress are also involved. Congress may override the decisions of an agency such as the Federal Trade Commission, and the courts interpret statutes and administrative rules and regulations when there is a question about a specific application. The agencies, however, are often delegated substantial authority by Congress, and have a wide range of discretion in implementing policy because their mandates are often broad and ill-defined in their enabling legislation. The Federal Trade Commission Act, for example, specifies that unfair methods of competition are illegal, but what specific methods are unfair is left up to the commission and courts to decide on a case-by-case basis. Thus the agencies make what is called administrative law through implementing the statutes passed by Congress. The application of a public policy passed by Congress can actually change the nature of the policy itself, as implementation often affects policy content.[29]

Policy evaluation, the last stage, involves an attempt to determine whether the policy has actually worked. Such an evaluation can lead to additional policy formulation to correct deficiencies. According to Anderson, Brady, and Bullock, there are two types of policy evaluation. The first is a seat-of-the-pants, or political evaluation that is usually based on fragmentary evidence and may be ideologically biased. The other is a systematic evaluation that seeks to measure the impact of policies objectively and see how well objectives are actually accomplished. Such an evaluation focuses on the effects a policy has on the problem to which it is directed.[30]

Preston and Post present other models of the public policy process that focus more on the dynamics of decision making than on stages of policy-making. They describe three models: optimization, incrementalism, and power bargaining. The optimization model is epitomized by most economists and many bureaucrats who regard the public policy process as the rational search for optimal solutions to well-defined problems. The elementary principles of such an approach are maximization (attaining the highest level of output for a given level of input) and minimization (incurring the least possible cost or inconvenience in order to achieve a given result). The optimization model is a useful analytical construct, but it is limited by its stringent analytic requirements and limited scope. It is an intellectual abstraction, according to Preston and Post, setting forth formal relationships among given conditions. But it takes no account of the way in which policy goals are articulated, alternatives proposed, and preferences discovered. Thus it is at best only a partial model of the public policy process.[31]

> The problem, of course, is that government is not supposed to be just a unified, efficient, economic machine but a responsive, disjointed, political apparatus that is accessible at many points and reflects the great variety of perspectives found in an open society.[32]

The incrementalist approach holds that policy formulation proceeds by small steps and changes rather than a comprehensive analysis in search of some optimal state of affairs. Incrementalism involves fragmenting an overly complex problem that no one fully understands into smaller manageable problems. Thus a piece of a larger problem is first coped with by a specific policy, then the consequences of this first policy are dealt with, and so on, until the larger problem is alleviated or is no longer of concern. Rather than adopting a comprehensive revision of the welfare system, for example, and searching for an optimal solution such as a guaranteed income or other sweeping change, welfare reform from an incrementalist perspective focuses on small changes in one or more programs such as food stamps or Medicaid, coping with the consequences of these changes, making other small changes, and so on, ad infinitum.

Some argue that incrementalism is the only possible approach to such large problems as poverty because of political constraints. Any suggestion of comprehensive reform exposes every aspect of the existing system to endless debate because of vested interests, guaranteeing political stalemate. Thus every administration is politically constrained to pursue an incremental strategy of reform.[33] Such a strategy, however, leaves much to be desired. Incrementalism has been called the science of muddling through, without a clear sense of direction or idea of what policy would be most preferred from the standpoint of some overriding principle or objective.

The power bargaining model is more of a political model, focusing on the strength and goals of various power centers within society, and on the processes of conflict bargaining and cooperation among them. Public policy is to be explained primarily in terms of the interaction of groups possessing some degree of social and political power. Conflict between these groups is resolved and an equilibrium reached through bargaining and compromise. The essence of power is the ability to impose penalties or distribute rewards. Thus the outcome of the policy process depends on the penalizing and rewarding abilities of conflicting groups.

Preston and Post then go on to describe what they call an institutional-systems model of the public policy process that integrates these three models into a comprehensive framework. (See Figure 4.1.) The primary initiative in identifying issues for public policy consideration in this model is based in society at large and its various constituent elements. Formal policy-making takes place within the constitutional and governmental system that defines the levels and branches of government, their responsibilities and power, and relationship to each other. These aspects of the system are of long duration

Figure 4.1

Institutional Systems Model of the Public Policy Process

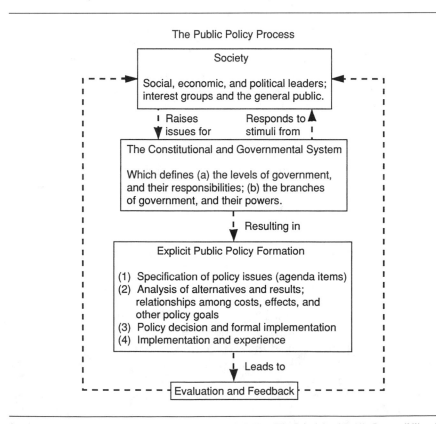

The Public Policy Process

Society

Social, economic, and political leaders; interest groups and the general public.

Raises issues for — Responds to stimuli from

The Constitutional and Governmental System

Which defines (a) the levels of government, and their responsibilities; (b) the branches of government, and their powers.

Resulting in

Explicit Public Policy Formation

(1) Specification of policy issues (agenda items)
(2) Analysis of alternatives and results; relationships among costs, effects, and other policy goals
(3) Policy decision and formal implementation
(4) Implementation and experience

Leads to

Evaluation and Feedback

Source: Preston/Post, *Private Management and Public Policy: The Principle of Public Responsibility,* © 1975, p. 72. Reprinted by permission of Prentice-Hall, Inc., Englewood Cliffs, NJ.

and subject to only incremental change. The process of explicit policy formation involves the stages of problem identification, analysis, policy decision, implementation, and experience. This last stage, experience, leads to evaluation and feedback to the society at large, which may require policy changes. This model accommodates the optimization model with its inclusion of analysis, acknowledges incrementalism in the relative permanence of the constitutional and governmental system, and includes power and bargaining at all stages.[34]

THE ADMINISTRATIVE PROCESS

To implement laws created by Congress, administrative agencies were created. The agencies with the most direct impact on business are the regulatory agencies. The first such agency was the Interstate Commerce Commission (ICC) created in 1887 to deal with the railroads. Then followed other regulatory agencies dealing with specific industries such as communications, transportation, and financial institutions. In the 1960s and 1970s, Congress enacted hundreds of laws dealing with the environment, civil rights, consumer issues, and other social matters, and created many new agencies to implement this legislation. This new type of regulation has come to be called social regulation to distinguish it from the earlier type of regulation that dealt with a specific industry. Figure 4.2 presents an historical perspective of agency growth, showing the growth of traditional industry regulation in the New Deal era, and the surge of social regulation that is of more recent vintage.

An administrative agency has been defined as "a governmental body other than a court or legislature which takes action that affects the rights of private parties."[35] These agencies may be called boards, agencies, or administrative departments, but in the regulatory area they are most often called commissions. The State Governmental Affairs Committee defined a regulatory commission as "one which (1) had decision-making authority, (2) establishes standards or guidelines conferring benefits and imposing restrictions on business conduct, (3) operates principally in the sphere of domestic business activity, (4) has its head and/or members appointed by the president . . . [generally subject to Senate confirmation], and (5) has its legal procedures governed by the Administrative Procedures Act."[36]

These regulatory commissions have specialized functions to implement governmental policy in specifically defined fields. Congress cannot immerse itself in all the details of each activity regulated or pass legislation that mandates specific forms of business behavior. Thus it passes laws that are broad in scope and more or less sets general goals to be accomplished. The task of implementing these laws is given to the regulatory agencies, which are largely composed of so-called experts in areas like safety and health or the environment. Congress, for example, gives the Environmental Protection

Figure 4.2

A Historical Perspective of Agency Growth

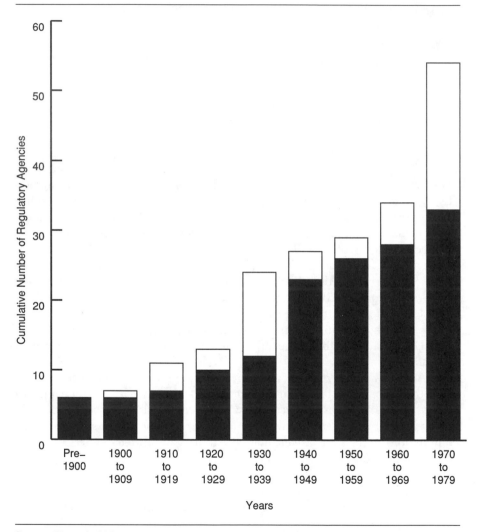

Source: Kenneth Chilton, *A Decade of Rapid Growth in Federal Regulation* (St. Louis, MO: Washington University, Center for the Study of American Business, 1979), p. 5. Reprinted with permission.

Agency (EPA) the power to set standards to improve air and water quality, but does not specify what kind of standards should be established and for what substances. It is up to the EPA to determine these standards based on its expertise. In this manner, the EPA and other regulatory agencies make public policy.

Congress creates an administrative agency by passing a statute that specifies the name, composition, and powers of the agency. This statute is called the enabling legislation for the agency. Thus the agencies are theoretically a creature of the Congress and accountable to Congress for agency activities. Congress can amend the enabling legislation to change agency behavior. Each House has oversight committees that review the work of the agencies, hold hearings, and propose amendments to the enabling legislation. Congress can also control agency activities through the appropriations process by attaching riders forbidding the agency to spend any money on particular cases.

Agencies are also subject to specific statutes that govern their activities. The Administrative Procedures Act (APA) passed in 1946 specifies formal procedures with which agencies must comply and establishes standards and prerequisites for judicial review of agency action. Agency actions that are going to affect the environment are subject to the National Environmental Policy Act (NEPA) that requires the development of an environmental impact statement before undertaking the action. Finally, the Freedom of Information Act (FOIA) and Government in the Sunshine Act require, with certain exceptions, that agency documents be publicly available and that agency proceedings be open to the public.[37]

Judicial review of agency action is important because many of the regulations issued by agencies that are opposed by business wind up in the courts. Despite congressional oversight, the primary task of assuring that agencies comply with congressional dictates has fallen on the courts. The courts may overturn an agency's action for any of the following reasons: (1) the agency failed to comply with the procedures specified in its enabling legislation, the APA, NEPA, or FOIA, (2) the agency's action conflicts with its enabling legislation and therefore exceeds the scope of its authority, (3) the agency's decision is premised on an erroneous interpretation of the law, (4) the agency's action conflicts with the Constitution, and (5) the agency erred in the substance of its action. The last reason has to do with standards of evidence to support an agency's findings and the consideration of all relevant factors in a decision.[38]

There are two general types of regulatory agencies. Some agencies are independent in the sense that they are not located within a department of the executive branch of government. Since they are not part of the legislative or judicial branch either, a fourth branch of government seems to have emerged that combines the functions of the other three in the making, interpreting, and implementing of legislation. In creating these agencies and making them independent, Congress sought to fashion them into an arm of the legislative branch and insulate them from presidential control. But many presidents have considered these commissions to be adjuncts of the executive branch and have argued that they should be able to coordinate and direct the independent agencies.[39]

Critics of this structure argue that the independent character of these commissions can hinder political monitoring by the executive branch and Congress that would make the agencies more responsive to social and economic change. Since Congress in particular does not exercise its oversight function very well in some cases, the agencies can become complacent in their functions. On the other hand, these agencies can also become too zealous in their efforts, requiring new congressional action to rein them in, such as recent efforts directed toward the FTC and its rule-making authority.[40]

Another criticism is that the independent character of administrative agencies has weakened them by removing the benefits of more direct congressional and presidential support. In the case of industry regulation, this makes the agencies more vulnerable to pressure from the regulated industries. They become timid in defending the public interest and developing effective regulatory programs. In the case of social regulation, the independence of the agencies makes them subject to pressures from various interest groups, which may make them ignore the economic impact of their actions.[41]

Other agencies are located within the executive branch in one of the cabinet departments. These agencies include the Food and Drug Administration (FDA) as part of the Department of Health and Human Resources, the Antitrust Division of the Department of Justice, the Labor-Management Services Administration and OSHA in the Department of Labor, and the National Highway Traffic Safety Administration (NHTSA) in the Department of Transportation. Even here, however, there is some question whether these agencies are subject to presidential influence and guidance or whether they are free to use the regulatory authority granted them by Congress. Some believe that the president's power to appoint and dismiss cabinet officers carries with it an implicit authority to direct actions by regulatory agencies within the executive departments. Others argue that these agencies may accept White House advice, but that ultimately they are as independent as the separate regulatory commissions.[42]

Regulatory activities may be pursued in a number of ways, but the rule-making procedure is generally preferred by the newer social regulatory agencies. Rule making is the process of promulgating rules, and results in regulations of greater certainty and consistency and broader input from the public. The APA definition of a rule is "an agency statement of general or particular applicability and future effect designed to complement, interpret, or prescribe law or policy."[43] Thus rule making is the enactment of regulations that will generally be applicable at some future time period.

Under the rule-making process, an agency must first publish a proposed regulation in the Federal Register. The Federal Register is a legal newspaper in which the executive branch of the U.S. government publishes regulations, orders, and other documents of government agencies. It was created by Congress for the government to communicate with the public about the administration's actions on a daily basis. This procedure provides an opportunity for public comment. Any interested individual or organization concerned with a pending regulation may comment on it directly in writing or orally at a hearing within a certain comment period.

The Federal Register gives detailed instructions on how, when, and where a viewpoint can be expressed. After the agency receives and considers the comments, it may publish a final version of the regulation in the Federal Register or discontinue the rule-making procedure. If a final regulation is published, the agency must also include a summary and discussion of the major comments it received during the comment period. The final regulation may take effect no sooner than 30 days following its publication. After a final rule has been adopted by the agency, it is also published in the Code of Federal Regulations. The code contains all the rules and regulations that any given agency has passed over the course of its existence.

On February 17, 1981, President Reagan issued an executive order that required agencies in the executive branch to prepare a Regulatory Impact Analysis for each major rule being considered. The purpose of this analysis was to permit an assessment of the potential benefits and costs of each major regulatory procedure. The executive order also required that agencies choose regulatory goals and set priorities to maximize the benefits to society and choose the most cost-efficient means among legally available options for achieving the goals. This Regulatory Impact Analysis must be submitted to the Office of Information and Regulatory Affairs (OIRA) located in the Office of Management and Budget (OMB). This analysis must pass OIRA's scrutiny before a regulation can be published. OIRA has the power to delay issuance of the regulation either in its proposed or final form.

Government agencies are very important actors in the public policy process. They combine the functions of the legislative branch in making administrative law, the executive branch through enforcing agency actions, and the judicial branch in adjudicating disputes. The administrative process has grown because of the need for specialized application of the laws Congress passes. The Congress did not wish to increase executive power by giving these functions to the president, and thus created administrative agencies as an alternative. These agencies are subject to control by the other three branches through congressional oversight, the presidential power of appointment and issuance of executive orders, and judicial review. But they also have shown a great deal of autonomy at times in formulating public policy. Thus business is surprised because a law passed by Congress often turns out to be quite different than anticipated when implemented by the agencies.

> Administrative agencies wield power because they constitute mobilizations of resources that can be used to allocate political values. They develop distinctive institutional points of view on what policies are deemed in the public interest. They push unabashedly within political arenas to advance these viewpoints. Moreover, agencies are supported by external political groups as well as opposed by them, and thus they engage fully in the political conflict that inevitably envelopes those possessing power.[44]

This political conflict limits the power agencies can exercise in the government. There are several features in the bureaucratic environment, some of which have been already mentioned, that limit the power of agencies. Because of the separation of powers concept, Congress and the executive branch have some ability to control agency behavior. The press makes the exposure of agency scandal a principal objective. The Freedom of Information Act requires agencies to open themselves to public scrutiny. The power of public interest lobbies and built-in mechanisms of client advocacy also provide limits on agency behavior. Statutory encouragement and protection of whistle blowing is also a factor in the environment. Finally, the institutionalization of citizen participation in decision making provides another check on agency power. This system of checks and balances led one author to comment that bureaucratic power in the United States is "probably more inhibited than in any other country on earth."[45]

ADMINISTRATIVE STRUCTURE FOR ENVIRONMENTAL POLICY

An administrative structure has been created at the federal level to implement laws related to the environment. Actually, when Congress passes environmental legislation, it is often quite broad so that it needs a great deal of interpretation. Regulations issued by agencies provide this interpretation and are quite specific regarding requirements and procedures to be followed. This process is something of a law-making function in and of itself. While the Congress passes statutory legislation regarding the environment, it is up to the agencies to implement them and in the process create what is called administrative law. There are two federal agencies that are responsible for attaining environmental objectives and developing policies to preserve the physical environment.

Council on Environmental Quality

The National Environmental Policy Act created the Council on Environmental Quality (CEQ), a three-member body located in the executive office of the president. (See Exhibit 4.2.) In general, the CEQ (1) evaluates all federal programs to see that they are consistent with the national policy on the environment, (2) advises and assists the president in environmental matters, and (3) develops national policies in the environmental area.

The CEQ is responsible for administering the environmental impact statement process through the issuance of regulations to federal agencies regarding their preparation. Beyond this, however, the CEQ has no administrative authority for pollution control. Its approach is entirely preventive in

Exhibit 4.2

Council on Environmental Quality

Purpose: To administer the environmental impact statement process and to develop and recommend to the President policies for protecting and improving environmental quality.

Regulatory Activity: The CEQ is responsible for issuing regulations to federal agencies on the preparation of environmental impact statements required under the National Environmental Policy Act. It also (1) monitors and appraises federal programs affecting the environment; and (2) assists in coordinating national environmental programs.

Established: 1969

Legislative Authority:
Enabling Legislation: National Environmental Policy Act of 1969 (83 Stat. 852)
                       National Environmental Improvement Act of 1970 (84 Stat. 114)
                       Water Quality Improvement Act of 1970 (84 Stat. 94)

Organization: The Council, located within the Executive Office of the President, consists of three members appointed by the President with the advice and consent of the Senate. The Office of Environmental Quality within the Department of Housing and Urban Development provides staff for the Council.

Budgets and Staffing
(Fiscal Years 1970–1990)

	75	80	85	86	87	88	(Estimated) 89	90
Budget ($ millions)	4	8	1	1	1	1	1	1
Staffing	50	32	11	13	13	13	13	13

Note: Budget and staffing figures include the Office of Environmental Quality.

Source: Ronald J. Penoyer, *Directory of Federal Regulatory Agencies,* 2nd ed. (St. Louis, MO: Washington University Center for the Study of American Business, 1980), p. 25. Reprinted with permission.

nature. Another function of the CEQ is preparation of the Environmental Quality Report, an annual report on the state of the environment. CEQ responsibility for this report is analogous to the Council of Economic Advisers and the Economic Report of the President.

Despite its lack of authority, the CEQ has symbolic importance and political value to environmental interests. The agency's presence in the president's executive structure gives it visibility and implies a high national priority to environmental problems. Its opportunities to influence the president directly give it the role of acting as the environmental conscience of the executive branch. However, the agency can exercise no more influence than the president cares to give it because the president can ignore any of its recommendations.

Environmental Protection Agency

The other federal agency involved in protecting and enhancing the physical environment and one with much more sweeping authority over various aspects of pollution control than the CEQ is the Environmental Protection Agency (EPA). Its responsibilities involve the development and implementation of programs that range across the whole domain of environmental management. The EPA began on July 9, 1970, when President Nixon sent a reorganization plan to Congress that took the various units dealing with the environment from existing departments and agencies and relocated them in a single new independent agency. The plan became effective on December 2, 1970, when the EPA officially opened its doors.

The EPA was formed from 15 separate components of 5 executive departments and independent agencies. Programs related to air pollution control, solid waste management, radiation, and drinking water were transferred to the EPA from the Department of Health, Education, and Welfare (now the Department of Health and Human Services). The water pollution control program was transferred from the Department of Interior and the authority to register and regulate pesticides from the Department of Agriculture. The responsibility to set tolerance levels for pesticides in food was transferred from the Food and Drug Administration and a pesticide research program came from the Department of the Interior. Finally, the responsibility for setting environmental radiation protection standards came from the old Atomic Energy Commission.

The EPA now has responsibility for pollution control in seven areas of the environment; air, water, solid and hazardous waste, pesticides, toxic substances, radiation, and noise. Its general responsibilities in these areas include (1) establishing and enforcing standards, (2) monitoring pollution in the environment, (3) conducting research into environmental problems and holding demonstrations when appropriate, and (4) assisting state and local governments in their efforts to control pollution. (See Exhibit 4.3.) The EPA is headquartered in Washington, D.C., with regional offices and laboratories located throughout the country. (See Figures 4.3 and 4.4.)

The research arm of the EPA is the Office of Research and Development (ORD), which directs the EPA's research program. About 70 percent of this program is in direct support of environmental problems of concern to the agency: the other 30 percent deals with long-term problems to address future regulatory needs. The major areas of research are monitoring, development of technology, determination of ecological effects, and definition of the health effects of environmental pollutants. In addition to its own research staff, a Science Advisory Board composed of preeminent non-EPA scientists was established by Congress to advise the agency on scientific issues.

Exhibit 4.3

Environmental Protection Agency

Purpose: To protect and enhance the physical environment.

Regulatory Activity: In cooperation with state and local governments, the agency controls pollution through regulation, surveillance, and enforcement in eight areas: air, water quality, solid waste, pesticides, toxic substances, drinking water, radiation, and noise. Its activities in each area include development of: (1) national programs and technical policies, (2) national emission standards and effluent guidelines, (3) rules and procedures for industry reporting, registration and certification programs; and (4) ambient air standards. EPA issues permits to industrial dischargers of pollutants and for disposal of industrial waste; sets standards which limit the amount of radioactivity in the environment; reviews proposals for new nuclear facilities; evaluates and regulates new chemicals and chemicals with new uses; and establishes and monitors tolerance levels for pesticides occurring in or on foods.

Established: 1970

Legislative Authority:

   Enabling Legislation: Reorganization Plan No. 3 of 1970, effective December 2, 1970
   The EPA is responsible for the enforcement of the following acts:

      Water Quality Improvement Act of 1970 (84 Stat. 94)
      Clean Air Act Amendments of 1970 (84 Stat 1676)
      Federal Water Pollution Control Act Amendments of 1972 (86 Stat. 819)
      Federal Insecticide, Fungicide and Rodenticide Act of 1972 (86 Stat. 975)
      Marine Protection, Research, and Sanctuaries Act of 1972 (86 Stat. 1052)
      Noise Control Act of 1972 (86 Stat. 1234)
      Provisions of the Energy Supply and Environmental Coordination Act of 1974 (88 Stat. 246)
      Safe Drinking Water Act of 1974 (88 Stat. 1661)
      Resource Conservation and Recovery Act of 1976 (90 Stat. 95)
      Toxic Substances Control Act of 1976 (90 Stat. 2005)
      Clean Air Act Amendments of 1977 (91 Stat. 685)
      Clean Water Act of 1977 (91 Stat. 1566)

Organization: This independent agency, located within the Executive branch, is headed by an administrator.

Budgets and Staffing
(Fiscal Years 1970–1990)

	70	75	80	85	86	87	88	(Estimated) 89	90
Budget ($ millions)	205	794	1360	1928	1860	2642	3109	3384	3664
Staff	3856	9144	11004	11615	12041	13197	13589	13739	14417

Note: Budget figures exclude construction grants.

Source: Ronald J. Penoyer, *Directory of Federal Regulatory Agencies,* 2nd ed. (St. Louis, MO: Washington University Center for the Study of American Business, 1980), p. 27. Reprinted with permission.

Figure 4.3 U.S. Environmental Protection Agency Organization Chart

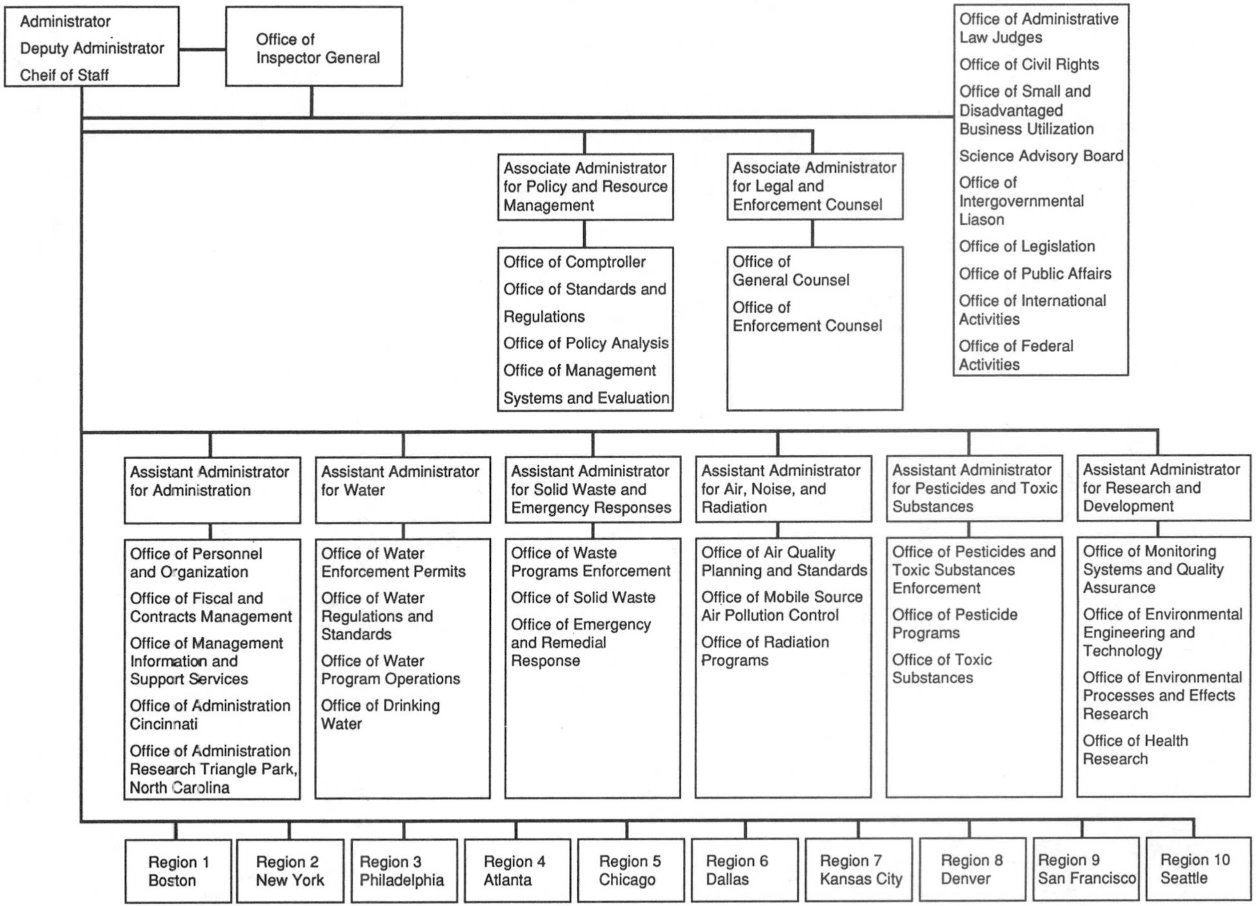

Source: Environmental Protection Agency, *Your Guide to the U.S. Environmental Protection Agency*, OPA212 (Washington, DC: Environmental Protection Agency, 1982), pp. 4–5.

Figure 4.4

U.S. Environmental Protection Agency Regional Organization

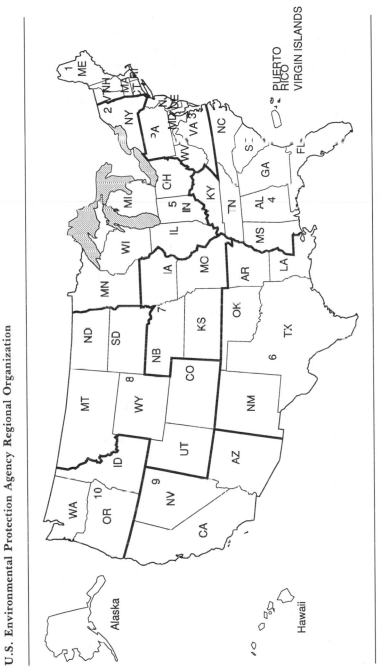

Source: *Finding Your Way Through EPA* (Washington, DC: Environmental Protection Agency, August 1979), p. 2.

The Office of Legal and Enforcement Council acts as the EPA's law firm and is responsible for carrying out all of its legal responsibilities and activities. The enforcement philosophy of the EPA is to encourage voluntary compliance with environmental laws by communities and private industry and to encourage state and local governments to perform enforcement actions when needed. If these efforts fail, the EPA is authorized to enforce the law through inspection procedures with respect to all aspects of its responsibilities and criminal investigation units with regard to hazardous waste disposal.

THE SOCIAL PROCESS

Our society is often characterized as pluralistic, meaning that it is relatively open as far as public participation is concerned. A pluralist society is composed of a number of groups, all of which, to varying degrees, wield influence in the public policy process. These organizations can quite properly be called interest groups because they form around shared interests. People organize such groups and join or support them because they share common attitudes and values on a particular problem or issue and believe they can advance their interests better by organizing themselves into a group rather than pursuing their interests individually. These groups compete for access to formal institutions of decision making and for the attention of key policymakers in the hope of producing policy outcomes that favor their interests.

Such interest groups are thus conveyers of certain kinds of demands that are fed into the public policy process. They fill a gap in the formal political process by representing interests that are beyond the capacities of individuals acting alone or representatives chosen by the people. At times they perform a watchdog function by sounding an alarm whenever policies of more formal institutions threaten the interests of their members. They generate ideas that may become formal policies of these institutions and help to place issues on the public policy agenda.

Americans seem particularly inclined to form groups to pursue their common interests. In 1980, there were nearly 15,000 nonprofit associations of one kind or another, and 28 percent of these were headquartered in Washington, D.C., a sure indicator of political interest. In 1981, approximately 40,000 people were employed by these Washington-based associations.[46] One study reported that 75 percent of all American adults belonged to at least one organization, and 57 percent were active in at least one group.[47] The importance of associations in American life was recognized by Alexis de Tocqueville many years ago in his famous book on American democracy.

> Americans of all ages, all conditions, and all dispositions, constantly form associations. They have not only commercial and manufacturing companies, in which all

take part, but associations of a thousand other kinds—religious, moral, serious, futile, extensive or restricted, enormous or diminutive. The Americans make associations to give entertainments, to found establishments for education, to build inns, to construct churches, to diffuse books, to send missionaries to the antipodes, and in this manner they found hospitals, prisons, and schools.[48]

These interest groups perform a variety of functions for their members. Groups may perform a symbolic function simply by giving members the opportunity to express the interests or values they hold. Such activity serves to reinforce one's identity or provide legitimacy for certain ideas, a valuable function in and of itself. Closely related is an ideological function, whereby groups may provide an outlet for people who hold strong beliefs about a particular aspect of American life, such as free enterprise, and need a way to appeal to these strongly held principles. A common function of interest groups is to promote the economic self-interest of their members, a function most often associated with business and labor groups. Groups also provide members with information, ranging from political information related to particular causes the group may be pursuing to more technical information in which members may be interested, such as information about stamps, coins, or antique cars. Most groups collect, analyze, and disseminate information to their members to some extent. Finally, groups can perform instrumental functions for their members—concrete goals that are noneconomic in nature. This goal can include the efforts of antismoking groups to ban smoking in public places or the right-to-life groups that seek to outlaw abortions.[49]

The way a problem gets identified in a pluralistic system, then, is for people who are concerned about the problem to organize themselves or join an existing organization to pursue their particular interests in the problem. If the problem is of widespread concern, and the group or groups dealing with it can attract enough financial and other kinds of support, the problem may eventually become public as people become aware of it and show varying degrees of support. Eventually government or other institutions may pick up on the problem and translate the issues being raised into formal legislation or other policy actions. These interest groups then continue to exercise influence in helping to design public policies to deal with these problems.

Thus in the pluralist model, problems are identified and policies designed in a sort of bottom-up fashion—concern about a problem can begin anywhere at the grass-roots level in society and eventually grow into a major public issue that demands attention. This is in contrast to the power-elite model, a sort of top-down process in which the upper class identifies the problems, designs public policy, and forces it on the rest of society. We could see the pluralistic process at work during the social revolutions of the 1960s. Various interest groups, such as the Southern Christian Leadership Conference, Nader's groups, and the Sierra Club, were active in identifying the problems of civil rights, consumerism, and pollution and in helping to shape public policies on these problems.

Public policy, then, reflects the interests of groups, and as groups gain and lose influence, public policy is altered to reflect the changing patterns of group influence. The public interest takes shape through the pulling and tugging that goes on between special interests. Public policy is the result of the relative influence of the group in the policy-making process, and results from a struggle of these groups to win public and institutional support. As one theorist claims, "What may be called public policy is the equilibrium reached in this [group] struggle at any given moment, and it represents a balance which the contending factions or groups constantly strive to weigh in their favor."[50]

In theory, a pluralistic system is an open system. Anyone with a strong enough interest in a problem can pursue this interest as far as it will take him or her. Membership in a particular social or income class or of a particular race does not shut anyone out from participating in the public policy process. Power is diffused in a pluralistic system and dominant power centers are hard to develop in such a competitive arrangement. The existence of many interest groups also provides more opportunities for leadership, making it possible for more people with leadership ability to exercise these talents. There are many opportunities for people to become political entrepreneurs who perform an organizing function by bringing people together with similar interests, analogous to that of economic entrepreneurs.[51]

But interest groups themselves, particularly as they become large, tend to be dominated by their own leadership. This leadership usually formulates policy for the group as a whole, and the public stance of an interest group often represents the views of a ruling elite within the interest group itself rather than all of the rank-and-file membership. Many interest groups may provide few, if any, opportunities for members to express their views on issues facing the group. Interest groups in many cases also draw most of their membership from better educated, middle- or upper-class segments of society. Many minorities and particularly the poorer elements of society are not adequately represented. Their problems are likely to be ignored, and some groups cannot advance their interests even in a pluralistic system unless championed by other people who are more likely to participate in public policy-making.

Improved public policy decisions should also result from such a structure, since more people, particularly those who are closest to the problem, have an input in decision making. Yet a pluralistic system is a system of conflict because interest groups compete for attention and influence in the public policy process, and such competing interests do not necessarily result in the best public policy decisions. Conflict can get out of control and result in social fragmentation, making a policy decision for society difficult to reach. This is particularly true when interest groups are unwilling to compromise, in which case reaching a public policy decision for society as a whole may be impossible. Furthermore, some interests, as we stated, are not adequately represented.

A pluralistic system does seem to allow, however, for more interests to be represented than alternative models. More people should have a chance to promote their particular values and interests and have a chance to govern society. This is a mixed blessing, however, as the more pluralistic a society becomes, the more diverse will be the interests represented, and the less clear will be the direction in which society is moving. The lack of central direction for society, which an elite provides, can be a disadvantage of pluralism as society is pulled to and fro by the competition of many different interests with varying degrees of power and influence. Thus a society may find it increasingly difficult to formulate possible solutions to complex policy questions.

The public choice school sees interest groups not so much as competitors against one another, but as competing against the public, which is largely unaware of what is happening. Interest groups are joint raiders on the U.S. Treasury and potential abusers of government's coercive power. As government expanded its activities, interests groups saw political competition rather than economic competition as the most effective way to ensure their economic survival. They have found it profitable to manipulate the political process to redistribute wealth and insulate them from the uncertainties of the market.[52]

Some observers have characterized our society as one of interest group pluralism, whereby the federal government is subject to the pressures of special interest groups. Because of the changes in the seniority system in Congress and the proliferation of subcommittees, Congress has become a collection of independent power centers. The interest groups can thus take their case directly to individual representatives and senators and establish close working ties with the subcommittee(s) in their areas of interest. The result is the infamous *iron triangle* composed of the interest groups, the congressional subcommittee, and the relevant federal agency, which becomes the focus of public policy-making. This kind of process encourages government to act on individual measures without attention to their collective consequences. Policy is not made for the nation as a whole, but for narrow autonomous sectors defined by the special interests. While these groups may claim to be acting in the public interest, such claims are suspect.

> . . . the problem with the so-called public interest groups is not their venality but their belief that they alone represent the public interest. The confidence these groups have had in pursuing their numerous and sometimes far-reaching missions is not always warranted, especially when their activities — and their demands — are scrutinized in the context of the full effects of the government regulations which they so often instigate or endorse with tremendous zeal.[53]

Another problem with interest group pluralism is the removal of public policy-making from public scrutiny. Decisions are made behind closed doors, effectively removed from popular control. As stated by Everett Carl Ladd, "The public cannot hope to monitor the policy outcomes that result from the individual actions of 535 Senators and Representatives operating through a maze of iron triangles."[54] The solution to this fractionalism, according to some observers, is a revitalized party system where the claims of interest groups can be adjusted to mesh with a coherent program that represents more of a national interest. The proliferation of interest groups makes necessary strengthened parties that can cope with the multiple organized pressures of interest group pluralism.

ENVIRONMENTAL GROUPS

There are several environmental groups that have been influential in the public policy process to place environmental issues on the agenda and support legislation and regulation to deal with environmental problems. Many of the ideas generated by these groups have found their way into laws and thousands of regulations that affect business. The groups employ lawyers, economists, ecologists, and systems analysts to press for additional laws and regulations to promote their interests. And they challenge official interpretations of environmental impacts regarding government projects and plans that affect the environment. A brief discussion of several of these groups will help you to understand their interests and how they operate in the public policy process.

The Sierra Club. This group lobbies Congress on dozens of different issues related to the environment ranging from nuclear energy to wetlands preservation. It opposes the licensing, construction, and operation of new nuclear fission plants, and favors the reduction of society's dependence on nuclear power. The club also is involved in a major effort to influence funding for environmental agencies and programs. The Sierra Club is one of the most influential environmental groups in the country.

The Friends of the Earth. Founded in 1971, the Friends of the Earth is a tax-funded environmentalist organization that is similar in outlook and activities to the Sierra Club. The group is a major participant in the no-growth movement and supports government ownership of land to ensure that wealth is wisely passed from generation to generation. It has been lobbying for a national population policy and eventual population stabilization.

The National Wildlife Federation. This organization is one of the largest environmental groups claiming over 4 million members in 1982 and having a budget of $37.1 million. Many of its achievements include legislation that prohibits individuals from owning and using private property, by banning various areas from private ownership and development. Other efforts have to do with blocking the use of coal, nuclear power, natural gas, and hydroelectric power.

Environmental Action. This group was founded in 1970 when it coordinated Earth Day, a series of teach-ins and protests across the nation. Since 1981, its major efforts have been directed toward helping dedicated grassroots environmentalists fight the propollution policies of the Reagan administration. Its ongoing efforts include the Dirty Dozen Campaign which focuses on 12 of the most obvious antienvironmental members of Congress, and the Filthy Five Campaign, which is intended to make voters and politicians aware of large polluting corporations.

Natural Resources Defense Council. The principal strategy of this group is to block economic development in the courts by suing firms for failure to pay adequate attention to the hundreds of environmental laws and regulations affecting their operations. The organization also sues the federal government over improper preparation of an environmental impact statement or for violations of the Endangered Species Act as well as for alleged violation of other laws and regulations. The Environmental Defense Fund is another litigious group that pursues similar strategies.

Environmental Defense Fund. Best known for its analysis and sponsorship of novel solutions to environmental problems, such as market-based incentives for pollution control. Effects change mainly through litigation, although it has been known to engage in lobbying efforts on certain occasions.

The Nature Conservancy. Rather than lobby or engage in other political action, this group raises money to buy land or accepts gifts of land to hold in its natural state. The organization tries to protect places that desperately need protection and preservation by caring for the land it comes to own and keeping it from being developed. In this manner the organization protects wetlands, remote desert areas, pristine lakes, and other areas of concern.

These and other interest groups dedicated to protection and preservation of the environment often seem to wield an influence far beyond what their numbers would suggest. Many of them formed a coalition during the years of the Reagan administration, called the Green Lobby, that was very effective in preventing many of the environmental laws from being repealed or watered down by Congress. They tried to mitigate the effects of the staff and budgetary cutbacks at the agency level. These groups were also effective in seeking the removal of the head of the EPA and the secretary of the Department of the Interior during the early years of the Reagan administration for their allegedly antienvironmentalist stance. They have also become more active in filing citizen suits against companies for violation of environmental laws and regulations.

CONFLICT RESOLUTION

Because the public policy process is open to public participation, and because of the existence of the powerful environmental groups we listed, there is often a great deal of conflict over the policies and programs of the government, as well as the shape of legislation and regulation that affects business. Major sources of conflict involve competing resource demands, differences in values regarding the relative worth of resources, and uncertainties regarding the costs, benefits, and risks involved in proposed actions. Because of the potential for conflict on environmental issues, techniques for resolution of conflict become of great importance in order to make efficient and effective decisions that will benefit the public at large and preserve our environmental resources. The choice of a decision-making technique can have a major effect on whether the decision achieves its objectives and is accepted by the publics that have a stake in the outcome.

There are several categories of conflict resolution, as shown in Exhibit 4.4.[55] The notion of conflict anticipation has to do with the early identification of potential sources of conflict so that these problems may be studied and mitigated if possible before positions become hardened and an adversarial

Exhibit 4.4

Types of Environmental Conflict Resolution

Type	Definition	Examples
Conflict anticipation	A third party identifies potential disputes before opposing positions are fully identified	Scoping or screening process in impact assessment identifies likely problems and affected groups
Joint problem solving	Ongoing group meetings discuss and clarify issues and resolve differences; agreements reached are informal	Structured workshops; adaptive environmental assessment; environmental planning citizens' advisory committees
Mediation	Formal negotiations between empowered representatives of constituencies; mediator facilitates but does not impose settlement.	Technical meetings to seek settlements; facilitator uses a variety of negotiating and mediating techniques
Policy dialogues	Meetings to discuss and resolve differences between conflicting policy-making agencies; results become advisory to official policy-making bodies	Interagency advisory committees; ad hoc meetings between members of different governmental agencies
Binding arbitration	Formal arguments presented by opposing parties; arbitrator imposes settlement that parties have previously agreed to abide by	Labor-management contract arbitration; court arbitration hearings

Source: Walter E. Westman, *Ecology, Impact Assessment, and Environmental Planning* (New York: Wiley, 1985), p. 120. Copyright © 1985 by John Wiley & Sons, Inc. Reprinted by permission of John Wiley & Sons, Inc.

situation develops. The scoping process in environmental impact assessment is an example of this kind of conflict resolution. Identifying potential conflicts before they get out of hand gives the disputing parties an opportunity to work out compromises and solutions at early stages of a project proposal. Even if disputes are not resolved at this stage, at least differences can be explored and put on the table, so to speak.

The technique of joint problem solving involves the making of an informal agreement among the contending parties, which can then be considered more formally for possible adoption by decision makers. This process typically starts early and continues throughout the full term that is necessary for a decision to be made. Thus ongoing group meetings are often held throughout the decision-making process to clarify issues and resolve differences in an informal manner. In this way the various positions can be aired without formal commitment, and the parties to the dispute can develop an acquaintance with each other and perhaps even come to develop some degree of trust, which would serve them well at later stages when formal decisions have to be made.

Environmental mediation is a formal process of negotiation among officially recognized representatives of affected constituencies. There has to be a shared willingness among the parties to a dispute to attempt negotiation or else the technique may not resolve differences. The mediator may be asked to clarify areas of agreement and disagreement and suggest possible solutions to the conflict and ways to implement these solutions. However, the final agreement must be made by a separate decision-making body in order for the decision to be binding on the parties involved. The mediator facilitates but cannot impose a settlement on the disputing parties. Mediation is often used in labor disputes and may also be helpful in environmental conflicts.

Policy dialogues involve informal forums for discussion where differences regarding governmental policies may be resolved and where advice may be provided to government agencies. The discussants could be representatives for the different agencies that are involved in the policy-making on an issue or outside experts who have been asked to submit a report to the policy-making body. Interagency advisory committees are an example of this type of conflict resolution. These committees are often formed when agencies differ over proposed actions and have no other way to resolve the dispute.

Finally, binding arbitration involves an agreement among the opposing parties to abide by the decision of the arbitrator. Thus the arbitrator imposes a decision on the parties to the dispute. This process gives the disputing parties a chance to have their side of the story heard, and the arbitrator makes the decision after he or she has heard all the contending positions. Choice of the arbitrator is crucial in this technique, which may be why it is not used very often to settle environmental disputes. It may be difficult to find objective arbitrators that don't already have some fairly strong positions on many environmental issues.

Questions for Discussion

1. Why are markets themselves not able to respond effectively to environmental issues? Is public policy a more useful concept to understand how the commons is managed in our society? Why or why not?

2. Which definition of public policy makes the most sense to you? What are the essential elements of the definition you chose? How does public policy differ from business policy?

3. What is the public policy agenda? How do issues get on the agenda? What environmental issues would you say are on the public policy agenda at the present time?

4. What values can be expressed through the public policy process that cannot be expressed through markets? Is there a difference between the way people act as consumers and the way they act as citizens?

5. Comment on the statement that "ideas or convictions that can be supported by reasons in the political process are different from wants and interests satisfied in markets." Do you agree or disagree?

6. What is the function of a political process? Why do people participate in this process? What is the task of a political system? What skills and abilities are necessary to function effectively in this process?

7. What are public goods and services? How do these differ from private goods and services? Why can't public goods and services be provided through market exchange? Give examples to support your answer.

8. How are value conflicts resolved in the public policy process? How does this process differ from the way value conflicts are resolved by the market? Which process is more efficient?

9. Describe the general models of the public policy process presented in the chapter. Which model do you like best? Which model do you think is most realistic? Do these models help you to understand how the public policy process functions?

10. Describe the administrative process. How does administrative law differ from statutory law? Does business have to concern itself with both levels of lawmaking? Why or why not?

11. Why are administrative agencies created? What functions do they perform? What laws or statutes govern the behavior of these agencies? What checks and balances exist as far as agency power is concerned?

12. How are regulatory activities carried out? What types of activities are generally used with respect to environmental regulation? How do these activities work, and where can business executives and citizens have an input to the process?

13. What is a pluralistic system? How does this kind of system work with regard to public policy? What are interest groups and what functions do they perform?

14. What are the advantages and disadvantages of a pluralistic system? On the whole, do you believe better public policy comes from this kind of system? What is interest group pluralism? Does this term adequately characterize our society?

15. What is conflict resolution? What are the different categories of conflict resolution presented in the chapter? Which seem most effective from your point of view? Which are most relevant to environmental policy-making?

16. Looking at the public policy process as a whole, would you say that the commons is managed as well as could be expected through this process? What are the major problems with regard to the public policy process? How could the system be improved?

NOTES

1. Mark Sagoff, *The Economy of the Earth* (Cambridge: Cambridge University Press, 1988), p. 70.

2. James E. Anderson, David W. Brady, Charles Bullock III, *Public Policy and Politics in America* (North Scituate, MA: Duxbury Press, 1978), pp. 4–5.

3. Ibid., p. 5.

4. Theodore J. Lowi, *Incomplete Conquest: Governing America,* 2nd ed. (New York: Holt, Rinehart and Winston, 1981), p. 423.

5. Thomas R. Dye, *Understanding Public Policy,* 3rd ed. (Englewood Cliffs, NJ: Prentice-Hall, 1978), p. 3.

6. Lee E. Preston and James E. Post, *Private Management and Public Policy: The Principle of Public Responsibility* (Englewood Cliffs, NJ: Prentice-Hall, 1975), p. 11.

7. Ibid.

8. Ibid.

9. Anderson, Brady, Bullock, *Public Policy,* p. 6.

10. B. Guy Peters, *American Public Policy: Promise and Performance,* 2nd ed. (Chatham, NJ: Chatham House, 1986), p. vii.

11. Ibid.

12. Sagoff, *The Economy of the Earth,* p. 8.

13. Ibid., p. 17.

14. Ibid., p. 53.

15. Ibid., p. 44.

16. Ibid., p. 56.

17. Ibid., p. 92.

18. Ibid., p. 121.

19. Dye, *Understanding Public Policy,* p. 23.

20. John Rawls, *A Theory of Justice* (Cambridge, MA: Harvard University Press, 1971), p. 266.

21. Gerald Sirkin, *The Visible Hand: The Fundamentals of Economic Planning* (New York: McGraw-Hill, 1968), p. 45.

22. James Buchanan, *The Demand and Supply of Public Goods* (Chicago: Rand McNally, 1968), p. 8.

23. See Michael J. Mandel, "How Much Is a Sea Otter Worth?" *Business Week,* August 21, 1989, pp. 59, 62.

24. William R. Greer, "Pondering the Value of a Human Life," *New York Times,* August 16, 1984, p. 16.

25. Alasdair MacIntyre, "Utilitarianism and Cost-Benefit Analysis: An Essay on the Relevance of Moral Philosophy to 'Bureaucratic Theory," Donald Scherer and Thomas Attig, eds. *Ethics and the Environment* (Englewood Cliffs, NJ: Prentice-Hall, 1983), pp. 145–146.

26. James E. Anderson, David W. Brady, and Charles Bullock III, *Public Policy and Politics in America* (North Scituate, MA: Duxbury Press, 1978), p. 7.

27. Ibid., p. 9.

28. Ibid., pp. 9–10.

29. Ibid., pp. 10–11.

30. Ibid., pp. 11–12. Evaluation is a problem in American government, because there is almost no incentive to evaluate federal programs. After going through the difficulty of getting a program started and funded, a federal bureaucrat is highly unlikely to agree to an independent evaluation that could allow political opponents a chance to have the program discontinued. Thus there have been few instances where an important policy initiative has been tried and tested in any rigorous manner. See "Intellectuals' Niche in Public Policy," *Insight,* September 19, 1988, pp. 62–63.

31. Lee E. Preston and James E. Post, *Private Management and Public Policy* (Englewood Cliffs, NJ: Prentice-Hall, 1975), pp. 62–64.

32. Charles T. Goodsell, *The Case for Bureaucracy: A Public Administration Polemic,* 2nd ed. (Chatham, NJ: Chatham House, 1985), p. 175.

33. See Frederick Doolittle, Frank Levy, and Michael Wiscman, "The Mirage of Welfare Reform," *The Public Interest,* No. 47 (Spring 1977), p. 77.

34. Preston and Post, *Public Policy,* pp. 67–73.

35. John D. Blackburn, Elliot I. Klayman, and Martin H. Malin, *The Legal Environment of Business: Public Law and Regulation* (Homewood, IL: Irwin, 1982), p. 65.

36. Robert E. Healy, ed., *Federal Regulatory Directory 1979–80* (Washington, DC: Congressional Quarterly, 1979), p. 3.

37. Blackburn, Klayman, and Malin, *Legal Environment,* p. 67–68.

38. Ibid., pp. 70–71.

39. Healy, *Regulatory Directory,* p. 25.

40. Ibid.

41. Ibid., p. 26.

42. Ibid., p. 31.

43. Blackburn, Klayman, and Malin, *Legal Environment,* p. 77.

44. Goodsell, *Bureaucracy,* p. 126.

45. Ibid., p. 133.

46. Robert H. Salisbury, "Interest Groups: Toward A New Understanding," *Interest Group Politics,* Allan J. Cigler and Burdett A. Loomis, eds. (Washington, DC: Congressional Quarterly, 1983), p. 357.

47. Samuel H. Barnes, "Some Political Consequences of Involvement in Organizations," paper presented at the 1977 annual meeting of the American Political Science Association, quoted in Raymond E. Wolfinger, Martin Shapiro, and Fred I. Greenstein, *Dynamics of American Politics,* 2nd ed. (Englewood Cliffs, NJ: Prentice-Hall, 1980), pp. 229–230.

48. Alexis de Tocqueville, *Democracy in America* (New York: Schocken, 1961), Vol. II, p. 128.

49. Norman J. Ornstein and Shirley Elder, *Interest Groups, Lobbying and Policymaking* (Washington, DC: Congressional Quarterly Press, 1978), pp. 29–34.

50. Earl Latham, *The Group Basis of Politics* (New York: Octagon Books, 1965), p. 36 as quoted in Anderson, Brady, and Bullock, *Public Policy and Politics,* p. 416.

51. Andrew S. McFarland, "Public Interest Lobbies Versus Minority Faction," *Interest Group Politics,* Allan J. Cigler and Burdett A. Loomis, eds. (Washington, DC: Congressional Quarterly, 1983), p. 327.

52. "The Political Economy of Interest Groups," *Manhattan Report,* Vol. IV, No. 2 (1984), p. 2.

53. Murray L. Weidenbaum, *The Future of Business Regulation* (New York: AMACOM, 1979), p. 146.

54. Everett Carl Ladd, "How to Tame the Special-Interest Groups," *Fortune,* Vol. 102, No. 8 (October 20, 1980), p. 72.

55. Walter E. Westman, *Ecology, Impact Assessment, and Environmental Planning* (New York: Wiley, 1985), pp. 120–123.

SUGGESTED READINGS

Anderson, James E. *Public Policy-Making,* 2nd ed. New York: Holt, Rinehart & Winston, 1979.

Buchanan, James. *The Demand and Supply of Public Goods.* Chicago: Rand McNally, 1968.

Carter, Lief H. *Administrative Law and Politics.* Boston: Little, Brown, 1983.

Dunn, William N. *Public Policy Analysis: An Introduction.* Englewood Cliffs, NJ: Prentice-Hall, 1981.

Dye, Thomas R. *Understanding Public Policy,* 6th ed. Englewood Cliffs, NJ: Prentice Hall, 1987.

Hartle, Douglas G. *Public Policy Decision Making and Regulation.* Montreal: Institute for Research on Public Policy, 1979.

Jones, Charles O. *An Introduction to the Study of Public Policy,* 3rd ed. Boston: Brooks-Cole, 1983.

Lineberry, Robert L. *American Public Policy.* New York: Harper & Row, 1978.

Olson, Mancur. *The Logic of Collective Action.* Cambridge, MA: Harvard University Press, 1977.

Paul, Ellen F., and Philip A. Russo, Jr. *Public Policy: Issues, Analysis, and Ideology.* Chatham, NJ: Chatham House, 1982.

Perry, Huey L. *Democracy and Public Policy.* New York: Wyndham Hall, 1985.

Peters, B. Guy. *American Public Policy: Promise and Performance,* 2nd ed. Chatham, NJ: Chatham House, 1986.

Portney, Kent E. *Approaching Public Policy Analysis.* Englewood Cliffs, NJ: Prentice-Hall, 1986.

Preston, Lee E., and Post, James E. *Private Management and Public Policy.* Englewood Cliffs, NJ: Prentice-Hall, 1975.

Robey, John S. *Public Policy Analysis.* New York: Garland, 1983.

Sirkin, Gerald. *The Visible Hand: The Fundamentals of Economic Planning.* New York: McGraw-Hill, 1968.

CHAPTER 5

GLOBAL PROBLEMS

~

The environmental problems that were of concern in the 1970s were global in the sense that every industrial society shared some of them. Air pollution existed in every country with factories and automobiles, and water pollution was a problem where manufacturing companies and municipalities disposed of large quantities of waste in lakes and rivers. The disposal of solid and hazardous waste also began to pose serious problems for many countries as the 1970s drew to a close. But these problems were dealt with largely on a national basis, often in cooperation with state and local authorities. The United States, for example, passed laws and regulations related to air and water pollution that were largely implemented by the states. The problem of waste disposal was dealt with on a federal level through laws and regulations related to solid and hazardous waste disposal. Every country that became concerned about these types of pollution passed some kind of laws or regulations to deal with the problem.

Theoretically, we could escape most of these problems by moving to a part of the country that was still in something of a natural state where the air was not polluted and the water was clean enough to drink. In the 1980s, however, problems appeared that affected people all over the world and required international cooperation to deal with effectively. No one can escape the effects of such problems as global warming, because there is nowhere to hide. We cannot go to Walden Pond to escape this type of problem, because the whole earth may be warming, not just certain parts of it, and Walden Pond will also be affected. Two problems of this nature that became of concern in the 1980s are global warming and ozone depletion.

GLOBAL WARMING

The phenomenon that goes by the name of global warming, sometimes also called the greenhouse effect, is believed to be caused by changes in the earth's atmosphere that are the result of industrial processes. Although there is some controversy about the causes of global warming, and indeed, whether global warming is actually taking place, many scientists believe there is some linkage between global warming and changes in the composition of the atmosphere. These changes in the atmosphere do not stem from modification in the major constituents of the atmosphere, but from increases in the levels of several of the atmosphere's trace gases. These trace gases include carbon dioxide, nitrous oxides, methane, and several compounds of chloroflorocarbons. Exhibit 5.1 provides information about the buildup of these trace gases.

These trace gases have increased as a result of intensified industrial activity. Thus the activities of humans account for most of the changes in the atmosphere over the past 200 years. Such activities include the combustion of fossil fuels for energy, industrial and agricultural practices, burning of vegetation, and deforestation. These activities are not only changing the chemistry of the atmosphere, but may also be driving the earth toward a climatic warming of unprecedented magnitude. Unwelcome surprises are a possibility as human activities continue to affect an atmosphere whose inner mechanisms and interactions with living organisms and nonliving materials are incompletely understood.[1]

The theory about global warming holds that these trace gases form a shield around the earth which prevents some of the infrared waves from the earth from escaping into the atmosphere. (See Figure 5.1.) These gases are relatively transparent to sunshine, which heats the earth, but trap heat by more efficiently absorbing the longer wavelength infrared radiation released by the earth.[2] These gases thus cause a warming effect by acting much like a greenhouse in keeping the heat of the sun in rather than letting it escape. As trace gases increase, particularly carbon dioxide, their heat-trapping ability also increases, further warming the earth. While there is some controversy over many of the particulars as well as whether a linkage actually exists between fluctuations in trace gases and global warming, the process has been described as an ongoing geophysical experiment.[3]

Warnings were stated as far back as 1890, when a Swedish chemist, Svante Arrhenius, began to fear that the massive burning of coal during the industrial revolution that pumped unprecedented amounts of CO_2 into the atmosphere might cause problems. He made a prediction that a doubling of atmospheric CO_2 would eventually lead to a 9°F warming of the earth, and suggested that glacial periods might have been caused by a diminished level of the gas. While his contemporaries scoffed at such an idea, he was right on

Exhibit 5.1

Greenhouse Gases at a Glance

Carbon Dioxide (CO₂)

- Accounts for about 50% of the greenhouse effect.
- Is generated from burning fossil fuels, especially coal, and from deforestation.

Chlorofluorocarbons (CFCs)

- Account for about 15% of the greenhouse effect.
- Leak into upper atmosphere from refrigerators, air conditioners, styrofoam packaging; remain for 75 to 100 years.
- Thousands of times more heat-absorbing than CO₂.
- Also responsible for nibbling away at the ozone layer, which protects the earth from too much ultraviolet radiation.
- In September 1987, 50 countries agreed to cut CFC production in half.

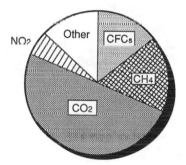

Methane (CH₄)

- Accounts for 15–20% of the greenhouse effect.
- Is a by-product of burning wood, and is released from natural sources such as cattle, wetlands, rice paddies and termite mounds.

Nitrous Oxides (NO₂)

- Accounts for about 5% of the greenhouse effect.
- Is formed when chemical fertilizers break down and when coal is burned.

Other

- Ozone (O₃), halons (CFC-like synthetic compounds), water vapor and other airborne particles.

Source: Sierra Club, "Global Warming," May 1989, p. 2.

Figure 5.1

Global Warming Theory and Uncertainties

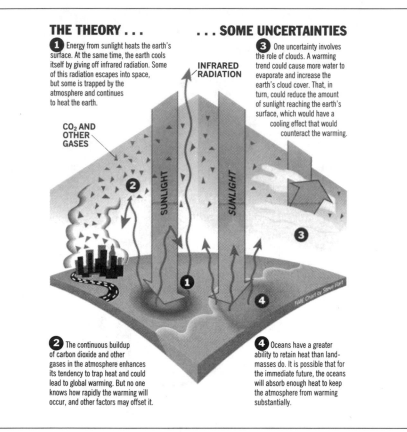

THE THEORY . . .

1 Energy from sunlight heats the earth's surface. At the same time, the earth cools itself by giving off infrared radiation. Some of this radiation escapes into space, but some is trapped by the atmosphere and continues to heat the earth.

CO₂ AND OTHER GASES

2 The continuous buildup of carbon dioxide and other gases in the atmosphere enhances its tendency to trap heat and could lead to global warming. But no one knows how rapidly the warming will occur, and other factors may offset it.

. . . SOME UNCERTAINTIES

3 One uncertainty involves the role of clouds. A warming trend could cause more water to evaporate and increase the earth's cloud cover. That, in turn, could reduce the amount of sunlight reaching the earth's surface, which would have a cooling effect that would counteract the warming.

4 Oceans have a greater ability to retain heat than land-masses do. It is possible that for the immediate future, the oceans will absorb enough heat to keep the atmosphere from warming substantially.

INFRARED RADIATION

SUNLIGHT   SUNLIGHT

Source: Charles P. Alexander, "A Sizzling Scientific Debate," *Time,* April 30, 1990, p. 84. Copyright 1990 The Time Inc. Magazine Company. Reprinted by permission.

track. During his time, CO_2 concentration was about 280 to 290 parts per million, but today the count stands at 340 parts per million.[4] Scientists have documented a 25 percent increase in carbon dioxide over the interglacial level in the past 100 years, and some scientists expect the present level to double by the year 2050. (See Figure 5.2.) Atmospheric methane has doubled during this same time period.[5]

The major culprit seems to be the burning of fossil fuels, particularly coal, which releases carbon dioxide into the atmosphere. Deforestation also adds carbon dioxide to the atmosphere because trees and other vegetation absorb CO_2 as they grow, and release an equal amount when they are burned or decay naturally. Further concentrations of trace gases depends on

Figure 5.2

Global Concentrations of Carbon Dioxide Have Risen 10 Percent Since 1958

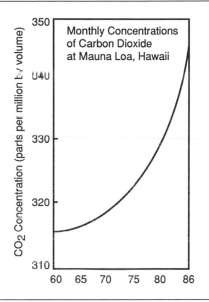

Source: United States Environmental Protection Agency, *Environmental Progress and Challenges: FPA's Update* (Washington, DC: U.S. Government Printing Office, 1988), p. 38.

the consumption of fossil fuels and the rate of deforestation. Growth in the use of fossil fuels will reflect population growth and the rate at which alternative energy sources and conservation measures are adopted. The rate of deforestation will depend on government policies with respect to continued exploitation of these resources around the globe. Assuming that fossil fuel consumption will continue to increase at about its present pace, CO_2 emissions are expected to increase between .5 and 2 percent a year for the next several decades. Other trace gases could contribute as much to global warming as CO_2 because they are much better able to absorb infrared radiation even though they are emitted in much smaller quantities. But predicting future emissions of these other gases is even more difficult than it is for carbon dioxide.[6]

During 1988, some 5.6 billion tons of carbon were produced by combustion of fossil fuels, which is more than a ton for each human being on earth. Another 1 to 2 billion tons of carbon were released by the felling and burning of forests around the world. Each ton of carbon emitted into the air results in 3.7 tons of carbon dioxide. Carbon emissions in 1988 went up 9.7 percent, the largest annual increase in almost a decade. The Third World currently burns fossil fuels at far lower rates than the industrial world, but if and when these countries overcome their economic problems, the potential for growth in fossil fuel use is enormous. Many developing countries now add far more carbon to the atmosphere through deforestation than through fossil fuel consumption. Brazil, for example, contributes some 336 billion tons of carbon each year through deforestation, over six times as much as through burning fossil fuels.[7]

Some of this increase will be absorbed by natural processes. Carbon dioxide in the atmosphere is continually being absorbed by green plants and by chemical and biological processes in the oceans. Because carbon dioxide is a raw material of photosynthesis, an increased concentration might speed the uptake by plants, which would counter some of the buildup. Increased uptake by the oceans may also slow the buildup to some extent. But the increased buildup of trace gases may also cause positive feedbacks that would add to the atmospheric burden. Rapid climate change could disrupt forests and other ecosystems and reduce their ability to absorb carbon dioxide from the atmosphere. Global warming could also lead to release of the vast amount of carbon held in the soil as dead organic matter.[8]

Effects

What effect will the continued buildup of these trace gases have on the earth's climate? To answer this question scientists rely on mathematical climate models. History offers no clear answer to this question, nor can climate be reproduced in a laboratory experiment. These models consist of expressions for the interacting components of the ocean-atmosphere system and equations representing the basic physical laws governing their behavior. To determine the effect of trace gas buildup, scientists specify the projected amount of greenhouse gases and compare the model results with a controlled simulation of the existing climate, based on present atmospheric composition.[9]

Constructing a model of anything involves making critical assumptions about how the world works. The more factors that are included in the model, the more assumptions have to be made, and the more complex the model becomes. In predicting climate change, scientists have to construct a model of the atmosphere. These models are called general circulation models (GCMs), and may contain as many as 100,000 computer instructions. Because of these complexities, skeptics believe that climate models have not yet been validated, cannot yet be trusted, and therefore cannot serve as guides for public policy decisions.[10]

There are several shortcomings to the modeling technique. Models are said to be inaccurate when it comes to dealing with atmospheric turbulence, precipitation, and cloud formation. Clouds, for example, have a net cooling effect, reflecting sunlight back to outer space. Present models reproduce only average cloudiness, but climate change may actually cause incremental change in cloud characteristics altering the nature and amount of feedback processes. Another problem is with the oceans, which may act as a thermal sponge slowing any initial increase in global temperature. Because of the complexities involved, the dynamics of oceans are simplified, treated at course resolution, or left out entirely.[11]

The main effect of an ocean on climate is the redistribution of heat on the earth's surface. Such heat can flow horizontally in large ocean currents, or up and down vertically, moving between the surface and the depths of the ocean. In most models, these effects have not been included, or have been included in such a way that they were not allowed to change in response to changes in the atmosphere. The same is true with respect to cloud formation. Many scientists have argued that if the earth warms, more water vapor will evaporate to form more clouds, which in turn will reflect more sunlight away from earth, so that the greenhouse effect will be reduced or completely nullified.[12]

Given all these problems, many scientists still believe that the models are well enough validated and other evidence of greenhouse-gas effects on climate is strong enough, that the increases in average surface temperature predicted by the models for the next 50 years is valid within a rough factor of two, meaning that it is better than an even bet that the changes will take place. Most of the models are in rough agreement that a doubling of carbon dioxide or an equivalent increase in other trace gases would warm the earth's average surface temperature by between 3.0° and 5.5°C. Such a change would be unprecedented in human history.[13]

Actual Warming

About half a degree of actual warming has taken place in the last 100 years, but the 1980s appear to be the warmest decade on record, with 1988, 1987, and 1981 being the warmest years in that order. There apparently was a rapid warming of the atmosphere before World War II, a slight cooling trend through the mid-1970s, and a second period of warming since then.[14] The new decade continued this trend, as scientists announced that 1990 was the earth's warmest year in the nearly two centuries that records have been kept. This meant that seven of the ten warmest years on record have occurred since 1980. Temperature in the 1980s was about one-third of a degree warmer than the globe's average temperature of the previous 30 years. This was a sharp increase when compared with long-term averages. And 1990 was another one-third of a degree warmer than 1980.[15]

There is some dispute about these figures. According to a federal study released in 1990, temperatures in the southeastern United States actually fell 1° in the past 30 years while rainfall has increased. This finding does not prove that global warming is not happening, because the fall in temperature may be due to the difficulty of calculating global warming on a regional scale.

But this data was expected to at least contribute to the debate about global warming. Other critics of the prevailing opinion suggested that temperature rises might be due to increasing urbanization where the temperatures are recorded, as city temperatures are higher than the surrounding countryside because of the concentration of people and their activities.[16]

In order to get a more accurate reading of actual climate change, scientists are experimenting with undersea sound waves to measure warming. At the beginning of 1991, scientists switched on a loudspeaker in the ocean near Heard Island, which is 2,550 miles southwest of Perth, Australia. Since the speed of sound varies with temperature, measuring the pace of this ocean music for 10 to 20 years may tell us whether the oceans are warming. Small variations in sea temperature are one factor in global weather and ocean current changes can have drastic effects.[17]

What would be the effects of such climate change? Should warming continue, coastal areas would undoubtedly face a rise in sea levels. A global temperature increase of a few degrees Celsius over the next 50 or 100 years would raise sea levels by between .2 and 1.5 meters as a result of the thermal expansion of the oceans, the melting of mountain glaciers, and the possible retreat of the Greenland ice sheet's southern margins. Many cities near low-lying coastal areas would be flooded, and people would have to either erect seawalls or move to another location. (See Figure 5.3.) Such a change would mean hot, dry summers for many parts of the world. There could be a decline in agricultural productivity in the Middle West and Great Plains as the corn and grain belts moved north by several hundred kilometers. Temperate zones would move further north leaving areas that were primary agricultural zones, such as the midsection of the United States, useless for growing crops. Such shifts would cause great hardships for some people and benefits for others.[18]

A rising sea level could flood dry lands in the Southeast, and increase the usage of water for irrigation in California's Central Valley, as spring runoff from the Sierras decreases. Costs to protect developed shorelines could reach $111 billion through the year 2100 if sea level rises 1 meter. Despite these efforts, an area the size of Massachusetts could be lost to water. And more summer heat will increase demand for electricity, which could require spending $325 billion to build new power plants. Animals and plant life will also be affected. While climate zones may move hundreds to miles to the north, animals and plants may not be able to migrate as quickly.[19]

The Debate

James Hansen, an atmospheric scientist who heads NASA's Goddard Institute, made national headlines when he testified before Congress in 1988 that the greenhouse effect had already begun and was no longer just a theory. During the first five months of 1988, he testified, average worldwide tem-

Figure 5.3

Areas of the World Vulnerable to a Rising Sea Level

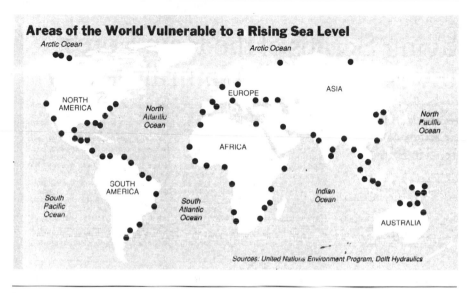

Areas of the World Vulnerable to a Rising Sea Level

Source: William K. Stevens, "Governments Start Preparing for Global Warming Disasters," *New York Times,* November 14, 1989, p. Y-21. Copyright © 1989 by The New York Times Company. Reprinted by permission.

peratures were the highest in all the 130 years of record keeping. He also stated that he was 99 percent certain that the highest temperatures were not just a natural phenomenon but were the direct result of a buildup of carbon dioxide and other trace gases from human-made sources. His findings were based on monthly readings at 2,000 meterological stations around the world.[20]

Most world climate models indicate that the world is already committed to a warming of several degrees over the next few decades, which represents a warming unprecedented in human history. There is something of a delayed reaction to the buildup of greenhouse gases, in that it takes 20 years for these gases to have an effect. So even if we stopped burning fossil fuels tomorrow, we would still be in for some degree of warming in future years. Thus any strategies developed to deal with the problem will have to provide plans to adapt to a warmer globe and prevent greater warming in the future.[21]

There are few objections to the theory as a whole, and everyone in the scientific community agrees that atmospheric concentration of carbon dioxide and other trace gases is on the rise. Many believe that this increase cannot help but have some effect on the climate.[22] But whether or not the greenhouse effect is already apparent and thus needs to be dealt with now, as

Hansen claimed, is a matter of some debate. Some scientists say that the buildup of carbon dioxide and the warming of the globe is circumstantial. The warming that has been experienced could be due to natural causes and attributable to atmospheric cycles or other naturally occurring factors.[23] The greenhouse theory has not been proven conclusively, and to take action at this time to reduce emissions of carbon dioxide or other trace gases may be spending a good deal of money unnecessarily.[24]

To deal with this problem would require international cooperation. All nations of the world would have to agree to limit the release of carbon dioxide and other trace gases in order to have a major effect on global warming. Thus far, the United States has taken a wait-and-see attitude, and continues to study the problem. But waiting for more direct evidence of the greenhouse effect could involve a commitment to greater climatic change than would be involved if action were taken now to slow the buildup of trace gases. In other words, waiting to solve the problem if the theory proves to be true would cost more money in the future than taking some steps now to cut back on carbon dioxide and other emissions.

This phenomenon of global warming thus presents policymakers with a dilemma. Waiting for conclusive and more direct evidence of global warming that would either confirm or deny the results of computer modeling is not a cost-free proposition. By then the world will be committed to greater climatic change than it would be if action were taken now to slow the buildup of greenhouse gases. But proposals for immediate action to slow the buildup of trace gases entail large investments as insurance against future events whose details are far from certain. Much money could be spent on such strategies that may not prove to have been necessary.[25]

Under the auspices of the United Nations, representatives from more than 130 countries met to start work on an international treaty aimed at slowing the buildup of greenhouse gases. Present plans call for the drafting of an international climate treaty in 1991, and for its formal adoption at a global environmental summit in 1992. The European Economic Community and Japan want to cap emissions of carbon dioxide at 1990 levels. But the United States opposes emission targets because they are too costly given the evidence so far on global warming. Other countries argue, however, that the cost of taking action now would be small compared with waiting too long before taking action. Developing countries that rely on subsistence agriculture and natural resources will be very vulnerable to climate changes of whatever direction and magnitude. The International Panel on Climate Change (IPCC) has recommended a policy of energy conservation and reforestation that makes economic sense even without climate change, a clear example of a tie-in strategy.[26]

To its credit, the Bush administration has taken several steps that will help combat global warming. The White House earmarked $1 billion for global climate research in 1991 and committed the United States to phasing out production of CFCs by the year 2000. It also vowed to plant a billion

trees that would absorb CO_2 from the atmosphere. But most of these measures were adopted for reasons that had relatively nothing to do with global
warming. Environmentalists advocate that the government should do much
more to discourage the burning of fossil fuels, but the White House worries
about the economic consequences of forcing sudden reductions in the use of
fossil fuels. While it is wise to consider the possible economic damage of such
strategies, the government could encourage energy conservation much more
than it has without destroying the economy.[27]

Strategies

Coping effectively with global warming will force advanced societies to
reverse trends that have dominated the industrial age up to this point. The
challenge cannot be met, according to some scholars, without a strong
commitment on the part of both individual consumers and governments to
promote greater energy efficiency, to use renewable energy sources, to
institute a carbon tax on fossil fuels, to reverse tropical deforestation, and to
eliminate CFC production more rapidly.[28] The EPA estimates that to stabilize atmospheric concentration of CO_2 at current levels, carbon emissions
must be cut by 50 to 80 percent, taking them back to the level of the 1950s.
Even a 20 percent cut would require a dramatic change in energy planning
and land-use policies around the world.[29]

   Any realistic strategy, according to Christopher Flavin, must start with
the fact that one-fourth of the world's population accounts for nearly 70
percent of the fossil fuel-based carbon emissions. The planet will never be
able to support a population of 8 billion people generating carbon emissions
at the rate of Western Europe today. Such emissions result in a concentration
of CO_2 three times preindustrial levels, which is well above doomsday
scenarios. But limiting carbon emissions in developing countries remains an
extraordinarily difficult issue. No one has begun to wrestle with the critical
equity issues this strategy entails.[30] The United States contributes about 25
percent of the world CO_2 emissions with only 6 percent of the world's
population. Thus the United States is in a good position to take global
leadership in combating the greenhouse effect with an ambitious energy
efficiency campaign and the export of new energy-efficient technology.[31]

   The atmospheric buildup of carbon dioxide results from burning gasoline in our cars and coal and oil in our power plants. These activities are
responsible for about half of the greenhouse effect, according to some
sources. Burning coal is said to produce twice as much carbon dioxide per
unit of heat as natural gas, and a third more than the burning of oil. It is said
that no global warming solution will be successful unless carbon dioxide
emissions from coal combustion are controlled. The best solution is to limit
the burning of coal through greater energy efficiency and the use of natural
gas and renewable energy resources like solar and wind power.[32]

   One scientist recommends that tie-in strategies be adopted, taking actions that will yield benefits even if climatic change does not materialize as predicted. Such a tie-in strategy is the pursuit of energy efficiency. More efficient use of fossil fuels will slow the buildup of carbon dioxide in addition to curbing acid rain, reducing urban air pollution, and lessening our dependence on foreign sources of supply. These benefits would accrue to our society even if the effects of carbon dioxide on global warming prove to be overstated. The same tie-in strategies would hold true for the development of alternative energy sources, revision of water laws, searching for drought resistant crop strains, and other such strategies. These steps would offer widespread benefits even in the absence of any climatic change.[33]

Another recommendation is for the implementation of a carbon tax on fossil fuels. The tax would allow market economies to consider the global environmental damage of fossil fuel combustion. Coal would be taxed the highest, oil next, and natural gas would follow. In countries that do not wish to raise total taxes, the carbon tax could be offset by a reduction in other taxes. Picking the correct tax would be a complicated undertaking, but the environmental costs of using a particular fuel could be assessed and then internalized though taxes. Such taxes would have to be agreed on internationally. Tax revenues could be used to develop permanent and stable funding for improving energy efficiency and developing renewable sources.[34]

The first step in a worldwide strategy, according to one expert, is the establishment of ambitious, but practical goals for the reduction of carbon emissions, particularly in those countries that currently use fossil fuels most heavily. Industrial countries will have to take the lead and reduce CO_2 emissions 20 to 35 percent over the next ten years. If emissions are kept at today's levels, Third World increases would raise global emissions 20 to 30 percent by the end of the decade, and 50 to 70 percent in 20 years.[35] Overall, carbon emissions would have to be reduced to a maximum of 2 billion tons per year in order to stabilize atmospheric concentrations of greenhouse gases by the middle of the twenty-first century. Production of CFCs must be ended and global carbon emissions must be cut by 10 to 20 percent over the next decade.[36]

The costs of some of these plans, however, are astronomical. According to economists Alan Manne of Stanford University and Richard Richels of the Electric Power Research Institute, costs to the United States alone would run from $800 billion to $3.6 trillion in cumulative costs over the next century. Annual costs could run as high as 5 percent of gross national product. By way of contrast, the nation is currently spending $85 billion a year, or about 2 percent of GNP, on all other environmental protection measures.[37] The Bush administration predicted that there would be a sharp reduction of economic growth around the world if trace gas emissions were reduced by 20 percent during the next 15 years. Another economist estimated that the cost of stabilizing these emissions would be about $50 billion a year for the United States and $150 billion annually for the rest of the world.[38]

GENERIC STRATEGIES

Wait and See

This strategy is basically the one the United States has adopted. There is time for further research, and indeed, further research is needed before policies are adopted. This strategy has the advantage of causing little economic dislocation at present and not taking actions that would later prove to have been unnecessary. Much money would be spent unnecessarily and jobs lost that could be avoided if more study were done. However, if the most pessimistic predictions about global warming prove to be true, the warming may be more severe if we wait and it may be more costly to deal with it in the future.

Assume the Worst and Act Accordingly

Such a strategy would probably involve a significant reduction in the use of fossil fuels, perhaps as much as 50 percent, a halt to deforestations, and the reforesting of millions of square miles of the earth's surface. This approach has the advantage of dealing with the worst case scenario immediately, and suffering whatever changes are necessary. But this strategy could cause enormous economic hardship, which may turn out to have been unnecessary if less pessimistic predictions turn out to be right.

No Regrets

This approach involves taking actions that make sense whether the warming predictions turn out to be true or false, in other words, this strategy is the same as the tie-in strategy mentioned earlier. Almost every effort to reduce air pollution and acid precipitation will also help reduce trace gas emissions. Further improvements in energy efficiency can make a big difference. Reduction of our dependence on foreign oil makes sense even without consideration of the greenhouse effect. This strategy has the advantage of avoiding unnecessary costs connected with the worst case strategy. But if the latter proves to be true, the "no regrets" response will be inadequate.

Source: James Trefil, "Modeling Earth's Future Climate Requires Both Science and Guesswork," *Smithsonian* magazine, Vol. 21, No. 9 (December 1990), p. 36.

What Can Be Done

There are several things that can be done to deal with global warming, and most of them would be beneficial to societies whether or not global warming proves to be of long-lasting concern. (See Exhibit 5.2.) Thus they are examples of techniques or technologies that could be implemented under a tie-in strategic approach to the problem. Most of these technologies are already available or are well along as far as research and development are concerned. Thus they could be implemented quickly if the proper incentives were provided.[39]

Exhibit 5.2

How to Beat the Heat

- Improve auto efficiencies by raising mileage-per-gallon standards for new cars and trucks, coupled with a gas-guzzler tax and a gas-sipper rebate.
- Accelerate research and development of solar and renewable energy-generating technologies, with multi-year authorizations.
- Provide federal assistance for least-cost state energy planning regulation.
- Accelerate CFC phaseout and CFC recycling.
- Implement reforestation projects domestically and aggressively discourage tropical deforestation internationally.
- Accelerate the rate of energy-efficiency gains in residential and commercial buildings through standards, market incentives, and, if necessary, government investment programs.
- Reconsider tax incentives for renewable resource development and investment.
- Implement a gas tax, and potentially, a tax on carbon dioxide emissions.
- Analyze all federal energy investments and actions in terms of their potential effect on CO2 emissions.

Source: Sierra Club, "Global Warming," May 1989, p. 3.

Cleaning Up Coal. Coal is used to produce over half the world's power, but pound for pound, coal can be up to 100 times as dirty, depending on the pollutant, as oil and natural gas. But technology does exist to reduce that pollution. Fluidized bed combustion, for example, sharply reduces oxides of nitrogen and sulfur dioxide emitted from coal burning. Massive fans keep powdered coal suspended in midair so it burns cleaner with less energy loss. Plants being built in Stockholm using a variant of this technique are estimated to achieve an efficiency of 85 percent by capturing waste heat and emit one-tenth the sulfur dioxide of plants in the United States and one-sixth the oxides of nitrogen.

The integrated gasification-combined cycle technology combines two concepts with regard to the burning of coal: (1) coal is turned from a solid into a gas, removing much of the sulfur in the process, and (2) the gas is used to run two turbines, one powered by the hot combustion gases and the other by steam. Finally, add-on cleaners can be used to clean up coal burning. Scrubbers are systems that can remove up to 95 percent of the sulfur from stack gases, and have been in widespread use throughout the world for nearly two decades. Technology for removing nitrogen pollution, such as selective catalytic reduction, is of more recent origin.

Natural Gas. Natural gas contains only half the carbon of coal, none of the sulfur, and less nitrogen. Simple conversion to natural gas could thus dramatically reduce unwanted trace gas buildup. The use of natural gas would also allow utilities to use new energy-efficient superturbines and plants. These turbines work like a jet engine bolted to the ground, and already turn 47 percent of their fuel into electricity compared to 38 percent efficiency for the best coal-fired plants. There are 31 such superturbines already in operation, under construction, or on order, and 210 slightly less efficient versions already running.

Conservation. Conservation measures can be applied either where electricity is produced or where it is used. Cogeneration is a demonstrated method for raising the efficiency of power plants. This technique puts heat that would otherwise be wasted to some use in warming homes and offices or even running manufacturing processes. Cogeneration is already common in Sweden and other parts of Europe where efficiency can rise to as high as 85 percent. Conservation measures by consumers can involve turning thermostats down and using more efficient light bulbs. According to some estimates, conservation measures by consumers alone could save one-third to one-half of the electricity produced in the United States. This kind of conservation would involve no reduction in living standards.

Energy Efficiency. More efficient use of energy has the immediate potential to cut fossil fuel use at least 3 percent annually in industrial countries. In developing nations, efficiency can be used to limit fossil fuel growth while economic development continues. Efficiency improvements worldwide between 1990 and 2010 could make a 3-billion ton difference in the amount of carbon being released into the atmosphere each year. Such a strategy implies an annual rate of energy efficiency improvement of 3 percent. No other approach, according to one source, offers as large an opportunity for limiting carbon emissions in the next two decades.[40]

Fuel Cells. Conventional power plants make steam to spin turbine blades that generate electricity, whereas fuel cells depend on chemistry rather than mechanics. The chemicals used vary, but the principle is the same: The fuel reacts chemically to decompose into water and carbon dioxide, giving off electricity in the process. The heat that is generated as a by-product can also be harnessed. These fuel cells already approach 50 percent efficiency and manufacturers say that 80 percent is achievable.

Renewable Sources. Renewable energy technology such as wind power, geothermal, solar thermal, photovoltaic, and various biomass technologies are likely to advance most rapidly in the years ahead.[41] These sources have several advantages over fossil fuels and nuclear power. They are inexhaustible, produce little or no pollution or hazardous waste, and pose few risks to public safety. They are entirely a domestic resource and thus would be virtually immune to foreign disruptions like the recent conflict in the

Persian Gulf produced. They also provide a hedge against energy price inflation caused by the depletion of fossil fuel reserves. And large-scale renewable energy technologies can be installed relatively quickly in six months to two years.

Building Cleaner Cars.   According to some sources, the potential for reducing carbon dioxide from cars and trucks is at least as great as from power plants. In the United States, where new cars are the least fuel efficient in the world, an increase in the average fuel efficiency of just 1 mile per gallon would reduce carbon dioxide emissions by about 40 billion pounds per year. This reduction is equivalent to the closing of six coal-fired plants. The current new-car auto fleet averages about 26 miles per gallon, but there have been attempts to raise this average significantly. The technology for improvements in car mileage is already here. In 1984, a Volvo design team produced a prototype four-passenger car that achieved 83 miles per gallon on the highway while designed to meet U.S. crash and pollution standards.

Reversing Deforestation.   Tropical deforestation is estimated to be the source of 20 to 25 percent of the gases that are warming the atmosphere. Policies to stop destruction of these forests would make a major contribution to slowing down the greenhouse effect. Even where slash-and-burn techniques have to be continued, carbon dioxide emissions can be reduced by between 90 and 98 percent by using different strategies. Villagers can be encouraged to reclaim land that had been cleared earlier and then abandoned. Younger forests contain less carbon than older more primary forests, thus torching second-growth trees can reduce pollution by about 90 percent. Second, farmers can be persuaded to use simple techniques to keep their land continually productive in a system of sustainable cropping. If existing land could be made more productive, it would not have to be abandoned to burn virgin forest elsewhere, cutting pollution another 90 percent.

Countries in temperate regions can also help restore the earth's carbon balance by planting trees. The challenges to a global reforestation plan include finding sufficient and appropriate land, raising needed financing, and mobilizing social institutions to accomplish reforestation. Large areas of marginal crop and grazing lands could be converted to trees, which stabilizes soils at the same time it increases the rate of carbon fixing. Tree planting can improve an urban environment by moderating summer heat and improving aesthetics. The real challenge facing these programs is maintaining the trees once they are in the ground.[42]

Phasing Out Chlorofluorocarbons.   CFCs were responsible for an added or estimated 25 percent of added greenhouse effect during the 1980s. In the United States, CFCs constituted 40 percent of the country's greenhouse emissions.[43] They are being phased out, however, and thus their effect in producing global warming will be gradually reduced. However, the timetable agreed on at Montreal is already believed to be outdated, and the elimination of these compounds needs to be speeded up, both to reduce global warming and protect the ozone layer. Companies like Du Pont have already adopted a strategy of phasing out CFCs faster than the treaty requires, and have found some substitutes that are being implemented.

Your Contribution To Global Warming

Industry isn't the only culprit; every light bulb you burn can send carbon dioxide into the atmosphere

HOW MUCH COAL does it take to turn on your light bulb? And how much of the carbon dioxide in our atmosphere can we blame on your light bulb? Too bad there are no punch lines; this is no joke. More than half the electricity consumed in this country is powered by coal. Coal burning is our main source of carbon dioxide, the primary greenhouse gas out of the quartet that also includes carbon monoxide, nitrogen oxides and chlorofluorocarbons.

Scientists estimate there is 25 percent more carbon dioxide in our atmosphere now than there was two centuries ago. They expect the present level to double by the year 2050. The subject, however, is not completely bleak. Our very ability to calculate how much coal we burn helps us understand how to burn less and reduce harmful emissions.

To figure out how your electricity use contributes to the greenhouse effect that many scientists believe is already warming our planet, you might first want to understand how your energy use is calculated. Your electric company bills you for kilowatts, or 1,000-watt units of electric power. If you leave a 100-watt light bulb on for 10 hours, you use one kilowatt hour (KWH) of electricity.

Let's suppose you use a 100-watt bulb as an outside night light for eight hours a night, 365 days a year. This bulb consumes 292 KWH a year. The energy probably comes from coal, especially since your light is on at night; during the day, oil and gas supplement coal at peaks of energy demand. The other two sources of electric power, hydro and nuclear, supply about a quarter of our electricity. But for the purposes of this exercise, let's assume that your light's power is from coal.

Each KWH used in your home requires the burning of an average of 1.28 pounds of coal (eastern coal has a slightly higher energy content than western coal). Since

ELECTRICAL CONNECTIONS TO POLLUTION

ELECTRICAL APPLIANCES		POUNDS OF CARBON DIOXIDE ADDED TO ATMOSPHERE*
Color Television	per hour	.64
Steam Iron	per hour	.85
Vacuum Cleaner	per hour	1.70
Air Conditioner, room	per hour	4.00
Toaster Oven	per hour	12.80
Ceiling Fan	per day	4.00
Refrigerator, frostless	per day	12.80
Waterbed Heater with thermostat	per day	24.00
Clothes Dryer	per load	10.00
Dishwasher	per load	2.60
Toaster	per use	.12
Microwave Oven	per 5-min use	.25
Coffeemaker	per brew	.50

*At room temperature and sea level, every pound of carbon dioxide occupies 8.75 cubic feet, about half the size of a refrigerator.

This rough guide to the emissions you may be causing is based on power requirements of common appliances, the average energy produced by eastern and western coal and the assumption that all the electricity comes from coal.

your light uses 292 KWH a year, it requires the burning of about 375 pounds of coal. And since carbon dioxide is made up of one carbon atom and two oxygen atoms—and coal is as much as 84 percent carbon—the total emission of carbon dioxide is about 1.8 times the weight of the coal, say 675 pounds for your light. Every pound of carbon dioxide occupies 8.75 cubic feet at room temperature and sea level. That means you are responsible for emitting about 6,000 cubic feet of carbon dioxide every year. And that's just one light. If you use 1,000 KWH a month, you add 28,062 pounds of carbon dioxide—or

245,540 cubic feet (one football field 5 feet deep)—to the atmosphere each year.

What can you do to help? Use other fuels? The burning of oil or natural gas also releases carbon dioxide and other pollutants, although neither releases as much carbon dioxide as coal. Nuclear power plants don't release carbon dioxide, but they are far more costly, release more waste heat, and pose serious environmental risks. Even if nuclear energy were perfectly safe, it takes about ten years to build a nuclear power plant. We can't wait that long to solve the greenhouse problem.

Here's how you can help. Replace that 100-watt night-light bulb with a tiny screw-in fluorescent tube that requires only 13 watts of power and uses 13 percent of the energy required by the old one—about 38 KWH a year instead of 292 KWH. Outdoors at night, you won't notice the slight difference in the amount of light. You'll reduce the amount of coal burned and the resulting carbon dioxide emissions by 87 percent—and save as much as $20 a year.

One light bulb may not sound like much, but if all the 100 million or so households in the United States did the same, we would prevent the annual release of 29.7 million tons of carbon dioxide. We could reduce our need for power by 8,500 megawatts—the equivalent of 17 coal-fired power plants of 500 megawatts each!

You can save even more energy and money with improved insulation and efficient major appliances. Buy the most energy-efficient refrigerators, freezers and air conditioners you can find. An air conditioner with an energy efficiency ratio (EER) of 12 will use only two-thirds as much electricity as one with an EER of 8.

Remember that one light bulb may not make much difference, but when we multiply by 100 million, perhaps we can have a last laugh after all.—*George Barnwell*

Source: National Wildlife, Vol. 28, No. 2 (February–March, 1990), p. 53.

Other companies that produce CFCs could follow suit, which would greatly reduce the threat of global warming.

Until modern times, the earth's climate was largely self-correcting and stable, letting in just the right amount and type of solar energy and providing just the right balance of temperature and moisture to sustain living things. Alternating cycles of warming and cooling, and lesser or greater concentrations of trace gases have forced some species into extinction. But these same changes have helped other species to evolve. Just as we have begun to discover the climatic rhythms that have gone on for hundreds of millions of years, we may also have begun to change them irrevocably. And how many more unexpected changes are waiting to be discovered?[44]

OZONE DEPLETION

Another global environmental problem that recently appeared is the depletion of the ozone layer in the stratosphere. This layer absorbs most of the harmful ultraviolet radiation that comes from the sun, and depletion of this layer allows higher levels of ultraviolet radiation to reach the surface of the planet. Too much ultraviolet radiation can damage plant and animal cells, cause skin cancer and eye cataracts in humans, reduce crop yields, deplete marine fisheries, cause damage to materials of various kinds, and kill many smaller and more sensitive organisms. Each 1 percent drop in ozone is projected to result in 4 to 6 percent more cases of skin cancer. Increased exposure to UV radiation also depresses the human immune system, lowering the body's resistance to attacking organisms.[45]

Terrestrial and aquatic ecosystems are also affected by ultraviolet radiation. Screenings of more than 200 different plant species, most of them crops, revealed that 70 percent were sensitive to ultraviolet radiation. Increased exposure may decrease photosynthesis, water-use efficiency, yield, and leaf area. Aquatic ecosystems are also threatened, as phytoplankton would decrease their productivity 35 percent with a 25 percent reduction in the ozone layer. Destruction of upper level ozone could add to the damage done by the same substance at lower altitudes, where ozone is a major air pollutant. As more ultraviolet radiation hits the earth's surface, the photo-chemical process that creates smog will accelerate. Overall, the risks to aquatic and terrestrial ecosystems and to human health because of an increase in ultraviolet radiation are enormous. (See Exhibit 5.3.) The present value of the benefits of controlling emissions through the year 2075 has been estimated at $6 trillion, which is some 240 times greater than the costs of controlling emissions of those gases that destroy the ozone layer.[46]

Ozone (O_3) is a form of oxygen that rarely occurs naturally in the lower atmosphere. It is created when ordinary oxygen molecules (O_2) are bombarded with ultraviolet rays in the stratosphere. This radiation breaks the oxygen molecules apart and some of the free oxygen atoms recombine with

Exhibit 5.3

What If the Shield Erodes?

The sun bombards the earth with photons, light rays of varying wavelengths. The shorter the wave-length, the more damage the rays can inflict. Among the most dangerous are wavelengths of ultraviolet light (UV) measuring from 200 to about 315 nanometers (a nanometer is a billionth of a meter).

The ozone layer blocks all of the most damaging UV light, the band from 200 to 290 nanometers known as UV-C. Without that protection, life on earth could not survive. Fortunately, only a drastic reduction of the ozone shield would allow any UV-C to filter through. The ozone also screens out much of the UV between 290 and 315 nanometers, the band called UV-B. But enough gets through to cause, even now, millions of cases of skin cancer every year.

It's the UV-B that has scientists worried. For every 1 percent drop in ozone, there's a 2 percent increase in UV-B intensity at the earth's surface. Most plants and animals have evolved under relatively constant UV-B. Any prolonged increase could set in motion far-reaching — and unpredictable — ecological changes.

When UV-B radiation strikes a living thing, it is absorbed by the outer layers of cells. Microscopic plants and animals lack such protection. Single-celled plants at the bottom of the marine food chain are the base on which much of the world's population ultimately depends for protein. Those plants suffer a drastic drop in photosynthesis when exposed to UV-B at levels found under the Antarctic ozone hole.

Nor is the effect limited to single-celled plants. When exposed to increased UV-B in experiments, many crop plants react negatively. Peas, beans, squash, cabbage, and soybeans show reduced nutrient content, slower growth, and lower yields, as well as impaired photosynthesis. Plants vary in their response to UV-B, though. Some weeds, especially, seem to love it.

In humans, exposed body parts usually have some protection from UV-B. Pigmentation in the skin's surface layer stops UV rays before they reach lower layers. In the eye, the cornea and lens block UV from reaching the retina, the light-sensitive tissue that UV would damage.

But inborn defenses against UV go only so far. Some sun-induced damage still occurs:

Skin cancer. Exposure to UV-B is linked to all forms of skin cancer — basal-cell carcinoma, squamous-cell carcinoma, and malignant melanoma. The first two are quite common, and usually curable. But melanoma, which represents only 3 percent of all skin cancers, accounts for two-thirds of skin cancer deaths. The EPA projects more than 60 million additional cases of skin cancer and about one million additional deaths among Americans alive today or born by the year 2075 if CFC usage continues to grow at its present rate.

Eye damage. Under extremely bright conditions, such as sunlight on snow, prolonged UV exposure can cause painful snowblindness, a temporary inflammation of the cornea. A rise in UV radiation may increase the frequency of such effects. Even more worrisome is the potential effect on the lens. Growing evidence suggests that chronic, life-time exposure to UV contributes to certain types of cataracts — opaque regions in the lens that interfere with vision. The EPA projects some 17 million additional cases in the future caused by CFC damage to the ozone layer.

Some scientists believe that increased UV-B exposure might affect certain immune-system processes, but any danger is still speculative. No doubt exists, however, that UV causes sunburn and premature aging of the skin. A rise in UV will probably increase the incidence and seriousness of those conditions.

O_2 to form ozone. This configuration gives oxygen a property it ordinarily does not have, that is, the ability to absorb ultraviolet rays. Thus the ozone layer is able to protect oxygen at lower levels from being broken up and keeps most of the harmful rays of the sun from penetrating to the earth's surface.[47] These vital functions are performed without most people even being aware of the ozone shield.

The Culprit

The culprit in ozone depletion was identified in 1974 by Mario Molina and Sherwood F. Rowland, two chemists at the University of California at Irvine, who theorized that chlorofluorocarbons (CFCs) eventually drift up to the stratosphere to react chemically with ozone molecules in a destructive fashion. While many chemicals that are released into the atmosphere decay in weeks or months, CFCs are so chemically inert that they can stay intact for a century. Normal disposal mechanisms have little or no effect on CFCs. Rain, for example, cannot wash them out of the atmosphere since they are not soluble in water. These characteristics give them ample time to rise through the atmosphere to reach higher altitudes and do their damage to the ozone layer. (See Exhibit 5.4.)

Exhibit 5.4

Ozone Destroyers

CFCs (or chlorofluorocarbons) are a whole family of chemicals that contain chlorine and fluorine. Some are more damaging to the ozone layer than others. Here are the most commonly used kinds:

CFC 11, CFC 12	The most common CFCs and the most destructive to the ozone layer. Also the most stable, with atmospheric lifetimes of 75 and 110 years, respectively.
CFC 22:	Used in air conditioners and refrigerators. Poses less danger to the ozone layer than CFCs 11 and 12 because it breaks down more rapidly.
CFC 113	A solvent for metals and circuit boards. Its use has increased dramatically in the last decade.
Halons:	Technically not CFCs, because they contain bromine. But represent a new and growing threat because bromine destroys ozone even faster than chlorine. Used in fire extinguishers.
"Safe" CFCs	Materials that contain hydrogen, making them break down faster. They include CFCs 123, 124, 133a and 502. A related safe chemical, which has no chlorine or bromine, is FC 134a.

Source: Douglas Starr, "How to Protect the Ozone Layer," *National Wildlife,* December-January, 1988, p. 27.

Because of the nature of the chemical reactions, CFCs release chlorine atoms when finally broken down by ultraviolet radiation from the sun, and these chlorine atoms act as a catalyst in a series of reactions that convert ozone into oxygen. (See Figure 5.4.) Because the chlorine acts as a catalyst rather than as a reagent, a single molecule of chlorine can destroy thousands of ozone molecules before it eventually gets washed out of the atmosphere. Another family of compounds called halons, which contain bromines, were discovered to be a hundred times more efficient than the chlorine compounds at ozone destruction.[48]

CFCs often take six to eight years to reach the upper layer of the atmosphere. The latest ozone measurements reflect only the response of the ozone layer to gases released through the early 1980s. The gases now rising through the lower atmosphere will take six to eight years to reach the stratosphere to do their damage. An additional 2 million tons of substances containing chlorine and bromine are trapped in insulation foams and appliances and fire-fighting equipment. Chlorine concentrations are expected to triple by 2075 while bromine concentrations are expected to grow faster, exhibiting a tenfold increase from current levels.[49]

When first discovered, CFCs proved to be remarkable compounds. Since they are inert, they do not react with other chemicals with which they are mixed. They are also neither toxic nor flammable at ground level. Chemists at General Motors are given credit for first discovering these compounds. The refrigeration industry needed a new refrigerant to survive in the 1920s, and in 1928, chemists at GM focused their attention on the strong carbon-fluorine bond of certain carbon-based compounds known as fluorocarbons. These fluorocarbons are chemically similar to hydrocarbon molecules, except that one or more hydrogen atoms are replaced by chlorine, fluorine, or bromine atoms. CFCs are fully chlorinated fluorocarbons, which

Figure 5.4

How Ozone Is Destroyed

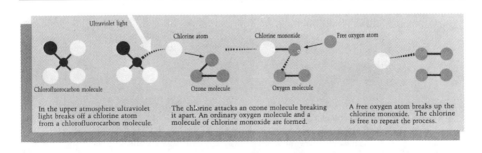

Source: U.S. Environmental Protection Agency, *Environmental Progress and Challenges: EPA's Update* (Washington, DC: U.S. Government Printing Office, 1988), p. 38.

means that they have no hydrogen atoms and are made of only chlorine, fluorine, and carbon.

After this initial discovery, the number of CFC compounds grew quickly into the dozens, and were used as a universal coolant, refrigerating 75 percent of the food consumed in the United States, as a blowing agent in rigid insulation forms, as an aerosol propellant, as a solvent to remove glue, grease, and soldering residues from micro-chips and other electronic products, and as a component of foam packaging containers. (See Table 5.1.) Between 1958 and 1983, the average production of some forms of CFC compounds grew 13 percent a year, and could have continued to grow more or less indefinitely.[50]

When chemists Molina and Rowland developed their theory, empirical validation was unavailable because of the difficulties of measuring actual levels of stratospheric ozone. But almost as soon as news of their work hit the popular press, consumers began switching to non-aerosol packaging for common household products such as deodorants. In 1978, the United States banned the use of CFCs as an aerosol propellant, but most of the rest of the world continued to use them for this purpose. At that time, the United States consumed about half of all CFCs manufactured worldwide, and aerosol uses accounted for about half of this consumption. Manufacturers of personal care products and of aerosol containers used in industry switched to other propellants including carbon dioxide and simple aliphatic hydrocarbons like propane and butane.[51]

Discovery of the Ozone Hole

Government and industry built computer models to simulate the chemical and physical processes that determine ozone levels in the stratosphere, some of which led scientists to believe that Molina and Rowland had overstated the

Table 5.1

Global CFC Use by Category, 1985

Aerosols	25%
Rigid Foam Insulation	19
Solvents	19
Air Conditioning	12
Refrigerants	8
Flexible Foam	7
Other	10
Total	100%

Source: Reprinted from STATE OF THE WORLD, 1989, A Worldwatch Institute Report on Progress Toward a Sustainable Society, Project Director: Lester R. Brown. By permission of W. W. Norton & Company, Inc. Copyright © 1989 by Worldwatch Institute.

problem. Thus no international action was taken to limit CFC usage until the discovery of the ozone hole over Antarctica. This phenomenon was first discovered in 1983 when the British Antarctic Survey discovered that concentrations of ozone in the stratosphere were dropping over Antarctica at a dramatic rate each austral spring to be replenished again by the end of the fall season. This discovery led to a $10 million scientific mission carried out by the United States under the combined sponsorship of NASA, the National Oceanic and Atmospheric Administration, and the Chemical Manufacturers Association to find out more about this phenomenon.[52]

By the spring of 1987, the average ozone concentration over the South Pole was discovered to be down 50 percent, and in isolated spots it had actually disappeared. The report on this discovery also indicated that the ozone layer around the entire globe was eroding much faster than any model had predicted. Ozone depletion was said to be occurring far more rapidly and in a different pattern than had been forecast. While the role of CFCs in ozone depletion had been hotly contested after the theory was formulated in 1974, within a matter of weeks the report's conclusions were widely accepted and the need for immediate policy changes became apparent to many of the world's leaders.[53]

In the spring of 1985, representatives of 21 nations met under the auspices of the United Nations Environment Program to consider worldwide restrictions of CFC usage. The Soviet Union, Japan, and the European Economic Community argued for a freeze on existing CFC levels only, but the United States, Canada, and Scandinavian countries pressed for a virtual phase-out of CFCs by the year 2000. The phase-out proposal, a personal initiative of the EPA administrator, was opposed by the Reagan White House. Interior Secretary Donald Hodel suggested that everyone could stay indoors or wear hats, sunglasses, and sunscreen for protection against increased ultraviolet radiation. The ridicule that greeted this proposal spurred a Senate resolution urging a two-stage phase-out of CFCs and halons. As a compromise, U.S. negotiators proposed a 50 percent reduction in CFC production and a freeze on halons. This plan formed the basis for the Montreal treaty.[54]

On September 16, 1987, after years of debate and heated negotiation, the Montreal Protocol on Substances That Deplete the Ozone Layer was signed by 24 countries. By mid-November of 1988, that total had increased to 35 countries. The agreement included a freeze on CFC production at 1986 levels to be reached by 1989, a 20 percent decrease in production by 1993, and another 30 percent cut by 1998. Halon production was also subject to a freeze based on 1986 levels starting in 1992. In order to obtain this many signatures, the treaty included extended deadlines for some countries, allowances to accommodate industry restructuring, and loose definitions of products that can legitimately be traded internationally. Developing countries were given a ten-year grace period past the industrial-country deadline during which CFC production could be increased to meet "basic domestic needs."[55]

The cumulative effect of the loopholes means that even with widespread participation, the protocol's goals of halving CFC use by 1998 will not be attained. Unless it is strengthened, the agreement will most likely not arrest ozone depletion, but merely slow its acceleration.[56] Since it takes CFCs as long as six to eight years to drift up to the ozone layer, there are still many in the pipeline, so to speak, that have yet to do their damage. But the Montreal treaty was an unprecedented effort to deal with a global problem and may provide a model for agreements to deal with other global problems such as the greenhouse effect.[57]

Twenty-four countries, plus the European Community Commission, signed the protocol in September 1987, with many other countries signing over the ensuing months. Six months after the protocol was signed, the U.S. Senate approved it by a vote of 83 to 0. After this action, President Reagan promptly signed the ratification agreement, making the United States the second nation to ratify the agreement. Entered into force on January 1, 1989, the treaty did try to distribute economic burdens fairly and was sensitive to special situations. It established periodic scientific, economic, and technical assessments so that specific provisions could be adapted to evolving conditions. There are even provisions for emergency meetings of signatories in case of unexpected and fast-breaking developments.[58]

In June of 1990, representatives from 75 countries met in London to sign an accord that strengthened provisions of the treaty. Projections showed that if industrialized countries phased out CFCs as scheduled, but the less developed countries did not go along, these countries' use of CFCs would soar from 15 percent to 50 percent of world usage by the end of the century. That increase would leave chlorine levels slightly above the current level even with reductions by developed countries. Thus the pact calls for eliminating CFC usage worldwide in a decade, and it will set up an international fund of $200 billion to help less-developed countries join the campaign. This aid will help subsidize purchase of CFC substitutes by less-developed countries, and build new plants to produce refrigerators and other products that use CFC substitutes.[59]

The impact on industry is expected to be severe. The estimated annual world production of the chemicals is worth about $2.2 billion and the industries that use them now have annual sales of many additional billions of dollars. In the United States alone, CFCs represent a $28 billion industry that employs about 715,000 people in 5,000 companies.[60] Manufacturers in the United States sell about $750 million of the compounds annually to about 5,000 customers in the refrigeration, air-conditioning, automotive, plastic-foam, and electronics industries. These industries, in turn, produce $27 billion each year in goods and services directly dependent on CFCs. Some $135 billion of installed equipment and products require the availability of CFC compounds for maintenance and repair. Thus the treaty jeopardized the life of existing equipment and undoubtedly will force industry to spend a good bit of money on engineering new products.[61]

CFCs are pervasive in the United States, contained in 100 million refrigerators, 90 million cars and trucks, 40,000 supermarket display cases, and 100,000 commercial building air conditioners. Du Pont estimated that banning CFCs would render useless or require altering capital equipment valued at $135 billion in the United States alone. Most substitutes seem to be either toxic to humans, corrode the metal machinery in which they are used, or are simply inefficient coolants. Others are potentially explosive. Companies may have to invest billions of dollars in new plant construction to make substitute products, so they want to be sure the substitutes aren't toxic and don't fail to serve the purpose as a reliable substitute.[62]

Strategies

Curtailing chlorine and bromine emissions enough to prevent widespread environmental damage requires a virtual phaseout of CFC and halon emissions as soon as possible. As previously noted even that would not prevent the damage. The releases of other compounds containing chlorine and bromine not currently covered under the treaty also need to be controlled and in some cases halted entirely. Governments around the world must provide money for research and development of substitutes. The results of this research, as well as new technologies and processes, need to be shared with developing countries. Valuable time was lost when governments and industries relaxed their regulatory and research efforts during the 1980s. This decrease in activity makes a crash program essential.[63]

In 1989, the U.S. Congress enacted an excise tax on ozone depleting chemicals (ODCs) with far-reaching effects. Congress hoped the tax would discourage the use of ozone depleting chemicals and encourage an expedited search for safe substitutes. The tax applies to any substance that at the time of sale or use by a manufacturer, producer, or importer is listed as a ODC and which is manufactured or produced in the United States or entered into the United States for consumption, use, or warehousing. The tax is generally $1.37 per pound, increasing to $1.67 per pound in 1992, and $2.65 per pound in 1993. Some ODCs are considered less depleting than others and are subject to a scaled-down rate. The tax was effective January 1, 1990, and affected manufacturers, wholesalers and retailers, and businesses that retain stocks of chemicals.[64]

Long-term reductions of CFCs involve alternative product disposal methods, use of substitute chemicals, and development of new process technologies. Use of CFC propellants in aerosols, which are still the largest source of CFC emissions worldwide, can be banned. Rapid evaporation of cleaning solvents can also be eliminated. Since CFCs are used only to clean the final product and are not incorporated in it, emissions can be reduced immediately. Capturing CFC emissions from flexible-foam manufacturing can also be accomplished fairly quickly, but requires an investment in new ventilation systems. Another area that offers significant savings at low cost is improved design, operating, and maintenance standards for refrigeration and air-conditioning equipment. Refrigerants that are drained during systems recharging can be recovered. But to recover CFCs from junked automobiles and other appliances years after they are produced requires either a collection system or a bounty scheme to encourage reclamation by salvagers.[65]

Even if emissions of CFCs are substantially reduced, however, there are other chlorine-based chemicals that will continue to cause problems if not controlled. They are methyl chloroform used as a degreasing agent for metals and electronics equipment parts, and carbon tetrachloride, which is used in the production of CFCs as well as in pesticides and dyes. Over the next century, methyl chloroform may account for 35 percent of the buildup of chlorine in the atmosphere unless it is controlled.[66] Other gases that may contribute to the problem are hydrogen chloride and hydrogen fluoride emitted during volcanic eruptions. Volcanoes eject an average of about 11 million tons of hydrogen chloride and 6 million tons of hydrogen fluoride into the atmosphere annually.[67]

Over the longer term, however, phasing out the use and emission of CFCs will require the development of chemical substitutes that do not harm the ozone layer. The challenge for business and government is to find alternatives that (1) perform the same function at a reasonable cost, (2) do not require major equipment modifications, (3) are nontoxic to workers and consumers, and (4) are environmentally benign. One of the major delays associated with new chemical compounds is the need for extensive toxicity testing that can run from five to seven years. In some cases, it may be possible that a new product design can eliminate or at least reduce the need for CFCs or substitute chemicals while providing additional benefits. Manufacturers must ask if the functions performed by CFCs are really necessary.[68]

Du Pont Company

The Montreal Treaty led the largest manufacturer of CFCs, Du Pont, to phase out the production of CFCs regulated under the protocol altogether. Du Pont was the world's largest manufacturer of CFCs, receiving $600 million in 1987 in revenues from this business. The Freon Products Division, which was involved in the production and sale of CFCs, had 1,200 employees, and was a self-contained profit center with its own production, marketing, and research and development staffs. Virtually all of its revenue came from the sale of various CFC compounds. Du Pont enjoyed international patent protection of CFCs through the late 1940s, and just as these patents expired, demand for the product skyrocketed as building and vehicular air conditioning and household aerosols became commonly used throughout the country.[69]

Du Pont was the only firm producing CFCs in all three major markets that included the United States, Europe, and Japan. While it did not begin manufacturing CFCs in Europe and Japan until indigenous firms had already become entrenched, by virtue of its early scientific leadership it was by far the world's largest producer and the only firm with a significant worldwide presence. In 1985, Du Pont produced 882 million pounds of CFCs in these three markets, with 706 million pounds being produced in the United States alone. U.S. sales of CFCs peaked in 1973, when concern began to develop about depletion of the ozone layer. Aerosol uses accounted for about half of CFC consumption in the United States, and when this use was banned in 1978 because it was a nonessential use of the product, consumption of CFCs fell by 50 percent, but began climbing slowly back toward mid-1970 levels as more uses were found and demand in nonaerosol sectors grew.[70]

As concern about CFCs and their role in depleting the ozone layer mounted, Du Pont led producers and users in opposing CFC regulation, citing scientific uncertainty as the primary reason for its opposition. In the absence of regulation, CFC use was expected to grow at about the level of GNP in the industrialized world, and somewhat faster in developing countries. When the initial furor over ozone depletion took place in the late 1970s, Du Pont was spending $3 to $4 million per year in attempts to identify substitutes. From 1981 to 1985, however, the company spent practically nothing on substitute development because it doubted that further regulatory restrictions on CFCs were forthcoming and because the substitutes were uniformly more expensive.[71]

All of these plans changed with the signing of the Montreal Protocol in 1987, where virtually all of the world's industrial nations agreed to cap production. The countries who signed the protocol could decide for themselves how to allocate production among CFC compounds and among producers, subject to an overall ceiling for each country that was expressed in terms of ozone depletion potential. The EPA regulations for implementing the protocol were proposed in December 1987, and would set limits on the amount of CFCs each firm could sell in the American market. The limit for each firm would be based on the firm's 1986 production, weighted according to the ozone depletion potential of each compound. Firms could transfer production and sales rights among themselves to take advantage of scale economies in production.[72]

While opposing regulation because of scientific uncertainty, Du Pont also made a public promise to change its position if the scientific case against CFCs should solidify. The company underwrote scientific efforts to examine the problem, and developed the first credible two-dimensional model of stratospheric ozone. This model showed that significant sustained increases in CFC emissions were likely to decrease the ozone layer over a period of time. These findings, coupled with the discovery of the ozone hole over Antarctica, led Du Pont to change its position. The company stated, "It would be prudent to limit worldwide emissions of CFCs while science continues to work to provide better guidance to policymakers." But only international action would be effective, the company argued, because unilateral action by the United States would provide an excuse for other nations to delay regulating their own producers. Thus Du Pont supported ratification of the Montreal Protocol.[73]

In early 1988, the company began to feel some pressure to cease production and sale of CFCs entirely. Some politicians reminded the company of the promises it had made to stop production should reputable evidence show that CFCs pose a health hazard. The company responded by stating, "At the moment, scientific evidence does not point to the need for dramatic CFC emission reductions." The company emphasized the continuing uncertainty of science, and argued that CFC markets needed time to develop and adapt to improved substitutes. To interfere with a smooth transition through drastic production cutbacks would be irresponsible.[74]

The issuance of the NASA Executive Summary Report on ozone depletion caused the company to reassess its position. This report described a fundamental change in the scientific understanding of the CFC-ozone connection. It presented hard evidence of reductions in stratospheric ozone concentrations over temperate populated regions as well as Antarctica, firmly established the link between CFCs and ozone depletion, and suggested that implementation of the Montreal Protocol would result in little net depletion of ozone and that continuing ozone decreases were expected even if the protocol were implemented. The statement made by the company only days before had been overtaken by events.[75]

In March 1988, Joe Glass, head of the Freon Products Division, decided to recommend that the company stop manufacturing the CFCs regulated under the protocol. Because of difficulties in developing substitutes and obtaining regulatory approval to produce them, this exit would be phased in over a ten-year period. But by 1999, when the protocol would require a cutback to 50 percent of 1986 levels, Du Pont planned to stop manufacturing regulated CFC compounds entirely.[76] The company received widespread accolades for this announcement; competitors either kept silent, or commented that they were still reviewing the evidence and were not at all sure that such drastic action was warranted.

Substitutes

Chemical companies such as Du Pont that made CFCs are now in a race to find and develop substitutes that can be mass produced at affordable costs to industry. (See Exhibit 5.5.) There are approximately 14 major chemical companies worldwide working on studies of possible substitutes. The key to substitutes or alternatives to CFCs may be in the use of hydrogen. If one or more hydrogen atoms are substituted for a chlorine or fluorine atom in a CFC molecule, the desirable thermodynamic properties may be retained. The new compound that is formed in this manner is less stable than CFCs, and most of it will break down in the lower atmosphere before reaching the

Exhibit 5.5

Ozone Uses and Substitutes

Uses	Chemical	What Industry Can Do	What You Can Do
Blowing bubbles into flexible foam for furniture, bedding, carpet padding, dashboards	CFC 11	Substitute methylene chloride (a suspected carcinogen) or CFC 123 as blowing agent.	Buy spring mattresses and nonfoam furniture.
Blowing bubbles into rigid foams for egg cartons, coffee cups, home insulation	CFC 11 CFC 12	Use pentane (which is flammable) for blowing or improve the recovery of CFC vapors.	Buy food in cardboard packaging. Use fiberglass or cellulose insulation.
Solvent for dry cleaning leather goods, cleaning printed circuit boards, degreasing metal	CFC 113	Substitute water for cleaning circuit boards and use other solvents for dry cleaning, or recycle CFCs.	Shop for washable fabrics.
Refrigerant in automobile air conditioners, the greatest single consumer source of CFCs	CFC 12	Substitute CFC 22 (which requires higher pressures) or FC134a (not yet commercially available).	Replace air-conditioner hoses every three years. Ask mechanics to drain coolant into bottles, rather than letting it evaporate.
Used in fire extinguishers for high-tech equipment	Halon	No good substitutes, but industry can recycle unused extinguishers.	Buy other types of extinguishers for home applications.

Source: Douglas Starr, "How to Protect the Ozone Layer," *National Wildlife* (December-January 1988), p. 28.

stratospheric ozone layer. But if too many hydrogen atoms are introduced, the compound may become flammable.

Five such hydrochlorofluorocarbons (HCFCs) have been developed and are used widely. One compound called HCFC-22 is the refrigerant used in most residential, window, and commercial rooftop air-conditioning systems and heat pumps. Compared with CFC compounds, HCFCs have far less effect on the ozone layer, something in the range of 2 to 5 percent of the ozone depletion potential on a weight basis. But the problems associated with use of HCFCs is that they degrade the varnish on motor windings and are flammable.

Since chlorine is the element that causes the major problem with CFCs, the ideal substitute would be comprised of only carbon, hydrogen, and fluorine. These compounds called hydrofluorocarbons (HCFs) have no potential to deplete the ozone layer. To date, at least three HCF compounds have been developed in limited quantities. They are being developed by Du

Pont as a replacement for CFC usage in automobile air-conditioning systems. At the present time, there are toxicity as well as lubrication problems associated with the compound, but if these problems can be solved, commercial production is scheduled for the early 1990s.

In mid-1990, Du Pont announced plans to design four world-scale plants to produce its line of HCFs which would become operational somewhere around the middle of the decade. These plants will be capable of producing more than 140 million pounds of HCFs annually and could supply most of the world's needs for the compounds through the end of the century. The company said that overall costs of commercializing its line of CFC alternatives could total more than $1 billion in research, development, and capital projects, including $240 million invested through 1990 and projected costs over the next ten years.[77]

Refrigerator makers were planning to make their product without using CFCs, an engineering challenge that will not be easy to solve. In a refrigerator that weighs 250 pounds and is priced at $700, CFCs weigh less than 3 pounds and cost no more than $5 to install initially. These CFCs served two important functions: (1) they circulated between the appliance's compressor and evaporator as a refrigerant, and (2) they made up part of the rigid foam insulation in the walls of the cabinet. Many of the substitutes reduced energy efficiency at a time when the industry was being asked to reduce the product's energy consumption. Recent gains in energy efficiency was largely a result of increased use of CFCs in the product. Other substitutes involved extensive retooling of compressors and potential liability from flammability.[78]

Early in 1990, Carrier Corporation, which manufactures heating and cooling systems, announced a recovery and recycling system for refrigerants that are responsible for 10 percent of American CFC emissions. The plan called for the company to invest $750 million to help phase out the use of CFCs in air-conditioning refrigerants and to recover and recycle existing CFC refrigerants. Most of the CFCs coming from this source are released into the air during routine maintenance of large cooling units. The new equipment, which looks like a home hot water tank turned on its side and mounted on wheels, is intended to be used by air-conditioning maintenance crews to drain, contain, and recycle refrigerants.[79]

In January 1991, Du Pont announced a family of refrigerator and air conditioner coolants as substitutes for CFCs to be used by General Motors in their 1994 models. The substitutes go under the trade name Suva and required an investment of $240 million in ten facilities that were either in operation or under construction. The substitute was expected to sell for around $10 a pound in comparison to the CFC compound previously used, which sold for $2.40 a pound including a $1.37 special tax instituted by Congress. To accommodate the new coolant, GM will have to develop a larger evaporator and condenser and redesign the compressor on its air conditioners. It was estimated that GM will have to spend up to $1 billion over the next two to three years to convert to the new coolant.[80]

Questions for Discussion

1. What are global problems? What makes these problems different from the more traditional environmental problems that have been around for some time? How can global problems be solved?

2. Describe the greenhouse effect. What are trace gases? Have these gases increased over the past several years? What predictions are made about future levels of these gases?

3. What are general climate models? What do they generally show with regard to global warming? What problems do these models have that raise some doubts about the validity of their predictions?

4. Given the evidence, has global warming actually taken place over the past decade? If so, is this warming attributable to the greenhouse effect? Why or why not? What other events could cause global warming?

5. What would be the effects of global climate change on the scale predicted by the models? What areas of the world would be most affected? What areas might benefit from such changes? Would you like to see these changes happen? Why or why not?

6. What are the risks involved in waiting any longer to take steps that would reduce trace gas emissions? What are the risks involved in cutting back on carbon dioxide emissions at this time given the current state of knowledge? Are more studies necessary? What kind of studies would be helpful to policymakers?

7. What is a tie-in strategy? Does this approach to global warming make sense? What specific measures would you advocate to implement this strategy? What other strategies would you recommend? What should business do about the problem at this time?

8. Prioritize the specific measures to deal with global warming described in the chapter. Which of these measures are most important to begin immediately, and which can wait until further information is discovered? Which would be most costly? Which would impact business organizations most severely?

9. What functions does the ozone layer perform? What will happen if this layer continues to deteriorate? What are some of the cost estimates regarding the damage that would be done by further depletion?

10. What are CFCs? What uses have they had in our society? Why were they such a useful substance? Was there any way business could have tested for the ozone depletion effects these substances are believed to possess?

11. Describe the story relative to the discovery of the effect CFCs have on the ozone layer. What role did theory and empirical evidence play in

this story? Are there any lessons to be learned here that could apply to global warming? Do you believe the full story has been discovered?

12. Describe the events that led to the Montreal Treaty. What impacts was the treaty predicted to have on industry? Why was it revised soon after it was passed and ratified? How did Du Pont react to the treaty? Was Du Pont a responsible corporate citizen?

NOTES

1. Thomas E. Graedel and Paul J. Crutzen, "The Changing Atmosphere," *Scientific American,* Vol. 261, No. 3 (September 1989), p. 66.

2. Stephen H. Schneider, "The Changing Climate," *Scientific American,* Vol. 261, No. 3 (September 1989), p. 70.

3. Ibid.

4. Michael D. Lemonick, "The Heat Is On," *Time,* October 19, 1987, p. 63.

5. Schneider, "The Changing Climate," p. 72.

6. Ibid., p. 73.

7. Christopher Flavin, "Slowing Global Warming," *State of the World 1990* (Washington, DC: Worldwatch Institute, 1990), p. 20.

8. Schneider, "The Changing Climate," p. 73.

9. Ibid., pp. 74–75.

10. James Trefil, "Modeling Earth's Future Climate Requires Both Science and Guesswork," *Smithsonian,* Vol. 21, No. 9 (December 1990), p. 33. See also Carolyn Lockhead, "Global Warming Forecasts May Be Built on Hot Air," *Insight,* April 16, 1990, pp. 14–18.

11. Schneider, "The Changing Climate," p. 75.

12. Trefil, "Modeling Earth's Future Climate," p. 34.

13. Schneider, "The Changing Climate," p. 75.

14. Ibid., p. 72.

15. "1990 Was Hot Year for Earth," *Times-Picayune,* January 10, 1991, p. A-10. See also "Hot Times," *Time,* January 21, 1991, p. 65.

16. Daniel Haney, "Study Bucks Theory of Global Warming," *Times-Picayune,* February 18, 1990, p. B-8.

17. John Carey, "Is the World Heating Up? Well, Just Listen," *Business Week,* February 4, 1991, pp. 82–83.

18. Schneider, "The Changing Climate," p. 77.

19. Paulette Thomas, "EPA Predicts Global Impact from Warming," *Wall Street Journal,* October 21, 1988, p. B-4.

20. David Brand, "Is the Earth Warming Up?" *Time,* July 4, 1988, p. 18. See also Bob Davis and David Wessel, "NASA Aide Says White House Made Him Dilute Testimony on Greenhouse Effect," *Wall Street Journal,* May 9, 1989, p. B-4.

21. Sierra Club, "Global Warming," May 1989, p. 3.
22. Bill McKibben, *The End of Nature* (New York: Random House, 1989), p. 29.
23. See Eugene Linden, "Big Chill for the Greenhouse," *Time,* October 31, 1988, p. 90.
24. See Carolyn Lockhead, "The Alarming Price Tag on Greenhouse Legislation," *Insight,* April 16, 1990, pp. 10–13.
25. Schneider, "The Changing Climate," p. 78.
26. John Carey, "Is the World Heating Up?" pp. 82–83.
27. Michael Duffy and Glenn Garelik, "A Sizzling Scientific Debate," *Time,* April 30, 1990, p. 84.
28. Flavin, "Slowing Global Warming," p. 18.
29. Ibid., p. 20.
30. Ibid., p. 22.
31. Sierra Club, "Global Warming," May 1989, p. 2.
32. Ibid.
33. Schneider, "The Changing Climate," p. 78.
34. Flavin, "Slowing Global Warming," p. 28.
35. Ibid., pp. 35–36.
36. Ibid., p. 37.
37. Carolyn Lockhead, "The Alarming Price Tag on Greenhouse Legislation," *Insight,* April 16, 1990, p. 10.
38. Bob Davis, "Bid to Slow Global Warming Could Cost U.S. $200 Billion a Year, Bush Aide Says," *Wall Street Journal,* April 16, 1990, p. B-5.
39. Curtis A. Moore, "Fixing the Atmosphere," *International Wildlife* (May-June 1989), pp. 19–23.
40. Flavin, "Slowing Global Warming," pp. 22–23.
41. Ibid., p. 25.
42. Ibid., p. 31.
43. Ibid., p. 32.
44. Lemonick, "The Heat Is On," p. 67.
45. Cynthia Pollock Shea, "Protecting the Ozone Layer," *State of the World 1989* (New York: Norton, 1989), p. 82.
46. Ibid., pp. 83–85.
47. Lemonick, "The Heat Is On," p. 61.
48. McKibben, *The End of Nature,* pp. 39–40. See also Amal Kumar Naj, "Bromines May Be Harming Ozone Layer as Much as Fluorocarbons, Report Says," *Wall Street Journal,* August 30, 1988, p. 37.
49. Shea, "Protecting the Ozone Layer," p. 87.
50. McKibben, *The End of Nature,* pp. 39.
51. National Wildlife Federation, "Du Pont Freon Products Division (A)," 1989, p. 6.
52. Lemonick, "The Heat Is On," p. 59.
53. Shea, "Protecting the Ozone Layer," p. 81.
54. "Can We Repair the Sky?" *Consumer Reports,* May 1989, p. 324.
55. Shea, "Protecting the Ozone Layer," pp. 93–94.

56. Ibid., p. 94.

57. Laurie Hays, "Du Pont Plans to Complete Phase-Out of Chlorofluorocarbons by Year 2000," *Wall Street Journal,* July 29, 1988, p. 16.

58. Richard Benedick, "Diplomacy and the Ozone Crisis," *The GAO Journal* Summer 1989, p. 37.

59. Vicky Cahan, "Fixing the Hole Where the Rays Come In," *Business Week,* July 2, 1990, p. 58.

60. Laurie Hays, "CFC Curb to Save Ozone Will Be Costly," *Wall Street Journal,* March 28, 1988, p. 5.

61. Elliott D. Lee, "Limits Worry Chlorofluorocarbon Firms," *Wall Street Journal,* September 15, 1987, p. 6.

62. Amal Kumar Naj, "As CFC Phase-Out Looms, Doubts on Substitutes Arise," *Wall Street Journal,* March 6, 1989, p. B-4.

63. Shea, "Protecting the Ozone Layer," pp. 94–96.

64. Grant Thornton, "National Tax Alert," February 23, 1990, pp. 1–3.

65. Shea, "Protecting the Ozone Layer," pp. 89–90.

66. Vicky Cahan, "Just When the Ozone War Looked Winnable . . . ," *Business Week,* June 12, 1989, p. 56.

67. "A Natural Culprit in Ozone Depletion," *Insight,* September 5, 1988, p. 57.

68. Shea, "Protecting the Ozone Layer," pp. 91–92.

69. National Wildlife Federation, "Du Pont," p. 10.

70. Ibid., pp. 4–7.

71. Ibid., p. 12.

72. Ibid., pp. 7–9.

73. Ibid., pp. 13–15.

74. Ibid., pp. 15–17.

75. Barbara Rosewicz, "New Ozone Study Shows Depletion Exceeds Estimates," *Wall Street Journal,* March 16, 1988, p. 43.

76. Mary Lu Carnevale, "Du Pont Plans to Phase Out CFC Output," *Wall Street Journal,* March 25, 1988, p. 2.

77. "Du Pont Co. Plans 4 Hydrofluorocarbon Alternatives Plants," *Wall Street Journal,* June 22, 1990, p. A-2.

78. Richard Koenig, "Refrigerator Makers Plan for Future Without CFCs," *Wall Street Journal,* December 15, 1989, p. B-1.

79. Charles W. Stevens, "Carrier Unveils Recycling Unit for Refrigerants," *Wall Street Journal,* January 9, 1990, p. B-3.

80. Amal Kumar Naj, "Du Pont Unveils Coolants to Substitute for CFCs; GM Plans Use in 1994 Cars," *Wall Street Journal,* January 22, 1991, p. B-4.

SUGGESTED READINGS

Abrahamson, Dean Edwin, ed. *The Challenge of Global Warming.* Washington, DC: Island Press, 1989.

Cogan, Douglas G. *Stones in a Glass House: CFCs and Ozone Depletion.* Washington, DC: Investor Responsibility Research Center, 1988.

Environmental Protection Agency. *The Potential Effects of Global Climate Change on the United States.* Washington, DC: EPA, 1988.

Fisher, David E. *Fire and Ice: The Greenhouse Effect, Ozone Depletion, and Nuclear Winter.* New York: Harper & Row, 1990.

Flavin, Christopher, "Slowing Global Warming," in *State of the World 1990.* Washington, DC: Worldwatch Institute, 1990.

Gribbin, John R. *Future Weather and the Greenhouse Effect.* New York: Delacorte Press/Eleanor Friede, 1982.

McKibben, Bill. *The End of Nature.* New York: Random House, 1989.

Mintzer, Irving M., et al. *Protecting the Ozone Shield: Strategies for Phasing Out CFCs During the 1990s.* Washington, DC: World Resources Institute, 1989.

Mitchell, George J. *World on Fire: Saving an Endangered Earth.* New York: Scribner's, 1991.

National Academy of Sciences. *Global Environmental Change.* Washington, DC: National Academy Press, 1989.

Oppenheimer, Michael, and Robert H. Boyle. *Dead Heat: The Race Against the Greenhouse Effect.* New York: Basic Books, 1990.

Roan, Sharon L. *Ozone Crisis.* New York: Wiley, 1989.

Schneider, Stephen H. *Global Warming: Are We Entering the Greenhouse Century?* San Francisco: Sierra Club Books, 1989.

Shea, Cynthia Pollack. *Protecting Life on Earth: Steps to Save the Ozone Layer.* Washington, DC: Worldwatch Institute, 1988.

Silver, Cheryl Simon, and Ruth S. Defries. *One Earth, One Future: Our Changing Global Environment.* Washington, DC: National Academy Press, 1990.

United Nations Environmental Program. *The Greenhouse Gases.* Washington, DC: Author, 1988.

CHAPTER 6

AIR POLLUTION

~

Just like other aspects of the environment, the air we breathe has a certain dilutive capacity, that is, it can absorb a certain amount of pollution without sacrificing its quality. But modern industrial processes have dumped such large amounts of pollutants in the air that its dilutive capacity has been exceeded, and the quality of the air seriously compromised. The air in certain places has become unhealthy to breathe and can cause serious illnesses if breathed continuously. Thus air pollution is a grave problem in many places in the world and can only be ignored at the risk of human health.

The air is so polluted in some cities in Poland, for example, that there are underground "clinics" in old uranium mines where the chronically ill can go to breathe clean air. Acid rain has so corroded railroad tracks in the country that trains are not allowed to exceed 24 miles an hour. Because of acid rain, it is believed that 15 to 20 percent of forests in former East Germany are dead, and another 40 percent are said to be dying. The air is so polluted in some cities that residents use their car headlights during the day, and visitors have been known to vomit from simply breathing the air. The government claims that nearly 40 percent of the population suffers ill effects from air pollution.[1]

About 99 percent of the air we breathe is gaseous nitrogen and oxygen. But as air moves across the earth's surface, it picks up trace amounts of various chemicals produced by natural events and human activities, minute droplets of various liquids, and tiny particles of various solid materials. These pollutants mix vertically and horizontally and often react chemically with each other or with natural components of the atmosphere. Continuous or repeated exposure to some of these pollutants can damage lung tissue, plants, buildings, metals, and other materials. The movement of the air and atmospheric turbulence help dilute many of these pollutants, but some of the more long-lived ones can be transported great distances before they return to the earth's surface.[2]

Pollutants can be classified as primary or secondary. A *primary air pollutant* enters the air as a result of natural events or human activities such as industrial processes. Substances such as carbon monoxide, carbon dioxide, sulfur dioxide, nitrogen oxide, most hydrocarbons, and most suspended particulate matter are examples of primary pollutants. *Secondary air pollutants* are formed in the air itself through a chemical reaction between a primary pollutant and one or more components of the air. Typical secondary pollutants are ozone, most nitrates and sulfates, and liquid droplets of chemicals such as sulfuric acid.[3]

Natural sources of air pollutants include forest fires, dispersal of pollen, volcanic eruptions, sea spray, bacterial decomposition of products of organic matter, and natural radioactivity. With the exceptions of large volcanic eruptions and buildup of radioactive radon gas inside buildings, most atmospheric emissions from widely scattered natural sources are diluted and dispersed throughout the world and rarely reach high enough concentrations to cause serious damage to the environment or to human health. The most serious threat comes from pollutants released into the air as a result of human activities. Much of the outdoor pollution in the United States comes from seven types of pollutants: carbon monoxide, hydrocarbons, lead, nitrogen dioxide, ozone, total suspended particulates, and sulfur dioxide. The nature and health effect of these pollutants are varied. (See Exhibit 6.1)

Major Air Pollution Problems

There have been several times in recent history when major problems with air pollution killed hundreds of people. In 1952, an air pollution incident in London killed 4,000 people, and further disasters in 1956, 1957, and 1962 killed a total of about 2,500 people. The first major air pollution disaster in the U.S. occurred in 1948 in the town of Donora in Pennsylvania's Monongahela Valley when fog laden with sulfur dioxide vapor and suspended particulate matter from nearby steel mills hung over the town for five days. About 6,000 of the town's 14,000 inhabitants fell ill and 20 were killed as a result of the pollution. In 1963, high concentrations of air pollutants accumulated in the air over New York City, killing about 300 people and injuring thousands.

Source: From *LIVING IN THE ENVIRONMENT: AN INTRODUCTION TO ENVIRONMENTAL STUDIES* 6/E by G. Tyler Miller, Jr. © 1990 by Wadsworth, Inc. Reprinted by permission of the publisher.

Exhibit 6.1

Major Air Pollutants and Their Health Effects

Pollutant	Major Sources	Characteristics and Effects
Carbon monoxide (CO)	Vehicle exhausts	Colorless, odorless poisonous gas. Replaces oxygen in red blood cells, causing dizziness, unconsciousness, or death.
Hydrocarbons (HC)	Incomplete combusion of gasoline; evaporation of petroleum fuels, solvents, and points	Although some are poisonous, most are not. Reacts with NO_2 to form ozone, or smog.
Lead (Pb)	Antiknock agents in gasoline	Accumulates in the bone and soft tissues. Affects blood-forming organs, kidneys, and nervous system. Suspected of causing learning disabilities in young children.
Nitrogen dioxide (NO_2)	Industrial processes, vehicle exhausts	Causes structural and chemical changes in the lungs. Lowers resistance to respiratory infections. Reacts in sunlight with hydrocarbons to produce smog. Contributes to acid rain.
Ozone (O_3)	Formed when HC and NO_2 react	Principal constituent of smog, Irritates mucous membranes, causing coughing, choking, impaired lung function. Aggravates chronic asthma and bronchitis.
Total suspended particulates (TSP)	Industrial plants, heating boilers, auto engines, dust	Larger visible types (soot, smoke, or dust) can clog the lung sacs. Smaller visible particles can pass into the bloodstream. Often carry carcinogens and toxic metals, impair visibility.
Sulfur dioxide (SO_2)	Burning coal and oil, industrial processes	Corrosive, poisonous gas. Associated with coughs, colds, asthma, and bronchitis. Contributes to acid rain.

Source: *Environment and Health,* 2nd ed. (Washington, DC: Congressional Quarterly Inc., 1982), p. 21.

Years of exposure to these pollutants can overload or deteriorate the natural defenses of the human body and cause or contribute to a number of respiratory diseases such as lung cancer, chronic bronchitis, and emphysema. Elderly people, infants, pregnant women, and persons with heart disease, asthma, or other respiratory diseases are especially vulnerable to air pollution. The World Health Organization (WHO) estimates that nearly a billion urban dwellers, or almost one of every five people on earth, are being exposed to health hazards from air pollutants. The EPA estimated in 1988 that 102 million Americans, or 42 percent of the population, were breathing unsafe air. Between 1970 and 1987, deaths in the United States from chronic lung diseases increased 36 percent. Air pollution costs the country at least $100 billion annually in health care and lost work productivity.[4]

Some of the air pollutants also cause direct damage to leaves of plants and trees and cause crop damage that can run into the billions of dollars. Chronic exposure to air pollutants interferes with photosynthesis and plant growth, reduces nutrient uptake, and causes leaves or needles to turn yellow and/or brown, and in some cases, to drop off altogether. Some kinds of air pollution can also leach vital plant nutrients from the soil and kill essential soil microorganisms. Trees can also be made more vulnerable to drought, frost, insects, fungi, mosses, and diseases by some kinds of pollutants. The effects of such chronic exposure of trees to multiple air pollutants may not be visible for several decades, but then suddenly large numbers begin dying because of nutrient depletion and increased susceptibility to other environmental elements.[5]

Air pollutants also damage various materials. The fallout of soot and grit on buildings and clothing requires costly sandblasting and cleaning to restore to a decent condition. Irreplaceable marble statues, historic buildings, and stained glass windows throughout the world have been pitted and discolored by air pollutants. Unless painted and maintained properly, iron and steel used in railroad tracks and to support bridges can become corroded and seriously weakened by air pollutants reacting with the metal. Various pollutants also damage leather, rubber, paper, paint, and certain kinds of fabrics.[6]

The total amount of pollution in the air over the United States at any given time adds up to hundreds of millions of tons. Table 6.1 shows the total emissions over several decades of the six most pervasive pollutants. The amount of these pollutants spewed into the air during some of these years was over 200 million metric tons (a metric ton is about 2,200 pounds), nearly a ton for every man, woman, and child in the country.[7] Table 6.2 shows the source of these pollutants for 1970, 1980, and 1986, the latest year for which figures are available. Certain kinds of sources predominate for different types of pollution. The internal combustion engine (autos and trucks) in 1986, for example, accounted for 70 and 40 percent of carbon monoxide and lead emissions, respectively. Stationary fuel burning (power, heating) accounted for 75 percent in 1970 and 81 percent in 1986 of sulfur oxide emissions.

REGULATION OF AIR QUALITY

Public policy measures designed to reduce air pollution date from the Air Pollution Act of 1955, which authorized the Public Health Service to undertake air pollution studies through a system of grants. This act created the first federally funded air pollution research activity. The Clean Air Act of 1963, which replaced the 1955 act, was aimed at the control and prevention of air

Table 6.1

National Air Pollutant Emmissions, 1940–1986

(In millions of metric tons, except lead in thousands of metric tons. Metric ton = 1.1023 short tons. PM = Particulates, SO₂ = Sulfur oxides, NO₂ = Nitrogen Oxide, VOC = Volatile organic Compound, CO = Carbon monoxide, Pb = lead)

Year	Emissions						Percentage Change[1]					
	PM	SO₂	NO₂	VOC	CO	Pb	PM	SO₂	NO₂	VOC	CO	Pb
1940	23.1	17.6	6.8	18.6	81.6	(NA)	(NA)	(NA)	(NA)	(NA)	(NA)	(NA)
1950	24.9	19.8	9.3	21.0	86.3	(NA)	7.8	12.5	36.8	12.9	5.8	(NA)
1960	21.6	19.7	12.8	23.8	88.4	(NA)	-13.3	-.5	37.6	13.3	2.4	(NA)
1970	18.5	28.3	18.1	27.5	98.7	203.8	-14.4	43.7	41.4	15.5	11.7	(NA)
1975	10.6	26.0	19.1	22.8	81.0	147.0	-42.7	-8.1	5.5	-17.1	-17.9	-27.9
1980	8.5	23.9	20.3	23.0	76.1	70.6	-19.8	-8.1	6.3	.9	-6.0	-52.0
1981	8.0	23.5	20.3	21.6	73.4	55.9	-5.9	-1.7	–	-6.1	-3.5	-20.8
1982	7.1	22.0	19.5	20.1	67.4	54.4	-11.2	-6.4	-3.9	-6.9	-8.2	-2.7
1983	7.1	21.5	19.1	20.9	70.3	46.3	–	-2.3	-2.1	4.0	4.3	-14.9
1984	7.4	22.1	19.7	21.9	69.6	40.1	4.2	2.8	3.1	4.8	-1.0	-13.4
1985	7.0	21.6	19.7	20.3	64.3	21.1	-5.4	-2.3	–	-7.3	-7.6	-47.4
1986	6.8	21.2	19.3	19.5	60.9	8.6	-2.9	-1.9	-2.0	-3.9	-5.3	-59.2

– Represents zero.

NA Not available.

[1]Percentage change from prior year shown.

Source: U.S. Department of Commerce, *Statistical Abstract of the United States 1989*, 109th ed. (Washington, DC: U.S. Government Printing Office, 1988), p. 200.

pollution. It permitted legal steps to end specific instances of air pollution and authorized grants to state and local governments to initiate control programs. The 1965 Amendments to the Clean Air Act (called the National Emissions Standards Act) gave the federal government authority to curb motor vehicle emissions and set standards, which were first applied to 1968 model vehicles. The Air Quality Act of 1967 required the states to establish air quality regions with standards for air pollution control and implementation plans for their accomplishment. The Clean Air Act Amendments of 1970 provided the legal basis for a new system of national air quality standards to be set by the federal government and called for a rollback of auto pollution levels. In the Clean Air Act Amendments of 1977, new deadlines were set for the attainment of air quality standards.

Thus the regulatory approach to pollution control is many faceted, and management of the commons we call the atmosphere is quite a complicated matter. The management system that has evolved over the years to control pollution and improve the quality of the air we breathe is complex and deals with various levels of control. The Clean Air Act Amendments of 1970 and 1977 laid out several different kinds of management methods to accomplish the goals of pollution control legislation with respect to air quality. These areas form a framework for understanding how the commons is being managed in the United States.

- Air quality management (ambient air quality).
- Limitations on industrial growth in areas where the air quality is better than the national standards, termed Prevention of Significant Deterioration (PSD).
- Restrictions on industrial growth and expansion in areas where national air quality standards have not been met (nonattainment areas).
- Limits on emissions from stationary sources (factories and power plants).
- Limitations on toxic emissions from industrial sources (primarily chemical plants).
- Limits on emissions from mobile sources (primarily cars and trucks).

Ambient Air Quality Management

To control ambient (that is, surrounding) air quality, the EPA set primary and secondary standards for seven pollutants. Six pollutants were initially identified by the EPA in 1971 as the most pervasive of artificial pollutants and in need of immediate reduction and control: sulfur dioxide, particulates, carbon monoxide, ozone, nitrogen dioxide, and hydrocarbons. In 1978, lead was added to the list of harmful pollutants. The primary standards concern the minimum level of air quality necessary to keep people from becoming ill

Table 6.2

Air Pollution Emissions by Pollutant and Source, 1970–1986

(In millions of metric tons, except lead in thousands of metric tons. Metric ton = 1.1023 short tons)

Year and Pollutant	Total Emissions	Controllable Emissions							Percentage of Total		
		Transportation		Fuel Combustion[1]		Industrial Processes	Solid Waste Dispoal	Misc. Uncontrollable	Transportation	Fuel Combustion[1]	Industrial
		Total	Road Vehicles	Total	Electric Utilities						
1970: Carbon monoxide	98.7	71.8	62.7	4.4	.2	9.0	6.4	7.2	72.7	4.5	9.1
Sulfur oxides	28.4	.6	.3	21.3	15.8	6.4	—	.1	2.1	75.0	22.5
Volatile organic compounds	27.5	12.4	11.1	1.1	—	8.9	1.8	3.3	45.1	4.0	32.4
Particles	18.5	1.2	.9	4.6	2.3	10.5	1.1	1.1	6.5	24.9	56.8
Nitrogen oxides	18.1	7.6	6.0	9.1	4.4	.7	.4	.3	42.0	50.3	3.9
Lead	203.8	163.6	156.0	9.6	.3	23.9	6.7	—	80.3	4.7	11.7
1980: Carbon monoxide	76.1	52.6	45.3	7.3	.3	6.3	2.2	7.6	69.1	9.6	8.3
Sulfur oxides	23.9	.9	.4	19.3	16.1	3.8	—	—	3.8	80.8	15.9

Volatile organic compounds	23.0	8.2	6.9	2.2	—	5.2	.6	2.9	35.7	9.6	.4
Particulates	8.5	1.3	1.1	2.4	.8	5.3	.4	1.1	15.3	28.2	38.8
Nitrogen oxides	20.3	9.2	7.2	10.1	6.4	.7	.1	.2	45.3	49.8	3.4
Lead	70.6	59.4	56.4	3.9	.1	3.6	3.7	—	84.1	5.5	5.1
1986: Carbon monoxide	60.9	42.6	35.4	7.2	.3	4.5	1.7	5.0	70.0	11.8	7.4
Sulfur oxides	21.2	.9	.5	17.2	14.3	3.1	—	—	4.2	81.1	14.6
Volatile organic compounds	19.5	6.5	5.3	2.3	—	7.9	.6	2.2	33.3	11.8	40.5
Particulates	6.8	1.4	1.1	1.8	.4	2.5	.3	.8	20.6	26.5	36.8
Nitrogen oxides	19.3	8.5	6.6	10.0	6.6	.6	.1	.1	44.0	51.8	3.1
Lead	8.6	3.5	3.3	.5	.1	1.9	2.7	—	40.7	5.8	22.1

— Represents zero.

[1]Stationary.

Source: U.S. Department of Commerce, *Statistical Abstract of the United States 1989*, 109th ed. (Washington, DC: U.S. Government Printing Office, 1988), p. 200.

and are aimed at protecting human health. These primary standards are intended to provide an "adequate margin of safety," which has been defined to include a "representative sample" of so-called sensitive populations such as the elderly and asthmatics. These standards are set without regard to cost or availability of control technology. The secondary standards are aimed at the promotion of public welfare and the prevention of damage to animals, plant life, and property generally. These standards are based on scientific and medical studies of the pollutants' effects. Table 6.3 shows the current standards that are in effect. As you can see, the primary and secondary standards for some of the seven pollutants are the same.

Because air pollution problems vary from place to place throughout the country, the EPA established 247 air quality control regions. An air quality control region is defined as "an area with definite pollution problems, common pollution sources, and characteristic weather."[8]

The states were responsible for drawing up plans called state implementation plans (SIPs) to attain the standards for the air quality control regions

Table 6.3

National Quality Standards for Ambient Air

Pollutant	Averaging Time	Primary Standards (Health)	Secondary Standards (Welfare, Materials)
Particulates	annual	75 μg/m^3	60 μg/m^3
	24 hour	260 μg/m^3	150 μg/m^3
Sulfur dioxide	annual	80 μg/m^3 (0.03 ppm)	
	24 hour	365 μg/m^3 (0.14 ppm)	
	3 hour	—	1,300 μg/m^3 (0.5 ppm)
Carbon monoxide	8 hour	10 mg/m^3 (9 ppm)	same as primary
	1 hour	40 mg/m^3 (35 ppm)	
Hydrocarbons (nonmethane)	3 hour (6–9 A.M.)	160 μg/m^3 (0.24 ppm)	same as primary
Nitrogen dioxide	annual	100 μg/m^3 (0.05 ppm)	same as primary
Ozone	1 hour	240 μg/m^3 (0.12 ppm)	same as primary
Lead	3 month	1.5 μg/m^3 (0.006 ppm)	

[1]In micrograms or milligrams per cubic meter—μg/m^3 and mg/m^3—and in parts per million—ppm.

Source: EPA, Environmental Protection Agency, *Cleaning the Air: EPA's Program for Air Pollution Control* (Washington, DC: June 1979), p. 10.

within their boundaries. The primary standards were initially to be attained by mid-1975 as required by the 1970 Clean Air Act. When that deadline came, however, only 69 of the 247 air quality control regions were in compliance with all the antipollution standards then in existence. Sixty regions failed the standards for particulates, 42 for sulfur dioxide, 74 for ozone, 54 for carbon monoxide, and 13 for nitrogen dioxide. Some interesting headlines appeared in the newspapers when these goals were not attained, among them, AIR TO BE ILLEGAL—BUT BREATHE ANYWAY.

Obviously some adjustments had to be made. In the 1977 amendments, the primary standards were to be attained as expeditiously as possible but not later than December 31, 1982, with extensions until 1987 for two pollutants most closely related to transportation systems (carbon monoxide and ozone) if the state required an annual automobile inspection of emission controls. Each state was also required to draw up specific plans for bringing each nonattainment region up to standard and for maintaining the purity of air in regions that already met the standards.

In order to enforce the deadlines, the EPA was authorized to impose sanctions on counties and cities failing to meet the standards. The law allowed the EPA to withhold millions of federal dollars for highway construction, new sewage treatment plants, and clean air planning grants as well as to ban construction or modification of most factories, power plants, and other major sources of air pollution. As the deadline approached, some 600 countries, about one-fifth of the total, were not in compliance with at least one of the standards and thus faced possible sanctions.

Congress proposed to amend the Clean Air Act in 1983 to give the EPA more discretion on where and when to impose sanctions and give the states more flexibility to determine how and when to clean up dirty air without the threat of federal action. But efforts to weaken the Clean Air Act became bogged down in politics, and no amendments from Congress were forthcoming. Subsequently, the EPA itself became embroiled in controversy that resulted in a change of leadership. The new EPA adopted a conciliatory approach, giving the states more time to meet national standards as long as the agency believed they were making a good faith effort to comply.[9] However, the EPA used the threat of sanctions to force some states and cities into compliance.[10] Thus the "action-forcing" strategy was continued.

As the 1987 deadline approached, at least 60 cities were expected to be out of compliance with the standards for carbon monoxide and ozone. About one-third of these cities qualified for extensions without incurring additional sanctions, and the EPA drew up a plan for coping with the other cities that were not in compliance. These cities would be subject to a construction ban, but would get new compliance deadlines depending on the seriousness of the problem. State and local officials were to begin reducing emissions immediately in those cities by an average of 3 percent annually. This plan gave the EPA considerable discretion in setting deadlines and instituting enforcement procedures, which, according to some environmental groups, made the necessity of passing new amendments to the Clean Air Act even greater.[11]

Early in 1985, the EPA announced a decision to cut allowable lead levels in gasoline more than 90 percent by January 1, 1986, and to consider a total ban as early as 1988 in light of evidence that airborne lead poses substantial health threats. Several studies discovered lead levels in blood (particularly in children) that could cause brain and nerve damage, mental retardation, anemia, and kidney disorders. Despite increased costs to refiners, the EPA administrator claimed that the reduction in lead content would produce a net saving of at least $6 billion in medical and automobile maintenance costs over the next seven years and would reduce lead usage from 33,000 tons to 5,500 tons a year.[12] A total ban on lead in gasoline proved to be impossible to attain because of damage to old car engines, but because of existing efforts ambient levels of lead in the air declined by 87 percent between 1977 and 1986, and emissions decreased by 94 percent.[13]

Prevention of Significant Deterioration

The 1977 amendments strengthened efforts to maintain air quality in regions where the air was already cleaner than the standards allow. Three kinds of regions were defined. A Class I region includes all national parks and wilderness areas and may include further areas named by the states. In these regions, no additional sulfur or particulate sources are permitted. Class II areas encompass every other Prevention of Significant Deterioration (PSD) region in the nation. In these areas, some industrial development is permitted up to a specified level. Class III areas can have about twice as much pollution from new sources, sometimes even up to the minimum federal standards. Any potential new pollution sources in these regions must obtain a permit before operating and meet a number of other conditions, such as using the best available control methods (BACT). Class III areas are created by reclassifying Class II areas. Thus far only one reclassification has taken place, in part because of the complexity of the reclassification system itself.

For nonattainment areas, the EPA adopted an offset policy. New industrial development is permitted as long as offsetting reductions are made from existing sources for the pollutants to be emitted by the new facilities. These existing sources must reduce their emissions more than enough to compensate for new sources of pollution. For example, in Oklahoma City, several oil firms agreed to put floating tops on large storage tanks to reduce hydrocarbon emissions so General Motors could build an automobile plant there.[14] Companies building new plants or expanding existing ones are also required to meet Lowest Achievable Emission Rates (LAER). This requires companies to limit emissions to the lowest rate achieved by any similar installation or plant anywhere in the United States, regardless of cost or circumstances.

Stationary Sources

Stationary sources of air pollution are also controlled. Typical stationary sources are power plant and factory smokestacks, industrial vents for gases and dust, coke ovens, incinerators, burning dumps, and large furnaces. The state plans required by the 1977 amendments must inventory these sources and determine how they should be reduced to bring the regions into conformance with ambient air quality standards. The EPA monitors the compliance status of about 30,000 stationary air pollution sources that are regulated by the states. Where standards are not being met, states are required to develop new plans and submit these to the EPA for review.

The law currently makes the EPA set emission limits for certain designated pollutants for selected categories of industrial plants and for those that are substantially modified. Control Technique Guidelines (CTGS) focus on retrofitting technology for existing plants. In addition, the EPA sets standards for all major stationary new sources. These limits are called "new source performance standards" (NSPS) and are specific to each industry. These standards set the maximum amount of each kind of pollutant that can be emitted from a new plant's stacks for each unit of the plant's production. As of 1981, the agency had listed 60 categories of sources, from power plants to grain elevators, for which it expected to develop standards. Rules had been issued for 33 sources, but the EPA failed to meet the 1982 deadline for developing NSPS for all 60 categories.

Although all air pollutants are hazardous to some degree, some are considered so dangerous to human health that they are limited individually through the setting of hazardous emission standards, called National Emissions Standards for Hazardous Air Pollutants (NESHAP). Presently such limitations apply to any discharge of asbestos, beryllium, mercury, benzene, arsenic, vinyl chloride, radionuclides, and coke oven emissions. The amounts of these substances that can be emitted into the atmosphere from stationary sources are strictly limited. Other substances are also being considered for this category of control including carbon tetrachloride, chromium, chloroform, and other suspected carcinogens.

In 1989, the EPA announced new rules to protect the public from cancer-causing vapors of benzene. These new regulations forced a broad range of companies, including coke producers, petroleum and chemical plants, and about 200,000 gasoline service stations, to cut emissions of benzene that pose cancer risks to workers and people living near the facilities. The new rules were expected to cost these various industries more than $1 billion. Most of this cost was expected to fall on half of all gasoline stations in the U.S. and on 15,000 bulk gasoline plants and 1,500 gasoline storage terminals. These regulations were considered important because they set a new policy for regulating all sorts of toxic air emissions. The new policy set out to limit chemical emissions so that the greatest number of people possible face no more than a one-in-a-million risk of contracting cancer.[15]

In 1982, the EPA adopted a new policy toward stationary sources of pollution called the bubble concept. This policy gives business more flexibility in meeting EPA standards. The agency assumes that an area which might include several plants is covered by an imaginary bubble. Companies within the bubble are allowed to expand their industrial operations so long as total emissions within the bubble don't increase. This approach gives plant engineers an incentive to find or develop the most inexpensive methods of limiting plantwide emissions of a particular pollutant to a level required in their permit to operate. Companies that reduce or limit their pollution are allowed to sell or trade credits to other companies that are already violating clean air standards and yet want to expand operations.[16]

As of December 31, 1983, the EPA had approved nine generic bubble rules allowing eight states to approve large classes of bubbles without prior EPA approval. Another generic bubble rule had been proposed for approval and 17 more were under development. As of the same date, 35 plant-specific bubbles had been approved by the EPA and eight had been proposed. The total savings resulting from bubbles proposed and approved were estimated at over $200 million. The total savings resulting from all bubbles approved, proposed, or under development were estimated to be over $700 million.[17] Table 6.4 shows several representative bubbles and the cost savings that resulted from them.

Table 6.4

Representative Control Cost Savings from Approved Bubble Transactions

Firm	Industrial Category	Type of ERC[1]	Cost Savings
3M Bristol, PA	Tape and packaging	Process change VOC	$3 million capital $1.2 million annual operating costs
Kentucky Utilities Muhlenberg, KY	Electric utility	Change in control SO_2	$1.3 million annual operating costs
General Motors Defiance County, OH	Foundry	Change in control TSP	$12 million capital costs
National Steel Corp. Weirton, WVA	Integrated steel	Change in control TSP	$30 million capital costs
U.S. Steel Fairless Hills, PA	Integrated steel	Change in control TSP	$27 million capital costs
J.H. Thompson Kennett Square, PA	Greenhouse	Fuel switch SO_2	$100,000 annual operating costs
Scott Paper Co. Chester, PA	Paper mill	Fuel Switch SO_2	$220,000 annual operating costs

[1] Emissions reduction credit.

Source: *Environmental Quality 1983: 14th Annual Report of the Council on Environmental Quality* (Washington, DC: U.S. Government Printing Office, 1984), p 191.

In 1986, the EPA expanded its bubble policy by announcing that it would approve bubbles in areas that had not met federal air pollution standards. Permission would be granted if pollution sources cut their emissions more than 20 percent below the allowable pollution level. Such bubbles must also be consistent with state air quality goals. Approval for new bubbles had ground to a halt over the previous 18 months as the EPA was in the process of revising the policy. When the policy was announced, about 125 bubble applications were pending in 29 states.[18]

Toxic Emissions

After the Bhopal, India, incident, there was increased pressure on the EPA to regulate toxic gas emissions, particularly from large plants. This incident brought long overdue attention to the health threat posed by airborne toxic chemicals from industrial sources. Such chemicals, which can cause cancer and birth and genetic defects, have often escaped regulation. In 1987, the EPA concluded that toxic air emissions may cause as many as 2,000 cancer deaths a year. Toxic air emissions, like acid depositions, can be carried great distances before falling to the ground, and are likely to rise rapidly in developing countries as new polluting factories are built.[19]

After several months of discussion, the EPA announced a new system to notify states about specific chemicals that may present substantial risk locally but little risk nationally. Each state would be required to monitor the major sources of these chemicals and publish the results, but would be free to regulate these emissions as they saw fit, meaning that regulations of a few hazardous pollutants could vary widely from state to state.[20] Also, SARA Title III, known as the Emergency Planning and Community Right-to-Know Act, was passed in 1986 as a response to the Bhopal accident. This title did not prescribe specific action that had to be taken by companies, but rather required them to reveal an unprecedented amount of information about the types and quantities of chemicals they produce, use, and routinely or accidentally release into the environment.[21]

This requirement enables government and the public to scrutinize company activities more closely, and has forced companies to communicate with local communities more fully. As a result, companies are voluntarily taking actions to protect public health and safety from toxic emissions, even though these actions are still in the early stages of development. Companies are driven by concern about their reputations and potential liability to better manage their activities that could result in serious environmental problems. Companies have also become motivated to provide more information about their products to consumers, enabling them to take more precautions in using the products.[22]

The first report of toxic emissions was released in 1989, and showed that emissions in eight states exceeded 100 million pounds. The total included 235 million pounds of carcinogens such as benzene and formal-

dehyde, and 527 million pounds of such neurotoxins as toluene and trichloroethylene. The EPA estimated that such air toxins cause more than
2,000 cases of cancer annually.[23] The 1990 report showed Louisiana to be the
worst polluter, topping Texas which topped the list the previous year. (See
Figure 6.1.) Companies in Louisiana released 716 million pounds of toxic
pollutants into the environment. Even at that, the state showed a 13 percent
drop from the previous year; nationwide, the decrease in toxic emissions was
about 9 percent.[24]

Figure 6.1

**The 20 States with the Largest Toxic Release Inventory Total Releases and
Transfers 1988**

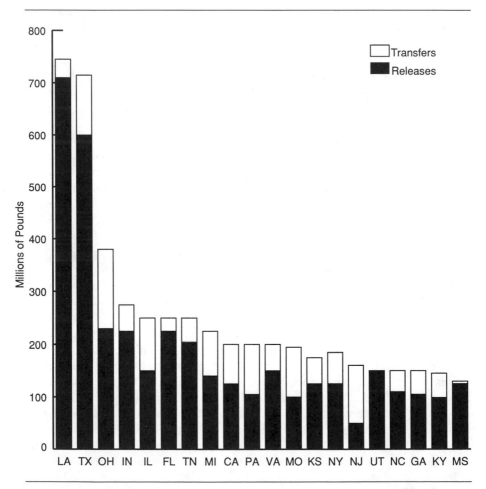

Source: United States Environmental Protection Agency, *Toxics in the Community: National and
Local Perspectives* (Washington, DC: U.S. Government Printing Office, 1990), p. 56.

Mobile Sources

For mobile sources of air pollution, the EPA sets standards for automobile, truck, and aircraft emissions. The motor vehicle emission standards in the Clean Air Act are directed at controlling nitrogen oxides, carbon monoxide, particulate matter, hydrocarbons, and lead. Although volatile organic compounds (VOCs) are not regulated as a criteria pollutant, emissions of these compounds are also controlled. This policy is based on the belief that control of these pollutants can best be accomplished by using control devices such as catalytic converters and electronic carburetors on autos and other vehicles. A near disaster was averted in 1977, when Detroit was producing 1978 model cars that were not in compliance with the standards for carbon monoxide and nitrogen oxides that were to go into effect that year. The auto industry claimed that the technology did not exist to meet these standards and asked for a relaxation that was finally granted, but not until a substantial number of cars had been produced for inventory.

The primary standards for carbon monoxide and hydrocarbons were set at a 90 percent reduction based on 1970 levels. Nitrogen oxide emissions were to be reduced 75 percent by 1985. The 90 percent reduction standard for hydrocarbons was achieved in 1980, and in 1981, the standards for carbon monoxide and nitrogen oxides were also achieved.[25] However, a study completed by the EPA in 1985 found that the percentage of cars meeting federal standards dropped to about 40 percent for the 1981 and 1982 model years, from about 65 percent in 1980, the year before tighter emission standards went into effect. Nevertheless, the agency didn't expect the rate of pollution-related recalls to increase, because most of the cars flunking the standards were close to compliance.[26]

In early 1990, the American Lung Association released a study stating that air pollution from motor vehicles is responsible for $40 to $50 billion in annual health care costs, and as many as 120,000 unnecessary or premature deaths. Annual health care costs actually range from as little as $4 billion to as much as $93 billion, but a $40 to $50 billion range appears to be the most realistic estimate. Release of the study was said to represent an attempt to identify the costs associated with leaving the nation's clean air standards unchanged, and make a strong case for more stringent vehicle controls on emissions.[27]

A controversial proposal for auto emission control was proposed by Don Stedman, a University of Denver chemist, after several years of research. "Modern cars are so clean that tightening standards or switching fuels is a total waste of money," he insisted. His research showed that only a tiny fraction of the cars on the road, perhaps as small as 8 percent, account for more than half the pollution. Instead of mandating lower emissions for new cars, he believed remote sensors that he had developed and used for his research should be used to spot gross polluters. Owners of these cars could then be sent notices to have their cars fixed. The cars causing the most pollution are those with broken or disabled pollution controls or those badly in need of a tune-up. Supporters say that his approach could reduce pollution in some cities by 30 percent or more, and be cheaper than many inspection programs.[28]

New Directions

The Bush administration in 1989 made a proposal for improving air quality to break the impasse that had existed for several years over amending the Clean Air Act. The proposal initially called for a 50 percent reduction in acid rain-producing sulfur dioxide emissions by the turn of the century, a 40 percent tightening of emissions standards for hydrocarbons from automobiles, a 75 percent cut in cancer-causing toxics emitted into the atmosphere over an unspecified period, and the use of alternative fuels that burn cleaner than gasoline.[29] Such fuels would be mandated in cities that have the worst smog problems. The proposal touched off a debate over its merit, and as the bill wound its way through the House and Senate, the inevitable compromises began to weaken some of the provisions[30]

The bill that eventually passed Congress and was signed by the president in 1990 limits the output of industrial pollutants that cause acid rain, calls for the elimination of chemicals that threaten the protective ozone layer, aims for a major reduction in the release of toxic and cancer-causing chemicals from chemical plants and other facilities, and requires a reduction in motor vehicle emissions that may require the sale of cleaner burning gasoline in the nine smoggiest cities in the country. In a pilot program that could eventually be expanded, auto manufacturers will have to build thousands of cars for Southern California that operate on alternative fuels such as natural gas or methanol.[31]

Specifically, sulfur dioxide emissions will have to be cut in half by the year 2000 to 10 million tons annually, and nitrogen oxides reduced by 33 percent to 4 million tons annually. These cuts will have to begin by 1992, and will cost coal-burning utilities about $3 billion a year to burn low-sulfur fuel or install scrubbers. Passenger cars will have to emit 60 percent less nitrogen oxides and 40 percent less hydrocarbons by the year 2003, and pollution control equipment must last ten years before it needs to be replaced. This provision will force oil companies to develop new kinds of gasoline and develop alternative fuels for automobiles. Consumers may have to pay 6 to 10 cents more for a gallon of gasoline and $600 more for a new automobile.[32]

The oil and gas industry claims that cleaner gas could require up to $30 billion in spending for new fuel tanks and retooled refineries. But the industry was said to have the capacity to make cleaner gas, and at least one company, ARCO, came out with a new cleaner burning formula that captured 33 percent of the market. The development of alternative fuels is another problem. These fuels, such as ethanol and methanol, improve combustion and reduce emissions of carbon monoxide and unburned hydrocarbons. But the alcohol in these fuels absorbs water when transported by pipeline, so it must be stored in separate tanks and blended with gasoline at terminals around the country. Ethanol, which comes from corn, could cost the oil companies $1 billion for each point of market share it captures.[33]

By the year 2003, there must be a 90 percent reduction in emissions of 189 toxic and cancer-causing chemicals. This provision will require most large manufacturers and utilities and many small businesses to invest heavily in new pollution control equipment that will raise the prices of many goods and services. Finally, CFCs and other ozone-destroying chemicals will have to be phased out of use entirely by the year 2000, a provision that will affect refrigerator and air-conditioner manufacturers and many other facilities that use these chemicals in products or in production processes.[34]

These new rules will be phased in over a 15-year period to protect jobs and the economy in general. Utilities that burn high-sulfur coal, which are concentrated in the Midwest, will be one of the industries most affected by the new regulations. For the first time, many small businesses, from dry cleaners to auto repair shops, will be required to invest in pollution control

---

The Pros and Cons of Alternative Fuels

Ethanol: Made from corn and other carbohydrate sources, has a higher octane rating than gasoline. Its higher oxygen content permits fuel to burn more efficiently, reducing carbon monoxide, benzene, and other toxics. It would reduce imports and benefit the farm economy. But, at least for now, its higher cost requires subsidies. It has a lower energy content than gasoline, is hard to ignite in cold weather, and is difficult to transport through pipelines.

Methanol: Made from natural gas and coal, reduces carbon monoxide and other pollutants, has more octane and mixes easily with gasoline. Its drawbacks include emissions of toxics like formaldehyde, its higher cost and lower energy content. Much of it is imported, so it would increase energy dependence.

Compressed Natural Gas: The least expensive alternative. It substantially reduces hydrocarbon and carbon monoxide emissions and requires no refining. There is an abundant domestic supply. But natural gas is less powerful. It has to be injected by hose in a slow process and requires large on-board compression tanks.

Electricity: Touted as the cleanest and quietest power source. Until recently it was considered a long way from commercial development. General Motors recently said it will mass-produce a battery-powered car, but they didn't say how soon. GM says the car, using an 850-pound battery that would charge in two hours, will accelerate from zero to 60 mph in eight seconds, run 125 miles before recharging.

Source: Copyright 1990, *USA Today*, May 22, 1990, p. 5A. Used with permission.

equipment. Because they were able to plead financial hardship successfully, steelmakers have until the year 2020 to eliminate cancer-causing emissions from their coke ovens, as long as they take interim steps to reduce that pollution. The total bill for the new regulations is expected to be about $25 billion a year or more, and will affect prices of many goods and services for consumers.[35]

In order to implement the new rules, the EPA expects to have its air program funding boosted as much as 30 percent to hire additional staffers and cover other program costs. The agency has its work cut out, as it has issued only seven regulations covering toxic air emissions in 20 years, but now is supposed to write scores of them quickly to tell industry how to comply with the new legislation. Purchase of new pollution controls will be difficult for business in a sluggish economy. And new regulatory schemes such as the market for pollution credits to control sulfur dioxide are completely untested. The bill is expected to cause plenty of pain and dislocation, and will undoubtedly require many adjustments as business complies with its many provisions.[36]

THE NEW CLEAN AIR BILL

Smog

Some 96 areas missed the deadline for meeting health standards for ozone, a main ingredient of smog. The new bill requires that all but nine areas comply by November 1999, all but Los Angeles, Baltimore, and New York by November 2005, Baltimore and the New York metropolitan area by November 2007, and Los Angeles by November 2020.

Areas that are moderately polluted or worse must cut smog 15 percent within six years. After that, areas that are seriously polluted or worse must make 9 percent improvements every three years until they meet the standards.

Tougher tailpipe standards are phased in starting with 1994 models to cut nitrogen oxides by 60 percent and hydrocarbons by 30 percent. Even deeper cuts are required for 2003 models if the EPA finds they're cost effective and needed. These standards have to be maintained for 10 years or 100,000 miles.

Warranties on pollution control equipment must last eight years or 80,000 miles for catalytic converters, electronic emissions control unit, and onboard emissions diagnostic equipment and two years or 24,000 miles for other pollution gear beginning with model year 1995.

Special nozzles are required on gasoline pumps in almost 60 smoggy areas. Also, more effective fume-catching canisters may be phased in on all new cars, starting in the mid-1990s. Devices are also required on cars to alert drivers to problems with pollution control equipment.

Industrial polluters that emit as little as 10 or 25 tons of smog-forming chemicals a year may have to make cuts, depending on the severity of smog in their area. The previous law sets the limit at 100 tons a year. Forty-three other categories of smaller pollution sources, including printing plants, are also regulated.

Alternative Fuels

Beginning in 1995, all gasoline sold in the nine cities in the United States with the highest ozone concentrations must be cleaner burning, reformulated gasoline that cuts emissions of hydrocarbons and toxic pollutants by 15 percent compared to gasoline sold in 1990. By the year 2000, the reductions must equal 20 percent.

Starting with 1998 models, a certain percentage of new vehicles purchased by owners of fleets of ten or more vehicles in the two dozen cities with the highest ozone and carbon monoxide concentrations must be capable of using clean fuels which will run considerably cleaner than today's autos. By the year 2001, even cleaner models must be produced.

By the model year 1996, car makers must begin producing at least 150,000 clean-fuel vehicles annually under a California pilot program designed to demonstrate vehicles that can run on nongasoline fuels, such as natural gas and methanol.

Toxic Emissions

Only seven chemicals have been regulated since 1970, but over the next ten years, the majority of polluting plants must use the best technology available to reduce their emissions of 189 toxic chemicals by 90 percent.

For any remaining cancer risks, the EPA is required to set health-based standards that produce ample margins of safety — a cancer risk of not more than about one in 10,000 — for people living near factories. Coke ovens are eligible for extensions until 2020 if they made extrastringent reductions in the first round.

The alternative fuels program should significantly reduce toxic emissions from vehicles. Additional cuts from cars or fuel is required after an EPA study. Benzene and formaldehyde must be controlled.

Acid Rain

In the first phase, the 111 dirtiest power plants in 21 states must cut sulfur dioxide emissions by 1995 for a total cut nationwide of 5 million tons. Two-year extensions can be given to plants that commit to buy scrubbing devices that allow continued use of high-sulfur coal.

In the second phase, more than 200 additional power plants must make sulfur dioxide cuts by 2000, for a total nationwide cut of 10 million tons. This deadline can be extended until 2004 for plants that use new clean coal technology.

An innovative trading system is created in which utilities that made extra-deep pollution reductions get credits they can sell or swap to utilities that want to increase their emissions. Bonus pollution credits are awarded to dirty utilities that install scrubbers and to power plants in high-growth and extremely low-polluting states plus the hard-hit Midwest.

A nationwide cap on utility sulfur dioxide emissions is imposed after the year 2000.

Utilities must cut nitrogen oxide emissions by 2 million tons a year, or about 25 percent, beginning in 1995.

No help is provided for rate payers beyond changes in the trading system. Coal miners and others put out of work because of clean air rules may quality for extra weeks of unemployment pay under a $250 million five-year job assistance program.

ACID RAIN

Acid rain is believed to be largely a human-made problem directly traceable to the burning of fossil fuels in power plants, factories, and smelting operations, and to a somewhat lesser extent, the burning of gasoline in automobiles. The burning of these fuels releases sulfur dioxide, nitrogen oxides, and traces of toxic metals like mercury and cadmium into the atmosphere to mix with water vapor. Acid rain then results from chemical reactions that follow to produce dilute solutions of nitric and sulfuric acids. These solutions, or acidic depositions, come down to ground level in the form of hail, snow, fog, rain, or even in dry particles. (See Figure 6.2.) Acid depositions are formally defined as having a pH level under 5.6 (a neutral solution has a level of pH 7, (See Figure 6.3).[37]

    Acid rain causes many serious environmental problems. When it enters a body of water, acid rain carries a deadly burden of toxic metals that can stunt or kill aquatic life. In the Adirondack Mountains in New York, more than 150 lakes that had previously supported trout life were thought to be fishless due to the high acid content of the lakes.[38] As the buffering effect of the acid-neutralizing minerals in the water diminishes, these lakes appear to die suddenly and turn clear and bluish. Surface waters that have a low acid-buffering capacity are unable to neutralize the acid effectively. Snowmelt in

Figure 6.2

Acid Rain

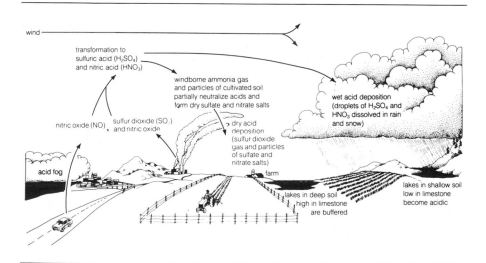

Source: From *Living in the Environment: An Introduction to Environmental Studies* 6/E by G. Tyler Miller, Jr. © 1990 by Wadsworth, Inc. Reprinted by permission of the publisher.

Figure 6.3

How Acid Is Acid Rain?

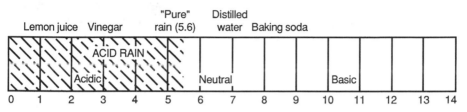

The pH scale ranges from 0 to 14. A value of 7.0 is neutral. Readings below 7.0 are acidic; readings above 7.0 are alkaline. The more pH decreases below 7.0 the more acidity increases.

Because the pH scale is logarithmic, there is a tenfold difference between one number and the next one to it. Therefore, a drop in pH from 6.0 to 5.0 represents a tenfold increase in acidity; while a drop from 6.0 to 4.0 represents a hundredfold increase.

All rain is slightly acidic. Only rain with a pH below 5.6 is considered "acid rain."

Source: Environmental Protection Agency, *Meeting the Environmental Challenge* (Washington, DC: U.S. Government Printing Office, 1990), p. 9.

northern areas can quickly kill a lake because all acids accumulated in the snow are released at once. Because of the freezing point depression phenomenon combined with the recrystallization of snow after it falls, the most acidic snow crystals will melt first thereby releasing 50 to 80 percent of the acids in the first 30 percent of snowmelt.[39]

When acid rain is absorbed into the soil, it can rob plants of nutrients because it breaks down minerals containing calcium, potassium, and aluminum. The aluminum may eventually reach lakes through water tables and streams and further contribute to the suffocation of fish.[40] Acid rain is suspected of spiriting away mineral nutrients from the soil on which forests thrive. Areas with acid-neutralizing compounds in the soil can experience years of acid rain without serious problems. But the thin soils of the mountainous and glaciated Northeast have very little buffering capacity, which makes them vulnerable to damage. Acid rain makes a corrosive assault on buildings and water systems that costs millions of dollars annually. It may also pose a substantial threat to human health, principally by contaminating public drinking water.[41]

Over 80 percent of sulfur dioxide emissions in the United States originate in the 31 states east of or bordering the Mississippi River, and more than half the acid rain falling on the eastern United States originates from the heavy concentration of coal-and-oil burning power and industrial plants in seven central and upper midwestern states. Prevailing winds transport these emissions hundreds of miles to the Northeast across state and national

---

Acid Rain

Acid rain is the term loosely used to refer to all forms of acid deposition which can occur in the forms of rain, snow, fog, dust, or gas. Man-made emissions of sulfur dioxide (SO_2) and nitrogen oxides. (NO_x) are the principal causes. These pollutants are transformed into acids in the atmosphere where they may travel hundreds of miles before falling in some form of acid rain. Acid rain has been measured with a pH of less than 2.0 — more acidic than lemon juice. The political implications of acid rain are an important issue, as the pollutants causing acid rain may originate within the political boundary, yet the effects of these pollutants are realized within another.

EPA research in the 1980s has increased scientific understanding of the effects of acid rain, including the sterilization of lakes and streams, detrimental reproductive effects on fish and amphibians, possible forest dieback and deterioration of man-made structures such as buildings and sculptures. These effects have been most obvious in the eastern U.S. and Canada, and in much of both western and eastern Europe. The Clean Air Act of 1970 helped to curb the growth of SO_2 and NO_x emissions in the U.S., and the 1990 Clean Air Act Amendments will bring significant additional reductions.

Source: Environmental Protection Agency, *Meeting the Environmental Challenge* (Washington, DC: U.S. Government Printing Office, 1990), p. 9.

---

boundaries. The acidity of the precipitation falling over much of this region has a pH of 4.0 to 4.2, which is 30 to 40 times greater than the acidity of the normal precipitation that fell on this region in previous decades. (See Figure 6.4.) Acid rain costs the United States at least $6 billion a year according to the National Academy of Sciences, and costs will rise sharply if strong action is not taken. The cost of reducing acid rain could run from $1.2 billion to $20 billion, depending on the extent of cleanup and the technology employed.[42]

The phenomenon of acid rain has caused a problem in the relations between the United States and Canada. Environmental officials in Canada have projected the loss of 48,000 lakes by the end of the century if nothing is done to reduce the emissions that produce acid rain. Some 2,000 to 4,000 lakes in Ontario have become so acidified that they can no longer support trout and bass, and some 1,300 more in Quebec are said to be on the brink of destruction. Canadians are also worried that acid rain will harm the forestry and related industries that provide jobs for one in every ten Canadians and earn $14 billion a year. The Canadian government contends that about 70 percent of the acid rain it receives comes from the United States, primarily from heavily industrialized areas in the Midwest. Thus they support legislation that would require a 50 percent cut in high-sulfur emissions from U.S. industrial sources.[43]

Figure 6.4

Areas Where Precipitation in the East Is Below pH5

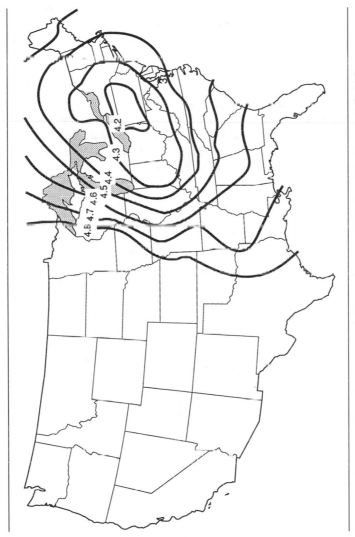

Source: Environmental Protection Agency, *Meeting the Environmental Challenge* (Washington, DC: U.S. Government Printing Office, 1990), p. 9.

Before the 1970 Clean Air Act, sulfur dioxide and nitrogen oxide emissions in the United States were increasing dramatically. (See Figure 6.5.) Between 1940 and 1970, annual sulfur dioxide emissions had increased by more than 55 percent and nitrogen oxide emissions had almost tripled. By 1986, however, annual sulfur dioxide emissions had declined by 21 percent and nitrogen oxide emissions had increased only 7 percent, even though the economy and the combustion of fossil fuels had grown substantially over the same time period. More reductions, however, need to be accomplished to solve the problem.[44]

Solving the problem of acid rain is not easy, because there are not only conflicts between nations, but between companies and certain regions of the country as well. Coal producers from the western states argue that the quickest and least expensive way to control acid rain is to require increased use of the low-sulfur coal that they produce. High-sulfur coal producers in the eastern part of the country argue that such a policy would cost them

Figure 6.5

Sulfur Dioxide Emissions 1940–1986

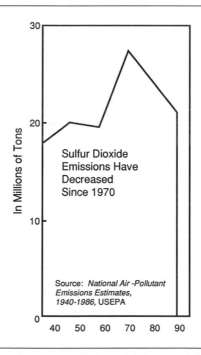

Sulfur Dioxide
Emissions Have
Decreased
Since 1970

Source: *National Air-Pollutant Emissions Estimates, 1940-1986*, USEPA

Source: Environmental Protection Agency, *Environmental Progress and Challenges: EPA's Update* (Washington, DC: U.S. Government Printing Office, 1988), p. 28.

billions of dollars in lost sales and force the layoffs of thousands of coal miners. They advocate that coal burning plants should install expensive pollution control equipment.[45]

Most utilities, however, are opposed to costly emission control programs. They argue that "(1) scientific data on acid rain are still fuzzy, especially in the crucial matter of precisely who is responsible; (2) costs of eliminating sulfur dioxide emissions by installing expensive scrubbers (which collect harmful substances before they are expelled) are prohibitive; and (3) it is questionable whether the situation is critical enough to justify immediate action."[46] Utilities in the Midwest, where most of the acid rain is said to be produced, say that if they are made to bear the full cost of emission controls, the economic backbone of the region will be broken. But a plan to impose a nationwide tax on all utilities, and thus spread the cost across consumers in the entire country, is opposed by utilities in the Southwest and the West who are unwilling to pay for solutions that will primarily benefit people in the Northeast and Canada.[47]

In November of 1983, there were at least ten acid rain bills already before Congress. The EPA administrator and White House officials were trying to draft compromise legislation. Their idea was to require cutbacks of between 25 to 50 percent in total sulfur dioxide emissions in a half dozen or so midwestern and eastern states in the next few years, with deeper cuts required later. Even a modest acid rain control plan, however, was estimated to cost between $1 and $2 billion annually in extra operating and capital costs.[48] Thus the costs for reducing acid rain aren't trivial.

In 1980, a National Acid Precipitation Assessment Program (NAPAP) was initiated to study the problem. Part of NAPAP included a National Surface Water Survey, which found the four subregions with the highest percentages of acidic lakes were the Adirondacks of New York, where 10 percent of the lakes were found to be acidic; the Upper Peninsula of Michigan where 10 percent of the lakes were also found to be acidic; the Okefenokee Swamp in Florida, which is naturally acidic; and the lakes in the Florida Panhandle where the acidity is unknown. The 1988 Stream Survey, which was also part of the program, determined that approximately 2.7 percent of the total stream reaches sampled in the mid-Atlantic and Southeast are acidic. The major cause of sulfates in streams was found to be atmospheric deposition.[49]

The study also found that air pollution is a factor in the decline of both managed and natural forests. But there seemed to be no direct impacts to seedlings by acidic precipitation or gaseous sulfur dioxide and nitrogen oxides at ambient levels. Ozone was suspected to be the leading pollutant that stressed regional forests and reduced growth. The NAPAP assessment also indicated that there are no measurable consistent effects on crop yield from the direct effects of simulated acidic rain at ambient levels of acidity.

Finally, the report concluded that there were too many uncertainties involved in assessing the effect of acid rain on materials or human health to be able to draw any firm conclusions.[50]

In general, the director of the project stated that "no apparent trend in the acidity of rainfall has been detected" in his testimony before Congress. "Because of complex atmospheric reactions, percentage reductions in emissions may not result in similar percentage reduction in depositions," he added. These statements challenged the claims made in a 1983 National Academy of Science report, which held that the relationship between emissions and depositions was proportional.[51] This latter report was widely used as the basis for proposals to cut sulfur dioxide emissions. The NAPAP report, however, did not calm fears about the effects of acid rain and the need to further cut sulfur dioxide and nitrogen oxide emissions.

The new Clean Air Act passed in 1990 contains provisions for large reductions in emissions of sulfur dioxide and nitrogen oxides to reduce acid rain to manageable levels. By the year 2000, SO_2 emissions are to be reduced nationwide by 10 million tons below 1980 levels, which is a 40 percent decrease. Emissions of NO_x will also be reduced by 2 million tons below levels that would occur in the year 2000 without new controls. This reduction represents about a 10 percent reduction from 1980 levels. These reductions will be achieved by instituting a variety of reforms aimed at limiting emissions after 1995 from electric power plants and other sources. These sources will be allowed to "trade and bank" their allowable emissions, something of a market-based approach to pollution control, which is hoped will achieve regional and national emission targets in the most cost-effective manner.[52]

There are two general methods of controlling emissions that cause acid rain: one focusing on the outputs of the combustion process by treating pollutants after they have already formed but prior to entering the atmosphere, the other focusing on inputs to the combustion process by changing the amount or composition of pollution-causing fuels. The most significant successes in terms of controlling outputs have been with the use of scrubber systems, which are included in the smokestacks of new coal-burning plants or retrofitted to the smokestacks of existing plants. Scrubbers work by forcing calcium-rich limestone into the flue emissions, where the calcium combines with the sulfur oxides and causes a neutralizing effect. Scrubbers are expensive to install, however, and create sludge, which has its own disposal problems.

Fluidized bed combustion is an example of an input approach aimed at changing certain qualities of the fuel before it is burned. This method involves mashing coal into a fine powder and then mixing it with certain chemicals, ultimately creating conditions where a more complete combustion of the fuel can be achieved. Another option is coal gasification and liquification where the fuel is turned into a liquid much like the fuel that was once used for streetlamps and certain coal-burning stoves. When this type of fuel is used, the emissions are in the form of a removable gas, which can be captured and treated. Another method called coal washing involves crushing the coal into a fine powder again and then "washing" it during combustion with calcium-based absorbents to soak up sulfur dioxide.[53]

INDOOR AIR POLLUTION

According to the EPA, there is a growing body of scientific evidence indicating that the air within homes and other buildings can be more polluted than outdoor air even in the largest and most industrialized cities that have serious outdoor air pollution. Indoor air pollutants include radon, asbestos, tobacco smoke, formaldehyde, airborne pesticide residues, chloroform, perchloroethylene (associated with dry cleaning), paradichlorobenzene (from mothballs and air fresheners), and a broad array of airborne pathogens (See Figure 6.6). The EPA has developed general information and specific guidelines designed to raise public consciousness about indoor air pollution and strategies to reduce and prevent such pollution. These guidelines include documents offering guidance on construction of new homes and rehabilitation of existing homes.[54]

The indoor air pollution problem is exacerbated in tightly constructed buildings that in the interest of saving energy do not let heat and cold escape. Thus indoor air pollutants are trapped. Since most people spend 90 percent of their time indoors, many may be exposed to unhealthy concentrations of pollutants. People most susceptible to pollution, the aged, the ill, and children, spend nearly all of their time indoors. The degree of risk depends on how well buildings are ventilated and the type, mixture, and amount of pollutants in the building. (See Exhibit 6.2.) Long-term effects of exposure range from impairment of the nervous system to cancer.[55]

Some experts believe our current indoor air pollution problems are partly the result of energy conservation measures implemented after the Arab oil embargo of 1973 when fuel prices skyrocketed. Homeowners and building managers sought ways to conserve energy resources. Ventilation standards were lowered in offices, for example, and 5 cubic feet of fresh air per minute per person became the recommended standard. The previous standard had been 10 cubic feet per minute per person. Windows that opened were replaced with mechanical ventilation systems. Homeowners caulked and weatherstripped around windows and doors and used new insulation products such as foams containing formaldehyde. Tightening up buildings reduced fuel bills, but also limited the natural ventilation that diluted stale and contaminated indoor air inside.[56]

The EPA is conducting research to identify and rank the health risks that result from exposure to individual indoor pollutants or mixtures of multiple indoor pollutants. More research is needed to find better methods

Figure 6.6

Air Pollution in the Home

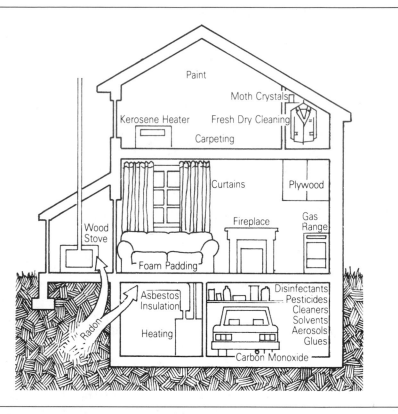

Source: Environmental Protection Agency, *Meeting the Environmental Challenge* (Washington, DC: U.S. Government Printing Office, 1990), p. 11.

for diagnosing building-related illnesses and correcting their causes. A variety of control measures need to be identified and analyzed, including product substitution or modification, and changes in building design and ventilation. The EPA is exploring strategies to address high-risk indoor air problems, which may include regulations as well as other approaches such as public education, technical assistance, and training programs.[57] Also needed are effective, easily operated, and commercially available devices to monitor personal exposure to indoor air pollution.

The EPA has taken action on asbestos, volatile organic compounds (VOCs) in drinking water, and certain pesticides. Schools are required to inspect for asbestos, to prepare management plans where there is a problem, and to take action when they find friable (easily crumbled) asbestos. Maxi-

Exhibit 6.2

Indoor pollution: The worst offenders

Pollutant	Danger	Source	Control
Formaldehyde	Eye, nose, and throat irritation, headaches, nausea. Possible cause of nasopharyngeal cancer.	Thousands of products and furnishings, including furniture, carpet, plywood, particleboard and urea-formaldehyde foam insulation.	Increase home ventilation, and seal sources such as particleboard. Test and seal walls containing urea formaldehyde foam.
Combustion Products	Headaches, dizziness, respiratory ailments. High concentrations of carbon monoxide can be fatal.	Gas stoves, furnaces, other fuel-burning appliances. Tobacco smoke.	Make sure appliances are properly maintained and vented to the outdoors. Install an exhaust fan above gas stove.
Household Products	Wide range of health effects, including resiratory irritation, damage to central nervous system, liver, or kidneys, possibly cancer.	Aerosol sprays, cleaning products, paints, solvents, glues, pesticides.	Follow the label and use with plenty of ventilation. Dispose of properly, preferably through a local household toxics collection program. Substitute nontoxic products.
Tobacco Smoke	"Passive smokers" may face greater risk of lung cancer, other cancers, heart disease. Children of smokers show increased prevalence of respiratory ailments.	Smokers.	Nonsmokers should avoid tobacco smoke. Smokers should isolate themselves, increase home ventilation and air filtration. Better yet, they can kick the habit.
Radon	Second leading cause of lung cancer in the United States.	Soil and rocks beneath home, some groundwater, some building materials.	Test your home, then seek professional guidance if necessary. An air-to-air heat exchanger can reduce radon concentrations. Sealing basement floors and openings around pipes and air ducts can prevent radon from entering homes.

Source: Make Lipske, "How Safe Is the Air Inside Your Home?" *National Wildlife*, Vol. 25, No. 3 (April-May, 1987), pp. 36–37.

What Should Be Done About Asbestos?

Asbestos is a group of minerals made up of tiny fibers. Unless completely sealed into a product, asbestos can easily crumble into a dust of tiny fibers small enough to become suspended in the air and inhaled into the lungs, where they remain for many years.

Considerable evidence indicates that exposure to even a small amount of asbestos fibers can cause lung cancer, mesothelioma (a cancer of the lung and abdominal lining), or asbestosis (a chronic lung condition that eventually makes breathing nearly impossible) 15 to 40 years later. Children are especially vulnerable.

The EPA estimates that exposure to asbestos in U.S. schools, shopping malls, office buildings, and apartment buildings causes 3,000 to 12,000 deaths a year from cancer and other illnesses. Workers who smoke and are exposed to asbestos have a much greater chance of dying from lung cancer than those who don't smoke.

Between 1900 and 1986, over 28 million metric tons (31 million tons) of asbestos were used in the United States for hundreds of purposes. Much of it was sprayed on ceilings and other parts of schools and public and private buildings for fireproofing, sound deadening, insulating heaters and pipes, and decorating walls and ceilings, until these uses were banned in 1974.

In 1989 the EPA ordered a ban on almost all other uses of asbestos such as brake linings, roofing shingles, and water pipes by 1997. This ban will eliminate 94% of the asbestos used in the United States. EPA officials estimate that the proposed ban would prevent at least 1,900 cancer deaths over the next 15 years. Higher costs for products made with asbestos substitutes would cost each consumer on the average a total of $10 during this period. Representatives of the asbestos industry in the United States and Canada (which produces most of the asbestos used in the United States) oppose the EPA ban and may challenge it in court. They contend that with proper precautions asbestos products can be safely used and that the costs of the ban outweigh the benefits.

In 1988 the EPA estimated that one of every seven commercial and public buildings in the United States contains easily broken asbestos. These buildings include Manhattan's World Trade Center, Chicago's John Hancock Building, Houston's Astrodome, and possibly a building you live or work in. In two-thirds of these buildings the asbestos has been so damaged that it is likely to become airborne and be inhaled. This is a potential threat to millions of people, including 15 million students and 1.4 million employees in elementary and secondary schools, especially those built between 1945 and 1978.

In 1986 Congress passed the Asbestos Hazards Emergency Response Act. It required all schools to have a qualified inspector check for asbestos and submit plans for containment or removal by May 8, 1989.* It is estimated that removing asbestos from schools will cost $3.2 billion and cleanup of all buildings will cost $51 billion. Financially strapped schools cannot afford such expenditures without increased local taxes or help from state and federal governments.

Some analysts argue that the benefits of asbestos removal from schools are not worth the costs, except in clear cases where ceilings and walls are deteriorating and releasing asbestos fibers. They call for sealing and other forms of containment instead of removal of most asbestos and point out that improper removal can release more hazardous fibers than sealing off asbestos that is not crumbling.

But some leading U.S. health experts, such as Dr. Irving Selikoff, contend that even the best available containment methods leave an unacceptable margin of risk for those exposed to asbestos fibers. What do you think should be done?

*For information on the control or removal of asbestos call the EPA's Toxic Substances Control Hotline at 1-(202) 554-1404 or write the EPA. You can also get a copy of *Asbestos in the Home* from the U.S. Government Printing Office, Washington, D.C. 20402.

Source: From *Living in the Environment: An Introduction To Environmental Studies* 6/E by G. Tyler Miller, Jr. © 1990 by Wadsworth, Inc. Reprinted by permission of the publisher.

mum contaminant levels have been issued for eight VOCs in water supplies serving more than 25 people. There are plans to issue 75 more drinking water standards for a wide variety of chemicals, which should reduce the levels of these compounds in indoor air. The EPA has also acted to control exposure to a number of pesticides that are believed to contribute to indoor air pollution.[58]

Exposure to indoor radon is also believed to be a serious environmental health problem, perhaps second only to smoking as a cause of lung cancer. Radon is a radioactive, colorless, odorless, naturally occurring gas that results from the radioactive decay of radium 226 found in many types of rocks and soils. It seeps through the soil and collects in homes by entering cracks in the foundation. When inhaled, radon can adhere to particles and then lodge deep in the lungs, increasing the risk of cancer. The EPA estimates that radon may be responsible for 5,000 to 20,000 lung cancer deaths per year, an estimate supported by a National Academy of Sciences study.[59] Radon problems have been identified in every state, and millions of homes throughout the country, according to the EPA, have elevated radon levels. In 1988, the EPA and the Surgeon General recommended that all Americans (other than those living in apartment buildings above the second floor) test their homes for radon.[60]

The radon program instituted by the EPA includes five major elements: problem assessment, mitigation and prevention, capability development, public information, and interagency cooperation. The EPA is conducting surveys to identify areas with high radon levels. (See Figure 6.7.) It is also developing techniques to reduce radon levels by sealing cracks, improving ventilation, and like measures. The agency also provides information on how to make radon measurements and how to evaluate health risks associated with different levels. Homeowners are also given information on ways to reduce radon levels in both indoor air and in drinking water.[61]

In office buildings, a phenomenon called the "sick building syndrome" began to emerge as a health hazard. (See Exhibit 6.3.) Complaints about headache, nausea, sore throat, or fatigue were commonplace among office

Figure 6.7 **Areas with Potentially High Radon Levels**

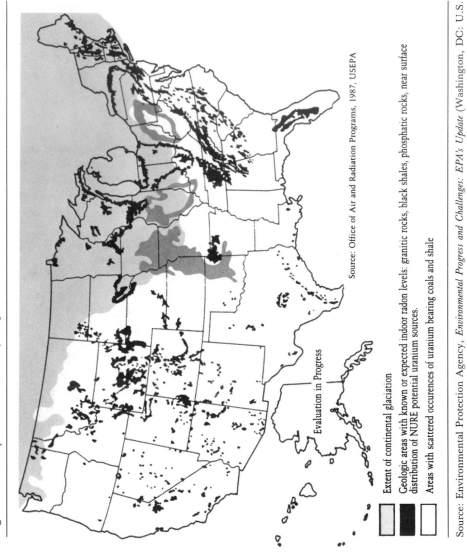

Source: Office of Air and Radiation Programs, 1987, USEPA

Extent of continental glaciation

Geologic areas with known or expected indoor radon levels: granitic rocks, black shales, phosphatic rocks, near surface distribution of NURE potential uranium sources.

Areas with scattered occurences of uranium bearing coals and shale

Evaluation in Progress

Source: Environmental Protection Agency, *Environmental Progress and Challenges: EPA's Update* (Washington, DC: U.S. Government Printing Office, 1988), p. 28.

Exhibit 6.3

What Are the Symptoms of a Sick Building?

The symptoms of "sick building" syndrome can mimic those of many diseases, from flu and colds to more serious lung disorders. Among the many signs of this malady are:

- Headaches
- Sinus problems
- Upper respiratory distress
- Eye irritation
- Runny nose
- Cough
- Dizziness
- Shortness of breath
- Nausea
- Tightness in the chest

One of the ways to help judge whether an illness might be related to a building or a home is to ask yourself the following questions:

- Do the symptoms go away when you leave your office? If so, there's a chance you are being exposed to some irritant in the work place.
- Are the symptoms worse as the week progresses, get better on the weekend and then become worse again Monday? Such a cycle could indicate a sick building-associated illness. One way to tell is by keeping a diary of your symptoms, recommends Dr. Rebecca Bascum, director of the University of Maryland's environtional research facility. "A lot of people get headaches and feel bad," Bascum says. "They notice their headaches more at work when they have to produce, but on looking at a diary realize that they have headaches other times and that it is not a building-related problem."

- Do any co-workers also suffer?
- Have you had any water problems in your office that might have left carpeting or a ceiling tile damp?
- Is your office new? New carpeting and furniture may emit formaldehyde or plasticizers for a few months.
- Has your office been painted recently, remodeled, cleaned extensively or exterminated? Any one of these can leave high levels of irritants that might be troubling to you.
- Do you work with smokers?

If you are concerned about your home, ask yourself the same questions, only keep in mind a different time frame. Do your symptoms get better when you are away from home? Are they worse on weekends and better during weekdays? If so, you may have a problem in your house. But remember that what people sometimes attribute to being part of the sick building syndrome can also be traced to other problems. If you work at a computer terminal for eight hours, chances are your eyes will be tired at the end of the day, explains Dr. Michael Hodgson of the University of Pittsburgh, and it could have absolutely nothing to do with indoor air pollution. — *Sally Squires*

Source: Mike Lipske, "How Safe Is the Air Inside Your Home?" *National Wildlife,* Vol. 25, No. 3 (April-May, 1987), p. 36.

workers, whose problems usually cleared up when leaving the building. Many buildings were found to have inadequate ventilation that allowed indoor contaminants from smoking and vapors from photocopying machines, cleaning liquids, and solvents to accumulate. The EPA estimated that the economic cost of indoor air pollution totaled tens of billions of dollars annually in lost productivity, direct medical care, lost earnings, and employee sick days.[62]

PROGRESS

Major improvements in air quality have been attained over the past two decades. (See Figure 6.8.) Atmospheric levels of sulfur dioxide, carbon monoxide, total suspended particulates, and lead have all been reduced. Between 1970 and 1988, sulfur dioxide emissions dropped 27 percent, particulate matter emissions were down 63 percent, and lead emissions dropped a dramatic 96 percent because of the phasing out of leaded gasoline. According to the EPA, emissions of nitrogen oxides increased slightly, some 7 percent since 1970, but all areas of the United States except Los Angeles were said to have met the nitrogen dioxide standard during the past ten years.[63]

Ozone, however, has proven to be particularly difficult to control. For example, in 1986, 76.4 million Americans continued to live in metropolitan areas with unhealthy levels of ozone. The American Lung Association estimates that 382 counties, which are home to more than half of all Americans, are currently out of compliance with the EPA ozone standard.[64] Studies released in 1986 suggested that ozone is harmful to human health at half the level previously thought, which would put a third of the U.S. population at risk. Recommendations were made to lower the present standard of .12 parts per million based on these findings.[65] Another study released in 1989 indicated that at the high levels existing in some cities, ozone could cause permanent damage, affecting lung tissue over many years and leading to a precipitous and irreversible loss of breathing power. Children's lungs were found to be particularly susceptible to permanent damage at levels below the federal standard.[66]

Carbon monoxide standards are also not being met in 41 metropolitan areas. Even in rural areas, emissions from woodstoves may create carbon

Figure 6.8

Comparison of 1970 and 1988 Emissions

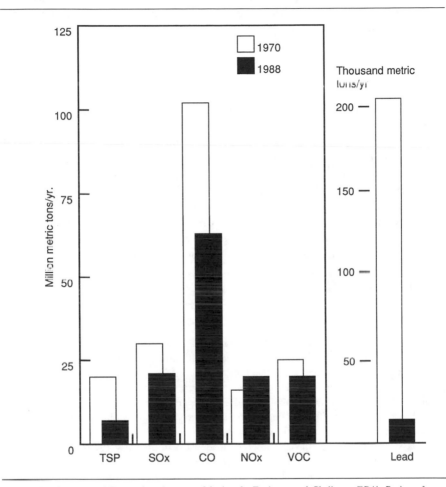

Source: Environmental Protection Agency, *Meeting the Environmental Challenge: EPA's Review of Progress and New Directions in Environmental Protection* (Washington, DC: U.S. Government Printing Office, 1990), p. 7.

monoxide problems. Controls on carbon monoxide and ozone-producing chemicals have reduced emissions from individual cars, gas stations, industries, and most other sources. These reductions are being offset, however, by rapid growth in the number of sources. The increase in cars and miles traveled each year, for example, keeps worsening the problem. The recent Clean Air Act Amendments contain provisions to strengthen federal and state ozone and carbon monoxide programs. The requirement for bringing cleaner burning gasoline and alternative fuels into the marketplace should help reduce these pollutants. The EPA is also preparing to set realistic timetables for controlling these pollutants, spell out the consequences for failure to attain them, and impose appropriate sanctions to bring nonattainment areas into compliance.[67]

There has been considerable progress, according to the EPA, in controlling particulate matter, but smaller particles still require more rigorous controls. Approximately 30 million people live in areas where concentrations of smaller particles exceed the standards. In July 1987, the EPA revised its standards relative to particulate matter to monitor only those particles that pose a risk to health because they are small enough to penetrate the most sensitive regions of the respiratory tract. Besides controlling industrial sources, the EPA's program also focuses on unconventional sources of particulate matter such as woodstoves, urban dust, and open burning for forest management and agricultural purposes.[68]

The drop in lead levels over the past decade, which has been dramatic, is mainly the result of mandated use of unleaded gasoline and reductions in the amount of lead permitted in leaded gasoline to the current limit of .10 grams per gallon. In the early 1970s, according to EPA figures, over 200 billion grams of lead were used in gasoline each year, but in 1989 less than 1 billion grams were used. This amounts to a reduction of over 99 percent.

The Dramatic Reduction of Lead in the Air

The dramatic reduction of lead in the air we breathe is one of the EPA's most important success stories. Lead has long been used in gasoline to increase octane levels to avoid engine knocking. Lead is a heavy metal that can cause serious physical and mental impairment. Children are particularly vulnerable to effects of high lead levels. Two efforts begun 15 years ago are responsible for a 95 percent reduction in the use of lead in gasoline.

Recognizing the health risks posed by lead, EPA in the early 1970s required the lead content of all gasoline to be reduced over time. The lead content of leaded gasoline was reduced in 1985 from an average of 1.0 gram/gallon to 0.5 gram/gallon, and still further in 1986 to 0.1 grams/gallon.

In addition to phasing down of lead in gasoline, EPA's overall automotive emission control program required the use of unleaded gasoline in many cars beginning in 1975. Currently, about 70 percent of the gas sold is unleaded.

These two efforts, combined with reductions in lead emissions from stationary sources such as battery plants and nonferrous smelters, have substantially reduced lead levels. This success has been one of the greatest contributions EPA has made to the nation's health.

Source: Environmental Protection Agency, *Environmental Progress and Challenges: EPA's Update* (Washington, DC: U.S. Government Printing Office, 1988), p. 16.

Lead emissions from stationary sources also have been substantially reduced through implementation of state plans designed to attain federal standards with respect to particulate matter and lead emissions. The EPA will focus its efforts on those few sources, mostly smelters, that are not yet in compliance.[69]

Regarding toxic emissions, the EPA's Toxic Release Inventory has prompted actions by industries and communities to address the problem. In 1990, nine major U.S. companies reached an agreement with the EPA to voluntarily reduce toxic air emissions at 40 chemical plants in 14 states. When fully implemented in 1993, this agreement will result in overall annual reductions from the plants involved of almost 83 percent, or 9 million pounds, the EPA claims. Also in the 1990s, the EPA will attempt to reduce by 50 percent the nationwide emissions of the 189 toxic pollutants listed in the Clean Air Act Amendments. Sources of these regulated pollutants will be required to achieve emission reductions comparable to similar facilities that have the best available controls. States will be given more responsibility to regulate these air toxins, and their capability to accomplish this regulation will be strengthened.[70]

STRATEGIES

Most of the approaches taken to date to reduce or control air pollution are considered by some experts to be nothing more than technological Band-Aids rather than efforts to address the roots of the problem, which is said to be inappropriate energy, transportation, and industrial systems. The most widespread technological innovation, for example, has been the introduction of electrostatic precipitators and baghouse filters for the control of particulate emissions from power plants. The predominant technique that has been used to reduce sulfur dioxide has been to put flue-gas desulfurization technology (scrubbers) on coal-burning power plants. These scrubbers can remove as much as 95 percent of a given plant's sulfur dioxide emissions. For the control of nitrogen oxide emissions from power plants, a variety of approaches have been used with mixed results. Clean coals technologies that lower emissions of both sulfur dioxide and nitrogen oxides during combustion are now under investigation.[71]

These technologies provide necessary immediate reductions to air pollution, but they are not the ultimate solution, according to some experts. They create environmental problems of their own, in many cases, and do little, if anything, to reduce carbon dioxide emissions that may contribute to global warming. They are best viewed as a bridge to the day when energy-efficient societies are the norm instead of the exception, and when renewable sources such as solar, wind, and water power provide the bulk of the world's energy.[72] The ultimate solution to the air pollution problem involves a major change in industrial societies and the industrial systems in these societies.

Efficient use of energy is an essential strategy for reducing emissions from power plants, which are a major source of many pollutants. Equally important, according to some experts, are the savings resulting from avoided power plant construction, which in some cases can more than offset the cost of emission controls at existing plants. It is essential that governments put economic incentives for energy reform into place as part of their air quality strategies. Industrial societies may also have to change their transportation systems. Reducing urban air pollution may require a major shift away from automobiles as the cornerstone of transportation systems. This may involve more experiments with alternative forms of transportation. In the meantime, societies must encourage the manufacture and purchase of automobiles that are both low in emissions and higher in fuel economy.[73]

Efforts to control toxic emissions will be most successful if they focus on waste minimization rather than simply on control of emissions after they have been created. Perhaps the most effective incentive for waste reduction is strict regulation regarding the disposal of these wastes into land, air, and water. This practice will force up the price of disposal, making it cost effective for industries to reduce waste generation. Public access to information about what chemicals a plant is emitting can be instrumental in spurring a response to this problem.[74]

Few policymakers, however, are considering implementation of comprehensive strategies that are necessary to reduce pollution for future generations. Los Angeles is one of the first regions in the world to really understand that lasting change will not come about unless a comprehensive plan to reduce air pollution is implemented.[75] In 1989, the South Coast Air-Quality Management District, a regional agency with authority over Los Angeles, adopted a sweeping 20-year antipollution plan that is 5,500 pages long. It calls for elimination of 70 percent of smog-producing emissions in the Los Angeles area by the year 2000.[76]

In the first phase, regulations will be issued to ban the use of aerosol hair sprays and deodorants and require companies to install the best antismog equipment available. These regulations will affect everyone, from Fortune 500 companies to local restaurants with charbroiler hoods and the corner dry cleaners. Later phases will impose stricter emission standards for automobiles and force employers to encourage car pooling. Eventually, the plan will require conversion of most vehicles to methanol and other cleaner burning fuels, and a massive switch to cars, buses, and trucks powered by electricity.[77] Officials say the cost of the plan will run $2.8 billion a year, or 60 cents a day for every person in the Los Angeles basin. But industry groups put the cost at more than $12 billion, or $2,200 annually per household for the initial stages alone. Some studies show job losses above 50,000 people.[78]

According to one expert, air pollution is an eminently solvable problem. But simply tinkering with the present system will not be adequate. The only strategy that will work is a comprehensive approach to the problem that focuses on pollution prevention rather than pollution control. As society is faced with ever mounting costs to human health and the environment, the question is not how society can afford to control air pollution, but how we can afford not to deal with the problem.[79]

~

Questions for Discussion

1. Distinguish between primary and secondary pollutants. What are natural pollutants? What substances are considered to be the most harmful as far as outdoor pollution is concerned?

2. What effects do these pollutants have on human health? How many people are exposed to health hazards because of these pollutants? What other damage is caused by these pollutants?

3. Describe the various levels of regulation with respect to air pollution. Are all these levels of control necessary? Why or why not? What would you recommend as an alternative system?

4. How is ambient air quality controlled? What are primary and secondary standards? What are air quality control regions? How are the regulations with respect to ambient air implemented? What adjustments were made in the 1977 amendments? Were these successful?

5. What are stationary sources of air pollution? How are these sources regulated? What is a bubble? Do you believe these bubbles are advantageous to business? Would you apply for one if you were responsible for air pollution control in your company? What factors would be important to consider in your decision?

6. Why are toxic emissions of concern? What does the new law (SARA) require with respect to these emissions? What long-term effect do you think these requirements will have on companies?

7. Study the new Clean Air Act in detail. What are its major provisions? What impact do you predict this bill will eventually have on industry? How will it affect your pocketbook? Will it affect your lifestyle? If so, in what ways?

8. What is acid rain? Is it as much of a problem as initially thought? What technologies exist to deal with the problem? How effective are they? How is the new Clean Air Act going to deal with acid rain? What incentives are provided in the legislation?

9. What are common sources of indoor pollution? How serious a problem is this kind of air pollution? What can be done about the problem? How

serious a problem is radon gas? What new evidence exists with respect to this problem?

10. What progress has been made with regard to outdoor air pollution? What problems remain to be solved? Will the new Clean Air Act adequately address these problems in your opinion? What else can be done?

∼

Notes

1. Thomas DiLorenzo, "Does Free Enterprise Cause Pollution?" *Across the Board* January-February 1991, p. 38.

2. G. Tyler Miller, Jr., *Living in the Environment* (Belmont, CA: Wadsworth, 1990), pp. 484–485.

3. Ibid., p. 485.

4. Ibid., pp. 497–498.

5. Ibid., p. 498.

6. Ibid., p. 501.

7. *Cleaning the Air: EPA's Program for Air Pollution Control* (Washington, DC: Environmental Protection Agency, 1979), pp. 3–4.

8. Ibid., p. 9.

9. Andy Pasztor, "EPA Puts Aside Action Against States and Cities," *Wall Street Journal,* October 3, 1983, p. 4.

10. See "EPA Proposes End to Highway Funds for Chicago Area," *Wall Street Journal,* May 2, 1984, p. 6, and "Detroit Faces Cutoff of Highway Funding Over EPA Standards," *Wall Street Journal,* June 12, 1984, p. 3. See also Robert E. Taylor, "U.S. Is Likely to Impose Growth Curbs in Areas Not Meeting Ozone Standard," *Wall Street Journal,* February 20, 1987, p. 6.

11. Barbara Rosewicz, "EPA Prepares Plan for Cities on Clean Air," *Wall Street Journal,* November 12, 1987, p. 64.

12. Robert E. Taylor, "Lead Content of Gasoline Must Be Cut by 90% by 1986, EPA Ruling States," *Wall Street Journal,* March 5, 1985, p. 46.

13. Jim Brady, "Leaden Gas' Demise Fuels Controversy," *Dallas Times Herald,* April 4, 1987, p. A-1.

14. EPA, *Clearing the Air,* pp. 10–11.

15. Barbara Rosewicz, "EPA Announces Steps to Protect Public from Cancer-Causing Vapors of Benzene," *Wall Street Journal,* September 1, 1989, p. A-3.

16. "EPA Is Set to Allow Factory Trade-Offs for Air Pollution," *Wall Street Journal,* April 2, 1982, p. 5.

17. *Environmental Quality 1983: 14th Annual Report of the Council on Environmental Quality* (Washington, DC: U.S. Government Printing Office, 1984), pp. 190–191.

18. Robert E. Taylor, "EPA Is Expanding Its 'Bubble' Policy for Air Pollution," *Wall Street Journal,* November 16, 1986, p. 18.

19. Hilary F. French, "Clearing the Air," *State of the World 1990* (Washington, DC: Worldwatch Institute, 1990), pp. 103–104.

20. Robert E. Taylor, "EPA Is Planning to Leave Regulation of Most Toxic-Gas Emissions to States," *Wall Street Journal,* June 4, 1985, p. 5.

21. "SARA Title III Brings Chemical Risk Issues to the Forefront of Corporate Management," *CEM Report,* Vol. 9 (Summer 1990), p. 1.

22. Ibid., p. 7.

23. Sharon Begley, "Is Breathing Hazardous to Your Health?" *Newsweek,* April 3, 1989, p. 25.

24. "Study: Auto Pollution Drives Up Health Costs," *Times-Picayune,* January 20, 1990. See also United States Environmental Protection Agency, *Toxics in the Community: National and Local Perspectives* (Washington, DC: U.S. Government Printing Office, 1990).

25. National Association of Manufacturers, *Perspective on National Issues: Clean Air and the Quality of Life,* (Washington, DC: Author, 1981), p. 3.

26. Robert E. Taylor, "EPA Finds Fewer Cars Are Meeting Emissions Limits," *Wall Street Journal,* May 28, 1985, p. 12.

27. Rick Raber, "La. Is Top Industrial Polluter," *Times-Picayune,* April 20, 1990, p. A-1.

28. John Carey, "If Don Stedman Is Right, The Clean Air Act Is All Wrong," *Business Week,* October 1, 1990, p. 40.

29. Michael Duffy, "Smell That Fresh Air!" *Time,* June 26, 1989, pp. 16–17.

30. Rose Gutfeld and Barbara Rosewicz, "White House and Senate Leaders Strike Clean-Air Bill Compromise," *Wall Street Journal,* March 2, 1990, p. A-3.

31. Michael D. Lemonick, "Forecast: Clearer Skies," *Time,* November 5, 1990, p. 33.

32. Ibid.

33. Mark Ivey, "Fuel Wars: Big Oil Is Running Scared," *Business Week,* June 4, 1990, p. 132. See also Caleb Solomon, "Shell Pumps Cleaner Gas in Dirtiest Cities in U.S.," *Wall Street Journal,* April 12, 1990, p. B-1.

34. Lemonick, "Forecast: Clearer Skies," p. 33.

35. Ibid.

36. Vicky Cahan, "A Clean-Air Bill Is Easy. Clear Air Is Hard," *Business Week,* November 5, 1990, p. 50.

37. "Storm over a Deadly Downpour," *Time,* December 6, 1982, pp. 84–86.

38. Anne LaBastille, "Acid Rain, How Great a Menace?" *National Geographic,* Vol. 160, No. 5 (November 1981), p. 653.

39. Betty Hiclman, "Acid Precipitation," *Environmental Science and Technology,* Vol. 15, No. 10 (October 1981), p. 1123.

40. Ibid., p. 1122.

41. "Storm over a Deadly Downpour," pp. 84–86.

42. Miller, *Living in the Environment,* pp. 496–497.

43. "Storm over a Deadly Downpour," pp. 84–86.

44. Environmental Protection Agency, *Environmental Progress and Challenges: EPA's Update* (Washington, DC: U.S. Government Printing Office, 1988), p. 28.

45. Andy Pasztor, "Search for Plan to Control Acid Rain Deeply Divides Industries, Regions," *Wall Street Journal,* November 10, 1983, p. 31.

46. "Storm over a Deadly Downpour," pp. 84–86.

47. Pasztor, "Search for Plan," p. 31.

48. Ibid.

49. EPA, *Environmental Progress and Challenges,* p. 29.

50. Ibid., pp. 29–30.

51. S. Fred Singer, "The Answers on Acid Rain Fall on Deaf Ears," *Wall Street Journal,* March 6, 1990, p. A-20.

52. Environmental Protection Agency, *Meeting the Environmental Challenge* (Washington, DC: U.S. Government Printing Office, 1990), p. 9.

53. Amal Kumar Naj, "Emission-Control Firms Seek Acid Tests," *Wall Street Journal,* August 17, 1989, p. A-4.

54. EPA, *Meeting the Environmental Challenge,* p. 11.

55. EPA, *Environmental Progress and Challenges,* p. 32.

56. Mike Lipske, "How Safe Is the Air Inside Your Home?" *National Wildlife,* Vol. 25, No. 3 (April-May 1987), pp. 37–39.

57. EPA, *Meeting the Environmental Challenge,* p. 11.

58. EPA, *Environmental Progress and Challenges,* p. 34.

59. Ibid., p. 32.

60. EPA, *Meeting the Environmental Challenge,* p. 10.

61. EPA, *Environmental Progress and Challenges,* p. 36.

62. Amy Docker Marcus, "In Some Workplaces, Ill Winds Blow," *Wall Street Journal,* October 9, 1989, p. B-1. See also David Holzman, "Elusive Culprits in Workplace Ills," *Insight,* June 26, 1989, pp. 44–45.

63. EPA, *Meeting the Environmental Challenge,* p. 7.

64. French, "Clearing the Air," p. 102.

65. Robert E. Taylor, "New Studies Indicate Ozone Is Harmful at Half Level Previously Thought Safe," *Wall Street Journal,* April 24, 1986, p. 4.

66. David Stipp, "Breathing Ozone at Cities' Current Levels May Injure Lungs, Research Indicates," *Wall Street Journal,* September 18, 1989, p. B-4.

67. EPA, *Meeting the Environmental Challenge,* p. 7.

68. Ibid., p. 8.

69. Ibid.

70. Ibid., p. 10. See also Rose Gutfeld, "EPA Says 9 Companies Agreed to Slash Toxic-Chemical Emissions at 40 Plants," *Wall Street Journal,* September 19, 1990, p. A-10.

71. French, "Clearing the Air," pp. 110–111.

72. Ibid., p. 111.

73. Ibid., p. 114.

74. Ibid. See also Amal Kumar Naj, "Some Companies Cut Pollution by Altering Production Methods," *Wall Street Journal,* December 24, 1990, p. A-1.

75. French, "Clearing the Air," pp. 117–118.

76. Philip Elmer-DeWitt, "A Drastic Plan to Banish Smog," *Time,* March 27, 1989, p. 65.

77. Ibid.

78. Carolyn Lockhead, "Pollutants Reined by Market Rules," *Insight,* July 3, 1989, p. 9.

79. French, "Clearing the Air," p. 118.

SUGGESTED READINGS

Brown, Michael. *The Toxic Cloud.* New York: Harper & Row, 1987.

Consumer Product Safety Commission. *The Inside Story: A Guide to Indoor Air Quality.* Washington, DC: CPSC, 1988.

Crandall, Robert W. *Controlling Industrial Pollution: The Economics and Politics of Clean Air.* Washington, DC: Brookings Institution, 1983.

Elliott, Thomas C., and Robert G. Schwieger, eds. *The Acid Rain Sourcebook.* New York: McGraw-Hill, 1984.

Environmental Protection Agency. *Environmental Progress and Challenges: EPA's Update.* Washington, DC: U.S. Government Printing Office, 1988.

Environmental Protection Agency. *Meeting the Environmental Challenge.* Washington, DC: U.S. Government Printing Office, 1990.

French, Hilary F. "Clearing the Air," *State of the World 1990.* Washington, DC: Worldwatch Institute, 1990.

Gibson, Mary, ed. *To Breathe Freely: Risk, Consent, and Air.* Totowa, NJ: Rowman & Allanheld, 1985.

Lafavore, Michael. *Radon: The Invisible Threat.* Emmaus, PA: Rodale Press, 1987.

Louma, Jon R. *Troubled Skies, Troubled Waters: The Story of Acid Rain.* New York: Viking Press, 1984.

MacKenzie, James J. *Breathing Easier: Taking Action on Climate Change, Air Pollution, and Energy Efficiency.* Washington, DC: World Resources Institute, 1989.

Ostmann, Robert, Jr. *Acid Rain: A Plague upon the Waters.* Minneapolis: Dillon Press, 1982.

Regens, James L., and Robert W. Rycroft. *The Acid Rain Controversy.* Pittsburgh: University of Pittsburgh Press, 1988.

Rousseau, David, et al. *Your Home, Your Health, and Well Being.* Vancouver, BC: Enwright, Hartley, and Marks, 1988.

Schmandt, Jurgen, and Hilliard Roderick. *Acid Rain and Friendly Neighbors: The Policy Dispute Between Canada and the United States.* Durham, NC: Duke University Press, 1985.

Stern, Arthur, et al. *Fundamentals of Air Pollution,* 2nd ed. New York: Academic Press, 1984.

Turiel, Isaac. *Indoor Air Quality and Human Health.* Stanford: Stanford University Press, 1985.

Wark, K., and C. F. Warner. *Air Pollution: Its Origin and Control,* 3rd ed. New York: Harper & Row, 1986.

Welburn, Alan. *Air Pollution and Acid Rain: The Biological Impact.* New York: Wiley, 1988.

CHAPTER 7

WATER POLLUTION

Water covers about 71 percent of the earth's surface, making it our most abundant resource. About 97 percent of this amount is salt water, most of which is contained in the oceans. Water is essential to all life and makes up 50 to 97 percent of the weight of all plants and animals and about 70 percent of the human body. Water is also a vital resource for agriculture, manufacturing, transportation, and many other human activities. Despite its importance, water is said to be one of the most poorly managed resources in the world. The human race wastes water indiscriminately, pollutes it with various contaminants, and charges too little for making it available. Consequently, even greater waste and pollution of this resource is encouraged.[1]

Although 3 percent of all the water in the world is fresh water, only a small amount of this percentage is usable. The rest is highly polluted, lies too far under the earth's surface to be extracted at an affordable cost, or is locked up in glaciers, polar ice caps, atmosphere, and soil in various places of the world. The usable fresh water still amounts to an average of 8.4 million liters (2.2 million gallons) for each person on earth. This supply of fresh water is continually collected, purified, and distributed in natural cycles, which works as long as we don't use water faster than it can be replenished and as long as we don't overload it with waste material.[2]

Our available fresh water comes from two sources: groundwater and surface-water runoff. Precipitation that does not soak into the ground or return to the atmosphere by evaporation is called surface water and becomes runoff that flows from the earth's surface into streams, rivers, lakes, wetlands, and reservoirs. This surface water can be withdrawn from these sources and used for human activities, but only part of the total annual runoff

195

is available for such purposes. Some of it flows in rivers to the oceans, and some must be left in lakes and streams for natural purposes.[3]

Some precipitation, under the influence of gravity, slowly soaks deeper into the earth where it fills pores and fractures in spongelike, or permeable, layers of sand, gravel, and porous rock such as sandstone. These porous, water-bearing layers of underground rock are called aquifers, and the water they contain is called groundwater. Aquifers are recharged or replenished naturally by precipitation, but this recharge process is usually quite slow compared to the more rapid replenishment of surface water supplies. If the withdrawal rate of an aquifer exceeds its recharge rate, the water in the aquifer is no longer a renewable resource.[4]

Water usage is measured in two ways: water withdrawal and water consumption. Water withdrawal occurs when water is taken from a ground-water or surface-water source and transported to a place where it is used in some fashion. Water consumption occurs when the withdrawn water is not available for reuse in the area from which it was withdrawn. About three-fourths of the water withdrawn worldwide each year is used for irrigation. The rest is used in industrial processes, in cooling electric power plants, and in homes and businesses. This use varies widely from country to country. In the United States, about three-fourths of the fresh water withdrawn each year comes from rivers, lakes, and reservoirs; the rest comes from groundwater aquifers. Almost 80 percent of this water is used for cooling electric power plants and for irrigation.[5]

Water withdrawal in the United States has more than doubled since 1950, because of increases in population, urbanization, and increased economic activity. About one-fourth of this water is consumed. The remaining three-fourths returns to replenish surface-water or groundwater supplies. Worldwide, up to 90 percent of all water withdrawn from rivers and lakes is returned to them for potential reuse, but about 75 percent of the water used for irrigation is consumed. Between 1985 and 2020, worldwide withdrawal of water for irrigation is projected to double, primarily because of increasing population pressures in less developed nations. Withdrawal for industrial processing and cooling electric power plants is projected to increase 20 times because of increasing industrialization in these countries, and withdrawal for public use in homes and businesses is projected to increase fivefold.[6]

CONTROLLING WATER POLLUTION

Fresh water can become so contaminated by human activities that it is no longer useful for some purposes and can be harmful to living organisms. Some of the fertilizers and pesticides that are applied to croplands run off into nearby surface waters or leach into aquifers far below the surface. Poor land-use policies accelerate the natural erosion of the soil that pollutes surface waters with sediment. Some of the sludge and other wastes we produce on land are dumped into the world's waters where they cause serious pollution problems. There are many different types and effects of water pollution (see box).[7]

Major Types and Effects of Water Pollutants

Disease-Causing Agents: Bacteria, viruses, protozoa, and parasitic worms that enter water from human, sewage and animal wastes and other sources.

Oxygen-Demanding Wastes: Organic wastes, which when degraded by oxygen-consuming bacteria, can deplete water of dissolved oxygen.

Water Soluble Inorganic Chemicals: Acids, salts, and compounds of toxic metals such as lead and mercury. High levels of such dissolved solids can make water unfit to drink, harm fish and other aquatic life, depress crop yields, and accelerate corrosion of equipment that uses water.

Inorganic Plant Nutrients: Water-soluble nitrate and phosphate compounds that can cause excessive growth of algae and other aquatic plants, which then die and decay, depleting water of dissolved oxygen and killing fish. Excessive levels of nitrates in drinking water can reduce the oxygen carrying capacity of the blood and kill unborn children and infants.

Organic Chemicals: Oil, gasoline, plastics, pesticides, cleaning solvents, detergents, and many other water-soluble and insoluble chemicals that threaten human health and harm fish and other aquatic life. Some of the more than 700 synthetic organic chemicals found in trace amounts in surface and underground drinking-water supplies in the United States can cause kidney disorders, birth defects, and various types of cancer in laboratory test animals.

Sediment or Suspended Matter: Insoluble particles of soil, silt, or other solid inorganic and organic materials that become suspended in water and that in terms of total mass are the largest source of water pollution. In most rivers, sediment loads have risen sharply because of accelerated erosion from cropland, rangeland, forestland, and construction and mining sites. Suspended particulate matter clouds the water, reduces the ability of some organisms to find food, reduces photosynthesis by aquatic plants, disrupts aquatic food webs, and carries pesticides, bacteria, toxic metals, and other harmful substances. Bottom sediment destroys feeding and spawning grounds of fish and clogs and fills lakes, reservoirs, river and stream channels, and harbors.

Radioactive Substances: Radioisotopes that are water soluble or capable of being biologically amplified in food chains and webs. Ionizing radiation from such isotopes can cause DNA mutations, leading to birth defects, cancer, and genetic damage.

Heat: Excessive inputs of heated water used to cool electric power plants. The resulting increases in water temperatures lower dissolved oxygen content and make aquatic organisms more vulnerable to disease, parasites, and toxic chemicals.

Source: From *Living in the Environment: An Introduction to Environmental Studies* 6/E by G. Tyler Miller, Jr. © 1990 by Wadsworth, Inc. Reprinted by permission of the publisher.

The world's rivers receive enormous amounts of natural sediment runoff, industrial discharges, human sewage, and surface runoff from urban and agricultural uses of land resources. Because rivers are moving bodies of water, many of them can recover rapidly from some forms of pollution, such as excess heat and degradable oxygen-demanding wastes, as long as they are not overloaded. Slowly degradable and nondegradable pollutants, however, are not eliminated by these natural purification processes. The ability of a river to recover depends on its volume, flow rate, temperature, acidic level, and the volume of incoming degradable waste material. Rivers that move slowly can easily be overloaded with oxygen-demanding wastes.[8]

Lakes and reservoirs, on the other hand, act as natural traps, collecting nutrients, suspended solids, and toxic chemicals in bottom sediments. They can take from 1 to 100 years to flush themselves compared to days and weeks for most rivers. This fact makes lakes more vulnerable to contamination with plant nutrients, oil, pesticides, and toxic substances that can destroy life at the bottom of the lake and poison fish in the lake. Eutrophication of lakes is a natural process, but the addition of phosphates and nitrates as a result of human activities can produce in a few decades the same degree of plant nutrient enrichment that may take thousands to millions of years by natural processes.[9]

Such cultural eutrophication is a major problem for shallow lakes and reservoirs. When large masses of floating algae die, dissolved oxygen in the surface layer of water is depleted as they fall to the bottom and are decomposed by aerobic bacteria. Then important game and commercial fish such as lake trout and smallmouth bass die of oxygen starvation, leaving the lake populated by carp and other less desirable species that need less oxygen. If excess nutrients continue to flow into the lake, the bottom water becomes foul and almost devoid of animals, as anaerobic bacteria take over and produce their smelly decomposition products.[10]

Controlling water pollution involves efforts in two areas of concern: (1) reducing the pollution of free-flowing surface waters and protecting their uses, and (2) maintaining the quality of drinking water. In the early 1970s, the impact of conventional pollutants on surface waters was recognized and programs were developed for their control. Later, the dangers posed by toxic pollutants on the nation's waters was recognized and steps were taken to eliminate their discharge. The need to protect drinking water became apparent in the mid-1970s as over 50 percent of the nation's drinking water was threatened by contamination from various sources such as underground storage tanks, fertilizers, pesticides, hazardous waste sites, and other sources.[11]

Thus a series of laws and regulations have been developed over the past several decades to protect our water resources. However, some of the laws relating to water pollution go back to the early years of the century or before. Laws to control water pollution actually began with the Rivers and Harbors

Act of 1899, which prohibited discharge of pollutants or refuse into or on the banks of navigable waters without a permit. The next public policy measure on water pollution was the Oil Pollution Act of 1924, which prohibited the discharge of refuse and oil into or upon coastal or navigable waters of the United States. These laws are still enforced in situations where their application is appropriate.

Modern efforts to control water pollution began with the Water Pollution Control Act of 1948, which declared that water pollution was a local problem and required the U.S. Public Health Service to provide information to the states that would help them coordinate research activities. The Water Pollution Control Act of 1956 contained enforcement provisions by providing for a federal abatement suit at the request of a state pollution control agency. The Water Pollution Control Act Amendments of 1961 broadened federal jurisdiction and shortened the process of enforcement by stating that where health was being endangered, the federal government did not have to receive the consent of all the states involved.

The Water Quality Act of 1965 provided for the setting of water quality standards that were state and federally enforceable. These became the basis for interstate water quality standards. This act also created the Water Pollution Control Administration within the Department of Health, Education and Welfare. The Clean Water Restoration Act of 1966 imposed a fine of $100 per day on a polluter who failed to submit a required report. Finally, the Water Quality Improvement Act of 1970 prohibited discharge of harmful quantities of oil into or upon the navigable waters of the United States or their shores. It applies to offshore and onshore facilities and vessels. The act also provided for regulation of sewage disposal from vessels.

SURFACE WATER

Pollution of surface water occurs when the quantity of wastes entering a body of water overwhelms its capacity to assimilate the pollutants these wastes contain. Thus the natural cleansing ability of oxygen contained in the water is compromised and the water can no longer break down organic pollutants. Excessive nutrients from agricultural activities and municipal sewage also cause eutrophications, which is a state of ecological imbalance where algae growth is favored at the expense of other forms of aquatic life. Large algae formations at the surface of the water deplete available oxygen and prevent sunlight from reaching submerged vegetation. Photosynthesis is seriously hampered, which reduces both support for aquatic life and the assimilative capacity of the water.

The major sources of surface water pollution are (1) organic wastes from urban sewage, farms, and industries, (2) sediments from agriculture, construction, and logging, (3) biological nutrients, such as phosphates in detergents and nitrogen in fertilizers, (4) toxic substances from industry and synthetic chemicals such as those found in pesticides, plastics, and detergents, (5) acid and mineral drainage from open-pit and deep-shaft mining, and (6) runoff containing harmful chemicals and sediment drained from streets and parking lots.[12] (See Table 7.1.)

There are both point and nonpoint sources of water pollution. Point sources are places where polluting substances enter the water from a discernible, confined, and discrete conveyance such as a sewer pipe, culvert, tunnel, or other channel or conduit. Point sources are those that come from industrial facilities and municipal sewage systems. Pollutants can also wash off, run off, or seep from broad areas of land. These are called nonpoint source pollutants because they cannot be located with much precision. Degradation of water from nonpoint sources is caused by the cumulative effect of all the pollutants that originate from large land areas within a single watershed. Common pollutants of the latter type are sediment eroded from soil exposed during construction of buildings and pesticides and fertilizers washed off cropland by rainwater. (See Figure 7.1.)

The wastewater from municipalities consists primarily of water from toilets and so-called gray water from sinks, showers, and other uses. This wastewater, which runs through city sewers, may be contaminated by or-

Table 7.1

Water Pollutants and Their Sources

	BOD	Bacteria	Nutrients	Ammonia	Turbidity	TDS	Acids	Toxics
Common Pollutant Categories								
Point Sources								
Municipal Sewage Treatment Plants	•	•	•	•				•
Industrial Facilities	•							•
Combined Sewer Overflows	•	•	•	•	•	•		•
Nonpoint Sources								
Agricultural Runoff	•	•	•		•	•		•
Urban Runoff	•	•	•		•	•		•
Construction Runoff			•		•			•
Mining Runoff					•	•	•	•
Septic Systems	•	•	•					•
Landfills/Spills	•							•
Silviculture Runoff	•				•	•		•

Abbreviations: Biological Oxygen Demand, BOD; Total Dissolved Solids, TDS.

Source: United States Environmental Protection Agency, *Environmental Progress and Challenges: EPA's Update* (Washington, DC: U.S. Government Printing Office, 1988), p. 70.

Figure 7.1

Point and Nonpoint Sources of Water Pollution

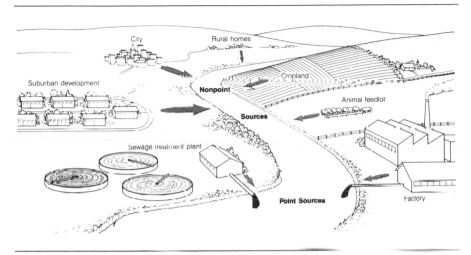

Source: From *Living in the Environment: An Introduction to Environmental Studies* 6/E by G. Tyler Miller, Jr. © 1990 by Wadsworth, Inc. Reprinted by permission of the publisher.

ganic materials, nutrients, sediment, bacteria, and viruses. Toxic substances used in the home such as paint and household cleaners and pesticides may also find their way into sewers. In some towns and cities, industrial facilities are hooked into the municipal discharge system and dump some of their wastes into this system. Finally, storm water sometimes enters the municipal system through street sewers, particularly in those old cities that do not have a dual system, and may carry with it residues, toxic chemicals, and sediments, and in worst cases, untreated sewage.[13]

Industrial sources, such as the manufacturing of steel and chemicals, produce billions of gallons of wastewater every day. Some of these pollutants are similar to those in municipal sewage, but often are more concentrated. Other pollutants from industrial sources are more exotic and include a great variety of heavy metals and synthetic organic substances. These pollutants may present serious hazards to human health and the environment, particularly when large quantities are discharged. The quantity of water that is discharged by industrial sources varies depending on the type of manufacturing process employed.[14]

The current system of water pollution control for surface water was established by the Federal Water Pollution Control Act Amendments of 1972, which mandated a sweeping federal and state campaign to prevent, reduce, and eliminate water pollution. This law proclaimed two general goals for the United States: (1) to achieve wherever possible by July 1, 1983, water that is clean enough for swimming and other recreational uses, and clean enough for the protection and propagation of fish, shellfish, and wildlife; and (2) by 1985, to have no discharges of pollutants into the nation's waters.[15] The goal of this act is to restore and maintain the chemical, physical, and biological integrity of the nation's waters. With this mandate, regulations and programs to reduce pollutants entering all surface water, including lakes, rivers, estuaries, oceans, and wetlands, were developed.

National Pollutant Discharge Elimination System

What is a NPDES permit? Under the Clean Water Act, the discharge of pollutants into the waters of the United States is prohibited unless a permit is issued by EPA or a state under the National Pollutant Discharge Elimination System (NPDES). These permits must be renewed at least once every five years.

What do NPDES permits contain? An NPDES permit contains effluent limitations and monitoring and reporting requirements. Effluent limitations are restrictions on the amount of specific pollutants that a facility can discharge into a stream, river, or harbor. Monitoring and reporting requirements are specific instructions on how sampling of the effluent should be done to check whether the effluent limitations are being met. Instructions may include required sampling frequency (i.e., daily, weekly, or monthly) and the type of monitoring required. The permittee may be required to monitor the effluent on a daily, weekly, or monthly basis. The monitoring results are then regularly reported to the EPA and state authorities. When a discharger fails to comply with the effluent limitations or monitoring and reporting requirements, EPA or the state may take enforcement action.

How are these effluent limitations developed? Congress recognized that it would be an overwhelming task for EPA to establish effluent limitations for each individual industrial and municipal discharger. Therefore, Congress authorized the agency to develop uniform effluent limitations for each category of point sources such as steel mills, paper mills, and pesticide manufacturers. The agency develops these effluent limitations on the basis of many factors, most notably efficient treatment technologies. Once EPA proposes an effluent limit and public comments are received, EPA or the states issue all point sources within that industry category NPDES permits using the technology-based limits. Sewage treatment plants also are provided with effluent limitations based on technology performance.

What are water quality-based limits? Limitations that are more stringent than those based on technology are sometimes necessary to ensure that state-developed water quality standards are met. For example, several different facilities may be discharging into one stream, creating pollutant levels harmful to fish. In this case, the facilities on that stream must meet more stringent treatment requirements, known as water quality-based limitations. These limits are developed by determining the amounts of pollutants that the stream can safely absorb and calculating permit limits such that these amounts are not exceeded.

Source: Environmental Protection Agency, *Environmental Progress and Challenges: EPA's Update* (Washington, DC: U.S. Government Printing Office, 1988), p. 50.

The act established a National Pollutant Discharge Elimination System (NPDES), which required permits for all point sources of pollution, providing the first major direct enforcement procedure against polluters. Under the system, it is illegal for any industry or municipality to discharge any pollutant into the nation's waters without a permit from EPA or from a state that has an EPA-approved permit program. When issued, the permit regulates what may be discharged (see box) and the amount of each identified pollutant allowed from a facility. The discharger must monitor its wastes and report on discharges, and comply with all applicable national effluent limits and with state and local requirements that may be imposed. If a plant cannot comply immediately, the permit contains a compliance schedule of firm dates by which the pollutants will be reduced or eliminated.

By 1988, 39 states were issuing permits under the NPDES structure, with the EPA itself issuing permits in the remaining states and on Indian reservations. While there are currently about 48,400 industrial and 15,300 municipal facilities that have NPDES permits, the EPA estimates that about 10 percent of the major facilities are in significant noncompliance with their permit conditions. (See box.) These facilities are subject to federal and state enforcement action, which can range all the way from an informal telephone call to formal judicial proceedings with possible financial penalties.[16]

This act was amended by the Clean Water Act of 1977, which made over 50 changes in the 1972 law. The most important from a business point of view was a change in the classification system of industrial pollutants and

---

What's a Pollutant?

It's illegal under the 1972 Federal Water Pollution Control Act to discharge pollutants into the nation's waters except under an NPDES permit.

Pollutants covered by this permit requirement are solid waste, incinerator residue, sewage, garbage, sewage sludge, munitions, chemical wastes, biological materials, radioactive materials, heat, wrecked or discarded equipment, rock, sand, cellar dirt, and industrial, municipal, and agricultural wastes discharged into water.

Excluded from the NPDES permit program are discharges of sewage from vessels; pollutants from vessels or other floating craft in coastal or ocean waters; discharges from properly functioning marine engines; water, gas, or other material injected into oil or gas wells, or disposed of in wells during oil or gas production, if the state determines that ground or surface water resources will not be degraded; agriculture projects; separate storm sewer discharges; and dredged or fill material.

Discharges excluded from the NPDES permit system are covered by other pollution control requirements.

Source: *Toward Cleaner Water* (Washington, DC: Environmental Protection Agency, 1974), p. 5.

the establishment of new deadlines. This change resulted in a much greater emphasis on the control of toxic pollutants. Toxic substances such as heavy metals and synthetic chemicals have rapidly contaminated the nation's waters. One major source of these substances is industrial discharges; therefore more attention to toxics was given in the amendments. These new categories and their deadlines as amended in 1987 are as follows:

> *Conventional pollutants.* These include BOD (biological oxygen demand), suspended solids, fecal coliforms, pH (acidity), and other pollutants so designated by the EPA. Industry is to have installed the "best conventional technology" (BCT) as expeditiously as practicable but in no case later than March 31, 1989, to control these pollutants.
>
> *Toxic pollutants.* The 1977 amendments specify an "initial list" of toxic substances to which EPA may add or subtract. Industry is to have installed the "best available" technology (BAT) not later than three years after a substance is placed on the toxic pollutant list and in no case later than March 31, 1989, to control toxic substances.
>
> *Nonconventional pollutants.* This category includes "all other" pollutants, that is, those not classified by the EPA as either conventional or toxic. The treatment required is the "best available" technology (BAT) as expeditiously as possible or within three years of the date the EPA established effluent limitations, but no later than March 31, 1989. A modification of these requirements is available under certain circumstances.

Rather than regulate surface water pollution on a substance-by-substance basis, as was done for air pollution, or establishing effluent limitations for each individual industrial and municipal discharger, Congress developed technology-based standards that apply to the broad categories of pollutants as mentioned. While there is some disagreement about exactly what these standards mean, in general "best conventional technology" means the average level of technology that an industry has installed to control that category of pollutants; "best available technology" means the most sophisticated technology that is currently available regardless of its cost and whether or not it is recognized as an industry standard.

In early 1987, Congress approved further amendments to the Clean Water Act by passing a $20 billion bill over the president's veto. The bill authorized $9.6 billion in grants and $8.4 billion in revolving construction projects for wastewater treatment plants; as much as $2 billion to clean up specific lakes, rivers, and estuaries; $400 million in grants to help states plan ways to reduce the toxic runoff from farmland and city streets; and funds to eliminate "hot spots" of toxic chemicals in waterways. The bill was backed by a coalition of construction companies, municipalities, and environmentalists.[17]

Nonpoint sources of pollution are regulated under Section 208 of the Clean Water Act. These nonpoint sources of pollution are a much more difficult problem to control. They generally cannot be collected and treated in some fashion, but can only be reduced by greater care in the management of water and land resources. One reason the United States did not meet the goals of the Federal Water Pollution Control Act was because a technology still does not exist to control nonpoint sources of pollution. These sources pour as much as 79 percent of all nitrates and 92 percent of all suspended solids into surface waters. Some major nonpoint sources of pollution are the following:

- Urban storm water; water running off buildings and streets, carrying with it oil, grease, trash, salts, lead, and other pollutants.
- Agricultural runoff: rain washing fertilizers, pesticides, and topsoil into water.
- Construction runoff: earth washed into streams, rivers, and lakes from erosion.
- Acid mine drainage: water seeping through mined areas.
- Forestry runoff: water washing sediments from areas where the earth has been disturbed by logging and timber operations.[18]

Section 208 requires that states and localities establish programs to control nonpoint source pollution. In contrast to point sources of pollution where uniform national standards have been developed, state and local governments have been assigned the major burden and responsibility for developing nonpoint source pollution controls. The reason for this approach is that soil conditions and types, climate, and topography (which are primary determinants of nonpoint source pollution) vary throughout the country. State and local authorities are required to develop a process for identifying significant nonpoint sources of pollution and to set forth control procedures, including, where appropriate, land-use regulations. Best Management Practices (BMPs) are to be identified and implemented to reduce the amount of pollution generated by nonpoint sources to a level compatible with water quality goals.

The efforts that have been made over the past few years to improve the quality of surface water have been encouraging. The EPA reports that in 1972, 36 percent of the nation's rivers that were assessed by the states met their water quality standards, but by 1988, that figure had increased to 70 percent. These rivers supported such beneficial uses as fishing and swimming. Between 1977 and 1988, the number of people served by adequate sewage treatment plants, which means secondary treatment or better, increased 84 percent, from 75 million to 138 million. Secondary treatment means 85 percent removal of conventional pollutants such as oxygen-demanding materials and suspended solids.[19]

However, the EPA reports that poorly treated sewage continues to cause pollution problems in many areas. Many cities and towns are still on construction schedules to reach secondary treatment levels. And new pollutants are gaining attention, such as minute amounts of toxic chemicals that are harder to identify and control. Nonpoint sources of pollution continue to be a problem. Toxics and other pollutants often come from many small sources that are widely dispersed and very difficult to control, such as urban runoff and drainage of pesticides, fertilizers, and animal wastes from farmland. These sources now appear responsible for most of the remaining damage to the nation's rivers, streams, and lakes.[20]

In 1990, the Great Lakes again made the national news when a third-year photography student at Ryerson Polytechnical Institute in Toronto claimed that Lake Ontario was so full of chemicals it can develop photographs. Lynch claimed that he had a portfolio of black-and-white pictures of the Toronto lakefront that had been developed in water from the lake with no chemicals added. The photographer said he had called provincial environmental officials to ask where he could find water heavily polluted with mercury and iron, chemicals necessary to develop pictures. When these officials refused to give this sort of information, he set out on his own and took samples of water near places that struck him as promising. He then exposed some film in each of these places and put it into film-developing canisters with his various water samples. The best sample proved to be one taken at a shipyard where a rusting old cargo vessel was apparently leaching a good bit of iron into the water.[21]

The current emphasis of surface water programs is on maintaining the gains that have been achieved nationwide, while expanding controls on nonpoint and toxic sources of pollution and targeting valuable threatened waters for additional action. Some key directions the EPA has enunciated include elimination of risks from selected highly toxic pollutants from point sources, significant reduction of risks from all other toxic pollutants, control of storm-water discharges including combined sewer overflows, and strong federal leadership and assistance to states in controlling nonpoint sources of pollution particularly in agriculture. The EPA is relying even more strongly on state and local governments to achieve the nation's water quality goals. They have recently been awarded $40 million in grants from the EPA to stem the flow of pollutants from nonpoint sources.[22]

DRINKING WATER

About one out of every two Americans and 95 percent of those living in rural areas depends on groundwater supplies for drinking water. About 75 percent of American cities rely on groundwater for their supply of drinking water. Water seeping from underground aquifers also provides nearly a third of the flow in U.S. streams and supplies much of the nation's other surface water. In 1982, the EPA found that 45 percent of the large public water systems served by groundwater were contaminated with synthetic organic chemicals that posed potential health threats. In 1984, at least 8,000 water wells throughout the nation were considered to have unusable or degraded water. The most common pollutants were solvents such as trichloroethylene (TCE), carbon tetrachloride, and chloroform. The EPA also documented groundwater contamination by 74 different kinds of pesticides in 38 states.[23]

Some bacteria and most suspended solid pollutants are removed as contaminated surface water seeps through the soil into underground aquifers. But this natural process of purification can also become overloaded by large volumes of wastes, and the effectiveness of this process varies with the type of soil involved. No soil is effective in filtering out viruses and some synthetic organic chemicals. Once such contaminants reach groundwater supplies, they are usually not effectively diluted and dispersed because the movement in most aquifers is slow and nonturbulent. Degradable organic wastes are not broken down as readily as in rapidly flowing surface waters because groundwater has little dissolved oxygen and a fairly small population of anaerobic decomposing bacteria. Thus it can take hundreds or thousands of years for contaminated groundwater to cleanse itself of degradable waste material. Slowly degradable and nondegradable waste material can permanently contaminate aquifers.[24]

Two major sources of groundwater contamination are leaks of hazardous organic chemicals from underground storage tanks and seepage of hazardous organic chemicals and toxic heavy metal compounds from landfills, abandoned hazardous waste dumps, and industrial waste storage lagoons located above or near aquifers. (See Figure 7.2.) Another source is accidental leaks from wells used to inject almost 60 percent of the country's hazardous wastes deep underground. Laws regulating injection of these wastes are weak and poorly enforced, making this a particularly threatening source of groundwater contamination. Wastes can escape during this process and permanently contaminate aquifers; thus some environmentalists and other believe this disposal process should be banned.[25]

The quality of drinking water is regulated by the Safe Drinking Water Act of 1974 as amended in 1977 and 1986, which gives the EPA authority to set national standards to protect drinking water. These standards represent the Maximum Contaminant Levels (MCL) allowable and consist of numerical criteria for specified contaminants. The states bear primary responsibility for enforcing drinking water standards assisted in part with federal funds.[26] The EPA also issues rules to protect underground sources of drinking water (aquifers) from contamination by underground injection of wastes and other materials.

The EPA took over the setting of drinking water standards from the U.S. Public Health Service in 1975, and in a ten-year period, set limits for

Figure 7.2 Sources of Groundwater Contamination

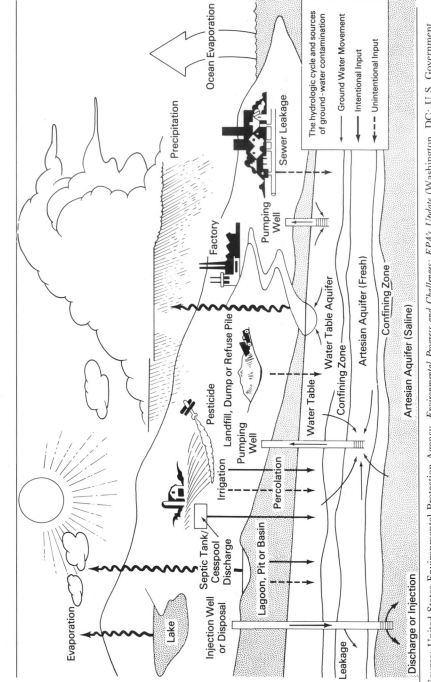

Source: United States Environmental Protection Agency, *Environmental Progress and Challenges: EPA's Update* (Washington, DC: U.S. Government Printing Office, 1988), p. 53.

208

only 25 contaminants. Critics complained that hundreds of widely used synthetic chemicals had not been included in drinking water standards. In response to this criticism and the growing evidence of drinking water contamination, the EPA, in late 1985, proposed standards to restrict the levels of eight additional chemicals found in public water systems, and 39 other compounds and 4 microbes found in drinking water. These standards were based on health effects of the chemicals, cost considerations, and feasibility of maintaining the limits. The EPA also proposed that water systems monitor 51 other compounds suspected of being harmful. It was estimated that about 1,300 community water systems would have to spend $280 million on treatment equipment and $21 million annually on operating expenses to meet the "maximum contaminant levels" in the proposed standards.[27]

Revisions to the Safe Drinking Water Act passed in 1986 provided money to protect aquifers that are the sole source of drinking water for an area and authorized the EPA to review any federally funded projects that may threaten or affect their quality. The revisions also required states to develop plans to safeguard other public water supplies, and gave the EPA five years to set maximum levels for at least 108 of the hundreds of contaminants currently found in drinking water. Twenty-five more standards were to be issued every three years thereafter. The EPA was also required to issue regulations within 18 months requiring public water systems to test for contaminants not yet regulated. Public systems would have to test their water at least once every five years thereafter for such contaminants.[28]

In early 1990, the EPA did issue new regulations for 25 additional chemicals that would cover an additional 2.5 million metric tons of waste or wastewater generated by 17,000 businesses each year. The rules were expected to affect 13 major industries and cost them an additional $200 to $400 million a year. The largest share of the costs would fall on petroleum refineries, pulp and paper mills, synthetic fiber plants, wholesale petroleum marketers, and organic chemical companies. Some 200 facilities that were disposing of industrial wastes in surface impoundments that could leak contaminants into groundwater were expected to close as a result of the new regulations.[29]

The EPA came under fire in the summer of 1990 and was accused of doing little to protect some 30 million Americans from exposure to potentially contaminated drinking water. The National Wildlife Federation (NWF) sued the EPA for relaxing rules that required states to comply with the Safe Drinking Water Act. The NWF cited a study by the Centers for Disease Control which found that between 1986 and 1988, 24 states reported dozens of outbreaks of acute illness due to contaminated water. This lawsuit was supported by a General Accounting Office report that concluded the water safety system is plagued by unreliable statistics on contamination, serious underreporting of violations, and falsification of data.[30]

By 1995, the EPA expects to set new standards for 108 contaminants and to work with the states to enforce them vigorously. Initial monitoring and regulations for lead and radionuclides will be completed and a plan to improve filtration of microbial contaminants will also be developed. The EPA will continue to establish controls on underground injection of waste material to regulate the permitting, construction, operation, monitoring, and closure of five classes of injection wells. Its Wellhead Protection Program (WHP) will also be continued, under which the EPA is developing a comprehensive approach for protecting these groundwater supplies from all sources of contamination. The costs of making all these improvements will be $1 to $2 billion per year, with the states needing an additional $200 million in onetime expenditures to install new programs and $131 million annually to maintain those new programs.[31]

In 1987, the EPA began to pay more attention to underground storage tanks that were said to be leaking motor fuels and chemical solvents into groundwater. Most of these tanks were made of bare steel without any corrosion protection, and were nearing the end of their useful lives. About 400,000 of these underground storage tanks were thought to be leaking. Rules were issued that required existing tanks to be monitored and repaired or replaced if leaking. Since existing tanks would also have to meet the minimum requirements for new tanks within ten years, it was expected that most of them would have to be replaced during this time period. The rules banned installation of new bare steel tanks that lacked corrosion protection, and required double-walled tanks for hazardous chemicals. These rules were expected to cost industry about $410 million annually.[32] Changes to these regulations in 1988 required phasing in of new tanks within five years instead of ten with the oldest tanks forced to comply within the first year. The new tanks were also to be installed with monitoring devices.[33]

Lead poisoning also became of concern in 1987. An EPA study estimated that some 42 million Americans may drink water that exceeded the standard the EPA was proposing. The standard had been set at a 50 parts per billion level of concentration, but the EPA was considering reducing the concentration level to 20 parts per billion.[34] This level of exposure may not be harmful to adults, but in children it can cause mental retardation, stunt growth, and even lead to death. The National Resources Defense Council claimed that high levels of lead in our water cost the society over $1 billion a year in hospital and child-care costs alone. Bringing the level down to 20 parts per billion would cost $115 to $145 million per year, but the resulting savings would more than offset that number.[35]

Unlike other chemical contaminations of the water supply, the introduction of lead usually occurs between the treatment facility and the tap where water is drawn. The major culprit is lead solder in water coolers and the use of lead in plumbing solder.[36] Some communities have taken steps to reduce lead in their drinking water. The city of Seattle, for example, added lime or soda to "harden" the water, reducing the lead to almost undetectable levels. It cost about 8 cents a month per person served for this treatment, with the cost increasing to about 25 cents for smaller communities.[37] When building a home, it has been suggested that homeowners should ask the plumber to use lead-free solder, which costs only a few dollars more than leaded solder. Running the tap water for a few seconds longer than usual will also flush most of the lead out of the system.[38]

OCEANS AND COASTAL WATERS

The deterioration of oceans and coastal waters was highlighted in 1988 and 1989 when beaches were closed that were littered with medical waste and contaminated with fecal coloform bacteria. The EPA reports that one-third of the nation's shellfish beds are closed because of pollution, resulting in millions of dollars of lost revenues. Twenty-five percent of monitored estuarine waters have elevated levels of toxic substances, and eutrophication is increasing the number of dead zones where fish cannot survive. Coastal fisheries, wildlife, and waterfowl populations have declined while population and industrial growth along coastal areas have increased dramatically over the past decades. Currently, more than 120 million Americans now live within 50 miles of the ocean shore.[39] Some estimates show that by the year 2000, 75 percent of the U.S. population will live within 50 miles of the coast.

The nation's near coastal waters encompass inland waters from the coast itself to the head of the tide, which is defined as the farthest point inland at which the influence of tides on water level is detected. These waters include bays, estuaries, and coastal wetlands, and the coastal ocean out to the point at which it is no longer affected by land and water uses in the coastal drainage basin. When considered as a whole, these ecosystems support a wide range of ecological, economic, recreational, and aesthetic uses that depend on good water quality.[40] But these near coastal areas bear the brunt of massive inputs of wastes into the ocean, which can overwhelm the natural dilution and degradation processes of these areas and destroy them as sources of food and recreational pleasure.

These coastal waters and accompanying wetlands are home to many ecologically and commercially valuable species of fish, shellfish, birds, and other wildlife. Some 85 percent of the nation's commercially harvested fish are dependent on near coastal waters at some point in their life cycle. Billions of dollars a year are generated as income from commercial and recreational fishing, tourism and travel, urban waterfront and private real estate development, and recreational boating, marinas, harbors, all involving coastal waters. Millions of people use the bays, beaches, and coastal ocean for swimming, boating, fishing, hiking, and for open space. These areas are thus very valuable to the nation as a whole.[41]

These coastal environments are susceptible to contamination because they act as sinks for large quantities of pollution discharged from municipal sewage treatment plants, industrial facilities, and hazardous waste disposal sites nearby. (See Figure 7.3.) Nonpoint source runoff from agricultural lands, suburban development, city streets, and combined sewer and storm-water overflows poses an even more significant problem than point sources of pollution. Activities such as dredging, draining and filling, dam construction, and the building of shorefront houses may further degrade these environments. Debris on beaches from sewer and storm drain overflows can cause public safety and aesthetic concerns and can result in major economic losses for coastal communities during the tourist season. Growing population pressures will continue to subject these coastal ecosystems to further stress. Thus coastal waters are subject to a number of serious environmental problems including toxic contamination, eutrophication, pathogen contamination, habitat loss and alteration, and changes in living resources.[42]

As just one example of what can happen to seafood from chemical pollutants (see Exhibit 7.1), there is a windswept inlet about halfway between Galveston and Corpus Christi, Texas, called Lavaca Bay, which used to be a fisherman's paradise. But in 1989, there was a 5-square-mile section of the

Figure 7.3

America's Troubled Coasts

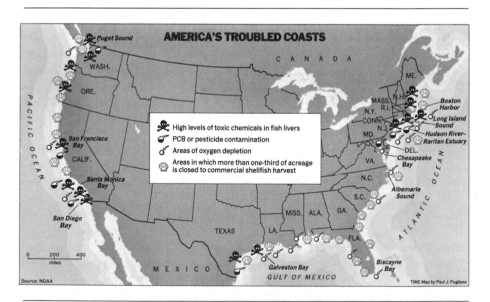

Source: Anastasia Toufexis, "The Dirty Seas," *Time,* August 1, 1988, p. 50. Copyright 1988 Time Warner Inc. Reprinted by permission.

bay that became so polluted with mercury that the finfish and crabs caught there were unfit for human consumption. The Texas Department of Health posted a warning declaring the area off-limits to fishing. The source of the mercury was a huge alumina plant on the bay operated by the Aluminum Company of America, which legally discharged mercury into the water from 1966 until 1970, an act that was thought harmless at the time, but was later found to have long-lasting impacts. When ingested in sufficient amounts, mercury can damage the human nervous system and kidneys.[43]

Exhibit 7.1

Contaminants Found in Seafood

Contaminant	Source	Possible health effects[1]
Methyl mercury	Industrial discharges	Impairment of immune system; kidney damage; central nervous system damage; reproductive system damage; hearing and vision loss
Lead	Industrial discharges; naturally occurring	Impairment of immune system nervous system damage; liver disease; reproductive damage; possible link to cancer
DDT[2]	Agricultural and urban runoff	Liver cancer; central nervous system damage; reproductive damage; tumor promotion; impairment of immune system
Chlordane[3]	Agricultural and urban runoff	Headaches; dizziness; excitability; confusion; lack of coordination; seizures; convulsions
Hepatitis A virus	Sewage	Acute inflammation of the liver; extreme fatigue; jaundice; nausea; vomiting and diarrhea
Vibrio bacteria	Naturally occurring	Mild to severe diarrhea; severe blood poisoning; skin contact with water can cause mild to severe infection of an open wound

[1] Many of the effects are based on animal studies. All depend on a variety of factors, including the form of the substance, the dose, the duration and frequency of exposure, the sensitivity of the individual, preexisting health conditions, age and genetic makeup. Many effects "probably would not occur upon the occasional ingestion of the toxicant in quantities commonly associated with food products," according to the Texas Department of Health.

[2] DDT was banned for use in the United States in 1972, but lingers in the environment and may still be used in Mexico and other countries.

[3] Banned in 1988.

Source: Texas Department of Health as reported in Jim Morris, "A Breeding Ground for Disease," *Dallas Times Herald,* July 9, 1989, p. A-17.

American shores are also being inundated by plastic debris. In one day in September 1987, volunteers collected 307 tons of litter, two-thirds of which was plastic, on the sands of the Texas Gulf Coast. This litter included 31,733 bags, 30,295 bottles, and 15,631 six-pack yokes. On a four-day trip from Maryland to Florida that ranged 100 miles offshore, a marine biologist spotted Styrofoam and other kinds of plastic trash on the surface of the water for most of the whole cruise. This kind of trash can cause serious waste disposal and pollution problems for coastal beaches and waters.[44]

Suffocating and sometimes poisonous blooms of algae, which are called red and brown tides, regularly blot the nation's coastal bays and gulfs. They usually leave a trail of dying fish and contaminated mollusks and crustaceans behind. Patches of water known as dead zones, where the oxygen in the water has almost been totally depleted, are proliferating. As many as a million fluke and flounder were killed in the summer of 1988 when they became trapped in anoxic water in the Raritan Bay in New Jersey. During the same summer, another dead zone, which was said to be 300 miles long and 10 miles wide, was adrift in the Gulf of Mexico.[45]

Regarding pollution of the oceans, dumping of dredged material, sewage sludge, and industrial wastes are major sources of pollution. Sediments dredged from urban harbors are often highly contaminated with heavy metals and toxic chemicals like PCBs and petroleum hydrocarbons. When dumped in the ocean, these contaminants can be absorbed by marine organisms.[46] The oceans also receive agricultural and urban runoff, atmospheric fallout, garbage and untreated sewage from ships, accidental oil spills from tankers and offshore oil drilling platforms, and intentional discharges of oil by tankers when they empty or clean their bilges.[47]

Should Ocean Dumping of Sewage Sludge Be Banned?

During the summer of 1988 hypodermic needles, IV tubing, blood sample vials, and other medical wastes washed ashore on beaches from Maine to North Carolina. Beaches in several states, especially New York and New Jersey, had to be closed.

In an election year the resulting public outcry prompted Congress to pass the Ocean Dumping Ban Act of 1988 banning all ocean sludge dumping by 1992. In 1988 New Jersey ordered an end to all ocean dumping of sludge by 1991, with the goal of protecting its $7 billion coastal tourism industry and its $100 million a year fishing industry.

Some elected officials and scientists oppose this ban. They argue that ocean disposal is safer and cheaper than land dumping and incineration, especially for areas such as New York City where there are not enough suitable sites for landfills or incinerators.

It is also argued that banning ocean sludge dumping will do little to prevent pollution of beaches because sewage sludge and the floatable solid waste that fouls beaches are two different things.

Proponents of ocean sludge dumping argue that debris found on beaches comes from

- combined sewers that mix storm runoff with municipal waste-water and over-flow during periods of heavy rain
- sewage treatment plants that occasionally malfunction
- illegal dumping of medical and other wastes
- floatable material that collects in streets and drains and is washed out by big storms or high tides
- garbage dumped at sea by commercial and pleasure boats
- debris thrown away by beach users

Potentially harmful medical waste represents less than 1% of beach litter. Most of the rest is plastic and paper debris dropped by beachgoers. Thus, if we want clean and safe beaches all of us will have to change our disposal-oriented lifestyles.

There is general agreement that the deep ocean is better equipped than land to handle sewage and some forms of industrial waste. But most scientists believe that the ocean should not be used for the dumping of slowly degradable or nondegradable pollutants like PCBs, some pesticides and radioactive isotopes, and toxic mercury compounds that can be biologically amplified in ocean food webs. Many of these materials are mixed with some types of sewage sludge and industrial waste being dumped into the ocean in large quantities.

There is concern that the site where sludge is dumped off the East Coast is the prime migratory path for species like tuna and marlin. The suspended sludge particles can also threaten the offshore spawning area for the bluefish, the region's number-one sport fish.

A 1988 study by NOAA scientists warned that because of the Gulf Stream currents at the deep-water site off the coast of New York, hazardous suspended solids dumped there could spread all the way to Cape Hatteras off North Carolina. Some NOAA scientists propose drilling 1.4 million 122-meter- (400 foot-) deep holes in a 26-square-kilometer (10-square-mile) section of the Atlantic floor and filling the holes with sludge from New York City.

Other scientists argue that the battering rams used to drill the holes and the debris produced would have harmful effects on shellfish and other aquatic life. Some NOAA officials argue that seabed burial is not the same as at-sea dumping and thus is not subject to the Ocean Dumping Ban Act.

Environmentalists favor requiring that sludge be treated to remove PCBs, toxic metals and other hazardous substances. Then the sludge would be safer to dispose of on the land or at sea or better yet could be used as a soil conditioner for forests, parks, and other areas not used to grow food. The small volume of highly toxic chemicals removed from the sludge could be disposed of in landfills designed for such wastes. What do you think should be done with sewage sludge?

Source: From *Living In The Environment: An Introduction To Environmental Studies* 6/E by G. Tyler Miller, Jr. © 1990 by Wadsworth, Inc. Reprinted by permission of the publisher.

The dumping of industrial wastes into the ocean declined from 5 million tons in 1973 to 0.3 millions tons in 1986, reflecting better control practices on the part of industrial facilities. (See Figure 7.4.) But sewage sludge dumping increased from 5 million tons in 1973 to 7.9 billion tons in 1986, largely due to construction and operation of new or improved sewage treatment plants that increased the production of such sludge. One of the major challenges facing the oceans will be the resolution of this kind of waste disposal crisis, where the oceans are often seen as a quick fix solution for

Figure 7.4

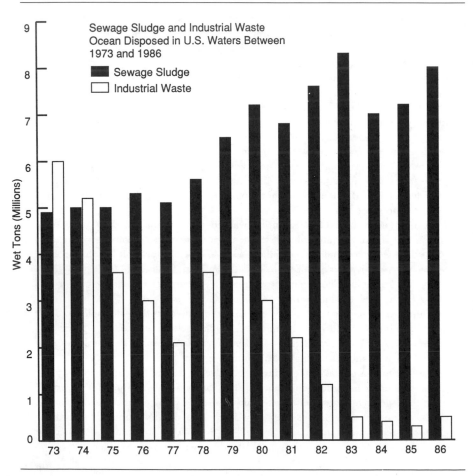

Note: For the purpose of this graph, Industrial Waste Category also includes Fish Waste and Construction Debris

Source: Office of Marine and Estuarine Protection. USEPA.

waste disposal problems. Cities will have to develop better and more ecologically sound ways to dispose of this waste material.[48] Every year barges and ships legally dump more than 172 million metric tons (189 million tons) of solid waste off the coasts of the United States where they mingle with vast amounts of agricultural and urban runoff. Countries could ban such dumping in waters under their control and an international treaty could ban dumping in international waters.[49]

Disposal of plastics from land and ships at sea has become a serious problem in the past several years. This nonbiodegradable debris can cause injury and death of fish, marine mammals, and birds. As many as 2 million seabirds and 100,000 marine mammals may die every year after eating or becoming entangled in the plastic debris. Sea turtles choke on plastic bags they apparently mistake for jellyfish. Sea lions become ensnared when they playfully poke their noses into plastic nets and rings, and unable to open their jaws in some cases, starve to death. Brown pelicans become enmeshed in fishing line and sometimes hang themselves. In Florida, people have seen them hanging from tree branches.[50]

Crude oil as it comes from the ground and refined petroleum can be accidentally or deliberately released into the ocean from a number of sources. Tanker accidents and blowouts at offshore drilling rigs are the best known sources because they receive a great deal of publicity when they occur. But about half of the oil reaching the oceans is said to come from the land as a result of runoff and dumping of waste oil by cities and industrial facilities. Tanker accidents account for only 10 to 15 percent of oil spilled into the oceans each year, but such spills can have severe ecological and economic impacts on the region where they occur. There has been a decrease since 1973 in the average annual number of major oil tanker accidents due to improved safety measures, better navigational equipment, and better training.[51] All of these factors were sadly lacking, however, during the Valdez oil spill in 1989, which was the largest such spill the United States had experienced in its waters.

Such accidents help to keep the focus on oil tankers and the dangers of transporting oil in this manner. (See Exhibit 7.2.) One possible solution is to require all tankers to have double hulls, which would reduce the danger of spills from groundings or collisions. President Jimmy Carter issued an executive order in 1976 requiring all tankers exceeding 20,000 tons that wanted to sail in American waters to be outfitted with double hulls and bottoms. Ship owners were given 5 years to comply, but 16 years later, this order has not been implemented. Oil companies are still lobbying strongly against legislation that would accomplish by 2005 what Carter wanted done by 1982, and have thus far been successful.[52]

The industry claims that such vessels would cost between 15 and 30 percent more than single-hulled vessels, and would result in an increase in shipping costs that would be passed on to consumers in higher costs for

Exhibit 7.2

The Perils of Transporting Oil by Sea

Among the most common problems and mishaps facing oil tankers:

- **Fires and Explosions,** which can happen at almost any stage of a tanker's journey, are most likely when the tanks are empty (the ballast voyage). Fumes trapped in the tanks are ignited by sparks generated by the cleaning process. Vapors can also build up in the pump room as was evidently the case in the Mega Borg spill.

- **Collisions** at the entrance to, or in ports. In the collision of the Phillips Oklahoma and another ship in the River Humber, England, in September 1989, its side tanks were penetrated and it lost 750 tons of crude oil.

- **Break Ups** in heavy weather. In 1988–89 three tankers: the Athenian Venture, carrying 30,000 tons of product, the Odyssey, carrying 130,000 tons of oil, and the Maasguar, carrying 30,000 tons of chemicals, all sank fully loaded, with the loss of all 79 crew members.

- **Running Aground** while entering or leaving ports has caused many spills including the disastrous Exxon Valdez spill in March 1989.

- **Overflows** while loading or discharging oil. In August 1989 the Minerva over-filled tanks and discharged 2 tons of crude into the Delaware River.

- **Hull Cracks** can occur, especially on large American tankers making the Alaska run; in January 1989 the hull of the Cove Leader cracked while loading in Alaska, spilling 10 tons of crude.

- **Poor Maintenance** has been a contributing factor in some accidents. Faulty maintenance and poor design may have contributed to the loss of a plate on the Pacificos, which spilled 10,000 tons of oil off the coast of Africa in October 1989.

- **Contact Damage,** such as hitting the dock or another ship, can rupture the hull. In 1989 the Stolt Sea was hit while moored at Avondale, La., on the Mississippi River, losing 200 tons of bunker fuel oil.

Source: Caleb Solomon and Daniel Machalaba, "Troubled Waters: Oil Tankers' Safety Is Assailed as Mishaps Occur Almost Daily," *Wall Street Journal,* June 20, 1990, p. A-1. Reprinted by permission of *Wall Street Journal* ©1990 Dow Jones & Company, Inc. All Rights Reserved Worldwide.

gasoline, heating oil, and other petroleum products. The American Petroleum Institute (API) put the cost of retrofitting the fleet of 653 American and foreign tank ships and 1,800 U.S. barges with double bottoms at $16.6 billion. The API also claimed that there would not be enough space in U.S. shipyards to meet the proposed deadline. It also stated that the cost of this action would have an inflationary effect on the U.S. economy.[53]

Congress was also considering oil spill liability legislation that would increase liability standards for oil spills, impose a bigger tax to finance a cleanup fund, and require better cleanup plans. Critics of this legislation claim that this bill would do little to fix the problem, which is that legal liability is now too uncertain and that too many regulatory layers conflict to allow rapid cleanups. Meanwhile, the oil industry proposed funding its own rapid-deployment force to clean up spills wherever they occur in U.S. waters. Twenty firms agreed to create a $35-million Petroleum Industry Response Organization to reduce the harmful effects of spills and the financial costs to shippers. There would be 5 regional response teams, according to this plan, and 19 other staging areas for quick cleanups.[54]

The effects of oil on ocean ecosystems depend on the type of oil, the amount released, the distance of the release from coastal areas, the time of year, weather conditions, the average water temperature, and ocean and tidal currents. After an oil spill, hydrocarbons such as benzene and toluene affect shellfish and nonmigratory fish, sometimes killing them in great numbers. Other chemicals remain on the surface and form floating tarlike blobs that adhere to marine birds, sea otters, seals, sand, rocks, and almost all objects they encounter. This oily coating destroys the animals' natural insulation and bouyancy, and most drown or die of exposure. Heavy oil components that sink to the ocean floor or wash into estuaries can have the greatest long-term ecosystem impact. These components can kill bottom-dwelling organisms such as crabs, oysters, mussels, and clams or make them unfit for human consumption. Oil slicks that wash onto beaches can have serious economic effects on coastal residents who lose income from fishing and tourist activities.[55]

In order to deal with pollution of the oceans and near coastal areas, the EPA established the Office of Marine and Estuarine Protection in 1984 to administer all the agency's ocean and coastal programs. Some of the most important achievements of this office include (1) continuation of the Great Lakes restoration program and startup of programs in the Chesapeake Bay and 17 estuaries that are part of the National Estuary Program, (2) progress toward a ban on ocean dumping of sewage, sludge, and industrial waste, (3) the creation of a Coastal and Marine Policy to promote coordination of coastal programs conducted by different federal and state agencies, and (4) the implementation of a near coastal waters plan for managing environmental problems in waters that are not included in the ongoing bay and estuary programs.[56]

In the next decade, the EPA intends to work with state and local governments to increase the acres of shellfish beds open to harvest, reduce fishery bans and advisories due to contamination, decrease beach closures, and eliminate ocean dumping of sewage and industrial wastes. The EPA also wants to strengthen nonpoint source management programs in all coastal counties and tighten controls on point source discharges of toxics, nutrients, and other pollutants to restore the quality of coastal waters. Storm-water discharge permits will be required for large cities in all coastal counties, and help will be provided to smaller municipalities with storm-water problems. State and local governments are being encouraged to manage coastal development so that it proceeds in an environmentally sound direction.[57]

The EPA is asking all types of offshore activities, such as oil and gas operations, to help protect marine waters and surrounding ecosystems from degradation. It is also taking enforcement actions to eliminate any illegal ocean disposal of waste material. Finally, the EPA and other federal agencies are working with international bodies such as the United Nations to assess the health of the world's oceans and develop an integrated approach to preventing their further degradation.[58] Such an approach is needed if we are to halt pollution of the oceans and ensure survival of the human race. As Jacques-Yves Cousteau commented, "The very survival of the human species depends upon the maintenance of an ocean clean and alive, spreading all around the world. The ocean is our planet's life belt."

SOLUTIONS

The potential solutions for ensuring safe drinking water and improving the quality of surface water are not cheap or, in most cases, easy to implement. But it seems the best solutions focus on inputs that cause contamination rather than trying to clean up contaminated water. Such an approach is more ecologically and, in most cases, economically sound than allowing water to become contaminated in the first place. Most people would agree that the most economical and surest way of ensuring safe drinking water, for example, is to make sure that existing wells and surface-water sources do not become contaminated. There are several actions that can be taken within this general approach.

1. *Reduce or eliminate the use of pesticides and fertilizers in agriculture.* According to a report published by the Office of Technology Assessment, 260,000 tons of active ingredients in pesticides and 42 million tons of fertilizer are spread annually over the equivalent of 280 million acres across the country.[59] Contamination usually occurs through conventional application on farmland and an increasingly common method of irrigation called chemigation, in which water is mixed with pesticides. In addition, fertilizers are also contaminating the groundwater in many communities that rely on agriculture to support their economy. Contamination in states such as Iowa is particularly worrisome to federal and state officials because Iowans rely on groundwater for over three-quarters of their drinking water supply. Five years ago, 40 public groundwater wells exceeded the federal standard for nitrates, a common fertilizer.[60]

Alternative means of pest control are available. One study done by the University of Nebraska has shown that crop yield can actually be increased without the use of pesticides.[61] This method involves a constant monitoring of insect and bird seasonal variations, planting techniques, and alternate field cycles of usage. It is not yet known if this method can be used on a large scale, but the results look promising. Alternatives to the use of fertilizer also exist that promise crop yields comparable to yields using fertilizer. If pesticide and fertilizer usage could be reduced, this action would have a major impact on the pollution problem regarding surface and drinking water.

2. *Increase the number of banned substances that can be disposed of in our nation's waterways.* Of the 65,000 chemicals in existence today, 40,000 are suspected to be carcinogenic. Yet only a handful have been banned from disposal in our nation's waterways. While the EPA plans on adding approximately 15 to 25 new chemicals to the banned list each year, this number pales in comparison with the thousand or so new chemicals that are introduced into the environment annually. The testing procedure must be speeded up so that more chemicals can be banned if necessary, and industry must take more precautionary steps to make sure the new chemicals they generate are environmentally safe and will not cause a water pollution problem.

3. *Promote industrial recycling throughout the country.* Water supplies for cities and industries are typically taken from a river or aquifer, used in a factory or home, and then released as "wastewater" to the nearest water source. As the demand for water increases, this approach easily overtaxes existing water sources.[62] Not only must large quantities of fresh water be made available, but natural waterways are used to dilute the wastes that are discharged. This traditional way of thinking and setting up industrial processes cannot continue because we are running out of water resources.

Recycling is an alternative that can help solve many of these problems, a technique that provides incentives for business. Some companies, such as the 3M Corporation, have already successfully employed a waste-recycling system. In such a closed-loop system, waste isn't simply dumped into a nearby stream or lake, but instead, chemical wastewater is separated and the different chemical compounds are returned to their original form. In this way, the chemicals that are recovered can be used to create new products.[63]

An Armco steel mill in Kansas City, Missouri, which manufactures steel bars from recycled ferrous scrap, draws into the mill only 9 cubic meters of water per ton of steel produced, compared with as much as 100 to 200 cubic meters per ton in many other steel plants. Besides cutting its total water needs by using recycled iron scrap rather than new metal, the Armco plant uses each liter of water 16 times before releasing it, after final treatment, to the river. There are other such success stories, such as a paper mill in Hadera, Israel, which requires only 12 cubic meters of water per ton of paper, whereas many of the world's paper mills use 7 to 10 times this amount.[64]

Even though several such stories can be told, the recycling of water in manufacturing plants has not been attempted on a large-scale basis. But this may change. Many industrial pollution control processes already recycle water by design. And because wastewater must be treated to a high-quality level to meet environmental standards, recycling partially treated water within a plant may become more economical than paying the high costs associated with treatment of discharges to the level required. As pollution control standards are made more stringent, the costs of industrial recycling tend to go down and become more economically feasible.[65]

4. *Require industrial pretreatment for discharge and reuse.* Pretreatment is a fancy word for cleaning up the discharge from industrial plants before it is discharged into municipal sewage systems, a practice that exists in many localities. Without pretreatment, many adverse effects can occur including the corrosion of collection systems or of the sewage treatment system due to corrosives in the wastewater, exposure of workers to toxic substances and hazardous fumes, limited to more expensive sludge disposal options, or the passing through of hazardous toxins to the water supply.

Such pretreatment programs can have beneficial effects for companies. These programs can also have some very important benefits for the environment. When a wastewater treatment facility treats water, it basically takes the unwanted organic material as well as some toxins out of the water and sends the treated water to customers or discharges it into lakes and rivers. What is left behind is a material called sludge, the organic and toxic waste taken from the water. This sludge has to be disposed of somehow, probably in a landfill or in an incinerator. Both of these methods of disposal have problems, but if this sludge does not contain any toxic material, it can be disposed of much more easily.[66]

5. *Encourage public recycling and conservation.* Probably one of the most ignored and forgotten methods of increasing the supply of fresh drinking water is the notion of conservation. Historically, conservation has been used only during short-term crises, such as drought-induced water shortages. But as cities grow and face severe physical and financial constraints to supply water to thirsty residents, conservation on a long-term basis makes more sense. Building new wastewater treatment facilities is an expensive proposition, as is the search for ever more distant water supplies and the transportation of those supplies where they are needed.

The U.S. Congressional Budget Office estimates that of the nation's 756 large urban water systems (those serving more than 50,000 people), 170 will need additional water supplies by 1992. The city of Tucson, for example, is expected to triple in size by 2025. The city currently relies solely on groundwater, of which 307 million cubic meters pumped out each year is not replaced.[67] The city of Los Angeles is facing severe water shortages due to its tremendous growth over the past several decades, and the fact that it has to get its water from sources many miles away. The city is facing challenges from small communities that also rely on the same water sources. Drought conditions only amplify an already serious problem.[68]

Washington, D.C., was able to conserve water through better management techniques. The city put into place a conservation-oriented rate structure, a public awareness program, implemented a new efficient water delivery network, and diverted some flood storage capacity to the water supply. These four programs made a $250 million investment unnecessary. The city of Boston launched a leak repair and detection program in 1988 to save water from leaking out of its system. Later it was determined that the program reduced water losses in the greater Boston area by more than 80 percent, from more than 25 million gallons per day to fewer than 4 million gallons. Florida, which was hard hit in the early 1990s with little rainfall, instituted fines and penalties to violators of the newly implemented state water resource laws, designed to curb waste and encourage recycling.[69]

Recycling is also playing a part in extending the nation's water supplies. The city of El Paso is experimenting with injecting treated wastewater into aquifers that supply water to that region. If the plan works, city officials believe they can save at least 15 percent of the current water supplies now used. The use of water-efficient fixtures can also save a great amount of water each day. The typical U.S. toilet, for example, turns about 5 gallons of high-quality water into wastewater each time it is flushed. This is a needless waste of water. There are currently a variety of fixtures on the market that can greatly reduce water usage. Substituting the most common water-saving varieties for a conventional model could reduce household water use by one-fifth. Use of extremely low-water fixtures could cut existing levels of water usage by as much as 50 to 70 percent, according to some estimates.[70]

Some experts recommend the use of markets to allocate shrinking water supplies and encourage conservation. In many instances, it is said, concerns about water do not stem from an absence of supplies, but from the absence of a proper market to ensure a balance between consumer demand and those supplies. If government regulations and subsidies distorting water use were to be eliminated, water markets would allow excess supplies to be sold or leased to those who were willing to pay for more water. Water quality could also be improved if Congress were to introduce a system of tradable pollution discharge permits, to be required for all public and private pollution discharges. The federal government would establish the maximum level of discharges for each water basin or drainage area, and then allow the states to meet discharge goals through the most cost-effective methods.[71]

A market for water would work like any other market; owners of water supplies would offer their water for sale and users would offer to buy it, with the two parties negotiating an agreeable price. Only by removing federal subsidies will the groups interested in water be forced to evaluate the true costs and benefits of projects. Besides achieving an equilibrium between existing supply and demand for water, markets would also (1) encourage conservation by requiring users to pay the full market price of supplies, which means prices would rise when supplies are short, (2) when facing high market costs for limited supplies, potential users, such as developers, would be forced to consider whether the cost of water made the development worthwhile, and (3) a market price would encourage users of artificially cheap water, such as farmers, to consider selling water to those who value it highly but cannot obtain supplies under the current system.[72]

What do people do if the water supply is already contaminated? Many wastewater treatment plants are ill equipped to remove toxic substances, as they were designed to remove mostly organic materials. What do people do if they suspect the water is unsafe to drink? Bottled water is one solution. In the United States, there are about 475 bottling plants in operation representing about 600 different brands. Americans spent about $2 billion on bottled water in 1989, making it the fastest growing segment of the entire American beverage industry.[73] But questions have to be raised about the safety of this bottled water. Much of it comes from the same aquifers that produce tap water. No one can say with confidence that the gallon of spring water we buy at the market isn't as contaminated as tap water.

For one thing, the Food and Drug Administration (FDA), not the EPA, regulates the bottled water industry. The FDA standards for bottled water are not as stringent as the EPA's standards for tap water, and the testing done by bottlers under FDA guidelines is not as frequent as testing done by the EPA for ground and surface water.[74] The point is that most water ultimately comes from the same source, and if one portion of this source is contaminated, the possibility exists that the entire supply for a region of the country is contaminated. Thus the use of bottled water may give consumers a false sense of security.

The point-of-use water purification market is one area that looks promising. This market involves the use of household water purification devices. There are three different technologies on the market today: (1) an activated carbon filtration system, in which contaminants attach themselves directly to the carbon's porous surface, (2) distillers in which the water is heated until it vaporizes and bacteria and suspended matter are removed, and (3) the reverse osmosis system in which water is forced through a semipermeable membrane that catches most dissolved components in the water. All three types of filtering techniques can be quite effective, but unfortunately, not all units will catch all different types of contaminants. The point-of-use market is expected to grow from its current level of $1.7 billion a year to over $3.8 billion by 1995, according to some reports.[75]

Regarding surface water, alternatives for cleaning up contaminated water are being developed. Scientists at the Sandia National Laboratories have devised a way to clean up polluted water with a sun-powered detoxification system. The unit may be able to remove most organic materials, including most industrial solvents, pesticides, dioxins, PCBs, and other chemicals. The process is radically different from conventional wastewater treatment processes that only remove toxins from water. It actually breaks down the toxins into smaller, safer molecules that can then be released into the water system. The unit takes ultraviolet light from the sun and concentrates it on the polluted water, which then separates into water, carbon dioxide, and some very dilute acids that can very easily be neutralized. The system cleans about 30 gallons of water a minute, and scientists believe that they can increase this by a factor of 2 to 3 within a few years.[76]

Another alternative to conventional sewage systems is already being used in some places. "Natural" sewage systems modeled after nature's own purifying powers are already treating the sewage of some communities. Cattails, reeds, and rushes in human-made marshes are extracting toxic chemicals and metals from highly polluted wastewater, canal lilies are cleaning up the discharge from backyard septic tanks, and in a New England greenhouse, snails, microorganisms, march plants, and fish are transforming raw sewage into fresh water.[77] Thus nature's way may provide some alternatives that more communities can adopt.

Since farming accounts for some 70 percent of global water use, irrigation is responsible for many environmental problems. Waterlogged and salted land, declining and contaminated aquifers, shrinking lakes and inland seas, and the destruction of aquatic habitats are some of the problems caused by excessive irrigation. Degradation of irrigated land from poor water management is forcing some land to be retired completely. Contamination of land and water by salts and toxic chemicals is only one indication that some irrigation is unstainable. The falling water table is a signal that groundwater withdrawals are exceeding the rate of replenishment. Visible ecological damage from large-scale irrigation projects has spawned strong opposition to the construction of new dams and diversion projects. New concerns are centered on the loss of free-flowing rivers, the destruction of fisheries from stream flow depletion, and damage to the marine and wildlife habitat.[78]

In conclusion, one expert recommends that any water management project should lean toward increasing the efficiency of water consumption rather than toward increasing the supply of water because the latter is often more costly and merely postpones a crisis situation. Mining of groundwater in order to increase the supply should be avoided at all costs, it is recommended, unless it can be guaranteed that the aquifer from which the water is being taken will be replenished in a reasonable period of time. Prevention of pollution and restoration of bodies of water that are already polluted should take precedence over the development of purification technologies. Purifying technology is becoming more complex and costly as the number of pollutants in the water increases. End-of-pipe remedies for industrial water pollution should be replaced by recycling and reuse. If sound principles of this kind are not followed in a water management system, it is all to easy to predict what will eventually happen to our water supply.[79]

$\sim$

Questions for Discussion

1. Where does the fresh water that we use come from, and how much is available on a per capita basis? What is an aquifer? How are aquifers recharged or replenished?

2. How can fresh water become contaminated? What are some of the main types of water pollutants and what are some of their effects? What factors affect the ability of a lake or river to recover from contamination by these pollutants?

3. What are the major sources of surface water pollution? Distinguish between point and nonpoint sources of water pollution. Give examples of each type. How are these kinds of sources controlled?

4. Describe the National Pollutant Elimination Discharge System. How does it work and what is required of business organizations? What kinds of sources are regulated in this manner?

5. What are technology-based standards? Describe the meaning of the technology categories currently in force. Are these relatively easy to understand and apply to business organizations? Can you think of any standards that might work better?

6. Give some examples of nonpoint sources of pollution. How are these sources controlled? Are these types of controls easy to apply? Why or why not? What incentives exist to comply with the regulations? What kind of a system might work better to control these sources of water pollution?

7. What are the major sources of groundwater contamination? How are these sources of pollution controlled? What kind of standards are in force to control these sources? Are you confident the system works well enough to protect your local drinking water supplies?

8. What kind of pressures exist with respect to our coastal waters? What pollution threats to coastal waters exist because of these pressures? What valuable economic benefits are provided by coastal waters? What ecological functions do they perform?

9. What is happening to our oceans? What are the most important sources of pollution of our oceans? How can such pollution be controlled? What threats do oil spills pose to oceans and how can they be prevented?

10. Evaluate the solutions to water pollution presented in the chapter. Which strike you as the most practical? Which are likely to be most effective? Which will impact business most severely? What would you recommend to deal with our water pollution problems?

NOTES

1. G. Tyler Miller, *Living in the Environment,* 6th ed. (Belmont, CA: Wadsworth, 1990), p. 238.

2. Ibid.

3. Ibid., pp. 238-239.

4. Ibid., p. 240.

5. Ibid., p. 242.

6. Ibid.

7. Ibid., p. 518.

8. Ibid., pp. 521-522.

9. Ibid., pp. 523-524.

10. Ibid., p. 525.

11. United States Environmental Protection Agency, *Environmental Progress and Challenges: EPA's Update* (Washington, DC: U.S. Government Printing Office, 1988), p. 45.

12. *Setting the Course: Clean Water* (Washington, DC: National Wildlife Federation, undated), p. 5.

13. *Environmental Progress and Challenges,* p. 46.

14. Ibid.,

15. *A Guide to the Clean Water Act Amendments* (Washington, DC: Environmental Protection Agency, 1978), pp. 1-2.

16. EPA, *Environmental Progress and Challenges,* p. 72.

17. Robert E. Taylor, "Senate Approves Clean Water Act, 86-14, Joining House in Overriding Reagan Veto," *Wall Street Journal,* February 5, 1987, p. 5.

18. *Clean Water and Agriculture* (Washington, DC: Environmental Protection Agency, 1977), pp. 2-3.

19. Environmental Protection Agency, *Meeting the Environmental Challenge* (Washington, DC: U.S. Government Printing Office, 1990), p. 2.

20. Ibid., pp. 2-3.

21. "Photos Are Developed in Lake Water," *Times-Picayune,* November 14, 1990, p. A-11.

22. EPA, *Meeting the Environmental Challenge,* p. 3.

23. Miller, *Living in the Environment,* p. 536.

24. Ibid., p. 537.

25. Ibid., pp. 537-538.

26. Andy Pasztor, "EPA Will Let States Retain Responsibility for Safety of Underground Water Supply," *Wall Street Journal,* December 30, 1983, p. 28.

27. Robert E. Taylor, "EPA's Plan to Regulate Contaminants of Water Isn't Seen Satisfying Congress," *Wall Street Journal,* October 14, 1985, p. 5.

28. Environmental Protection Agency, *Safe Drinking Water Act: 1986 Amendments* (Washington, DC: U.S. Government Printing Office, 1986), pp. 1-5.

29. "EPA Expands Rules in Battle to Control Water Contamination," *Wall Street Journal,* March 7, 1990, p. A-8.

30. "The Year of the Deal," *National Wildlife,* Vol. 29, No. 2 (February-March 1991), p. 36.

31. EPA, *Meeting the Environmental Challenge,* p. 2.

32. Robert E. Taylor, "EPA Plans to Require the Replacement of Many Storage Tanks Within 10 Years," *Wall Street Journal,* April 3, 1987, p. 4. See also "Costly Cleanups at The Gas Pump," *Business Week,* April 20, 1987, pp. 28–29.

33. Paulette Thomas, "EPA Issues Rules to Prevent Leaks in Storage Tanks," *Wall Street Journal,* September 14, 1988, p. 52.

34. Terrance Monmaney, "Poison in the Plumbing?" *Newsweek,* December 21, 1987, p. 56.

35. Stanley Weilborn, "Pouring Lead from the Tap," *U.S. News & World Report,* August 3, 1988, p. 35.

36. Barbara Rosewicz, "Electric Coolers May Add Unsafe Levels of Lead to Drinking Water, Study Finds," *Wall Street Journal,* December 10, 1987, p. 11. See also Barbara Rosewicz, "Water Coolers Focus of Inquiry on Lead Risk," *Wall Street Journal,* February 4, 1988, p. 21.

37. Weilborn, "Pouring Lead from the Tap," p. 35.

38. Ibid.

39. EPA, *Meeting the Environmental Challenge,* p. 4.

40. EPA, *Environmental Progress and Challenges,* p. 65.

41. Ibid.

42. Ibid., pp. 65–68.

43. Jim Morris, "A Breeding Ground for Disease," *Dallas Times Herald,* July 9, 1989, p. A-17.

44. Anastasia Toufexis, "The Dirty Seas," *Time,* August 1, 1988, p. 47.

45. Ibid., p. 46.

46. EPA, *Environmental Progress and Challenges,* p. 68.

47. Miller, *Living in the Environment,* p. 529.

48. EPA, *Environmental Progress and Challenges,* p. 69.

49. Miller, *Living in the Environment,* pp. 531–533.

50. Toufexis, "The Dirty Seas," p. 47.

51. Miller, *Living in the Environment,* p. 533.

52. William P. Coughlin, "Shippers Hold Out Against Double-Hull Tankers," *Times-Picayune,* May 27, 1009, p. A-8.

53. Ibid.

54. "Cleaning Up Oil," *Wall Street Journal,* March 30, 1990, p. A-10. The Oil Pollution Act passed by Congress in 1990 began to take effect in 1991 as tankers calling at U.S. ports were required to pay 5 cents a barrel for each barrel delivered. These fees are earmarked to pay or help pay for damage from spills. In addition, tanker operators face unlimited liability in connection with spills under the new law. See Edgar Poe, "Billion Dollar Settlement in the Exxon Valdez Case," *Wall Street Journal,* March 16, 1991, p. B-7.

55. Miller, *Living in the Environment,* pp. 534–535.

56. EPA, *Meeting the Environmental Challenge,* p. 4.

57. Ibid., p. 5.

58. Ibid.

59. "No More Pesticides?" *CBS Newsmagazine 60 Minutes,* March 24, 1990, p. 14.

60. Ibid.

61. "University of Nebraska Study Shines New Light on Alternatives to Pesticides," *Agribusiness News,* June 1987, p. 27.

62. Sandra Postel, "Water for the Future: On Tap or Down the Drain," *The Futurist,* March-April 1986, p. 18.

63. See Robert P. Bringer, "Pollution Prevention Plus," *Pollution Engineering,* Vol. XX, No. 10 (October 1988), pp. 84–89.

64. Postel, "Water for the Future," p. 18.

65. Ibid.

66. Anthony Ladd, Lecture at Loyola University, New Orleans, March 25, 1990.

67. Postel, "Water for the Future," pp. 19–20.

68. Richard Martin, "A Fight to Rescue a Dying Lake," *Insight,* October 17, 1988, pp. 20–21.

69. Postel, "Water for the Future," p. 21.

70. Ibid., p. 19.

71. Kent Jeffreys, "How Markets for Water Would Protect the Environment," *The Heritage Foundation State Backgrounder,* September 26, 1989, pp. 1–10.

72. Ibid.

73. Gina Bellafante, "Bottled Water: Fads and Facts," *Garbage,* January-February 1990, pp. 46–50.

74. Ibid. See also "Tap Water May Be Safest, Officials Say," *Times-Picayune,* April 11, 1991, p. D-1.

75. *U.S. Water News,* March 1990, p. 75.

76. Robert Pool, "Sun-Powered Pollution Clean Up," *Science,* Vol. 245 (March 1988), p. 23.

77. Janet Marinelli, "After the Flush, The Next Generation," *Garbage,* January-February 1990, pp. 24–35.

78. Sandra Postel, "Saving Water for Agriculture," *State of the World 1990* (Washington, DC: Worldwatch Institute, 1990), p. 47.

79. J. W. Maurits la Riviere, "Threats to the World's Water," *Scientific American,* Vol. 261, No. 3 (September 1989), p. 94.

SUGGESTED READINGS

Baker, Brian. *Groundwater Protection from Pesticides.* New York: Garland, 1990.

Borgese, Elisabeth Mann. *The Future of the Oceans.* New York: Harvest House, 1986.

Conservation Foundation. *Groundwater Pollution*. Washington, DC: Conservation Foundation, 1987.

King, Jonathan. *Troubled Water: The Poisoning of America's Drinking Water*. Emmaus, PA: Rodale Press, 1985.

Kneese, Allen V., and Blair T. Bower. *Managing Water Quality: Economics, Technology, Institutions*. Washington, DC: Resources for the Future, 1984.

Marx, Wesley. *The Oceans: Our Last Resource*. San Francisco: Sierra Club Books, 1981.

National Academy of Sciences. *Oil in the Sea*. Washington, DC: National Academy Press, 1985.

National Academy of Sciences. *Drinking Water and Health*. Washington, DC: National Academy Press, 1986.

National Wildlife Federation. *Setting the Course: Clean Water*. Washington, DC: National Wildlife Federation, undated.

Office of Technology Assessment. *Protecting the Nation's Groundwater from Contamination*. Washington, DC: U.S. Government Printing Office, 1984.

Office of Technology Assessment. *Wastes in Marine Environments*. Washington, DC: U.S. Government Printing Office, 1987.

Patrick, R. E. Ford, and J. Quarles, eds. *Groundwater Contamination in the United States*. Philadelphia: University of Pennsylvania Press, 1987.

United States Environmental Protection Agency. *A Ground-Water Protection Strategy*. Washington, DC: EPA, 1984.

United States Environmental Protection Agency. *Environmental Progress and Challenges: EPA's Update*. Washington, DC: U.S. Government Printing Office, 1988.

United States Environmental Protection Agency. *Meeting the Environmental Challenge*. Washington, DC: U.S. Government Printing Office, 1990.

CHAPTER 8

PESTICIDES
AND TOXIC SUBSTANCES

∽

Pesticides and toxic substances, which have proven useful for many purposes, both contain chemicals that may be dangerous to human health and the environment. Their toxic effects need to be investigated and regulated if necessary to protect human beings and the environment from serious damage. Even though pesticides and toxic substances are subject to different sets of laws and regulations, they warrant treatment in the same chapter.

PESTICIDES

Pests destroy crops worth billions of dollars each year, and with a steadily expanding population and a decrease in available land, farmers worldwide have used more and more pesticides to control these pests and maintain high crop yields. A pest is considered any unwanted organism that directly or indirectly interferes with human activity. Weeds are also a problem when they invade gardens, croplands, and other areas and compete for soil nutrients and water. Since about 1945, gardens and fields of crops have been treated with a variety of chemicals called pesticides. These are substances that can kill undesirable organisms and weeds. The most widely used types of pesticides are the following:

- *Herbicides:* Used to kill weeds, which are unwanted plants that compete with crop plants for soil nutrients.
- *Insecticides:* Used to kill insects that consume crops and food and transmit diseases to humans and livestock.

- *Fungicides:* Used to kill fungi that damage crops.
- *Rodenticides:* Used to kill rodents, mostly rats and mice.[1]

Many people believe that there is no alternative to pesticide use, given existing technology, to raise crops on the scale required to feed an ever growing human population. Besides helping in the production of greater quantities of food, pesticides also help reduce loss of food in storage and control disease carriers. Each year, about 3 billion pounds of pesticides are used for these and other purposes. Agriculture accounts for the greatest percentage, followed by industry, forestry, and government, and home

---

Common Usages of Pesticides

- Fiber crops—cotton and hemp, for example.
- Specialized field crops, such as tobacco.
- Crops grown for oil, such as castor bean and safflower.
- Ornamental shrubs and vines, like mistletoe.
- General soil treatments, such as manure and mulch.
- Household and domestic dwellings.
- Processed nonfood products—textiles and paper, for example.
- Fur and wool-bearing animals such as mink and fox, laboratory and zoo animals, pet sprays, dips, collars, litter, and bedding treatments.
- Dairy farm milk-handling equipment.
- Wood production treatments on railroad ties, lumber, boats, and bridges.
- Aquatic sites, including swimming pools, diving boards, fountains, and hot tubs.
- Uncultivated nonagricultural areas, such as airport landing fields, tennis courts, highway rights-of-way, oil tank farms, ammunition storage depots, petroleum tank farms, sawmills, and drive-in theaters.
- General indoor/outdoor treatments, bird roosting areas, mosquito control.
- Hospitals, including syringes, surgical instruments, pacemakers, rubber gloves, bandages, and bedpans.
- Barber shops and beauty shops.
- Mortuaries and funeral homes.
- Preservatives in paints, vinyl shower curtains, and disposable diapers.
- Articles used on the human body, such as human hair wigs, contact lenses, dentures, and insect repellents.
- Specialty uses, such as mothproofing and preserving specimens in museums.

Source: Environmental Protection Agency, *Environmental Progress and Challenges; EPA's Update* (Washington, DC: U.S. Government Printing Office, 1988), p. 128.

gardening and lawn usage.[2] Pesticides are used for many purposes, as the following list illustrates, and not all pesticides are used in agriculture, as is commonly thought.

Yet in poisoning pests, humans may also be poisoning themselves. Pesticides persist in the environment for long periods of time, and move up through the food chain from plankton or insects to animals and humans, making dietary exposure unavoidable in many situations. They also move downward through soil to contaminate groundwater used for drinking. Through these exposures, pesticides cause cancer, birth defects, and other health and environmental problems. Worldwide, about 2.3 million metric tons (2.5 million tons) of pesticides are used each year, or an average of a pound for each person on earth. About 85 percent of pesticides are used in developed countries, but use in developing nations is growing rapidly.[3]

Pesticide use has increased as industrialized agricultural practices have become more widespread throughout the world. Diverse ecosystems containing small populations of many species are replaced with greatly simplified agricultural ecosystems that contain large populations of only one or two desired plant species. In such simplified ecosystems, some organisms that would be controlled naturally in more diverse systems can grow in number and achieve the status of pests that pose serious threats to crops. As a result, the human race has to spend a great deal of time and money controlling these pests through the use of pesticides.[4]

In the United States, about 700 biologically active ingredients and 1,200 inert ingredients are mixed to make some 50,000 individual pesticide products. About 77 percent of these products are applied to commercial cropland, 11 percent to government and industrial lands, another 11 percent is used by households, and 1 percent is used in forest lands. Herbicides account for 85 percent of all pesticide use in the United States and 88 percent of the pesticides used for farmland. Insecticides make up about 10 percent of pesticide use in the United States, and fungicides another 5 percent. About 20 percent of the pesticides used each year in the United States are applied to lawns, gardens, parks, and golf courses. About 91 percent of all U.S. households use pesticides indoors, with the average homeowner applying about five times more pesticide per unit of land area than farmers.[5]

One of the first people to point out the dangers of pesticides was Rachel Carson. In her book *Silent Spring,* she presented information about the dark side of pesticide use to the public.[6] Before this, pesticides were by and large seen as an unqualified benefit, but after her book, fear began to spread throughout society that pesticides were unmanageable poisons. Concerns increased as more studies were done substantiating the dangers of unregulated pesticide usage. The World Health Organization (WHO), for example, estimated that at least 1 million people worldwide are poisoned by pesticides and 3,000 to 20,000 of them die each year because of exposure. At least half of those poisoned and 75 percent of those killed are farm workers in developing nations where warnings are not adequate and regulation is either lax or nonexistent.[7]

In the United States, some estimates claim that at least 313,000 of the 7 million farm workers become seriously ill from exposure to pesticides each year and at least 25 of them are killed. Some 20,000 Americans, the majority of whom are children, become sick because of unsafe use or storage of pesticides in and around the home each year. After medicines, pesticides are the second most frequent cause of poisoning in young children. Accidents and unsafe practices in plants manufacturing pesticides can expose workers, their families, and sometimes entire communities to harmful levels of pesticides or chemicals used in their manufacture.[8]

Scientists are concerned about possible long-term effects of continuous, long-term exposure to very low levels of pesticides. These chronic effects, if they exist, will not show up for several decades after exposure, making early detection impossible. It is said that traces of almost 500 of the 700 active ingredients used in pesticides in the United States show up in the food most people eat every day. Pesticide residues are likely to be found on tomatoes, grapes, apples, lettuce, oranges, potatoes, beef, and dairy products. In 1987, the National Academy of Sciences reported that exposure to pesticides in food could cause up to 20,000 cases of cancer a year in the United States, in a worst-case scenario. The same year the EPA ranked pesticide residues in foods as the third most serious environmental problem in the country.[9]

These concerns erupted in the spring of 1989, when the National Resources Defense Council (NRDC) released a report stating that apples treated with the pesticide Alar were exposing children to dangerously high levels of daminiozide, a possible carcinogen. The NRDC claimed that daminiozide use may cause 1 case of cancer for every 4,200 preschoolers, 240 times the acceptable standard.[10] The story was shown on *60 Minutes* and actress Meryl Streep made several appearances on talk shows and Capitol Hill attacking pesticides. Soon after these incidents, apples were ordered removed from school cafeterias in New York City, Los Angeles, and Chicago. Other school systems followed suit, and signs were posted above produce bins all over the country advertising Alar-free apples. The state of Washington, where 50 percent of the nation's apples are grown, faced huge economic losses.[11]

REGULATION

As a direct result of this growing concern about the dangers of unregulated pesticide usage, federal pesticide regulation was toughened and enforcement responsibility transferred from the Department of Agriculture, which promoted chemical pest control, to the Environmental Protection Agency (EPA). Congress also passed the Federal Insecticide, Fungicide, and Rodenticide Act (FIFRA) in 1972, which required that all commercial pesticides be approved for general or restricted usage. Since the passage of this law, the EPA has banned over 40 pesticides because of their potential hazards to human health. The use of DDT was banned in 1972, and several other pesticides such as aldrin, dieldrin, toxaphene, and ethylene dibromide have been suspended or banned since that time.[12] (See Exhibit 8.1.) Over the past 20 years, the EPA has canceled the registrations of 35 potentially hazardous pesticides and eliminated the use of 60 toxic inert ingredients in pesticide products.[13]

Pesticides are thus regulated by FIFRA, which assigned EPA the responsibility for protecting human health from any commercially available product used to kill germs, insects, rodents, and other animal pests, as well as weeds and fungi. Such products cannot be sold until they are first registered with the agency.[14] If test data show that a pesticide may be harmful to human health or the environment, the EPA can refuse to register it, restrict its use to certain applications, or require that only certified applicators apply the pesticide. Once they are registered, manufacturers of the product must use appropriate labels showing the approved uses of the pesticide. Over 50,000 pesticides have been registered since FIFRA was enacted.[15]

Exhibit 8.1

Pesticides Taken Off the Market

Pesticides	Use	Concerns
Aldrin	Insecticide	Oncogenicity
Chlordane (Agricultural uses; termiticide uses suspended or cancelled)	Inseciticide/ Termites, Ants	Oncogenicity; reduction in non-target and endangered species
Compound 1080 (Livestock collar retained, rodenticide use under review)	Coyote control; Rodenticide	Reductions in non-target and endangered species; no known antidote
Dibromochloropropane (DBCP)	Soil Fumigant — Fruits and vegetables	Oncogenicity; mutagenicity; reproductive effects
DDT and related Compounds	Insecticide	Ecological (eggshell thinning); carcinogenicity
Dieldrin	Insecticide	Oncogenicity
Dinoseb (in hearings)	Herbicide/Crop dessicant	Fetotoxicity; reproductive effects; acute toxicity

Exhibit 8.1 (Cont.)

Pesticides	Use	Concerns
Endrin (Avicide use retained)	Insecticide/Avicide	Oncogenicity; teratogenicity; reductions in non-target and endangered species
Ethylene Dibromide (EDB) (Very minor uses and use on citrus for export retained)	Insecticide/Fumigant	Oncogenicity; mutagenicity; reproductive effects
Heptachlor (Agricultural uses; termiticide uses suspended or cancelled)	Insecticide	Oncogenicity; reductions in non-target and endangered species
Kepone	Insecticide	Oncogenicity
Lindane (Indoor smoke bomb cancelled; some uses restricted)	Insecticide/Vaporizer	Oncogenicity; teratogenicity; reproductive effects; acute toxicity; other chronic effects
Mercury	Microbial Uses	Cumulative toxicant causing brain damage
Mirex	Insecticide/Fire Ant Control	Non-target species; potential oncogenicity
Silvex	Herbicide/Forestry, rights-of-way, weed control	Oncogenicity; teratogenicity, fetotoxicity
Strychnine (Rodenticide use and livestock collar retained)	Mammalian predator control; rodenticide	Reductions in non-target and endangered species
2, 4, 5, -T	Herbicide/Forestry, rights-of-way, weed control	Oncogenicity; teratogenicity; fetotoxicity
Toxaphene (Livestock dip retained)	Insecticide—Cotton	Oncogenicity; reductions in non-target species; acute toxicity to aquatic organisms; chronic effects on wildlife

Oncogenicity—Causes tumors   Teratogenicity—Causes major birth defects
Mutagenicity—Causes mutation   Fetotoxicity—Causes toxicity to the unborn fetus
Carcinogenicity—Causes cancer

Source: Environmental Protection Agency, *Environmental Progress and Challenges: EPA's Update* (Washington, DC: U.S. Government Printing Office, 1988), p. 118.

Before a pesticide is registered for use on food or feed crops, a *tolerance,* or legally enforceable residue limit must be set by the agency. Both domestically produced and imported foods are monitored to make sure they comply with the established tolerances. This procedure was instituted to protect consumers from exposure to unsafe levels of pesticide residue on the food they purchase in the marketplace. While initially the EPA was only able to determine tolerances for the general population, its new system takes into account differences in susceptibilities within the general population such as differences in age and geographic location.[16]

There are also different standards for different types of food. For example, raw foods are evaluated by weighing the risks of pesticide exposure against the benefits of pesticide usage. Processed foods, on the other hand, are subject to a more stringent standard, which states that food additives including pesticide residues must pose zero risk of cancer regardless of their benefit. Because of these differences, some existing chemicals in raw foods would be prohibited in processed foods.[17] If confidence can be established in this kind of program, it may reduce consumers' fear about product safety. Progress has been made in the exposure of humans to pesticides that have been banned. (See Figure 8.1.)

Amendments to the act in 1978 required the EPA to reregister the 35,000 pesticides previously registered and already on the market because the long-term health and environmental effects of many of these pesticides was poorly understood. The EPA was required to do a cost-benefit analysis on these products taking into account new information. If this analysis revealed that a particular product posed an unreasonable risk to human health or the environment when weighed against its benefits to agriculture and society, it had to be removed from the marketplace or restrictions had to be placed on its use as a pesticide.

There are three ways the EPA can remove a pesticide from the market. If the agency determines that a pesticide poses "unreasonable" adverse effects, it can issue a notice of intent to cancel the pesticide, at which time the affected registrant may request a hearing before an administrative law judge. If the judge disagrees with the EPA, the administrator of the EPA can make the final decision to cancel without any obligation to indemnify holders of a cancelled product. During this decision-making process, which can take several years, the pesticide can continue to be produced, sold, and used. Even after a final decision, remaining stocks of the pesticide can generally be used.[18]

The EPA can also suspend a pesticide's registration, but in order to do so, it must determine that the pesticide poses an "imminent hazard," meaning that the short-term risks of continued use outweigh any possible benefits. Registrants can dispute the suspension, but production of the pesticide has to cease until final action is taken. Sales and use of the pesticide could continue during this period. If the final decision is to prohibit sale and use of the

Figure 8.1

Levels of Pesticides in Humans

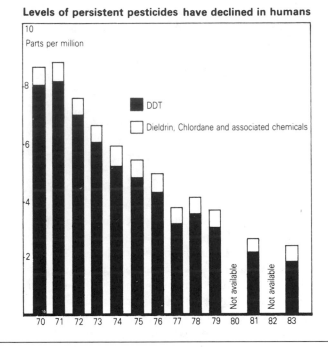

Levels of persistent pesticides have declined in humans

Source: Environmental Protection Agency, *Meeting the Environmental Challenge* (Washington, DC: U.S. Government Printing Office, 1990), p. 19.

product, the agency must indemnify at market value prior to the suspension holders of any remaining stocks.[19]

Finally, the EPA can order an emergency suspension if it finds that the pesticide poses an imminent hazard to humans and the environment. This suspension order precedes any hearing that is taking place and prohibits the sale and use of the pesticide immediately. After taking a final action to suspend the pesticide because it poses this kind of hazard, the EPA must also indemnify holders of remaining stocks of the pesticide. This method of removing a pesticide from the market has been used on only a few occasions to remove pesticides such as 2,4,5,T/Silvex, EDB, and Dinoseb.[20]

The 1972 law required the EPA to proceed on a product-by-product basis, even though many products have similar chemical properties. Further amendments to FIFRA in 1978 allowed the EPA to take a "generic" approach to registering pesticides. Using this approach, the agency is able to make one regulatory decision for an entire group of pesticides that have similar chemical ingredients rather than looking at them separately. It was estimated that using this method the agency would have to consider fewer than 600 active ingredients contained in the 45,000 different commercial products on the marketplace. Standards could be set for these 600 ingredients, and products would be registered according to whether they measure up to these standards.

Further amendments passed in 1988 were designed to speed up reregistration and remove potential threats to the budget of the EPA that could thwart its efforts to protect the public. These amendments require the EPA to complete reregistration by 1997, at least ten years earlier than would have been required without the amendments. This expedited reregistration requirement and the financial commitment to make it possible are the most important provisions of the amendments. The amendments also involve changes in the procedures for dealing with the recall, storage, and disposal of older pesticides when cancellation or the demands of reregistration force them off the market. Most of the financial burden of disposal was shifted to the pesticide industry, and the EPA was given additional authority to require holders of cancelled pesticides to dispose of the products and specify the means of disposal.[21]

In 1989, the agency was attacked for its system of setting pesticide standards. Critics contended that the agency was slow to revise standards for older pesticides, and takes a far too limited view in evaluating the dangers of new pesticides. When it sets pesticide tolerances, some experts claimed that the agency was grossly underestimating the risk to the public. Children, in particular, were said to be exposed to dangerously high cancer risks. One of the problems concerned the treatment of inert ingredients, which are used to dissolve, dilute, or stabilize the active agents. These inerts are excluded from the EPA's risk calculations, and only those ingredients the manufacturer lists as active are examined. Chemical makers claimed that these inerts were trade secrets and so shouldn't be reviewed, but it was believed by certain experts that some of these inerts were often more toxic than the active agents.[22]

While the initial health concern regarding the regulation of pesticides was whether a chemical used in pesticides could cause cancer, pesticides are now tested for a variety of potential problems including reproductive, immunological, and neurological effects. All new and previously registered pesticides are also screened for their potential to contaminate groundwater. Groundwater may be more vulnerable to contamination in some areas because of geological or other factors. In 1986, a survey indicated that 30 states had found wells contaminated with one or more of 60 different pesticides. These concerns were one of the major reasons that ethylene dibromide (EDB) and dibromochloropropane (CBCP) were taken off the market. In 1984, the agency issued a request for groundwater data on another 140 registered pesticides.[23]

Pesticides also harm fish and wildlife, which feed on contaminated fields and other water or prey on other contaminated organisms. Some chemicals such as DDT were found to persist in the environment and accumulate in the tissues of wildlife, causing the thinning of eggshells, which prevented the successful hatching of chicks. Since the 1960s, the use of a number of chemicals that were harmful to fish and wildlife have been cancelled, and a number of species threatened with extinction have since shown signs of recovery. These include the California brown pelican, the bald eagle, and the peregrine falcon. Nonetheless, problems remain (see box) that the EPA is attempting to address.[24]

The agency is currently evaluating some chemicals because of concerns about their effects on fish and wildlife, rather than focusing solely on whether a chemical could cause harm to humans. Manufacturers are required to submit information regarding the effects of pesticides on wildlife through laboratory studies and to demonstrate the actual impacts of a pesticide in the environment. The EPA is also developing better methods for determining the effects of pesticides on entire ecosystems as well as on individual organisms. The agency has begun a five-year research program to improve computer models of ecosystems in different environments across the country.[25]

Under the EPA's pesticide program, more than a million private users, mostly farmers, and 250,000 commercial applicators have been trained and certified in the safe use of pesticides. This program trains people in the proper use, handling, storage, and disposal of pesticides, including provisions for protective clothing, warning about treated areas, and waiting periods after spraying. Only such certified users are allowed to use pesticides that have a "restricted use only" classification. In late 1984, the EPA adopted a tougher policy toward pesticides thought to be hazardous by banning or restricting the use of eight high-volume pesticides, and proposing more stringent controls on about 25 other widely used pesticides that were suspected of posing health hazards for consumers and farm workers. This action was expected to cost manufacturers millions of dollars as they supplied the government with more extensive, up-to-date health and environmental test data on these substances.[26]

Despite these efforts, the risks to farm workers continued. It was estimated that in the course of a 30-day harvesting season, the typical farm worker might be exposed to 15 different compounds at various times, making the process of identifying which pesticide is to blame for a particular health problem impossible. Little is known about the chronic effects of many pesticides, and several of the studies that have been conducted can be faulted for one reason or another, thus making proof of a link between a specific pesticide and cancer difficult to establish. The benefit of the doubt has always gone in favor of manufacturers and users of pesticides rather than the workers, and pesticides have often been assumed safe until proven otherwise. To cope with this problem, the EPA issued new regulations to protect farm workers in 1988, which some believed were still inadequate.[27]

Endangered Species Return but Still Require Protection from Pesticides

By the early 1970s, the bald eagle had all but vanished from many areas of its natural range. At that time, only about 1,000 nesting pairs of eagle were found in the entire United States. Too few offspring were hatching successfully, and evidence pointed to the use of DDT and other persistent pesticides as the likely factor responsible for this condition. These pesticides and their by-products had affected calcium metabolism, making eggshells so thin that they broke under the weight of the nesting birds. Our national symbol, the bald eagle, became an endangered species.

Although still endangered, the bald eagle has shown remarkable signs of recovery since the ban on DDT in 1972. Today, there are almost 2,000 nesting pairs of bald eagles in the United States. The majority of birds seem to be producing normal eggs, even though problems with eggshells have been reported for some nests. The California brown pelican and peregrine falcon, also threatened with extinction by the persistent pesticides, have been recovering slowly as well.

Although the bald eagle and other birds have been recovering since the ban on DDT, there are still many thousands of species listed as endangered. These species usually have become endangered for a variety of reasons other than pesticides contamination; they nonetheless are particularly vulnerable to added stresses such as pesticides. Pesticides may kill wildlife directly, or may contaminate the food, water, and habitat of the wildlife.

Under the Endangered Species Act, EPA is required to consult with the Fish and Wildlife Service to ensure that pesticides do not jeopardize endangered species and their habitat. If the Fish and Wildlife Service determines that a pesticide is likely to be harmful to endangered species, it suggests alternatives to EPA for preventing damage to the species. It usually recommends not using the pesticide where endangered species would be exposed.

EPA is developing an approach to implementing these restrictions through the pesticide label. As proposed in the Federal Register, pesticide labels would list the counties that have limitations on use in endangered species habitats. Labels would refer users to county bulletins that contain maps indicating the portions of the county where pesticide use is limited. At first these limitations would apply to the four groups of pesticides that already have been evaluated: certain crop pesticides, pasture and rangeland pesticides, forestry pesticides, and mosquito larvicides. Information currently is being gathered for maps that would identify the location of potentially affected endangered species.

Because the presence of endangered species may vary within a state and even within a single county, states will have a particularly important role in determining where limitations are needed. Several states already have proceeded to develop recommendations for implementing the program. By working with agriculture and wildlife experts and government officials, we hope to ensure that pesticides pose minimal threats to endangered species.

Source: Environmental Protection Agency, *Environmental Progress and Challenges: EPA's Update* (Washington, DC: U.S. Government Printing Office, 1988), p. 136.

The EPA has also established the National Pesticide Telecommunications Network, which provides a toll-free number to obtain information on the use and disposal of pesticides, and information on how to recognize and manage pesticide poisonings. In 1990, the EPA completed a nationwide survey to determine the extent of pesticide contamination of groundwater and developed a program called Pesticides in Groundwater Strategy to protect drinking water sources from becoming contaminated. Such a focus will help protect the nation's drinking water supplies and give people some confidence that the EPA is concerned about this problem.[28]

In October of 1984, the EPA took its first step toward regulating pesticides created by gene splicing or other methods of biotechnology. The EPA issued rules requiring all companies or individuals planning to test the effectiveness of pesticides produced by genetic manipulation to notify the agency at least 90 days before the tests are conducted. The EPA can then deny experimental permits for tests that the agency determines may pose "substantial health concerns." These rules were the first phase of a comprehensive set of proposed policies and regulations that would spell out the EPA's authority to regulate the commercial testing and use of all such pesticides in the future.[29] A framework for coordinating federal regulation of biotechnology was established in 1986 that built on existing legislation and practices, but imposed additional levels of federal review for certain applications, particularly relating to new microorganisms. Further regulations were expected to be issued that would build on this policy statement.[30]

Under both the Toxic Substances Control Act and FIFRA, the EPA has instituted a process for carefully evaluating proposals for field testing of genetically altered products. Before permission for such an experiment is granted, information about the experiment is evaluated and shared with other agencies. If the experiment is approved, conditions are specified for conducting the experiment and results are required to be submitted to the EPA so that effects can be monitored and the decision reevaluated. Several tests of genetically engineered microorganisms outside the laboratory have been approved including tests on strawberries and potatoes using a microorganism modified to retard frost formation on plants. There are many developments in biotechnology (see box) that promise great benefits to the public, but also need to be regulated to prevent adverse effects to humans and the environment.[31]

In 1989, President Bush unveiled plans to accelerate the process for removing unsafe pesticides from the market and toughen penalties for misusing pesticides.[32] The National Academy of Science also issued a report recommending that a "negligible risk" standard be adopted. This report challenged the zero-risk standard of the Delany Clause and would replace it with a standard that allowed approval of pesticides in cases where they would produce tumors in fewer than one out of every million people exposed. The panel that produced the report stated the new standard would eliminate 98 percent of the cancer risk from 28 pesticides that the EPA has linked to cancer. Current standards were said to eliminate only about half the estimated cancer risk from these compounds.[33]

In 1990, the state of California placed the most sweeping environmen-

Some Developments in Biotechnology

There are many potential uses of genetically altered microorganisms. Some of the most exciting developments in biotechnology are described below.

- **Tracking the release of genetically altered bacteria.** A microorganism has been developed that can be tracked in the environment to provide information on its behavior. The microbe is formed by inserting two genes from a common bacterium into another microorganism. When these genes are present, the bacteria form blue colonies when exposed to a certain sugar, thereby allowing scientists to follow the survival of the genetically changed microbes both inside and outside the test area. The marking system can be used to mark other microorganisms and should help allay public concerns about potential consequences of releasing such microorganisms in the environment. EPA approved field tests of the bacteria on wheat and soybeans.

- **Developing bacteria to protect plants against frost.** EPA approved field tests of a bacteria designed to protect strawberry and potato plants from mild frosts. The new bacteria are the same as those that normally colonize these plants, except that they lack a protein that promotes the formation of ice crystals. Scientists expect that these new bacteria can help plants resist frost if the bacteria are applied before the normal bacteria can establish themselves.

- **Using bacteria to enhance alfalfa yield.** EPA also is examining the design of an experiment to test the effectiveness of genetically engineered bacteria to enhance the yield of alfalfa. This experiment will be conducted in Pepin County, Wisconsin, and will use an altered form of the bacteria that occur naturally in the soil. These altered bacteria work together with the roots of legumes (such as alfalfa, soybeans, and peas) to convert nitrogen gas into a form that can be used by the plants.

- **Using dead bacteria as a pesticide.** An innovative approach to pesticide development involves the insertion into another microbe of the genes that contain the code for a protein toxin. These altered microbes subsequently are grown in cultures to produce large quantities of the toxic protein. When these bacteria are killed, they can be administered as a pesticide. Small-scale field trials currently are underway to determine the effectiveness of these dead bacteria as pesticides.

- **Using bacteria for toxic waste disposal.** Researchers currently are working on the development of bacteria that can metabolize specific compounds in toxic wastes, such as PCBs, dioxin, and oil spills. For example, an EPA scientist has developed a strain of bacteria that can metabolize several components of crude oil. This development may enable us to control oil spills using only one bacteria rather than several different types. Bacteria also are being developed to extract toxic metals from landfills, mines, and wastewater.

Source: Environmental Protection Agency, *Environmental Progress and Challenges: EPA's Update* (Washington, DC: U.S. Government Printing Office, 1988), p. 140.

tal protection initiative ever conceived before the voters. The proposition was called "Big Green" because it bundled a number of environmental proposals into one huge package. One of the propositions in the package would have banned the sale of any food containing residues of cancer-causing pesticides within the state. In some cases a five-year phaseout of the pesticide would be put into effect immediately; in other cases, a phaseout would only occur only if manufacturers failed to dispel concerns about the pesticide through further testing. Because California has such a huge market, other food-producing states and countries that wanted access to this market would probably have to adopt similar restrictions. The economic stakes were high: In 1987, 600 million pounds of pesticides were sold in the state. The initiative failed, however, and so for now the issue is tabled.[34]

Pesticide use appears to have leveled off in recent years after steadily increasing in the 1960s and 1970s. (See Figure 8.2.) To encourage this trend, the EPA is supporting the development of new integrated pest management practices, which will hopefully reduce the reliance on chemicals by using a variety of pest control methods. A new farm bill could also further reduce agricultural use of pesticides by promoting more environmentally sound crop rotation practices, increasing funds for sustainable agriculture, promoting research and education, and providing incentives for farmers to adopt more environmentally compatible farming methods.[35]

The EPA is also encouraging the development of safer pesticides: Cancelled pesticides have been replaced by products that tend to be less persistent in the environment, are more precise in attacking given target pests, and require lower rates of application. The agency is also implementing a program targeted at endangered species, and is developing regulations for the storage and disposal of pesticides and pesticide containers. It will also promulgate new pesticide worker-protection standards to deal more effectively with this problem, and propose new applicator certification and training regulations.[36]

Regarding use of pesticides overseas, the EPA claims to be making some efforts to prevent pesticide misuse and overuse in other countries. The United States is an important exporter of pesticides and, in some cases, has sold pesticides overseas that have been banned or restricted in this country. But the United States is also a major importer of food commodities, and thus oftentimes pesticide use overseas returns to us as residues on the food we import.[37] Thus the United States has an interest in ensuring that pesticides are used responsibly throughout the world. To achieve this level of protection, the EPA has developed goals for international pesticide activities and wants to harmonize U.S. and international pesticide standards. The agency has also proposed a policy that would restrict the export of pesticides banned in the United States and is actively involved in related legislative efforts.[38]

Figure 8.2 U.S. Pesticide Usage

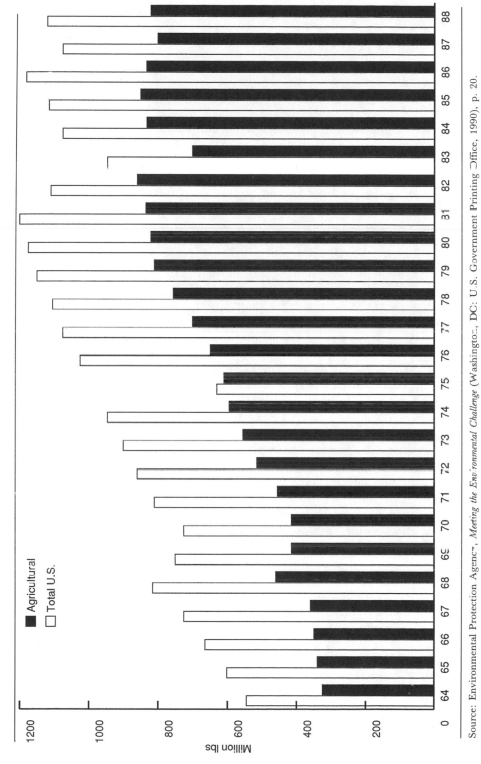

Source: Environmental Protection Agency, *Meeting the Environmental Challenge* (Washington, DC: U.S. Government Printing Office, 1990), p. 20.

ALTERNATIVES

Those who are opposed to the widespread continued use of pesticides point out that there are many safer and more effective ways to control pests and weeds that deserve consideration. Some of these alternatives can be grouped under the general heading of modifying cultivation procedures. One of these methods is crop rotation, where the types of crops planted in fields are changed from year to year so that populations of pests that attack a particular crop don't have time to multiply to naturally uncontrollable sizes. Planting rows of hedges or trees in and around crop fields can act as barriers to invasions by pests and provide habitats for their natural enemies. Planting times can also be adjusted so that most major insect pests starve to death before the crop is available. Crops can also be grown in areas where their major pests do not exist.[39]

Certain methods of biological control can be used, such as the introduction of various natural predators and pathogens (disease-causing bacteria and viruses). More than 300 biological pest control projects have been successful worldwide. A tiny wasp was used in Africa to stop devastation of cassave crops by a mealybug. Other examples of biological control include using guard dogs to protect livestock from predators, ducks to devour insects and slugs, geese for weeding orchards and for controlling grass in gardens and nurseries, birds and spiders to eat insects, and allelopathic plants which produce chemicals naturally that are toxic to their weed competitors or that repel or poison their insect pests.[40]

However, 10 to 20 years of research may be required to understand how a particular pest interacts with its various enemies and thus to determine the best biological control agent. Mass production of such agents is often difficult, and farmers have found that they are slower to act and harder to apply than pesticides. Such agents must also be protected from pesticides sprayed in adjacent fields, and there is the charge that some of these agents may also become pests in their own right. Some pest organisms develop genetic resistance to viruses and bacterial agents used for biological control and some may devour other beneficial insects.[41]

Males of some insect pest species can be raised in the laboratory and sterilized by radiation or chemicals. They can then be released into the environment in large numbers to mate unsuccessfully with wild females and thus eventually reduce the pest population. This method works best if the females mate only once and if the infested area is relatively isolated so that it does not become repopulated with nonsterilized males and defeat the program. Chemical hormones can also be used to prevent insects from maturing completely and make it impossible for them to reproduce. But they must be applied at exactly the right time in the life cycle of the target insect and they sometimes affect natural predators and other nonpest species.[42]

Food can also be irradiated to kill and prevent insects from reproducing in certain foods after harvest, which extends the shelf life of some perishable foods and destroys parasitic worms and bacteria. The FDA approved the use of low doses of ionizing radiation on spices, fruits, vegetables, and fresh pork in 1986, and it may soon approve it for use on poultry and seafood. Irradiated foods are already sold in 33 countries, but surveys show that consumers in the United States will not buy food labeled as irradiated because of fears about radiation exposure. But a food does not become radioactive when it is irradiated, just as exposure to X rays does not make the body radioactive. Thus there is some controversy over the use of this method.[43] (See box.)

Many pest control experts believe that the best way to control crop pests is through using a carefully designed integrated pest management (IPM) program. (See box.) In this approach, each crop and its pests are evaluated as an ecological system and a program is developed using a variety of cultivation, biological, and chemical methods to control pests that threaten the

---

Pro/Con Should Food Be Irradiated?

According to the FDA and the World Health Organization, over 1,000 studies show that foods exposed to low radiation doses are safe for human consumption. However, critics of irradiation argue that not enough animal studies have been done and that tests of the effects of irradiated foods on people have been too few and brief to turn up any long-term effects, which typically require 30 to 40 years to be evaluated.

The focus of this controversy is the fact that irradiation produces trace amounts of at least 65 chemicals in foods, some of which cause cancer in test animals. The FDA estimates that 58 of these chemicals are also found in nonirradiated foods and assumes that the concentrations of all 65 chemicals in irradiated food is too small to affect human health. Opponents of food irradiation say this assumption is unwarranted until these chemicals have been identified and thoroughly tested.

Opponents also fear that more people might die of deadly botulism in irradiated foods. Present levels of irradiation do not destroy the spore-enclosed bacteria that cause this disease but they do destroy the microbes that give off the rotten odor that warns of the presence of botulism bacteria. Critics also note that irradiation can be expensive, adding as much as five cents a pound to the price of some fresh vegetables.

Proponents, however, respond that irradiation of food is likely to reduce health hazards to people by decreasing the use of some potentially damaging pesticides and food additives. What do you think?

Source: From *Living in the Environment: An Introduction to Environmental Studies* 6/E by G. Tyler Miller, Jr. © 1990 by Wadsworth, Inc. Reprinted by permission of the publisher.

crops. The overall aim of an IPM is not to eradicate the pests totally, but to keep the population of pests just below the level at which they cause economic loss. When this level is reached, biological and cultural controls are first applied. Small amounts of pesticides are applied only when absolutely necessary, and a variety of chemicals are used even then to retard development of genetic resistance.[44]

This approach allows farmers to escape from the pesticide treadmill and at the same time minimize hazards to human health, wildlife, and the environment in general. By 1984, these programs were being used for nearly 40 crops in 15 states on about 8 percent of U.S. harvested cropland. It has been estimated that farmers using these programs saved $579 million more

Cockroaches — A Case Study in Integrated Pest Management

Cockroaches carry viruses and bacteria that can cause hepatitis, polio, typhoid fever, plague, and salmonella. Attempts to control the cockroach consume one third of the pest control budget for urban sites and represent the largest expenditure for a single pest in U.S. homes and other establishments. Because of its growing resistance to many pesticides, however, the cockroach is not likely to be eliminated from homes and other buildings in the near future.

Both the professional pesticide applicator and the average consumer can control cockroaches by using the principles of Integrated Pest Management (IPM). A blend of old-fashioned practices and new technology, IPM is an ecological approach to pest management that takes into account the biology of the pest and its interaction with the environment. Although IPM may include the use of chemical pesticides, it considers all available options to achieve the greatest control with the least possible hazard.

Controlling cockroaches with IPM involves estimating the extent of the cockroach population, and then using a range of techniques to achieve tolerable levels. The basic control measure is to modify cockroach habitats by lowering the temperature, removing food, eliminating moisture, reducing clutter, and filling hiding spaces such as cracks and crevices. If these actions do not provide enough control, the appropriate pesticides may

be used. Recent studies have shown that the most effective, least toxic, and least expensive method to control cockroaches is to apply 99 percent boric acid dust in cracks and crevices. The cockroaches ingest the powder while grooming themselves and die three to ten days later. (Because boric acid may be harmful if ingested by children, it should be used cautiously if children may be exposed.)

The IPM approach is being demonstrated for use in managing a variety of other pests, such as termites, grasshoppers, and aquatic weeds. Much of this work is done cooperatively with other federal and state agencies, pesticide user groups, universities, and the agricultural chemical industry. IPM is also viewed as a primary tool for managing pest populations that have become resistant to pesticides. Toward this end, we are working with the states to promote the use of innovative methods for dealing with pest resistance.

Source: Environmental Protection Agency, *Environmental Progress and Challenges: EPA's Update* (Washington, DC: U.S. Government Printing Office, 1988), p. 133.

than they would have by using traditional methods of pest control. These programs can (1) reduce inputs of fertilizer and irrigation water, (2) reduce preharvest pest-induced crop losses by 50 percent, (3) reduce pesticide use and control costs by 50 to 90 percent, and (4) increase crop yields and reduce crop production costs.[45]

However, use of IPM programs requires expert knowledge about each pest-crop situation and is slower acting and more labor intensive than the use of conventional pesticides. While long-term costs may be lower, initial costs may be higher than the use of pesticides. Methods that work in one area may not be applicable to another area with slightly different growing conditions, making each program more or less tailor-made to each situation. So far, this method has not been widely used in the United States because of many factors. Current federal funding of integrated pest management programs is only about $20 million a year, which is about half of what it costs to develop just one new chemical pesticide. Only about 2 percent of the Department of Agriculture's budget is spent on integrated pest management programs. These programs are strongly opposed by agricultural chemical companies who see little profit to be made from most alternative pest control methods.[46]

The term *sustainable agriculture* has taken on a new meaning in the current environment. Once the term referred to organic farming, which was a trendy program to grow crops without using synthetic chemicals. But more recently the effort has come to include efforts to curb soil erosion by modifying plowing techniques to protect water supplies by minimizing, if not eliminating, use of artificial fertilizers and pest controls. In addition to using new planting methods, farmers are also experimenting with novel ways to control pests without using chemicals. Thus the definition of sustainable agriculture has been considerably broadened so that it is acceptable to more people and has opened up an opportunity for dialogue for alternative farming methods.[47]

> "The 1990s are the beginning of the end of the chemical era," says Dave Dyer, executive director of American Farmland Trust. "Agrichemicals will shift from being the driving force to being the helping hand. The vision of such a future — one in which farmers cease to be among the nation's leading polluters of streams and groundwater, consumers no longer worry about eating an apple a day, the topsoil regenerates itself and the richest farmland on Earth becomes even richer — is too compelling to ignore.[48]

The movement toward sustainable agriculture faces stiff resistance, however, from farm communities all over the nation and draws ridicule from mainstream agriculture. There is a lack of reliable research into low-chemical methods, and thus many farmers say the new techniques simply won't work on modern giant farms. These methods would raise production costs, say critics, and make it impossible for U.S. farmers to compete on world markets. Others see the movement as a step backward that could lower farm yields and income from agricultural activities, by replacing the mechanical and scientific advancements of the past 50 years with more sweat and a lower standard of living. And still others worry that the movement could lead to increased government regulation of pesticides.[49]

TOXIC SUBSTANCES

The high standard of living many enjoy in the United States would not be possible without the thousands of chemicals that are produced and used in various products. Most of these chemicals are not harmful if used properly, but others may cause health effects ranging from cancer to birth defects and may seriously degrade the environment. Even exposure to some of these chemicals in minute amounts may cause harm. Reducing or eliminating exposure to these harmful chemicals is one of the major goals of the regulatory process regarding toxic substances.

The health hazard posed by a chemical after it enters the environment depends on its toxicity and the extent humans are exposed to it. Knowledge about the harmful effects of synthetic organic compounds has lagged far behind their introduction to the marketplace. The vast majority of chemicals in use have not been fully tested for toxicity, which requires animal experiments that can take several years and can cost more than $500,000 per chemical. Cancer induced by toxic substances may appear decades after the exposure and will usually be indistinguishable from a cancer caused by other means.[50]

While pesticides account for only a small share of the chemicals in common usage, they pose some of the greatest potential hazards. As we mentioned in the previous section, they pose risks not only to farm workers, but to the general population through residues on food and drinking water contamination. The relative threat posed by pesticide poisoning, food residues, and contaminated drinking water varies with the type of pesticide used and the care taken during application.[51]

Industrial wastes are the other major source of toxic substances because hazardous waste sites dot the countryside. Data on the generation and disposal of hazardous waste material are sketchier and more confusing than for pesticides. Countries apply different definitions to what is called "hazardous," "special," or simply "industrial" waste. Thus comparison between countries is difficult if not impossible. But most practices for disposing of hazardous waste still reflect the "out-of-sight, out-of-mind" mentality that has dominated waste disposal all over the world. This mindset exposes the public to unnecessary risks of contamination by toxic chemicals.[52]

But it is not only human beings that are affected by toxic chemicals. Wildlife is also exposed to the dangers of toxic substances. Researchers found that toxic compounds phased out in the 1970s continue to enter the waters of

Lake Michigan, for example, as they leach from the soil or are carried by the wind. Such chemicals have tainted nine of ten lake trout, and have rendered one of four unfit for human consumption. Forty percent of chinook salmon in the lake are said to exceed public health standards for safe levels of PCBs, and also contain DDT, mercury, dieldrin, and other toxins.[53]

When PCBs were phased out in the 1970s, the levels of these compounds in fish in the Great Lakes were ten times higher than today. But there are still plenty of them in the lakes because old dump sites containing PCBs continue to leak the chemical into the lakes. Also, PCBs in bottom sediments are long-lived because they are only slowly converted to nontoxic compounds. Dredging to deepen ship channels through the lakes has stirred up such persistent chemicals trapped in these sediments. PCB concentrations have also increased in recent years because of the drop in lake levels.[54]

REGULATION

There are 7 million known chemical compounds, 65,000 of which are in substantial commercial use and available on the market. Some 1,000 new chemicals are put into production each year and thus into the environment. Those chemicals that are harmful must be identified and steps taken to reduce the risks associated with them. The EPA has a number of legislative tools to use in controlling exposure to toxic chemicals by regulating their release into the air, water, and land. (See Exhibit 8.2.) This chapter focuses on the Toxic Substances Control Act (most of the other acts are covered in other chapters).

Before the Toxic Substances Control Act (TSCA), previous laws that dealt with these substances authorized the government to act only after widespread exposure and possibly serious harm had already occurred. One major concept underlying TSCA is that the government has the authority to act before a substance can harm human health or the environment — the substance is, in effect, guilty until proven innocent. Under TSCA, the EPA reviews risk information on all new chemicals before they are manufactured or imported, and decides whether they should be admitted, controlled, or denied access to the marketplace.

Because of TSCA, the entire chemical industry was put under comprehensive federal regulation for the first time. The law applies to virtually every facet of the industry — product development, testing, manufacturing, distribution, use, and disposal. In addition, importers of chemical substances are treated as domestic manufacturers, thus extending EPA's control to certain aspects of the international chemical trade.[55]

The initial impact of TSCA was in the area of inventory reporting. The act required the EPA to compile and publish an inventory of chemical substances manufactured, imported, or processed in the United States for

Exhibit 8.2

Major Toxic Chemical Laws Administered by the EPA

Statute	Provisions
Toxic Substances Control Act	Requires that EPA be notified of any new chemical prior to its manufacture and authorizes EPA to regulate production, use, or disposal of a chemical.
Federal Insecticide, Fungicide and Rodenticide Act	Authorizes EPA to register all pesticides and specify the terms and conditions of their use, and remove unreasonably hazardous pesticides from the marketplace.
Federal Food, Drug and Cosmetic Act	Authorizes EPA in cooperation with FDA to establish tolerance levels for pesticide residues on food and food products.
Resource Conservation and Recovery Act	Authorizes EPA to identify hazardous wastes and regulate their generation, transportation, treatment, storage, and disposal.
Comprehensive Environmental Response, Compensation and Liability Act	Requires EPA to designate hazardous substances that can present substantial danger and authorizes the cleanup of sites contaminated with such substances.
Clean Air Act	Authorizes EPA to set emission standards to limit the release of hazardous air pollutants.
Clean Water Act	Requires EPA to establish a list of toxic water pollutants and set standards.
Safe Drinking Water Act	Requires EPA to set drinking water standards to protect public health from hazardous substances.
Marine Protection Research and Sanctuaries Act	Regulates ocean dumping of toxic contaminants.
Asbestos School Hazard Act	Authorizes EPA to provide loans and grants to schools with financial need for abatement of severe asbestos hazards.
Asbestos Hazard Emergency Response Act	Requires EPA to establish a comprehensive regulatory framework for controlling asbestos hazards in schools.
Emergency Planning and Community Right-to-Know Act	Requires states to develop programs for responding to hazardous chemical releases and requires industries to report on the presence and release of certain hazardous substances.

Source: Environmental Protection Agency, *Environmental Progress and Challenges: EPA's Update* (Washington, DC: U.S. Government Printing Office, 1988), p. 113.

commercial purposes. The inventory was compiled from reports that manufacturers, importers, processors, or users of chemical substances were required to prepare and submit to the agency.[56] The first inventory was published in 1979 and contained information on over 62,000 chemicals that came from manufacturers and importers and included production volume and plant location. In 1986, manufacturers and importers were required to report current data for a subset of substances on the inventory and update the information every four years thereafter. During fiscal year 1987, the EPA received over 25,000 reports on 8,500 substances.[57]

After publication of the initial inventory, the premanufacture provisions of TSCA went into effect. These provisions require a manufacturer who has developed a new chemical not on the inventory list to submit a notice to the EPA at least 90 days before beginning manufacture or importation of a new chemical substance for commercial purposes other than in small quantities solely for research and development. The information that has to be given the EPA includes a description of the new chemical substance, the estimated total amount to be manufactured and processed, and so on.[58]

In addition to this information, submitters must append any test data in their possession or control and descriptions of other data concerning the health and environmental effects of the substance. The EPA encourages, but does not require, the submitter to follow the premanufacture testing guidelines the EPA has published. In any event, all test data are to be submitted regardless of their age, quality, or results. About 80 percent of the new chemicals received appear to present no unreasonable risks to human health or the environment, but the rest must go through a more detailed review. This review includes a structure-activity analysis where a chemical's physical and chemical behavior is predicted by comparing the chemical's molecular structure with that of other chemicals for which the behavior is already known.[59]

The EPA administrator has a number of options available after receipt of this information: extending the 90-day premanufacture review period for an additional 90 days for good cause, requiring additional testing of the substance, or initiating no action within the 90-day period because the chemical is deemed not to present a hazard to health or the environment. If a hazard is believed to exist, the administrator may issue a proposed order to take effect on the expiration of the notification period to prohibit or limit the manufacture, processing, or distribution in commerce, use, or disposal of such substance or to prohibit or limit any combination of such activities.

If a total ban on the substance is not necessary, the administrator can issue further directives regarding regulation of the substance. Possibilities include setting concentration levels, limiting the use of the chemical, requiring warnings or instructions on its use, requiring public notice of risk or potential injury, and regulating methods of disposal. If the administrator has reason to believe the method of manufacture rather than the chemical itself is at fault, the manufacturer may be ordered to revise quality control procedures to the extent necessary to remedy whatever inadequacies are believed to exist.

In its 1990 report, the EPA claimed to have reviewed more than 15,300 new chemicals proposed for commercial use since TSCA was enacted. The majority of these chemicals were determined to present no unreasonable risk to human health or the environment. Several hundred of these cases, however, were targeted for additional regulatory action and hundreds more were withdrawn by their manufacturers in the face of anticipated regulatory action. While specific data for actions through 1990 are not available, Table 8.1 shows new chemical actions that were taken by the EPA through September 1987, and thus gives you some idea of the process new chemicals have to go through.

In addition to these premanufacture notification provisions, other sections of TSCA deal with testing, evaluation, and control of existing substances. The act empowers the EPA administrator to require manufacturers or processors of potentially harmful chemicals already in use to conduct tests on these chemicals. The need for such testing must be based on the following criteria: (1) the chemical may present an unreasonable risk to health or the environment, or there may be substantial human or environmental exposure to the chemical, (2) there are insufficient data and experience for determining or predicting the health and environmental effects of the chemical, and (3) testing of the chemical is necessary to develop such data.[60]

The overall goal of the Existing Chemicals Program is to reduce unreasonable risks of injury to health or the environment from chemicals that are already in commerce. An interagency committee has been established by the act to assist the administrator to determine chemicals that should be tested, but the administrator's actions are not limited to these recommendations by the committee. This committee may designate, at any one time, up to 50

Table 8.1

New Chemical Actions Mid-1979 to September 30, 1987

Actions	Aggregated Total To Date
Total New Chemical Substance Submissions Received (PMNs; Applications for Exemptions)	10,842
Valid Pre-Manufacture Notifications (PMNs) Received	9,132
PMNs Requiring No Further Action	7,166
Voluntary Testing in Response to EPA Concerns	149
Voluntary Control Actions by Submitters	45
PMNs Withdrawn in face of regulatory action	183
PMNs Subject to control pending data	349
PMNs Resulting in prohibition or restrictions	4
PMN Exemption Applications Received	1,710
Granted	1,473
Withdrawn	147
Denied	12

Source: Environmental Protection Agency, *Environmental Progress and Challenges: EPA's Update* (Washington, DC: U.S. Government Printing Office, 1988), p. 126.

chemicals from its list of recommended substances for testing. Within one year, the administrator must either initiate testing requirements for these designated chemicals or publish in the Federal Register any reasons for not initiating such requirements.

The law also allows the EPA to require companies to submit unpublished health and safety data on a list of specified chemicals that are suspected of causing cancer or other health effects. These data are used to evaluate risks associated with exposure and to determine whether toxicity testing should be done if it has not been conducted.[61] Chemical manufacturers, processors, and distributors are also required to inform the EPA immediately when they obtain evidence that a chemical poses a substantial risk of harm to human health or the environment. Such notices may include unpublished toxicity and exposure studies and may lead to further action by the EPA or other agencies. In its 1988 report, the EPA claimed that it had received over 700 of these substantial risk notices.[62]

The EPA is also authorized to monitor the exposure of humans and the environment to chemicals in order to identify potential hazards. Since 1960, for example, the agency has monitored the levels of PCBs and chlorinated pesticides such as DDT in humans, and developed improved methods for monitoring chemicals in human tissues and fluids such as a method that was developed to measure dioxin in fatty tissue. The agency also has conducted a number of chemical exposure studies in order to determine the risk humans may face from exposure to certain substances.[63]

By the end of 1987, the EPA had requested additional health and environmental testing by the manufacturers of 63 chemical groups for possible regulatory control. Congress and the EPA determined that several chemicals posed such a high risk that they needed to be regulated more stringently. In 1978, for example, the EPA instituted regulatory controls over the manufacture, use, and disposal of polychlorinated biphenyls (PCBs) and banned the aerosol uses of chlorofluorocarbons (CFCs). In 1989, the agency banned the manufacture of most asbestos products.[64]

RESULTS

Some of the actions taken under the provisions of TSCA have shown dramatic results. Restrictions on the use and disposal of PCBs, for example, have resulted in a significant decline of these residues in the environment, food, and human tissues. The number of individuals with high PCB levels has declined from over 8 percent to less than 1 percent of the population.[65] (See Figure 8.3.) The EPA has also taken a number of actions to control dioxin contamination including canceling all uses of dioxin containing pesticides.

Figure 8.3

PCB Levels

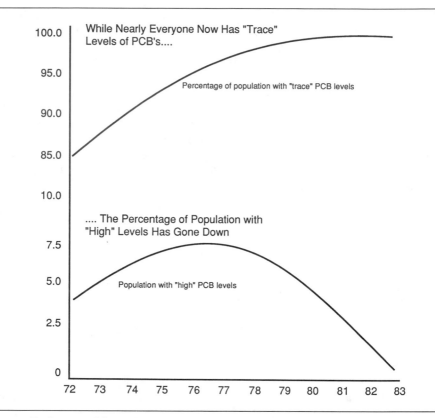

Source: Environmental Protection Agency, *Environmental Progress and Challenges: EPA's Update* (Washington, DC: U.S. Government Printing Office, 1988), p. 121.

   The PCB situation provides an example of the problems that existing chemical substances can present. The term *PCB* refers to a widely used group of 209 different toxic, oily, synthetic chlorinated hydrocarbon compounds known as polychlorinated biphenyls. These substances were used in many commercial activities, especially as heat transfer fluids in electrical transformers and capacitors. They were also used as hydraulic fluids, lubricants, and dye carriers in carbonless copy paper, and in paints, inks, and dyes. Over time, PCBs began to accumulate in the environment because of leaking electrical equipment and other sources. They eventually reached humans through the food chain and caused serious health problems in high concentrations.[66]

   The release of PCBs into the environment went largely unchecked from the late 1920s until the 1970s, but after that, the toxic effects of PCBs were recognized. They are one of the most ubiquitous of all contaminants. Tissue assays of more than 4,000 samples from humans in the 1970s showed that the entire U.S. population is carrying some burden of the substance. In 1973, the Food and Drug Administration (FDA) first established tolerances in PCBs for certain foods, and in 1979, those tolerances were lowered. These tolerances cover milk and manufactured dairy products, poultry and eggs, finished animal products and animal feed components, fish and shellfish, and infant and junior foods.[67]

In 1976, Congress directed the EPA to ban the manufacture, processing, distribution, and use of PCBs except in totally enclosed electrical equipment. The agency also imposed requirements to reduce the risk of PCB transformer fires, which can expose people in office buildings, apartment complexes, shopping malls, and other areas to severe risks. During a transformer fire, highly toxic furans and dioxins produced by the combustion of PCBs can spread throughout a building. The EPA has also established regulations for the safe disposal of PCBs and for the cleanup of PCB spills. New technologies, such as the use of incinerators and chemical and biological methods for detoxifying PCBs, have been promoted.[68]

Asbestos is another substance that was widely used for many useful purposes such as fireproofing and pipe and boiler insulation in schools and other buildings. Asbestos was often mixed with a cementlike material and sprayed on ceilings and other surfaces. Asbestos can break down into tiny fibers or dust that can be inhaled and lodge in lung tissue where it can cause lung cancer and asbestosis, which is a chronic scarring on the lungs that hinders breathing. The EPA has worked to reduce the exposure of schoolchildren to asbestos through two laws passed since 1984 that require schools to implement asbestos control projects. The agency has also studied asbestos in public and commercial buildings and has made recommendations on how to address the problem, and has implemented measures to protect state and local government workers involved in asbestos removal.[69]

NEW DIRECTIONS

After the Bhopal tragedy, community right-to-know bills were introduced into more states and both houses of Congress. Under Title III of the Superfund Amendments and Reauthorization Act (SARA) of 1986, also known as the Emergency Planning and Community Right-to-Know Act, facilities that manufacture, process, or use any of 309 designated chemicals in greater than specified amounts must report routine releases of those chemicals. The EPA is required to make information from these reports available to the public. This Toxics Releases Inventory, as it is called, is designed to assist citizen groups, local health officials, state environmental managers, and the EPA to identify and control toxic chemical problems. (See box.) One

---

Required Elements of a Local Emergency Plan

An emergency plan must do the following:

- Use the information provided by industry to identify the facilities and transportation routes where hazardous substances are present.
- Establish emergency response procedures, including evacuation plans, for dealing with accidental chemical releases.
- Set up notification procedures for those who will respond to an emergency.
- Establish methods for determining the occurrence and severity of a release and the areas and populations likely to be affected.
- Establish ways to notify the public of a release.
- Identify the emergency equipment available in the community, including equipment at facilities.
- Contain a program and schedules for training local emergency response and medical workers to respond to chemical emergencies.
- Establish methods and schedules for conducting "exercises" (simulations to test elements of the emergency response plan).
- Designate a community coordinator and facility coordinators to carry out the plan.

Source: Environmental Protection Agency, *Chemicals in Your Community: A Guide to the Emergency Planning and Community Right-to-Know Act* (Washington, DC: U.S. Government Printing Office, 1988), p. 5.

---

of the EPA's challenges is to interpret this information to help state and local officials evaluate and manage the risks posed by substances present in their communities.[70]

In addition to reporting routine releases, the law also provides for emergency notification of chemical accidents and releases, planning for chemical emergencies, and reporting of hazardous chemical inventories. With regard to accidental releases, the information that must be reported includes (1) the name of the chemical, (2) the location of the release, (3) whether the chemical is on the "extremely hazardous" list, (4) how much of the substance has been released, (5) the time and duration of the incident, (6) whether the chemical was released into the air, water, or soil, or some combination of the three, (7) known or anticipated health risks and necessary medical attention, (8) proper precautions, such as evacuation, and (9) a contact person at the facility.[71]

There are four groups of chemicals that are subject to reporting under this law, and some chemicals appear in several of these groups. The first group is extremely hazardous substances that because of their extremely toxic properties may be of immediate concern to the community. Releases of these chemicals must be reported immediately. The second group is labeled hazardous substances as listed under previous Superfund hazardous waste cleanup regulations. Releases of these chemicals above certain amounts must also be reported immediately. Hazardous chemicals are defined by the Occupational Safety and Health Administration (OSHA) as chemicals representing a physical or health hazard. Under this definition, many thousands of chemicals can be subject to reporting requirements. Inventories of these chemicals and material safety data sheets for each of them must also be submitted. Finally, the category of toxic chemicals includes those chemicals that have chronic or long-term toxicity effects. Estimates of releases of these chemicals into all media — air, land, and water — must be reported annually and entered into a national database.[72]

Companies reporting under this law can, under very limited conditions, request that the identity of specific chemicals in their reports not be disclosed to the public. In order to protect a chemical's identity in this fashion, companies must be able to prove that the information has not been reported under any other environmental regulation, and that it is a legitimate trade secret, that is, disclosure could damage the company's competitive position. If this protection is granted, the company must still report the chemical's identity to the EPA, but the agency keeps the original reports in a confidential file and "sanitized" versions, with the chemical name deleted, are made available to the public. Health professionals can obtain access to trade secret chemical information if they need it to diagnose and treat patients or to do research.[73]

The law's purposes are to encourage and support emergency planning for responding to chemical accidents and to provide local governments and the public with information about possible chemical hazards in their communities. It requires that detailed information about the nature of hazardous substances in or near communities be made available to the public. This law is different from many other federal statutes, in that it does not preempt states or local communities from having more stringent or additional requirements. More than 30 states have such laws giving workers and citizens access to information about hazardous substances in their workplaces and communities.[74]

Several new strategies are being pursued by the EPA including one that focuses agency attention on the highest risk toxic chemicals. Some 60,000 chemicals are being used in the United States, and most of these were in use before laws existed that required they be evaluated for health and environmental risks prior to being manufactured. The agency recently made a special effort to revitalize the review of these existing chemicals and make it a major priority. This strategy includes chemical screening that will be linked more directly to risk management. The EPA will be screening groups of chemicals, developing rules for these groups wherever possible. This procedure should greatly speed up the review process regarding existing chemicals.[75]

Cleaning Up the Toxic Mess One Small Step at a Time

1. *Do Your Homework — Gather the Facts.* Familiarize yourself with your community's environmental health by studying Toxic Release Inventory reports for your state, county, and community. Ask companies, state environmental agencies, and the EPA to verify the data and to give you more information on local pollution.

2. *Try to Picture the Problem.* Examine all the data on toxic releases to develop a broad view of the pollution scene. Find out if the information is complete and how the chemical releases were measured. Compare current figures with those from the previous year and with findings from other areas. Is progress being made?

3. *Alert Friends and Neighbors.* Strength comes from commitment, numbers, and diversity. Seek out other people who have worked to clean up toxics in your community, or organize a network of citizens who are interested in combating pollution.

4. *Seek the Advice of Experts.* Ask scientists, lawyers, and other experts to help you make a stronger case for reducing pollution. Local, state, and national environmental organizations can provide technical expertise. Colleges and universities also are excellent resources for free advice.

5. *Get Out and Spread the Word.* When you've gathered enough facts, issue a press release or hold a conference and present your ideas for cutting chemical waste. Winning in the court of public opinion often can be more effective than winning in a court of law.

6. *Confront the Pollution Problem Head-On.* Arrange meetings with industry representatives. First, gather the facts. Ask about methods of monitoring data and calculating chemical releases, accident records, and emergency response plans. Later, set goals to reduce toxic releases and improve monitoring in the factory and the community.

7. *Push for a Commitment.* Ask industry to "take the pledge" to use and release fewer toxic chemicals. Monsanto Corporation promised to cut airborne toxic emissions by 90 percent within four years. Polaroid pledged a 10 percent reduction in hazardous chemicals every year for five years.

8. *Size Up the Safety Net.* Industry may report that conditions have improved, but who backs up those claims? Make sure your community has a safety net, or an early warning system for monitoring pollution. If not, work to have one implemented. Does your community have an independent environmental planning and advisory board?

9. *Find Ways to Get Involved.* Participate in your community's emergency planning to reduce the risks of chemical accidents. Help establish limits for chemical releases according to the Clean Air Act, the Resource Conservation and Recovery Act, and other environmental regulations.

10. *Work For Better, Tougher Laws.* In many cases, industry's release of toxic chemicals is legal. Do existing state laws and local ordinances go far enough to assure your safety? If not, lobby for laws with sharper teeth to ensure the bite is put on pollution.

Source: Bill Lawren, "How Safe Is Your World? You Have a Right to Know," *National Wildlife,* Vol. 28, No. 2 (February-March 1990), pp. 18–19.

Under TCSA's information-gathering authority, the EPA was given a means to develop an integrated approach to the control and management of toxic chemicals all over the country. The agency shares such information among all its regulatory programs as well as with other agencies. An outreach service has been established to help the regional offices and states improve their risk assessments. This service is called the Chemical Assessment Desk and provides other parts of the agency with toxicity and risk information of the chemicals that have been reviewed in the toxic substances program. The EPA is also working with other countries to coordinate the gathering, testing, and evaluation of existing chemicals of common concern. This work is being done through the Organization for Economic Cooperation and Development, and through such efforts, it is hoped that a coordinated and comprehensive regulation of toxic chemicals can be developed.[76]

In 1983, a new agency was formed to study chemical dangers. This agency, called the Agency for Toxic Substances and Disease Registry, is located in the Public Health Service of the Department of Health and Human Services. It was created in response to a suit filed by the Environmental Defense Fund demanding intensive government health research into the effects of toxic chemical contamination. One purpose of the agency was to develop a list of all areas in the nation that have been closed or restricted for use because of chemical contamination and registries of people who have been exposed to toxic substances.[77]

Also in 1983, the state of New Jersey passed a worker right-to-know bill that, among other things, required business organizations to disclose to their employees and the public the names of toxic substances used in the manufacturing process. Several states have laws mandating disclosure to employees, but this was the first law mandating disclosure to both workers and nearby communities. Under the law, companies have 18 months to label all containers used by workers that contain any of about 1,000 hazardous substances and file publicly available papers with county health departments itemizing those substances. The New Jersey Business and Industrial Association estimated that it would cost state businesses about $20 million to comply and that it would put them at a serious competitive disadvantage.[78]

Courts are lending a more sympathetic ear to claims for compensation based on the fear of cancer. Residents of Hardeman County, Tennessee, discovered that their drinking wells had been contaminated with chemicals linked to cancer and other diseases. The Velsicol Chemical Corporation was blamed for the problem, as it had used a site in the area to dump waste from a nearby plant that manufactured pesticides. A group of 128 people sued the company in state court over alleged injuries such as liver and kidney damage. But the Hardeman County residents also demanded compensation for their fear of contracting cancer in the future.[79]

In earlier years, most courts would have dismissed such claims, but in August 1988, a federal appeals court approved the awarding of $207,000 for "cancerphobia" to five people serving as representatives of the class action.

Awards for other class members were to be determined by a trial judge if the amounts are not settled out of court beforehand. Some lawyers claimed that the number of such claims has proliferated in the past two or three years, and cancerphobia charges are becoming routine in large toxic injury cases. And the courts, as the preceding case illustrates, are showing signs of going along with these cases and awarding damages.[80]

Also in 1988, Proposition 65 that was passed by California voters in 1986 began to be implemented. This proposition required that California consumers be warned about products which contain chemicals known to the state to cause cancer or other reproductive harm or birth defects. The law requires prominent warnings on products that expose people to certain toxic substances unless the substances are at levels the state has deemed to be of "no significant risk" in causing cancer or birth defects. The levels are set so that a daily dose of the substance over a lifetime would be expected to produce no more than 1 excess cancer per 100,000 people. Companies that fail to issue such warnings face fines of as much as $2,500 per day for each violation.[81]

The purpose of the law was to force business organizations to examine closely their products and process to reduce exposure levels to below the state standards. There is some evidence that increased sensitivity to these problems is taking place. Such major companies as Gillette, Dow Chemical, and Sara Lee have replaced noxious chemicals in correction fluids, spot removers, and waterproofing sprays with new formulas that are touted as safer, and in some cases, even more effective. Other companies are being quiet about their reformulations to avoid calling attention to dangerous chemicals in their old products.[82]

In 1990, attention turned to the effects of toxic chemicals on children. Environmental groups began to cite scientific evidence suggesting that the nation's 63 million youngsters are significantly more endangered by toxic chemicals than adults. Children are believed to be more susceptible to toxins because the poisons quickly become more concentrated in small bodies. Their less developed detoxifying organs also raise the risk, as do rapidly developing cells which increase the danger from carcinogens and neurotoxins. To protect children, environmentalists are asking the government to set new safety standards for pesticides, toxins, and air pollutants taking children into account. The government has largely failed to do this up to the present time.[83]

Despite sharp reduction in childhood lead poisoning in the past 20 years, millions of children are said to still be at risk from lead levels that were once considered safe. Long-term effects of lead exposure are increasingly being observed at lead levels much lower than previously believed harmful. It is believed that children with immature bodies and a habit of carrying dust, dirt, and grime from hand to mouth are at greatest risk for lead poisoning. And pregnant women can also transmit lead to their unborn children. Lead residue in soil and dust and from old lead-based paint and other products poses significant risks for children. It was expected that remedying these problems will be difficult and expensive.[84]

STRATEGIES

Most of the toxic chemicals released into the environment come from pesticide use in agriculture and from the disposal of hazardous industrial waste material. Strategies that reduce pesticide use as indicated in the first part of this chapter and that minimize industrial waste generation offer cost-effective approaches to lessening risks from toxic substances. The quick fixes of pesticide spraying and end-of-pipe pollution control must be replaced with new production systems aimed at reconciling economic profits and environmental protection. Some experts believe that with technologies and methods now available, pesticide use could probably be halved and the creation of industrial waste cut by a third or more over the next decade.[85]

Detoxifying the environment involves the development of policies and establishment of funding priorities that actively promote new methods of production in agriculture and industry. Greater public commitments to research and development are needed, some experts believe, in the areas of biological, cultural, and genetic methods of pest control. Developing countries, in particular, may need to stop subsidizing chemical pesticides so heavily, which only encourages farmers to apply more chemicals than is economically justified and increases all risks associated with toxic farm chemicals.[86]

With regard to disposal of industrial wastes, more research and development money must focus on waste-reducing technologies. Virtually no country, according to one expert, has yet designed an effective, long-term strategy to reduce industrial chemical wastes. By investing in waste reduction, governments can avoid future problems and costs arising from waste mismanagement, shortfalls in treatment capacity, and public opposition to siting new disposal facilities. Few developing countries have even established the basic foundations for a hazardous waste management system, and most have no regulations governing toxic waste disposal or facilities that are capable of adequately treating and disposing of such materials.[87]

Perhaps the most promising strategy is to make industries assume more responsibility for the societal costs and risks associated with hazardous substances. Some experts think this strategy is crucial to fostering a transition to safer chemicals and products. If industries all over the world, for example, had to prove that chemical substances were safe, and if they faced strict liability for damages caused from the manufacture, use, and disposal of their products, the risks might diminish throughout the chemical cycle. Such a process would weed out risky substances in industrial laboratories before they are introduced into the environment, rather than waiting for a regulatory agency to correct abuses after many years of using the chemical.[88]

The Chemical Manufacturers Association (CMA) established a "Responsible Care" initiative to improve the performance of the industry health, safety, and the environment. This initiative was signed by over 170 leading chemical companies, representing more than 90 percent of the industrial chemical production in the country. The CMA promised to report progress in implementing the initiative, and asked residents who lived near chemical companies to be active participants in the initiative. The initiative was said to be the industry's way of making sure it was not part of the problem but part of the solution. The initiative listed the following principles:[89]

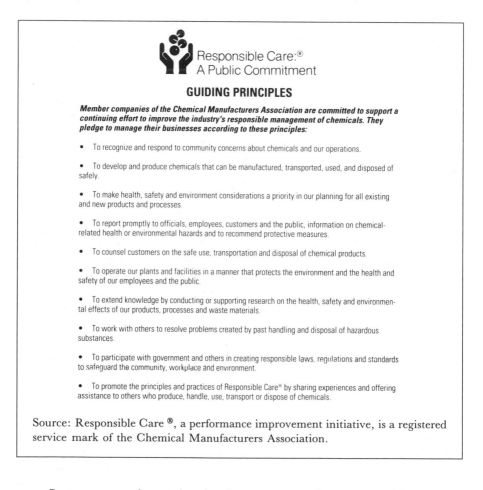

Responsible Care:®
A Public Commitment

GUIDING PRINCIPLES

Member companies of the Chemical Manufacturers Association are committed to support a continuing effort to improve the industry's responsible management of chemicals. They pledge to manage their businesses according to these principles:

- To recognize and respond to community concerns about chemicals and our operations.

- To develop and produce chemicals that can be manufactured, transported, used, and disposed of safely.

- To make health, safety and environment considerations a priority in our planning for all existing and new products and processes.

- To report promptly to officials, employees, customers and the public, information on chemical-related health or environmental hazards and to recommend protective measures.

- To counsel customers on the safe use, transportation and disposal of chemical products.

- To operate our plants and facilities in a manner that protects the environment and the health and safety of our employees and the public.

- To extend knowledge by conducting or supporting research on the health, safety and environmental effects of our products, processes and waste materials.

- To work with others to resolve problems created by past handling and disposal of hazardous substances.

- To participate with government and others in creating responsible laws, regulations and standards to safeguard the community, workplace and environment.

- To promote the principles and practices of Responsible Care® by sharing experiences and offering assistance to others who produce, handle, use, transport or dispose of chemicals.

Source: Responsible Care ®, a performance improvement initiative, is a registered service mark of the Chemical Manufacturers Association.

Some suggest that society has begun to turn from an uncritical acceptance of a chemically driven culture. The focus of industry has begun to shift toward a fairly widespread adoption of the waste management hierarchy of source reduction, recycling, treatment, and minimal residual storage and disposal. Perhaps the time has come, from the perspective of the environmental and health communities, to restrict the use of many toxic materials, and even prohibit some of them outright. While zero discharge may be unrealistic, this goal suggests the direction in which environmentalists are heading. Industry is approaching a similar position, but for largely different reasons. The high costs of waste disposal, combined with increased liability, make source reduction an economic imperative. Thus business is being led in the same direction as environmental and health advocates.[11]

Questions for Discussion

1. What are the most widely used types of pesticides? For what purposes are they used? What percentages are used for major categories of usage? Do these figures surprise you to any extent?

2. Who was one of the first to point out the danger of pesticide usage? What particular pesticide were focused on, and what dangers were highlighted? What was the effect of this action?

3. Describe the Alar incident. What organization raised the initial concern? What role did the media play? What was the result? What does this incident say about the public's perception of pesticides?

4. What threats do pesticides pose to human health and the environment? Describe the present regulatory system with regard to pesticides. Do you believe this system adequately protects human health and the environment? Why or why not? Who is most at risk from pesticides?

5. What risks do pesticides created by biotechnology pose for society? What regulatory system is evolving to control these risks? What more needs to be done in this area?

6. What alternatives to pesticides exist? Are these alternatives effective? What is an integrated pest management system? What are the advantages and disadvantages of this method? What does the future hold with regard to pesticide usage?

7. What threats do toxic substances pose to human health and the environment? Name some chemicals that you have heard about which are dangerous. What risks do these chemicals pose to human health and how have they been controlled?

8. Describe the Toxic Substances Control Act. What are its major provisions? How does the act work with respect to new and existing chemicals? What impacts has it had on the chemical industry? On the whole, do you think it is a good piece of legislation?

9. What are Community-Right-to-Know bills and what do they normally contain? What is a Toxic Release Inventory and what has been its effect on communities and on the chemical industry? Do these requirements help communities plan for emergency situations?

10. What new strategies are being pursued with respect to toxic chemicals? Do you believe these strategies hold much promise? What direction do courts seem to be taking? Is this a development that bears watching?

11. Describe the California approach to toxic chemical control. What does "significant risk" mean? Is this kind of law likely to be passed by other states? Why or why not? What was the impact of this approach on business?

12. What long-term strategies make the best sense regarding toxic chemicals? What additional things should industry do to protect the public and the environment? Examine the responsible care initiative of the Chemical Manufacturers Association. What do you think of these principles? Can they be implemented?

~

NOTES

1. G. Tyler Miller, *Living in the Environment,* 6th ed. (Belmont, CA: Wadsworth, 1990), p. 549.

2. *Your Guide to the U.S. Environmental Protection Agency,* OPA 212 (Washington, DC: Environmental Protection Agency, 1982), p. 9.

3. Miller, *Living in the Environment,* p. 550.

4. Ibid., pp. 551–552.

5. Ibid., p. 550.

6. Rachel Carson, *Silent Spring* (Greenwich, CT: Fawcett, 1962).

7. Miller, *Living in the Environment,* p. 554.

8. Ibid.

9. Ibid., p. 555.

10. Anastasia Toufexis, "Watch Those Vegetables, Ma," *Time,* March 6, 1989, p. 57.

11. Gisela Bolte, Dick Thompson, and Andrea Sachs, "Do You Dare to Eat a Peach?" *Time,* March 27, 1989, pp. 24–27.

12. Allen A. Boraiko, "The Pesticide Dilemma," *National Geographic,* Vol. 157, No. 2 (February 1980), p. 151. See also "Pesticides Leave Enduring Trail, Causing Disagreement," *Dallas Times Herald,* July 20, 1986, p. A-53.

13. Environmental Protection Agency, *Meeting the Environmental Challenge* (Washington, DC: U.S. Government Printing Office, 1990), p. 19.

14. *1978 Report: Better Health and Regulatory Reform* (Washington, DC: Environmental Protection Agency, 1979), p. 29.

15. Environmental Protection Agency, *Environmental Progress and Challenges: EPA's Update* (Washington, DC: U.S. Government Printing Office, 1988), pp. 114–115.

16. EPA, *Meeting the Environmental Challenge*, p. 19.

17. EPA, *Environmental Progress and Challenges*, p. 129.

18. "Pesticide-icides," *Regulation*, Nos. 3/4, 1987, p. 9.

19. Ibid.

20. Ibid.

21. Scott Ferguson and Ed Gray, "1988 FIFRA Amendments: A Major Step in Pesticide Regulation," *Environmental Law Reporter*, 19 ELR, 2-89, pp. 10070–10082.

22. Sonia L. Nazario, "EPA Under Fire for Pesticide Standards," *Wall Street Journal*, February 17, 1989, p. B-1. See also Jim Stiak, "Pesticides and Secret Agents," *Sierra*, May/June 1988, pp. 18–21.

23. EPA, *Environmental Progress and Challenges*, pp. 128–129.

24. Ibid., p. 134.

25. Ibid., pp. 134–135.

26. Andy Pasztor and Barry Meier, "EPA Has Started to Crack Down on Use of Pesticides Thought to Be Hazardous," *Wall Street Journal*, December 6, 1984, p. 7.

27. David Holzman, "Farm Workers Reap Cancer Risks," *Insight*, September 4, 1989, pp. 52–53.

28. EPA, *Meeting the Environmental Challenge*, p. 19.

29. "EPA Issues Rules on Pesticides Made by Biotechnology," *Wall Street Journal*, October 5, 1984, p. 37.

30. EPA, *Environmental Progress and Challenges*, p. 140.

31. Ibid., pp. 139–140.

32. Rae Tyson, "Bush Aims to Assure 'Safest Food'," *USA Today*, October 27, 1989, p. 1-A.

33. Robert E. Taylor and Art Pine, "Science Academy Urges Major Revision in U.S. Standards on Pesticides in Food," *Wall Street Journal*, May 21, 1987, p. 28.

34. Dennis Farney, "Sweeping Agenda: Environmental Plan in California Alarms Farm, Business Groups," *Wall Street Journal*, October 22, 1990, p. A-1; Richard Koenig, "Pesticide Makers Face Virulent Threat," *Wall Street Journal*, October 22, 1990, p. B-1.

35. EPA, *Meeting the Environmental Challenge*, p. 20.

36. Ibid., p. 19.

37. See David Weir and Constance Matthlesson, "Will the Circle Be Unbroken?" *Mother Jones*, June 1989, pp. 20–27.

38. EPA, *Meeting the Environmental Challenge*, p. 20.

39. Miller, *Living in the Environment*, p. 558.

40. Ibid., p. 559.

41. Ibid., p. 560. See also Amal Kumar Naj, "Can Biotechnology Control Farm Pests?" *Wall Street Journal*, May 11, 1989, p. B-1.

42. Miller, *Living in the Environment,* p. 561.

43. Ibid., p. 562.

44. Ibid.

45. Ibid., p. 563.

46. Ibid.

47. J. Madeleine Nash, "It's Ugly, But It Works," *Time,* May 21, 1990, p. 30.

48. Jeanne McDermott, "Some Heartland Farmers Just Say No to Chemicals," *Smithsonian,* Vol. 21, No. 1 (April 1990), p. 127.

49. Sue Shellenbarger, "Back to the Future: A Movement to Farm Without Chemicals Makes Surprising Gains," *Wall Street Journal,* May 11, 1989, p. A-1.

50. Sandra Postel, "Controlling Toxic Chemicals," *State of the World 1988* (New York: Worldwatch Institute, 1988), p. 124.

51. Ibid., p. 121–122.

52. Ibid., p. 120.

53. Peter Steinhart, "Innocent Victims of a Toxic World," *National Wildlife,* Vol. 28, No. 2 (February-March 1990), p. 21.

54. Ibid., p. 23.

55. EPA, *Better Health and Regulatory Reform,* p. 21.

56. Environmental Protection Agency, *Office of Toxic Substances, Reporting for the Chemical Substance Inventory* (Washington, DC: Environmental Protection Agency, 1977), p. 1.

57. EPA, *Environmental Progress and Challenges,* p. 123.

58. Appendix I to Premanufacture Notification Draft Guideline, *The Chemical Reporter* (Washington DC: Bureau of National Affairs, 1978), p. 1124.

59. EPA, *Environmental Progress and Challenges,* p. 126.

60. Environmental Protection Agency, *The Toxic Substances Control Act,* 1976, p. 2.

61. EPA, *Environmental Progress and Challenges,* p. 123.

62. Ibid., p. 124.

63. Ibid.

64. EPA, *Meeting the Environmental Challenge,* p. 18.

65. EPA, *Environmental Progress and Challenges,* p. 116.

66. Ibid., p. 120.

67. Paul N. Cheremisinoff, "Focus on High Hazard Pollutants," *Pollution Engineering,* February 1990, p. 75.

68. EPA, *Environmental Progress and Challenges,* p. 120. See also Amal Kumar Naj, "Battle Against Toxic PCBs Gains Ground as Bacteria Are Found That Eat Them," *Wall Street Journal,* November 9, 1988, p. B-4.

69. Ibid., pp. 120–121.

70. Ibid., p. 124.

71. United States Environmental Protection Agency, *Chemicals in Your Community: A Guide to the Emergency Planning and Community Right-to-Know Act* (Washington, DC: U.S. Government Printing Office, 1988), p. 7.

72. Ibid., p. 15.
73. Ibid., p. 14.
74. Ibid., pp. 2–4.
75. EPA, *Meeting the Environmental Challenge,* p. 18.
76. EPA, *Environmental Progress and Challenges,* p. 125.
77. "New Agency to Study Chemical Dangers," *Dallas Times Herald,* May 28, 1983, p. 4-A.
78. "New Jersey Bill Signed Forcing Public Listing of Toxic Substances," *Wall Street Journal,* August 30, 1983, p. 2.
79. Paul M. Barrett, "Courts Lend Sympathetic Ear to Claims for Compensation Based on Cancer Fears," *Wall Street Journal,* December 14, 1988, p. B-1.
80. Ibid.
81. John R. Emshwiller, "California Ushers in Environmental Law Placing Warning Levels on 29 Substances," *Wall Street Journal,* February 23, 1988, p. A-2.
82. Randolph B. Smith, "California Spurs Reformulated Products," *Wall Street Journal,* October 1, 1990, p. B-1. See also Eric Felten, "Gillette Quickly Covers Its Mistake," *Insight,* November 27, 1989, pp. 50–51.
83. Sonia L. Nazario, "Children Become Centerpiece of Efforts to Set Tighter Restrictions on Pollutants," *Wall Street Journal,* October 15, 1990, p. B-1.
84. "Lead Poisoning Poses Risk to U.S. Children Despite Precautions," *Wall Street Journal,* August 19, 1988, p. B-9.
85. Postel, "Controlling Toxic Chemicals," p. 118.
86. Ibid., pp. 133–134.
87. Ibid., pp. 134–135.
88. Ibid., p. 136.
89. "Handle with Responsible Care," *Wall Street Journal,* April 11, 1990, p. A-9.
90. Daniel Mazmanian and David Morell, "The Elusive Pursuit of Toxics Management," *The Public Interest,* No. 90 (Winter 1988), pp. 92–93.

SUGGESTED READINGS

Bogard, William. *The Bhopal Tragedy: Language, Logic, and Politics in the Production of a Hazard.* Boulder, CO: Westview Press, 1989.

Bosso, Christopher John. *Pesticides and Politics: The Life Cycle of Public Issue.* Pittsburgh: University of Pittsburgh Press, 1987.

Carson, Rachel. *Silent Spring.* Greenwich, CT: Fawcett, 1962.

Crone, Hugh D. *Chemicals and Society.* Cambridge, MA: Cambridge University Press, 1986.

Doniger, David D. *The Law and Policy of Toxic Substances Control: A Case Study of Vinyl Chloride.* Baltimore: Johns Hopkins University Press, 1978.

Dover, Michael J. *A Better Mousetrap: Improving Pest Management for Agriculture.* Washington, DC: World Resources Institute, 1985.

Edelstein, Michael R. *Contaminated Communities: The Social and Psychological Impacts of Residential Toxic Exposure.* Boulder, CO: Westview Press, 1988.

Gips, Terry. *Breaking the Pesticide Habit.* Minneapolis: IASA, 1987.

Hallenbeck, William H. *Pesticides and Human Health.* New York: Springer-Verlag, 1985.

Horn, D. J. *Ecological Approach to Pest Management.* New York: Guilford Press, 1988.

Kurzman, Dan. *A Killing Wind: Inside Union Carbide and the Bhopal Catastrophe.* New York: McGraw-Hill, 1987.

Marco, G. J., et al. *Silent Spring Revisited.* Washington, DC: American Chemical Society, 1987.

Postel, Sandra. "Controlling Toxic Chemicals," *State of the World 1988.* New York: Worldwatch Institute, 1988.

Postel, Sandra. *Defusing the Toxics Threat: Controlling Pesticides and Industrial Waste.* Washington, DC: Worldwatch Institute, 1987.

Scott, Ronald M. *Chemical Hazards in the Workplace.* New York: Lewis, 1989.

Segel, Edward, et al. *The Toxic Substances Dilemma: A Plan for Citizen Action.* Washington, DC: National Wildlife Federation, 1985.

United States Environmental Protection Agency. *Chemicals in Your Community: A Guide to the Emergency Planning and Community Right-to-Know Act.* (Washington, DC: U.S. Government Printing Office, 1988).

Watterson, Andrew. *Pesticide Users Health and Safety Handbook.* New York: Van Nostrand Reinhold, 1988.

Weir, David, and Mark Schapiro. *Circle of Poison: Pesticides and People in a Hungry World.* San Francisco: Institute for Food and Development Policy, 1981.

Van den Bosch, Robert. *The Pesticide Conspiracy.* Berkeley: University of California Press, 1989.

CHAPTER 9

WASTE DISPOSAL

∽

Every American household generates more than a ton of rubbish per year on average. Add to this total 60 million tons from commercial activities and 90 million tons from industry, thus making a total of around 400 million tons of solid waste produced each year in American society. On top of this figure, there is a further 250 million tons of hazardous waste generated annually that requires special treatment. Until the mid-1970s, this rubbish was largely handled by small firms or local government. Most of it was trucked to out-of-town sites and dumped. The dangerous waste was simply buried. Nobody really cared what happened to all this waste material as long as it was out of sight.[1]

Disposal of these wastes, especially those considered to be hazardous, is a costly and time-consuming business, requiring complex measures to control. Uncontrolled waste presents environmental and health risks that necessitates action to prevent degradation of water, soil, and air, and to protect human health. Initial concerns regarding waste disposal focused on the fire hazards posed by solid wastes and on the particulates generated by open burning. In the mid-1960s, for example, legislation was enacted to restrict open burning of garbage.

In the latter half of the 1970s, attention focused on the problems negligent hazardous waste disposal was causing for the environment and human health because of leaching, contamination, corrosion, and poisoning of land, water, vegetation, and animals as well as humans by toxic chemicals and heavy metals. Investigations disclosed that between 1950 and 1979, over 1.5 trillion pounds of hazardous wastes had been dumped in about 3,300 sites around the country. Fifty-three chemical companies in 1978 alone had dumped 132 billion pounds of industrial waste. Incidents such as Love Canal heightened public apprehension about the hazardous waste problem.[2]

As a result of concern about hazardous waste, federal and state governments have passed strict environmental standards related to its disposal. The solid waste problem became the subject of increasing attention as more and more waste was generated and traditional disposal methods became unacceptable. These developments led to the formation of waste disposal companies that have the ability to meet new environmental standards requiring safer and costlier methods of disposal.[3] These companies generally use the following four methods to dispose of solid and hazardous waste safely:

1. *Landfills:* These burial sites for waste are high-tech operations lined with impermeable materials and constantly monitored. Trenches are built into the base of the landfills to collect noxious fluids that could leak out and contaminate drinking water. These are then pumped to the surface where they are made inert. Landfills that do not meet such stringent standards are being closed all over the country.

2. *Incineration:* There are over 100 incinerators in the United States today that burn waste material and in some cases generate energy from this burning. Hazardous waste is burned at very high temperatures in special incinerators. These incinerators must have the technology to capture noxious fumes that are generated in the process of burning. Some of these incinerators have been in operation for several years and may need to be modernized.

3. *Recycling:* Some hazardous waste is recycled, but the problems with respect to recycling hazardous waste are even greater than the problems involved with recycling solid waste. The EPA wants to build a nationwide waste exchange to facilitate the exchange of both solid and hazardous waste and promote recycling of this material.

4. *Storage:* Some hazardous waste is simply stored in covered facilities that are not in close proximity to populated areas. Proper protection must be provided for leaking drums that might threaten groundwater supplies, and the stored material must be constantly monitored for leakage and other potential problems.

The costs of disposing of waste material has increased dramatically over the past several years. In 1978, for example, it cost about $2.50 to have a ton of hazardous waste dropped into a safe hole in the ground. In 1987 the cost of disposing of hazardous waste in this fashion ranged from $200 a ton upward. Burning the waste cost $50 a ton in 1978; in 1987 fees ran at over $200 a ton and $2,000 a ton for really nasty waste. Garbage companies a decade ago only charged $3 a ton to get rid of common or garden rubbish. Today an area like Long Island, which ships out nearly all of its household rubbish, pays $130 a ton to have the stuff removed.[4]

Even though operating margins of the garbage companies have increased making them quite profitable, the industry has problems with regulators and the public. The laws regulating disposal are inconsistent, laxly monitored, and seldom enforced, which creates distortions in the market. Definitions of hazardous waste differ and national laws on air, water, and soil pollution are seldom mutually coherent. Companies find it difficult to get permits for landfill sites and incinerators because of the "not in my back yard" (NIMBY) syndrome. Nations and communities alike object to the importation of waste from other countries and communities.[5]

SOLID WASTE

Nonhazardous solid waste can be defined as any unwanted or discarded material that is not in liquid or gaseous form. These wastes include municipal garbage and industrial refuse as well as sewage, agricultural refuse, demolition wastes, and mining residues. About 98.5 percent of this nonhazardous solid waste comes from mining, oil, and natural gas production and industrial activities. Mining waste is often left piled near mine sites where it can pollute the air, surface water, and groundwater. This waste material consists of overburden, which is the soil and rock cleared away before mining, and the tailings that are discarded during ore processing. Industrial waste consists of scrap metal, plastics, paper, fly ash from electrical power plants, and sludge from industrial waste treatment plants. Much of this waste is disposed of at the plant site where it is produced.[6]

Waste from homes and businesses in or near urban areas makes up the remaining 1.5 percent of nonhazardous solid waste produced in the country. Almost 160 million tons of this municipal solid waste are discarded in the United States every year, or about 400,000 tons every day. This is enough waste to fill the Astrodome in Houston more than twice daily for a year. This waste stream has increased 80 percent since 1960 and is expected to increase another 20 percent in the next ten years. The average amount of municipal solid waste generated per person in the United States is about two to five times that in most other developed nations.[7]

Americans throw out about 4 pounds of trash a day consisting mainly of paper products and yard wastes, which make up about 59 percent of all municipal solid waste.[8] (See Figure 9.1.) Most of the rest consists of glass, plastic, aluminum, iron, steel, tin, and other nonrenewable mineral resources. Only about 10 percent of these potentially reusable resources are recycled in this country. The rest is hauled away and dumped or burned at a cost of almost $5 billion a year. Each year these wasted resources have enough aluminum in them to rebuild the country's entire commercial air fleet every three months, enough iron and steel to supply the nation's automobile companies, and enough wood and paper to heat 5 million homes for 200 years.[9]

Figure 9.1

Composition of Municipal Waste

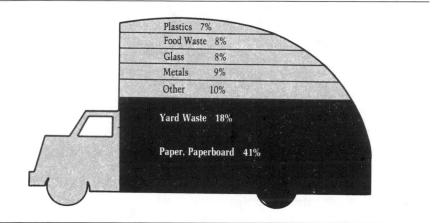

Plastics 7%
Food Waste 8%
Glass   8%
Metals   9%
Other   10%
Yard Waste 18%
Paper, Paperboard 41%

Source: Environmental Protection Agency, *Meeting the Environmental Challenge* (Washington, DC: U.S. Government Printing Office, 1990), p. 14.

DISPOSAL OPTIONS

Disposal of this amount of solid waste poses problems for our society that will only grow in magnitude. There is a problem with space as urban land grows more expensive, making it too costly to open new landfills. A second problem concerns the leachate, which is the distillation of chemicals in the waste material that percolates into the soil and groundwater. Third is the problem of organic decomposition, which is unsightly and smelly and a producer of methane gas as air and sunlight decompose some of the material. There is an ethical problem related to future generations who will have to deal with the trash we have disposed of in many cases, and who will have fewer resources to use because we have wasted them. And finally there is a political problem, consisting of the negative response most people have toward the building of more landfills and incinerators. A closer look at each of the disposal methods will more clearly indicate the nature of the problem.

Landfills

About 80 percent of waste material is disposed of in landfills. Before the Resource Conservation and Recovery Act (RCRA) was passed in 1976, much of the solid waste in this country was discarded into open dumps or burned in crude incinerators. These open dumps created health hazards, polluted surface water and groundwater, and often caught fire and filled the air with pollutants. The RCRA banned all open dumps and required land-fills to be upgraded to sanitary landfills. These sanitary landfills are disposal sites in which wastes are spread out in layers, compacted, and covered with a fresh layer of soil after each day's activity.[10]

Open burning of solid waste is not allowed in these landfills, odor is seldom a problem, and rodents and insects cannot thrive underneath the layers of garbage. These landfills are also constructed so they reduce water pollution from runoff and leaching. Semi-impermeable clay under the land-fill and a collection pipe as well as a subterranean trench around the site trap most of the leachate. Pumps then send it back to the top of the landfill where some of the chemicals are filtered out. Instruments constantly monitor the leachate to make sure it is not leaking into groundwater. This kind of landfill can be put into operation quickly, generally has a low operating cost, and can handle massive amounts of solid waste. After they have been filled and allowed to settle for a few years, the land can often be used for some constructive purpose such as a park, a golf course, an athletic field, or a wildlife area.[11]

Many people assume that the trash buried in a landfill eventually decomposes. But in fact, most of the garbage in a landfill is virtually mummified. The layers of dirt covering the garbage and the landfill's bulk tend to keep air and rain from reaching the garbage, and as a result, oxygen-loving bacteria play only a limited role in transforming ordinary household garbage into decomposed earth. Other bacteria do digest biodegradable material, but this process takes a long time and may stop altogether under extremely dry conditions. The average landfill is often like a pyramid where the trash buried there lies embalmed.[12]

Research into actual landfills shows that some food debris and yard waste does degrade, but at a very slow rate—only 25 percent in the first 15 years with little or no additional change for at least another 40 years. Most of the remaining trash seems to retain its original weight, volume, and form for at least four decades. Newspapers were found to be the largest single com-modity in landfills, taking up as much as 16 percent of the volume of waste dumped at the average site. Most of these newspapers, no matter what their age, come out in remarkably readable shape. Plastics constituted less a percentage of garbage than was suspected, growing only from 10 percent in the 1960s to 13 percent at present. It was surmised that today's plastic products are made thinner and lighter, allowing them to be squashed flat and thus to take up less space.[13]

The problem with this method of waste disposal is that many of these landfills are close to overflowing—almost 70 percent of such landfills are expected to reach capacity in 15 years. In more than 40 states, rising land costs, technical risks, new EPA regulations, leachate problems, increasing space scarcity, and an escalating number of NIMBY movements are forcing the closing of landfills. Communities where old landfills have reached capacity are having trouble siting new landfills.[14] Some cities without enough landfill space are shipping their trash elsewhere. But officials in southern states with large areas for landfills do not want to become the nation's garbage dump and are restricting garbage imports from other states. Increasingly, communities will have to accept responsibility for the wastes they produce instead of trying to make these wastes somebody else's problem.[15]

In March 1987, the infamous garbage barge that left Long Island City in New York loaded with 3,100 tons of refuse illustrates this problem. The owners of the barge had initially hoped to dispose of its load in a landfill in Moorehead City, North Carolina, but because of public outrage, the barge continued on a two-month journey along the Atlantic Coast and into the Gulf of Mexico, only to be turned away at every port at which it landed. Eventually the barge had to return home to where it started, and its load of garbage was finally going to be incinerated. The incident received national news coverage and called the nation's attention to the solid waste disposal problem.[16]

Many landfills leak pollutants that threaten groundwater supplies. To deal with this problem, the EPA proposed new regulations in 1988 that would force all municipal landfills to monitor hazardous wastes and methane gas, ban discharges of harmful wastes into underground water, and strengthen controls on rodents, insects, fire, and odor. The EPA estimates that these rules, to take full effect in 1991, would add $800 to $900 million a year to the nation's garbage disposal bill now estimated at $4 to $5 billion annually. These added costs will undoubtedly force more landfills to close and prevent other ones from opening, further contributing to the problem of solid waste disposal.[17]

Incineration

Alternative disposal methods include incineration, which can reduce garbage weight as much as 75 percent and reduce the volume by as much as 90 percent. Waste-to-energy incinerators also produce heat that can be sold to generate electricity which helps to reduce the cost of incineration. These incinerators do not pollute groundwater and add little to the air pollution problem if equipped with effective pollution control devices. But many U.S. incinerators built in the 1960s and 1970s were equipped with poorly maintained and ineffective pollution controls. Controls proposed by the EPA in 1988 required all new incinerators to use the best available technology to remove 95 percent or more of the air pollutants generated in the incineration of solid wastes.[18]

Incineration, however, still leaves about 25 percent of the original waste material in the form of toxic ash residues. This ash, which is usually disposed of in ordinary landfills, can be contaminated with hazardous substances such as lead, cadmium, mercury, dioxins, and other toxic metals. Environmentalists want the EPA to reclassify incinerator ash as a hazardous material, which would mean it would have to be disposed of in landfills designed to handle hazardous wastes. When disposed of in ordinary landfills, such waste can pose problems for human health and the environment.[19]

Incineration competes with the long-term goal of reducing waste because this method involves the commitment of a certain amount of garbage to be profitable, providing incentives to produce more rather than less garbage. The costs to the community of building an incinerator can be high as property values will go down if the facility is located near residential areas. The costs of building the facility itself can also be expensive, then it will have to be mothballed after 20 to 30 years of useful life. All of these technological uncertainties discourage investment in new methods that might result in better incineration technology.

At the end of 1989, there were 111 trash-to-energy incinerators operating in 40 states, and 210 others were being built or planned. By the end of the century, incinerators are projected to be burning about 30 percent of U.S. solid waste. But many of these facilities may be halted by the NIMBY movement that makes it hard to find new sites for incinerators. People are concerned about the air pollution generated by incinerators and the ash disposal problem. Conservationists also oppose dependence on incinerators because they encourage continuation of a throwaway approach that wastes resources. The use of incineration encourages people to continue tossing away paper, plastics, and other burnable materials rather than looking for ways to recycle and reuse these resources and to reduce waste production.[20]

Composting

Since yard waste constitutes a significant percentage of municipal solid waste, these wastes can be decomposed in backyard compost bins and used in gardens and flower beds. Currently, only about 1 percent of the yard waste generated in the United States is composted, but this method of disposing of yard wastes has the potential of reducing the solid waste stream by almost 18 percent. Degradable solid waste from slaughterhouses, food processing plants, and kitchens can also be composted, as can organic waste produced by animal feedlots, municipal sewage treatment plants, and various industries. Much of this material can be collected and degraded in large composting plants, and sold at a profit as a soil conditioner and fertilizer.[21]

One company believes that composting could handle up to 60 percent of the country's municipal solid waste, and is spending $20 million on research to develop disposable diapers that break down in composting systems. Disposable diapers pose a particular problem as they constitute a significant percentage of solid waste, and by holding out composting as a solution, the company hopes to encourage the construction of new garbage-handling systems. The commercial process advocated relies on the same biological degradation of material as in the backyard process. Such plants can turn garbage into compost under controlled temperature in 3 to 14 days. After this process, the compost must cure for 30 to 180 days before it can be used for landscaping or farming. There are only ten such plants in the United States at present, but it is hoped that local government will be motivated to build more systems of this kind, particularly if diapers are a major element of the process.[22]

Recycling

Another option is recycling, which is being pursued by an increasing number of communities. At least 22 states have already passed legislation either promoting or requiring the recycling of residential garbage and 9 states have passed mandatory deposit laws on beverage containers.[23] Other bills seek to impose bans on various solid waste elements, implement packaging taxes or restrictions, mandate some degree of source separation and recycling, or establish state procurement guidelines for recycled products.[24] Some experts have suggested that recycling and composting could reduce the amount of solid waste going to landfills by 70 percent and save $110 million a year compared to incineration. Japan has the world's most comprehensive waste management and recycling program.[25] (See box.)

How Japan Is Handling Its Solid Waste

Japan has one of the most sophisticated overall systems for managing waste in the world. Perhaps this came about because they ran out of landfill space 35 years ago, but nonetheless, they have been a pioneer in integrating the use of waste burning with maximum materials recycling. Japan recognizes recyclable materials as "resources" and not as waste, as is the common practice in the United States and other industrialized countries. Japanese citizens recycle 40 percent of their total solid waste stream, including 50 percent of all paper, 55 percent of glass bottles, and 66 percent of food and beverage cans.[26]

Many Japanese communities sort recyclables into a number of categories. For example, the residents of Zentsuji separate trash into 32 different categories and haul it to collection centers.[27] After sorting the recyclables, the hazardous elements requiring special treatment or disposal are removed from the remaining waste stream. The third category which is sorted contains materials that require direct landfilling, such as ceramics and nonrecyclable glass. The remaining category, soiled combustibles, are then incinerated.[28]

This latter category comprises 30 percent of the country's solid waste. Every Japanese community thus has its own incinerator or access to one nearby. To protect against hazardous emissions from incinerators, Japan requires the use of all possible operating practices and technologies to reduce air pollution and protect human health and the environment. Under optimal conditions, 99 percent of all measurable pollutants are removed, with the exception of mercury, which can be controlled in a range of 91 to 97 percent.

Resources can be recycled using high or low technology approaches. In the former approach, machines shred and separate urban waste to recover glass, iron, aluminum, and other useful materials. These materials are then sold to manufacturing industries as raw materials for the production process. The remaining trash, which consists of paper, plastics, and other combustible wastes, are either recycled themselves or incinerated. The heat produced by this incineration can be used to produce steam or electricity to run the recovery plant and for sale to industries and residential developments. Very few of these resource recovery plants are in existence today.[29]

The low technology approach involves homes and businesses separating various kinds of waste and disposing of it in separate containers. Paper, glass, metals, and plastics are usually separated in this manner, and picked up by compartmentalized city collection trucks, private haulers, or volunteer recycling organizations and then sold to scrap dealers, compost plants, and manufacturers. This method is used to recycle most solid waste in this and other countries. Studies have shown that it takes the average American family only 16 minutes a week to separate trash in this manner.[30]

This low technology approach to recycling produces little air and water pollution and has low start-up costs and relatively moderate operating costs. This approach also saves energy and provides jobs for unskilled workers. Recycling creates three to six times more jobs per unit of material than landfilling or incineration. Collecting and selling cans, paper, and other materials for recycling is an important source of income for many people all over the world, especially the homeless and the disadvantaged. In some developing nations, small armies of poor go through urban garbage disposal sites and remove paper, metals, and other items and sell them to factories to earn some money for themselves.[31]

Using scrap iron instead of iron ore to produce steel requires 65 percent less energy and 40 percent less water, and produces 85 percent less air pollution and 76 percent less water pollution. Recycling aluminum produces 95 percent less air pollution and 97 percent less water pollution, and perhaps most importantly, requires 95 percent less energy than mining and processing bauxite. Increasing the recycling rate of paper is a key to preventing further clearing and degradation of forests and reducing the unnecessary waste of timber resources. Thus recycling has tremendous advantages when it comes to resource and energy conservation.[32]

Nearly 30 percent of all paper products consumed in the United States are recycled, which amounts to 26 million tons a year. Recycled paper is made into new paper, cereal boxes, toilet tissue, and bedding for farm animals. Nationwide, demand is greater for high-quality white ledger paper than for newsprint and magazine paper because of the volume collected that can be made into these products. The greatest problem facing the recycled paper market has been that the supply of paper available to recycle is much greater than the immediate demand for the end products. Perhaps incentives need to be created for recycled products until a market is created that can then function on its own as demand and supply come into balance.[33]

One of the most troublesome problems with recycling is the increasing use of plastic packaging, which is difficult to burn or recycle. Because it is not biodegradable plastics will clog landfills for centuries. Many state and local governments have taken steps to ban or tax certain forms of plastic packaging and others are studying the problem. Bills have been introduced in Congress that would ban nondegradable beverage loops or would require all plastic products that pose a threat to fish and wildlife to be degradable or recyclable. But recycling has yet to take hold. Plastic can't legally be recycled into new food containers because of the possibility of contamination. And the economics of the situation doesn't favor other uses because consumers can buy new material for less than they would pay for recycled products.[34]

There is some evidence, however, that this situation is changing as some companies are finding ways to make a profit from plastics recycling.[35] The nation's largest recycler of plastic and fiber wastes, Wellman, Inc., saw sales top $300 billion in 1988, which was up from $260 million in 1987, showing that profits can be made from plastics recycling. The company buys about 100 million of the 150 million pounds of soft drink bottles reclaimed nationwide each year. There is still a long way to go, however, as the soft drink industry produces close to 900 million pounds of plastic bottles each year. Wellman uses the plastic scrap to produce polyester fibers that are then used as stuffing for ski jackets and sleeping bags, bedspreads, and furniture cushions. The company thinks that its fibers are found in 35 percent of all carpets made in the country, and stated that the market for its recycled fibers is so strong that it could utilize twice the number of scrap bottles if they were available.[36]

Some companies have made a switch from plastic containers to other paper-based packaging because of the recycling problem. In 1990, for example, McDonald's announced it was phasing out its foam sandwich containers, which accounted for about 75 percent of the foam packaging used by the company. Environmentalists had long complained that the polystyrene-based containers were difficult to recycle and did not degrade in a landfill, contributing to the waste disposal problem. The company had been engaged in an expensive campaign to show that foam containers could be recycled, sponsored by the chemical industry that manufactured polystyrene, but eventually gave into the critics of the packaging. The paper wrap it now uses takes up less volume and weighs about a third of the old polystyrene container.[37]

The chemical industry is concerned about finding ways to recycle plastics before the movement to ban or switch products grows any larger. But the task isn't easy, and researchers are trying a number of different approaches. Different plastic resins don't mix, and most plastic products are made up of several different resins. Thus the plastics have to be separated before recycling, which can be costly and time consuming. Nonetheless, almost all the major chemical companies have plunged into recycling ventures.[38] And one company claimed to have developed the first biodegradable plastic by using starch that can be derived from potatoes, corn, rice, or wheat. The material could be used, so it was claimed, to replace some of the nonbiodegradable plastic derived from petrochemicals.[39]

Other obstacles to recycling are even more serious. American attitudes will have to change to make recycling a more comprehensive approach to the waste disposal problem. The average American has been conditioned by advertising and example to a lifestyle that involves a throwaway attitude toward waste. Waste is something bad to be discarded and is not seen as a resource. The out-of-sight, out-of-mind approach to waste is prevalent. We emphasize making, using, and replacing more and more items to increase economic wealth regardless of the environmental costs to society. Because environmental costs are not reflected in market prices, consumers have little incentive to recycle and conserve renewable resources.[40]

Recycling to Reduce Large Quantities of Wastes

Recycling is an increasingly attractive option for handling our municipal wastes as municipal dumps fill up and communities become more resistant to new landfills and incinerators. Other countries such as Japan already have a recycling system in place. Japan recycles 50 percent of its wastes, and in one community they have shown that recycling can reduce garbage volume by as much as 65 percent.

In the United States, a few states have mandatory, statewide recycling laws (see map). In these states, residents have their recyclables picked up at the curb, much like regular garbage collection. A few states have new laws yet to be implemented, and as many as 8,000 localities have their own programs. Nine states have "bottle bills," whereby consumers pay a small deposit on cans and bottles, which is returned to them upon redemption. The cans and bottles then are collected by the distributor and recycled. Many states are considering taxes on both packaging and products made with nonrecyclable materials. These materials make up 33 percent of the garbage we throw out.

The federal government, to encourage use of recycled materials, will soon purchase paper and paper

Recycling paper increases energy savings by 95% and reduces solid waste.

products containing the highest possible percentage of recycled materials. It is also considering purchasing cement and concrete made with incinerator ash and asphalt made from used tires and re-refined lubricating oils. EPA has recycled its own office paper for years and has plans to start

recycling newspaper, bottles, and aluminum cans.

There is strong momentum for recycling around the country. EPA plans to capitalize on it through educational programs, providing technical assistance, encouraging market forces, and helping states develop solid waste/recycling plans.

Source: Environmental Protection Agency, *Environmental Progress and Challenges: EPA's Update* (Washington, DC: U.S. Government Printing Office, 1988), p. 91.

Public policy also hinders recycling efforts. Primary mining and energy industries get tax breaks, depletion allowances, and other tax-supported federal subsidies to encourage extraction and use of virgin materials. In contrast, recycling industries get few tax breaks and other subsidies. While the EPA has set a goal of recycling 25 percent of municipal solid waste by 1992, many believe the United States could easily recycle and reuse up to 35 percent of municipal garbage by the year 2000, and perhaps as much as 50 percent a decade later.[41] What is needed is a change in attitude that is reflected in market prices and public policy measures to support recycling.

The EPA is in the process of building a nationwide database to facilitate waste exchange and encourage companies to think of waste as a resource. While the idea is not necessarily new, as there are already some 18 regional nonprofit waste exchanges in the United States and Canada, the EPA's national focus may help to spread the use of exchange. As one example of how exchange can be useful, an upstate New York company used to spend $575 on hauling and tipping fees each time it dumped a truckload of scrap wood in a landfill hundreds of miles from its plant. Now for less than $200 it takes each load of scrap wood to a company in Pennsylvania that grinds it into an assortment of scented chips used as an air freshener. The EPA hopes to facilitate such exchanges with its computerized system that will be updated daily to end delays in getting rid of waste material.[42]

Reusable Products

The reuse of products involves using the same product over and over in its original form. Examples of reusable products are glass beverage bottles that can be collected, washed, and refilled by bottling companies. Up until 1975, most beverage containers in the United States were refillable glass containers. Today they make up only 15 percent of the market; nonrefillable aluminum and plastic containers have taken over. Another product is cloth diapers that can be washed and reused to replace disposable diapers that cause such a serious landfill problem. Carrying lunches in lunch boxes that can be reused instead of in onetime paper bags or baggies is another example.[43]

Since one of the largest components of municipal solid waste is packaging, reusable packaging holds great promise to reduce the garbage disposal problem. Although containers and packaging account for 30 percent of the total waste stream by weight, they account for a larger percentage of the volume, as packaging is generally bulky. To make matters worse, a majority of packaging contains foil or plastics, making the material difficult, if not impossible, to recycle. The small juice box that has become so popular because of its size and convenience is made up of so many different materials, it is not cost efficient to try and separate the materials so they can be recycled. The package has been banned in several states.[44]

Reuse of products extends resources and reduces energy use and pollution even more than recycling. Refillable glass bottles are the most energy-efficient beverage container on the market. Three times more energy is needed to crush and remelt a glass bottle to make a new one than is required to clean and refill a bottle. If reusable glass bottles replaced the 82 billion throwaway beverage cans produced in the United States every year, it is estimated that enough energy would be saved to supply the annual electricity needs of 13 million people. Countries like Denmark have taken this approach seriously and have banned all nonreusable beverage containers from the market.[45]

Source Reduction

Perhaps the best method of dealing with the solid waste disposal problem is not to produce so much waste in the first place. Reducing unnecessary waste of nonrenewable mineral resources can extend supplies of these resources even more dramatically than recycling or reuse. This method generally saves more energy than recycling and reduces the environmental impact of disposing of waste material. Manufacturers can conserve resources by using less material per product. They can also make products that last longer and abandon the planned obsolescence approach that may contribute to short-term profits but has long-term implications for resource availability. Products can also be designed so that they are easy and inexpensive to repair. Thus their useful life can be extended.[46]

INTEGRATED WASTE MANAGEMENT

The basic problem with waste disposal is cultural. Societies generate and dispose of waste based on cultural values that are exemplified in lifestyles and methods of manufacture. Exhibit 9.1 shows three different approaches to the waste disposal problem that reflect three different cultures. The sustainable approach would seem to make the most sense given the increasing costs of garbage disposal and the near exhaustion of some of our nonrenewable resources. The movement toward this kind of society, however, involves a change of basic values and notions of economic wealth that are not going to change overnight. But change of some sort seems inevitable given the dimensions of the waste disposal problem.

The ultimate disposal of solid waste involves combining various methods into an integrated management system that emphasizes certain management practices consistent with each community's demography and waste stream characteristics. In such an integrated waste management system, each component is designed so that it complements, rather than competes, with the other components in the system. These components must be

Exhibit 9.1

Three Systems for Handling Discarded Materials

Item	For a High-Waste Throwaway System	For a Moderate-Waste Resource Recovery and Recycling System	For a Low-Waste Sustainable Earth-System
Glass bottles	Dump or bury	Grind and remelt; re-manufacture; convert to building materials	Ban all nonreturnable bottles and reuse (not remelt and recycle) bottles
Bimetallic "tin" cans	Dump or bury	Sort, remelt	Limit or ban production; use returnable bottles
Aluminun cans	Dump or bury	Sort, remelt	Limit or ban production; use returnable bottles
Cars	Dump	Sort, remelt	Sort, remelt; tax cars lasting less than 15 years, weighing more than 818 kilograms (1,800 pounds) and getting less than 13 kilometers per liter (30 miles per gallon)
Metal objects	Dump or bury	Sort, remelt	Sort, remelt; tax items lasting less than 10 years.
Tires	Dump, burn, or bury	Grind and revulcanize or use in road construction; incinerate to generate heat and electricity.	Recap usable tires; tax or ban all tires not usable for at least 96,000 kilometers (60,000 miles)
Paper	Dump, burn, or bury	Incinerate to generate heat	Compost or recycle; tax all throwaway items, eliminate overpackaging
Plastics	Dump, burn, or bury	Incinerate to generate heat or electricity	Limit production; use returnable glass bottles instead of plastic containers; tax throwaway items and packaging
Yard wastes	Dump, burn, or bury	Incinerate to generate heat or electricity	Compost; return to soil as fertilizer; use as animal feed

Source: From *Living in the Environment: An Introduction to Environmental Studies* 6/E by G. Tyler Miller, Jr. © 1990 by Wadsworth, Inc. Reprinted by permission of the publisher.

combined in a cost-effective manner which is beneficial to each community and meets the need for safe garbage disposal that will continue to be effective for future generations.[47]

For example, a small town in a rural area may depend completely on landfilling to dispose of its waste; large cities may come to rely more heavily on recycling to reduce the burden on their landfills. Some cities utilize a complete integrated waste management system by stressing source reduction, mandating a recycling program, incinerating the remaining combustible trash, and landfilling the residual ash and any other items not suitable for incineration. Each community will need to tailor the system to meet its individual needs and take advantage of its resources.

The final report of the Municipal Solid Waste Task Force provided a valuable framework for apportioning municipal waste disposal responsibilities among federal, state, and local authorities. It emphasized voluntary efforts as opposed to increased federal regulation, and saw the EPA playing largely a role of information provider. According to this report, the EPA could develop technical and educational guidance, data collection and research and development programs, and act as a national clearinghouse for this information. The Task Force envisioned a cooperative effort by all levels of government to track volumes and types of wastes, with the EPA taking the lead in conducting research and development in technical areas related to combustion, landfilling, recycling, and source reduction. Six national objectives were identified as part of a national agenda to solve the municipal solid waste problem:[48]

1. Increase the waste planning and management information (both technical and educational) available to states, local communities, waste handlers, citizens, and industry, and increase data collection for research and development.

2. Increase effective planning by waste handlers, local communities, and states.

3. Increase source reduction activities by the manufacturing industry, government, and citizens.

4. Increase recycling by government and by individual and corporate citizens.

5. Reduce risks from municipal solid waste combustion in order to protect human health and the environment.

6. Reduce risks from landfills in order to protect human health and the environment.[49]

To accomplish these objectives, the use of more market incentives has been encouraged. Perhaps the greatest "market failure" with respect to solid waste disposal is the distortion of market incentives that results from municipal systems which charge flat fees for garbage collection. Wastefulness is encouraged by systems that charge such a single fee regardless of the amount of trash put out by households. Consumers are not being made aware of the true disposal costs resulting from their buying and discarding habits. If consumers were charged per pound for the type of garbage they generate, the proper signals would be sent so that their purchasing choices are affected by disposal costs.[50]

> Economic incentives also provide a way out of the NIMBY syndrome. Citizens do not want recycling centers, incinerators, and landfills in their backyards because they reduce property values and adversely affect other nonpecuniary aspects of home ownership—a quiet neighborhood, less traffic congestion and the like. The simple (but not easy) solution is to compensate property owners for their losses. An indirect form of compensation is to provide a public benefit—a firehouse, a park or civic center, or road improvements. Or restitution can be more direct, such as a lump-sum payment, or payment of property taxes for the homeowners. The point is that those enjoying the benefits of the waste disposal facility should offset at least some of the costs that are imposed on the areas surrounding the facility.[51]

The city of Seattle instituted a successful recycling program that fundamentally uses market incentives to change consumer behavior. Residents of the city are faced with a "pay-as-you-throw" system of garbage disposal. Homeowners pay $10.70 a month for a 19-gallon mini-can, but pay $31.75 for three full-size 32-gallon cans. Curbside recycling of plastic beverage bottles, glass, cans, newspapers, and other waste paper is free to homeowners. Four out of five households in the city recycle their trash, and 90 percent put out one or fewer cans of garbage a week. While volunteer efforts have received a great deal of attention, it is clearly market incentives in the form of high incremental costs for additional garbage cans that have changed the behavior of Seattle residents.[52]

HAZARDOUS WASTES

While initial concerns regarding waste disposal focused on the fire hazards posed by solid wastes, hazardous wastes began to get more and more attention as dumpsites were discovered all around the country that posed potential threats to groundwater supplies, as well as threats to wildlife and the environment in general.[53] There was little concern about this problem until 1977, when is was discovered that hazardous chemicals leaking from an abandoned waste dump in Niagara Falls, New York, were contaminating Love Canal, a suburban development. The publicity surrounding this problem made the public at large and especially public and elected officials aware of the dangers that buried hazardous wastes could pose for human health and the environment. The incident made the headlines for years, and the name of Love Canal became a household word that brought to mind untold dangers lurking beneath the surface in many parts of the country. (See box, p.288.)

Disposal of hazardous wastes is a costly and time-consuming business, requiring complex measures to control. Uncontrolled waste presents environmental and health risks that necessitate action to prevent degradation of water, soil, and air, and to protect human health. The total quantity of hazardous wastes produced in the country is difficult to estimate. The EPA estimates that 264 million tons are produced each year; the Office of Technology Assessment (OTA) has a much higher estimate of 400 million tons annually. About 95 percent of this waste is generated and either stored or treated on site by large companies such as chemical manufacturers, petroleum companies, and other industrial facilities.[54]

Hazardous wastes have been defined as wastes that (1) cause or significantly contribute to an increase in mortality or an increase in serious irreversible or incapacitating reversible illness, or (2) pose a substantial present or potential hazard to human health or the environment when improperly treated, stored, transported, or disposed of or otherwise managed.[55] They are wastes that cannot be managed by routine procedures because if they are improperly managed, they can cause a threat to public health and the environment. Improper disposal of hazardous wastes has also been responsible for other kinds of environmental damage — fires, explosions, pollution of surface water and air — as well as posing serious threats to human health through poisoning via the food chain or through direct contact.[56]

Hazardous wastes include wastes that pose a fire hazard (ignitable), dissolve materials or are acidic (corrosive), are explosive (reactive), or otherwise pose dangers to human health and the environment (toxic). (See Figure 9.2.) The characteristics of ignitability include liquids with a flash point (the temperature at which a vapor easily ignites in air) of less than 140°F, materials that burn so vigorously and persistently when ignited that they create a hazard, and ignitable compressed gases. Corrosive materials include aqueous wastes with a pH of less than or equal to 2 or greater than or equal to a pH of 12.5, and liquid wastes that corrode steel at a rate equal to or greater than .25 inch per year at a test temperature of 130°F.[57]

Reactive materials include those that react violently with water, form potentially explosive mixtures when combined with water, or when mixed with water will generate toxic gases, fumes, or vapors in quantities sufficient to endanger human health or the environment, and materials that are capable of detonation or explosive reactions if subject to a strong initiating source or if heated under confinement. Finally, toxic materials are those which have deleterious biological effects, such as poisoning, on human beings and other animal life.[58]

Hundreds of potentially dangerous substances can be found in hazardous waste, but as shown in Exhibit 9.2, the most common are few in

Love Canal

The Love Canal incident provides a horror story related to the disposal of hazardous wastes. Love Canal, located in Niagara Falls, New York, was an uncompleted, abandoned nineteenth-century waterway. It had been used as an industrial dump site since the 1930s, and in 1947 was purchased by Hooker Chemical and Plastics Company to dispose of drums of toxic chemical wastes. The site was covered and sold to the Niagara Falls Board of Education in 1953, who proceeded to build an elementary school and a playing field on the site. Part of the site was also sold to a developer who built several hundred homes on the periphery of the old canal.[59]

In 1976, after some years of unusually heavy rains and snow, the chemicals began seeping into basements of the houses. The canal itself overflowed and chemicals that had leaked from the decayed drums entered the environment. In August 1978, the New York State Department of health declared the Love Canal area "a grave and imminent peril" to the health of those living nearby. Investigations were conducted into complaints about an abnormal number of miscarriages, birth defects, cancer, and a variety of other illnesses. Eleven different actual or suspected carcinogens, including the dreaded dioxin, were found among the many chemicals leaching into the air, water, and soil. Air monitoring equipment found pollution levels ranging as high as 5,000 times the maximum safe level. Finally, President Carter declared Love Canal a disaster area, making federal disaster relief aid available to the residents, and signed an emergency order under which the federal government and New York State would share the cost of relocating the area families.[60] By July 1979:

- Two hundred and sixty-three families had been evacuated; 236 homes had been purchased by the state; 1,000 additional families had been advised to leave their homes;
- Housing values had dropped to nil;
- Almost $27 million had been appropriated by municipal, state, and federal agencies for providing temporary housing, closing off the contaminated area, and containing the leachate (including digging a trench, installing a drain pipe to catch the leachate, and covering the canal with a clay cap to seal it); and
- Nine hundred notices of claims had been filed against Niagara Falls, Niagara County, and the Board of Education for a total of more than $3 billion in damages to health and property, and other suits had been filed against Hooker Chemical Company.[61]

In 1982, the EPA released a three-volume, $5 million report suggesting that the Love Canal area was again safe for residents. The EPA Found "no clear evidence of environmental contamination" in most of the area around Love Canal that could be "directly attributable to migration of substances" from the dump itself. With the exception of houses closest to the site, the EPA said that the level of pollution found in the soil and underground water was "comparable" to other highly industrialized sites in upstate New York and the rest of the country. The study was sharply criticized by lawmakers and New York state officials including Hugh L. Carey, then governor of the state.[62]

These findings could have an affect on damage suits totaling more than $650 million filed by the state and the federal government against Hooker Chemical. Private parties also sued Hooker for hundreds of millions of dollars in additional damages. In October of 1983, Hooker claimed that it had reached out-of-court settlements on most of the personal-injury claims brought by residents of the Love Canal area. The company said it had settled with 1,345 of the 1,431 original claimants who sought a total of $16 billion in compensatory and punitive damages. The claims were for personal injury, wrongful death, or property damage resulting from exposure to chemical residues. The company ended up paying about $5 to $6 million with insurance companies paying about $25 million more.[63]

number. While there are about 14,000 regulated producers of hazardous waste, by far the majority are chemical manufacturers and allied industries. Ninety percent of the hazardous waste produced in the country comes from facilities that generate large quantities of more than 2,200 pounds per month. A much smaller amount comes from small quantity generators that produce between 220 and 2,200 pounds per month.[64]

The continuing problem of dealing with waste generation is complex and expensive. The EPA won't estimate what portion of the 264 metric tons of hazardous waste generated annually is disposed of improperly, but some

Figure 9.2

Characteristics of Hazardous Waste Materials

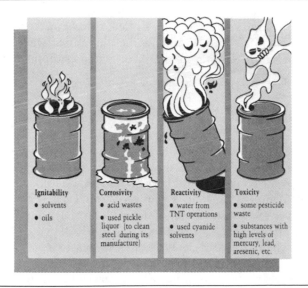

Ignitability	Corrosivity	Reactivity	Toxicity
• solvents • oils	• acid wastes • used pickle liquor (to clean steel during its manufacture)	• water from TNT operations • used cyanide solvents	• some pesticide waste • substances with high levels of mercury, lead, aresenic, etc.

Source: Environmental Protection Agency, *Environmental Progress and Challenges: EPA's Update* (Washington, DC: U.S. Government Printing Office, 1988), p. 85.

Exhibit 9.2

Common Hazardous Wastes

Chemical	Use	Manufacturing Hazard
C-56	Bug and insect killer	Acutely toxic, suspected carcinogen
Trichloroethylene (TCE)	Degreaser	Suspected carcinogen
Benzidene	Dye industry	Known human carcinogen
Curene 442	Plastics industry	Suspected carcinogen
Polychlorinated biphenyls (PCBs)	Insulators, paints, and electrical circuitry	Acutely toxic, suspected carcinogen
Benzene	Solvent	Suspected carcinogen
Tris	Fire retardant	Suspected carcinogen
DDT	Bug and insect killer	Acutely toxic
Vinyl chloride	Plastics industry	Known human carcinogen
Mercury	Multiple uses	Acutely toxic
Lead	Multiple uses	Acutely toxic, suspected carcinogen
Carbon tetrachloride	Solvent	Acutely toxic, suspected carcinogen
Polybrominated biphenyls (PBBs)	Fire retardant	Effects unknown

Source: Council on Environmental Quality, *Environmental Quality 1980* (Washington, DC: Government Printing Office, 1981), p. 217.

estimate that one out of every seven companies producing toxic wastes may have dumped illegally in recent years. No doubt huge quantities of such wastes go into streams, pastures, or vacant lots, where the risk of human contamination is high and the chance of detection slim.[65] Perhaps the best solution is for manufacturers to reduce the amount of waste generated by using new materials, adopting new processes and equipment, and reusing waste material in some fashion.[66]

REGULATION

Responsibility for control and eradication of hazardous waste disposal problems is lodged in the EPA's Office of Solid Waste and Emergency Response. This office implements two federal laws related to hazardous waste disposal, the Resource Conservation and Recovery Act (RCRA), which regulates current and future waste practices, and the Comprehensive Environmental Response, Compensation, and Liability Act (CERCLA), commonly called Superfund, which provides for cleaning up of old waste sites. Legislation thus focuses on preventing future contamination from improper waste disposal and the cleanup of existing waste sites where hazardous waste was disposed of improperly and poses a threat to human health and the environment.

The Resource Conservation and Recovery Act (RCRA)

RCRA, originally passed in 1976, controls the generation, transportation, storage, and disposal of wastes at existing or future waste facilities. Each year about 3,000 facilities manage 275 million metric tons of RCRA waste in the country. Specifically, the law provides for (1) federal classification of hazardous waste, (2) a "cradle-to-grave" manifest (tracking) system for waste material, (3) federal safeguard standards for generators and transporters, and for facilities that treat, store, or dispose of hazardous wastes, (4) enforcement of standards for facilities through a permitting system, and (5) authorization of state programs to replace federal programs.[67]

The basic purpose of RCRA is to protect groundwater from toxic pollution. The law provides cradle-to-grave control of hazardous waste material, from point of production through point of disposal. (See Figure 9.3.) Those who produce wastes have to obtain a permit to manage them on their own property. When shipping them to a treatment, storage, or disposal facility, they have to provide a manifest containing basic information about the waste material. All treatment, storage, and disposal operations are required to meet minimum standards to protect public health and the environment.[68]

Regulations to implement RCRA were developed in phases. The first phase included identification of solid wastes considered to be hazardous and the establishment of reporting and record keeping for the three categories of hazardous waste handlers: generators, transporters, and owners or operators of treatment, storage, and disposal (TSD) facilities. (See box.) In November 1980, these regulations became effective. By July 31, 1985, the EPA had identified 52,864 major generators of hazardous wastes, 12,343 transporters, and 4,961 TSD facilities.[69]

The second phase involved the development of technical standards related to the design and safe operation of the various types of treatment, storage, and disposal facilities. These standards serve as the basis for issuing permits to such facilities. Technical standards have been issued for incinerators and for new and existing land disposal facilities, along with financial responsibility and liability and insurance requirements for all facilities. Landfills, for example, must now include double liners, leachate detection and collection systems, and groundwater monitoring.

Congress intended the states to eventually assume responsibility for the RCRA hazardous waste program. The EPA is authorized to approve qualified state plans for hazardous waste management. To receive final authorization to operate the entire RCRA program, states must adopt regulations fully "equivalent to" and "consistent with" federal standards. Mississippi became the first state to receive full authorization to operate its own program. States can be granted interim authorization by setting regulations that are "substan-

Figure 9.3

The Hazardous Waste Manifest Trail

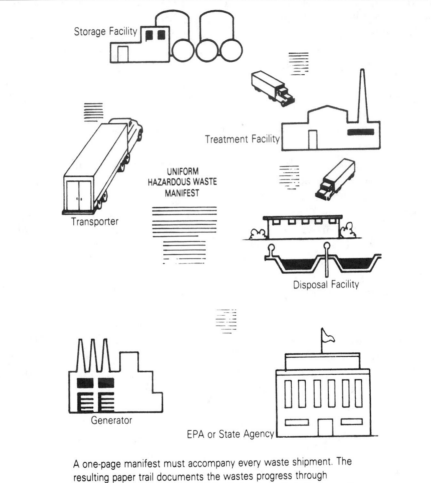

Storage Facility

Treatment Facility

UNIFORM
HAZARDOUS WASTE
MANIFEST

Transporter

Disposal Facility

Generator

EPA or State Agency

A one-page manifest must accompany every waste shipment. The
resulting paper trail documents the wastes progress through
treatment, storage and disposal. A missing form alerts the generator
to investigate, which may mean calling in the state agency or EPA.

Note: a manifest is unnecessary for waste treated and disposed of at the point
of generation.

Source: United States *Environmental Protection Agency, Environmental Progress and Challenges: EPA's
Update* (Washington, DC: U.S. Government Printing Office, 1988), p. 88.

tially equivalent to" EPA's regulations. All 50 states were expected to seek
final authorization to manage their own hazardous waste programs.

Congress reauthorized RCRA in late 1984 (these revisions were called
the 1984 Hazardous and Solid Waste Amendments, or HSWA), imposing

---

Responsibilities for Hazardous Waste

Generators must

- Determine if waste is hazardous.
- Apply for permit for waste handled on site.
- Originate and follow up manifest for waste moving off site.
- Keep records.

Transporters must

- Deliver hazardous waste to designated facility.
- Carry manifest with the shipment.
- Report and clean up spills.

TSD Facilities must

- Apply for permit from EPA.
- Meet Interim Status Standards until permit approved or denied.
- Meet permit conditions after permit is issued.

Source: *The Resource Conservation and Recovery Act: What It Is; How It Works,* SW-967 (Washington, DC: U.S. Environmental Protection Agency, 1983), pp. 5-6.

---

new and far-reaching requirements on the 175,000 enterprises that generate small amounts of waste per month (between 220 and 2,200 pounds) and those that own or operate underground storage tanks. The former are called small quantity generators (SQGs), and rules implemented in 1985 and modified in 1986 require any business producing or using hazardous materials or chemicals to register with the agency, and to be able to prove that the wastes from these materials are being disposed of properly.[70]

The revisions also required treatment of all hazardous wastes to EPA-specific levels or methods before they could be disposed of in landfills. Because of this "land ban," it was expected there would be more treatment of hazardous waste. For those wastes that are landfilled, the EPA established more stringent requirements for land disposal facilities which were expected to reduce the number of landfills that were permitted. Finally, the revisions required facility owners to clean up leaks of waste material that occurs at their facilities, and gave the EPA broadened authority to implement this requirement.[71]

The Comprehensive Environmental Response, Compensation, and Liability Act (CERCLA)

Commonly called Superfund, CERCLA provides money to the EPA and gives it authority to direct and oversee cleanup of old and abandoned waste sites that pose a threat to public health or the environment. The law provides funding for the government to clean up inactive waste sites where responsible parties cannot be found or where those responsible are unable or unwilling to perform the cleanup, and creates liabilities for parties who were associated with waste sites, either to perform the cleanup or to reimburse the EPA for the cost of the cleanup. Superfund was first authorized in 1980 for $1.6 billion, with the amount of money dependent on the size of the National Priority List, the extent of cleanup necessary, responsible party contributions, scope of the fund, and the amount of money the EPA could manage efficiently.

Superfund imposes liability on responsible parties for the costs of removal or remedial action, costs of response by other parties or entities, and for damage to, or destruction of, natural resources. The liability of the law is joint and several, that is, a single party may be held responsible for all cleanup costs even if other parties are involved. This might occur where other parties have disappeared or become insolvent, defunct, or bankrupt. Liability also attaches to a party without regard to fault or negligence. These costs can be high, for example, for a facility other than a vessel or vehicle, liability includes the total of all response costs plus up to $50 million for damages.[72]

The first phase of this effort was to conduct a nationwide inventory of such sites and establish priorities for cleanup. In ranking these dumpsites, the EPA takes five exposure pathways into account: (1) the population put at risk, (2) the hazard potential of substances at the sites, (3) the potential for contamination of drinking water, (4) the possibility of direct human contact, and (5) the potential for destruction of sensitive ecosystems. The EPA has broad discretion under the law in determining the appropriate remedial action to be taken in a specific instance. Once sites have been identified, the EPA can require owners of old or abandoned dumps to perform the cleanup work themselves, or, where this is not possible or where immediate action is needed, the EPA and the states can step in and do the cleanup. Proposed actions need to be cost-effective, environmentally sound remedies that are feasible and reliable from an engineering standpoint. No action can be taken in cases where attempting to clean up a dumpsite would present more danger to human health and the environment than leaving it alone.[73] (See box.)

Steps in Cleaning Up an Uncontrolled Waste Site

After someone alerts EPA about a potential problem site, what happens? If the site is found to present a release or threat of release to public health or the environment that must be addressed quickly, EPA may take emergency measures to remove the threat. These removal actions range from installing security fencing to digging up and removing wastes for safe disposal at a RCRA approved facility. Such actions may be taken at any site, not just those on the National Priority List (NPL). These actions can take place at any time during investigation or cleanup at a site when a determination is made that response should not be delayed.

1. **Identification and Preliminary Assessment.** If response can be delayed without endangering public health and the environment, we can take additional time to evaluate the site further. We collect all the available information on the site from our files, state and local records, and U.S. Geological Survey maps. We analyze the information to determine the size of the site, parties most likely to have used it, local hydrological and meteorological conditions, and the impact of the wastes on the environment.

2. **Site Inspection.** Inspectors then go to the site to collect sufficient information to rank its hazard potential. They look for evidence of hazardous waste, such as leaking drums and dead or discolored vegetation. They may take samples of soil or water. Inspectors analyze the ways hazardous materials could be polluting the environment, for example, through runoff into nearby streams. They also check to see if the public (especially children) have access to the site.

3. **Ranking Sites for the National Priorities List.** Sites are evaluated according to the type, quantity, and toxicity of wastes at the site, the number of people potentially exposed, the pathways of exposure, and the importance and vulnerability of the underlying ground-water supply. This information is used to determine the Hazard Ranking System score. If the score is 28.5 or above, the site may be proposed for listing on Superfund's National Priorities List. Each state may also propose one site for listing if it is the top priority site in the state.

4. **Negotiating with Potentially Responsible Parties.** After the parties potentially responsible for the contamination are identified, EPA notifies them of their potential liability. We then negotiate with them to reach an agreement to undertake the studies and subsequent cleanup actions needed at the site. If negotiations are not successful, EPA may use its enforcement authorities to require responsible parties to take action, or the Agency may choose to clean up the site and seek to recover costs at a later date.

5. **Remedial Investigation.** The objective for hazardous waste sites placed on the NPL is long-term cleanup. To select the cleanup strategy best suited to each unique site, a more extensive field study or remedial investigation is conducted by EPA, the state, or the responsible parties. This study includes extensive sampling and laboratory analyses to generate precise data on the types and quantities of wastes present at the site, the soil type and water drainage patterns, and resulting environmental or public health risks.

6. **Feasibility Study and Cleanup.** Cleanup actions must be tailored exactly to the needs of each individual site. The feasibility study analyzes those needs and evaluates alternative cleanup approaches on the basis of their relative effectiveness and cost. Remedial actions must use permanent solutions and alternative treatment to the maximum extent practicable. They may include technologies such as ground-water treatment or incineration.

7. **Post-Cleanup Responsibilities.** After cleanup, the state is responsible for any long-term operation and maintenance required to prevent future health hazards or environmental damage.

Source: Environmental Protection Agency, *Environmental Progress and Challenges, EPA's Update* (Washington, DC: U.S. Government Printing Office, 1988), p. 97.

Approximately 32,506 potentially contaminated sites that may pose a threat to human health or the environment have been identified nationwide. (See Figure 9.4.) Over 29,000 preliminary assessments have been conducted, and on the basis of these assessments, 17,800 sites have been determined to require no further action, but many of these sites will be cleaned up by the states. As of 1990, 1,246 sites were listed or proposed for listing on the national priorities list (NPL), which is a prerequisite for cleanup activities that would use federal Superfund money. (See Figure 9.5.) For sites listed on the NPL, further studies are conducted to determine the nature and extent of contamination. Such studies have been initiated at over 500 of the sites currently on the NPL, and over 251 long-term cleanups have been initiated at Superfund sites around the nation. Cleanup work has been completed at 52 such sites around the country.[74] (See Figure 9.6.)

Figure 9.4

Hazardous Waste Sites

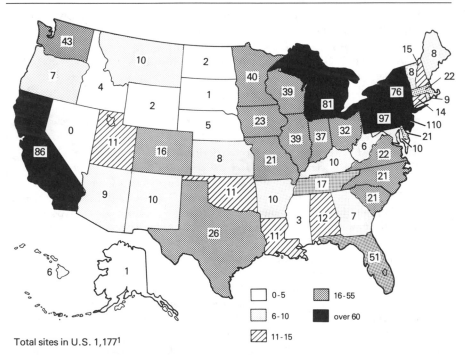

Total sites in U.S. 1,177[1]

Represents final and proposed sites on National Priority List.
[1]Includes nine in Puerto Rico; and one in Guam.

Source: U.S. Department of Commerce, *Statistical Abstract of the United States 1989.* 109th ed. (Washington, DC: Government Printing Office, 1988), p. 202.

Figure 9.5

Initial Assessment of Hazardous Waste Sites

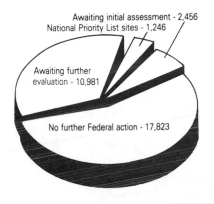

Source: Environmental Protection Agency, *Meeting the Environmental Challenge* (Washington, DC: U.S. Government Printing Office, 1990), p. 15.

Figure 9.6

Status of Work on Priority Sites

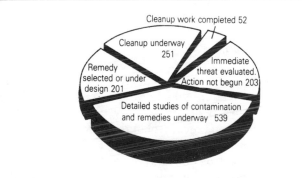

Source: Environmental Protection Agency, *Meeting the Environmental Challenge* (Washington, DC: U.S. Government Printing Office, 1990), p. 15.

The Office of Technology Assessment estimated that there may be at least 10,000 hazardous waste sites in the United States that pose a serious threat to public health and should be given priority in any national cleanup. The cost could easily reach $100 billion, or more than $1,000 per household. The General Accounting Office (GAO) estimated that 378,000 waste sites may require corrective action.[75] The EPA estimated that cleaning up abandoned waste dumps would cost another $11.7 billion beyond that already authorized. This estimate assumed that the cost of cleaning up an individual site varied between $6 to $12 million, that 1,500 to 2,500 sites would need cleanup, and that companies generating the wastes would pay 40 to 60 percent of the costs.[76]

The original Superfund authorization ran out in October 1985, and proposals were introduced into Congress to raise the amount of money in a reauthorization that ranged from $5.3 billion to $10 billion. The chemical industry lobbied hard to oppose any increase in the $300 million a year in special taxes that were required to contribute to Superfund, and most proposals contained provisions that would spread the cost of the cleanup of abandoned hazardous waste sites to all U.S. manufacturers instead of just oil and chemical companies. Proposals were made for a .08 percent value-added tax levied on the manufactured goods of companies with more than $10 million in sales with an exemption for processed foods.[77]

Because of the inability to agree on a financing plan, no new bill was passed before the old one expired, thus the administration was not able to collect any more taxes to support the cleanup effort. As the money began to run out, the EPA had to abandon new cleanup projects and put ongoing projects on hold. Without additional funds by April 1, 1986, the EPA would have been forced to terminate all cleanup contracts and start the furlough process of 1,500 Superfund personnel.[78] On April 1, 1986, the president signed a two-month extension that provided $150 million in stopgap funding through May 31, 1986, enough to keep the program going while Congress continued to seek a compromise on a comprehensive five-year reauthorization plan.

Finally, in October 1986, a new $9 billion Superfund program, called the Superfund Amendments and Reauthorization Act of 1986 (SARA), was passed and signed into law by the president. (See box.) The measure sets more stringent toxic waste cleanup guidelines and permits the formation of risk retention groups to offer pollution liability coverage. It also directs communities to enhance their emergency planning efforts for chemical accidents and allows citizens to sue businesses and the EPA for violations of the measure. To fund the bill, petroleum taxes were to be increased to $2.75 billion with a higher burden placed on imports. Another $2.5 billion will be raised from a broad-based corporate surtax levied at a rate of 0.12 percent on corporate alternative minimum taxable income exceeding $2 million. Other sources of funding include a $1.4 billion tax on chemical feedstocks, $1.25 billion from general revenues, and $0.6 billion from interest and recoveries from companies responsible for toxic dumps.[79]

As part of SARA, Congress directed the EPA to focus more of its efforts on finding permanent remedies for Superfund sites and less on simply containing existing untreated wastes. Treatment of wastes is not a major component of the remedies being selected at many of these sites, and efforts

The Superfund Amendments and Reauthorization Act of 1986

The 1986 amendments of CERCLA, known as the Superfund Amendments and Reauthorization Act (SARA), authorized $8.5 billion for both the emergency response and longer term (or remedial) cleanup programs. The Superfund amendments focused on:

- **Permanent remedies.** EPA must implement permanent remedies to the maximum extent practicable. A range of treatment options will be considered whenever practicable.
- **Complying with other regulations.** Applicable or relevant and appropriate standards from other federal, state, or tribal environmental laws must be met at Superfund sites where remedial actions are taken. In addition, state standards that are more stringent than federal standards must be met in cleaning up sites.
- **Alternative treatment technologies.** Cost effective treatment and recycling must be considered as an alternative to the land disposal of wastes. Under RCRA, Congress banned land disposal of some wastes. Many Superfund site wastes, therefore, will be banned from disposal on the land; alternative treatments are under development and will be used where possible.
- **Public involvement.** Citizens living near Superfund sites have been involved in the site decisionmaking process for over five years. They will continue to be a part of this process. They also will be able to apply for technical assistance grants that may further enhance their understanding of site conditions and activities.
- **State involvement.** States and tribes are encouraged to participate actively as partners with EPA in addressing Superfund sites. They will assist in making the decisions at sites, can take responsibility in managing cleanups, and can play an important role in oversight of responsible parties.
- **Enforcement authorities.** Settlement policies already in use were strengthened through Congressional approval and inclusion in SARA. Different settlement tools, such as de minimis settlements (settlements with minor contributors), are now part of the Act.
- **Federal facility compliance.** Congress emphasized that federal facilities "are subject to, and must comply with, this Act in the same manner and to the same extent . . . as any non-government entity." Mandatory schedules have been established for federal facilities to assess their sites, and if listed on the NPL, to clean up such sites. We will be assisting and overseeing federal agencies with these new requirements.

The amendments also expand research and development, especially in the area of alternative technologies. They also provide for more training for state and federal personnel in emergency preparedness, disaster response, and hazard mitigation.

Source: Environmental Protection Agency, *Environmental Progress and Challenges: EPA's Update* (Washington, DC: U.S. Government Printing Office, 1988), p. 95.

are underway to develop new technologies that will ensure permanent cleanup remedies. New technologies are being evaluated that will destroy, immobilize, or reduce the volume of hazardous waste material, and the EPA states that it is committed to increasing the number of such technologies that are available to deal with contaminated soils and groundwater.[80]

The EPA is also implementing a strategy for the better management of cleanups that calls for eliminating acute health threats as a first priority. This has been accomplished at all sites currently on the NPL list, and will be the first step accomplished at all new sites added to the list. Long-term, more permanent cleanups are then being conducted on a priority basis. To speed up and expand the cleanup process, the agency is planning greater emphasis on encouraging or enforcing cleanup by those responsible for causing the problem, and expanding the role of the communities near the sites in cleanup decisions.[81]

Despite these efforts, progress under Superfund is slow, as there is little incentive in the program for companies to develop new cleanup technologies and a great deal of incentive for companies to spend millions of dollars on lawyers to put off spending hundreds of millions on actual cleanup. For example, Shell Oil along with its insurers spent $40 million in legal fees before agreeing to spend several hundred million dollars to clean up a site near Denver. Five companies spent $16 million in legal fees before coming to an agreement to clean up a site near St. Louis that cost $14 million. Companies sue each other over their share of the liability and sue their insurance companies to make them financially responsible. The EPA has even gone beyond site owners, operators, and transporters and has sued lenders in some situations. All of this legal maneuvering takes a considerable amount of time and money.[82]

The question of liability took on a new twist in the late 1980s when businesses that purchased land had to take greater steps to protect themselves from being stuck with the bill for cleanup should that land later turn out to contain hazardous wastes. Insurance to cover this risk became increasingly difficult to purchase as insurers found coverage of such risks difficult to quantify. Under Superfund, current owners of contaminated property can be held liable for cleanup even if the previous owners were to blame for the problem. Companies began to use environmental auditors in increasing numbers to check the land and any buildings that may be on the property for hazardous wastes before buying. Such auditing, however, was not foolproof and attracted many questionable people who wanted to cash in on the demand for their services.[83]

In 1990, a decision by a court of appeals expanded the notion of lender liability under Superfund law, when it ruled that a bank foreclosing on contaminated property could be held liable as an owner for cleanup of the site. The question before the court was what level of activity would expose a holder of a security interest to liability? The court answered that under

Superfund a lender may be liable for the entire cost of the cleanup if its involvement with the borrower ever put it in a position to "affect hazardous waste disposal decisions" if it so chose. It did not matter to the court when the contamination took place or when the loan was made, even if these actions took place decades before the Superfund law was enacted. Because of joint and several liability, one bank could also be held liable for the entire cost of the cleanup if it was the only bank in the group that lent money which was still solvent. Thus loans of only thousands of dollars could conceivably generate liabilities in the millions.[84]

Because of the huge sums often involved in liability for hazardous waste cleanup, the issues of disclosure of such potential liability in financial statements is of concern. The Securities and Exchange Commission (SEC) mounted a disclosure study in 1988 that was intended to develop disclosure guidelines with respect to liability for cleanup, but any flagrant violations it discovered will be referred to the proper authorities for enforcement action. Companies claimed they would not know the full extent of their liabilities for several years, because of litigation with insurance companies and other potentially responsible parties. But the SEC believed that companies that had potential liability at several sites could at least disclose the minimum cost of cleanup at these sites.[85]

MANAGEMENT OPTIONS

The National Academy of Sciences outlined three ways to deal with hazardous waste: (1) waste prevention by waste reduction, recycling, and reuse, (2) conversion to less hazardous or nonhazardous material, and (3) perpetual storage. (See Figure 9.7.) The first approach is considered by many to be the most desirable. The best way to deal with waste of any kind is simply not to produce so much in the first place. The goal of waste prevention is to reduce the amount of waste produced by modifying industrial or other processes and by reusing or recycling the hazardous wastes that are produced.[86]

Companies that have tried to reduce their wastes often find that waste reduction and pollution prevention save them money. The Minnesota Mining and Manufacturing Company (3M) has had a waste reduction program in place since 1975, and in 1978 claimed that its waste production was cut in half, saving it $300 million. Most firms have little incentive to reduce their wastes, however, because of the small percentage that waste disposal amounts to in comparison to the total value of the products they produce. Some states have tried to encourage waste reduction by offering technical assistance, providing a database of information about waste material, and providing matching grants to large and small companies and communities wanting to implement waste reduction projects.[87]

According to EPA estimates, at least 20 percent of the hazardous waste generated in the United States could be recycled, reused, or exchanged so

Figure 9.7

Options for Dealing with Hazardous Waste

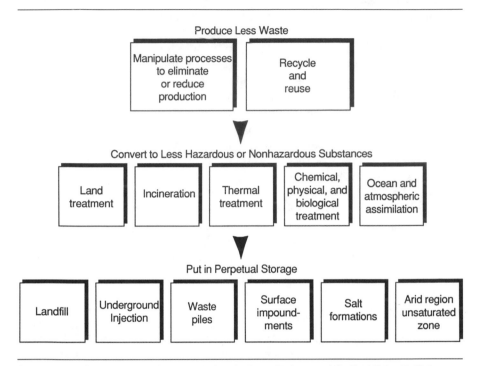

Source: From *Living in the Environment: An Introduction to Environmental Studies* 6/E by G. Tyler Miller, Jr. © 1990 by Wadsworth, Inc. Reprinted by permission of the publisher.

that one industry's waste becomes another's raw material, yet about only 5 percent of such waste is managed in this manner. As mentioned previously, the EPA is developing a computerized network to facilitate such exchanges. There is much more that could be done to encourage recycling and reuse of hazardous wastes, yet the EPA's budget typically allocates a very small percentage of money to promote recycling, reflecting the priorities of the government, which lean toward burial of waste material and incineration.[88]

Conversion of hazardous wastes to less hazardous or nonhazardous materials could include spreading degradable wastes on the land to let them degrade over time, burning them on land or at sea in specially designed incinerators, thermally decomposing them, or treating them chemically or physically. Over 60 percent of the hazardous wastes generated in this country could be incinerated, according to the EPA, but this is an expensive method of waste disposal, and has waste disposal problems of its own because of the toxic waste residue. Much of the waste material generated abroad is detoxified in large treatment plants, but these facilities have not been used to dispose of much of the waste generated in this country.[89]

Bioremediation techniques began to offer some promise in dealing with the hazardous waste problem. This technique involves using of bacteria to get rid of toxic components of hazardous waste and leave behind harmless substances. Bioremediation takes longer than more conventional cleanup methods, and may thus be inappropriate where fast action is needed, but the technique does have a decided cost advantage. In addition to being under attack as potentially unsafe, incineration can cost up to $1,000 per ton, whereas bioremediation costs less than $100 a ton in some cases. Use of this process may also be safer, as bioremediation eliminates the problem rather than relocating it somewhere else. Before it can be used on a large scale, however, several problems must be solved.[90]

The last phase of hazardous waste management involves placing these wastes in perpetual storage. Such storage methods can involve the use of secured landfills or underground vaults, which should be located in a geologically and environmentally secure place that is carefully monitored for leaks. The costs of using this method are high, and the toxic waste disposal and management industry has been expanding by 20 to 30 percent per year to handle waste material. Much waste material is also injected into deep wells that are theoretically drilled beneath aquifers that are tapped for drinking water and irrigation. While these disposal methods are safer than they were in previous years, they are still prone to leakage and other dangers.[91]

Finally, the development of an international hazardous waste trade must be mentioned. In order to save money and avoid regulatory hurdles, cities and waste disposal companies in the United States and other industrialized countries ship large amounts of hazardous waste to other countries. Most of these American legal exports go to Canada and Mexico. To ship waste to these and other countries, all U.S. companies have to do is to notify the EPA of their intent to ship this material, get written permission from the recipient country, and file an annual report with the agency.[92] Such lax provisions encourage countries such as the United States to transport its hazardous wastes problems to other countries.

These legal shipments of hazardous wastes may be only the tip of the "sludgeberg," as it is called, because there is evidence of a growing trade in illegal shipments of hazardous wastes between countries. Waste disposal firms can charge high prices for picking up hazardous wastes from companies that generate them, and if they can dispose of them legally or illegally in other countries at low cost, they can make large profits. Most of the recipient countries, however, are beginning to realize that importation of hazardous waste can threaten the health and environment of their country and weaken long-term economic growth. Many are adopting a "Not In Our Country" (NIOC) attitude similar to the NIMBY phenomenon in this country.[93]

In late 1990, it was reported that millions of tons of toxic waste were being dumped in Latin America each year, leaving poisonous residues that will endanger lives for decades. Everything from household trash to radioactive sludge was said to be sent to the region because lax antipollution laws

---

Treatment and Disposal of Hazardous Wastes

Treatment and disposal differs for organic and inorganic substances. Organic substances are made principally of carbon, hydrogen, and oxygen. Some of these materials can be broken down into relatively harmless substances such as water and carbon dioxide. In contrast, no matter what type of treatment is used on certain inorganic substances, they can only be broken down into components that still pose a potential risk. For instance, metals can never be broken down beyond their basic metallic elements, therefore, they ultimately require land disposal.

Landfilling of wastes is the last stop in the waste management chain and is one method of waste disposal. Only a small portion of waste is ultimately land-filled. The long-term goal of a landfill is to serve as an indefinite holding place for wastes and to minimize the potential of exposure. Hazardous wastes often are disposed of by injection as a liquid into the ground in specially designed wells. Approximately 20–35 million metric tons (about 10 percent by weight) of dilute, hazardous waste is disposed of annually into deep-well injection systems. These wells penetrate to depths well below drinking water sources where natural brine makes water unusable.

The vast majority of the hazardous waste managed annually is treated in man-made surface ponds (or impoundments) and wastewater treatment plants. The volume of wastewater disposal into surface waters is great, but these wastewaters can be regulated by the Clean Water Act (see section titled "Surface Water" in the Water Chapter). A relatively small amount—about 2 million metric tons—is incinerated. A number of different treatment technologies are used on hazardous wastes to render them less toxic before final disposal:

- Wastewaters are made less hazardous by biological decomposition, chemical neutralization, precipitation, or steam stripping. Steam stripping converts the hazardous constituents to gas, which is then captured in air pollution control equipment.

- The only alternative for metals and inorganics is recycling or solidification. Solidification involves combining the waste with a stabilizing agent, such as cement, to create a solid, impermeable material which lessens the likelihood of leaching into the soil.

- Enclosed incinerators primarily burn liquid organic waste and some sludges at high enough temperatures so that virtually complete combustion takes place.

Source: Environmental Protection Agency, *Environmental Progress and Challenges: EPA's Update* (Washington, DC: U.S. Government Printing Office, 1988), p. 87.

---

there made disposal of such waste easier and cheaper. Scientists in Brazil called the dumping of hazardous waste in their country an illicit trade that is shrouded in secrecy and often done by small and unregistered companies. This dumping was devastating the environment and said to cause cancer, birth defects, nerve damage, and blood disorders. According to Greenpeace,

Latin America made a perfect dumping ground as there was lots of space, loads of corrupt inspectors, and widespread ignorance of the problem.[94]

Leaders from 116 countries drafted an international treaty in 1989 that was designed to help control the export of hazardous waste material. The treaty would ban such exports unless the government of the receiving country gives prior written permission to receive the waste material. Many environmentalists want Congress to ban all exports of hazardous waste to other countries, believing that the United States has an ethical obligation to take care of its own waste material and not export the problem where it will affect the health and environment of other countries.[95]

~

Questions for Discussion

1. Describe the solid waste problem. How is most of this waste disposed of currently? What is the problem with this method of disposal? How much time is left?

2. What happens to waste material in landfills? Are consumers being misled about products advertised as biodegradable? Why or why not? What would you do about this advertising if it were part of your company's marketing strategy?

3. What problems exist with incineration as a method of waste disposal? Would you recommend this method as a viable one to deal with the solid waste problem? Why or why not? What can be done to improve incineration?

4. Is recycling the answer to the solid waste problem? What types of recycling exist? What can be done to develop more recycling programs across the country? What kinds of materials are a particular problem when it comes to recycling?

5. What is an integrated waste management system? What incentives can be used to dispose of waste more effectively? Is it realistic to think that waste will be seen as a resource in our country?

6. Describe the Love Canal incident. What questions did this incident raise about hazardous waste disposal? Was Hooker Chemical at fault? What could they have done differently?

7. What characteristics does hazardous waste possess? What are some of the most common hazardous wastes? Why are they so difficult to dispose of appropriately?

8. Describe the Resource Conservation and Recovery Act. What are its major provisions? What is cradle-to-the-grave control? How is this

accomplished? What responsibilities does business have under this system?

9. Describe the Superfund program. To what problem is it directed? What is joint and several liability? Why was the law constructed in this manner? Does this provision pose a particular problem for business?

10. How many sites have been identified as potentially dangerous? How many are on the National Priorities List? What steps are involved in cleaning up such sites? Why does the process of cleanup take so long?

11. What are the important provisions of the Superfund Amendments (SARA)? How is the new program funded? Does this method of funding seem more fair to you than the previous program? What new developments are taking place with respect to liability?

12. What options exist for dealing with hazardous waste? What is the best approach in your opinion? What are some companies doing to reduce the waste they produce? Do waste reduction techniques have widespread applicability?

NOTES

1. "The Garbage Industry: Where There's Muck There's High Technology," *The Economist,* April 8, 1989, p. 23.

2. Samuel Epstein, et al., *Hazardous Wastes in America* (San Francisco: Sierra, 1982), p. 303.

3. "The Garbage Industry," p. 23.

4. Ibid., p. 24.

5. Ibid., pp. 24–26.

6. G. Tyler Miller, *Living in the Environment,* 6th ed. (Belmont, CA: Wadsworth, 1990), p. 351.

7. Environmental Protection Agency, *Environmental Progress and Challenges: EPA's Update* (Washington, DC: U.S. Government Printing Office, 1988), p. 87.

8. Ibid.

9. Miller, *Living in the Environment,* p. 351.

10. Ibid., p. 359.

11. Miller, *Living in the Environment,* p. 359.

12. Richard Wolkomir, "I Learned That It Just Keeps Getting Deeper," *Smithsonian,* Vol. 21, No. 1 (April 1990), p. 152.

13. Dan Grossman and Seth Shulman, "Down in the Dumps," *Discover,* April 1990, pp. 39–40.

14. EPA, *Environmental Progress and Challenges,* p. 87.

15. Miller, *Living in the Environment,* p. 360.

16. Terri Thompson and Mimi Bluestone, "Garbage: It Isn't the Other Guy's Problem Anymore," *Business Week,* May 25, 1987, p. 150.

17. George J. Church, "Garbage, Garbage, Everywhere," *Time,* September 5, 1988, pp. 81–82.

18. Miller, *Living in the Environment,* p. 361.

19. Ibid.

20. Ibid.

21. Ibid., pp. 361–362.

22. Zachary Schiller, "Turning Pampers into Plant Food?" *Business Week,* October 22, 1990, p. 38.

23. Bill Eldred, "Changing Economics Revives Recycling," *American City and Country,* No. 102 (1987), pp. 57–63.

24. Paul Frumkin, "A Looming Crisis," *Restaurant Business,* No. 88 (1989), pp. 143–154.

25. Miller, *Living in the Environment,* p. 361.

26. Melinda Beck and Mary Hager, "Buried Alive," *Newsweek,* November 27, 1988, p. 70.

27. Ibid.

28. Joanna Underwood, "How Japan Is Handling Its Solid Waste," *EPA Journal,* March/April 1989, p. 43.

29. Miller, *Living in the Environment,* p. 363.

30. Ibid., p. 365.

31. Ibid.

32. Ibid.

33. Beck and Hager, "Buried Alive," p. 75.

34. Elliott D. Lee, "Opposition to Plastic Packaging Is Intensifying as the Nation's Solid-Waste Problem Grows Acute," *Wall Street Journal,* November 25, 1987, p. 38.

35. Susan Dillingham, "New Answers to a Plastic Life-style," *Insight,* January 30, 1989, p. 44

36. Ibid.

37. Scott Kilman, "McDonald's to Drop Plastic Foam Boxes in Favor of High-Tech Paper Packaging," *Wall Street Journal,* October 2, 1990, p. A-3.

38. Amal Kumar Naj, "Chemists Seek Ways to Recycle Plastics Before Movement to Ban Products Grows," *Wall Street Journal,* September 26, 1989, p. B-1. See also Richard Koenig and Mary Lu Carnevale, "Dow Chemical Domtar Plan Recycling Pact," *Wall Street Journal,* September 27, 1988, p. 6.

39. Michael Waldholz, "New Plastic Is Promoted as a Natural," *Wall Street Journal,* January 24, 1990, p. B-1.

40. Miller, *Living in the Environment,* p. 368.

41. Ibid.

42. Evan I. Schwartz, "A Data Base That Truly Is Garbage In, Garbage Out," *Business Week,* September 17, 1990, p. 92.

43. Miller, *Living in the Environment,* p. 369.

44. Gary McWilliams, "The Big Brouhaha over the Little Juice Box," *Business Week,* September 17, 1990, p. 36.

45. Miller, *Living in the Environment,* p. 369.

46. Ibid., p. 370.

47. Kenneth Chilton, *Talking Trash: Municipal Solid Waste Mismanagement* (St. Louis, MO: Washington University Center for the Study of American Business, 1990), pp. 7–8.

48. Ibid., p. 18.

49. EPA Municipal Solid Waste Task Force, *The Solid Waste Dilemma: An Agenda for Action* (Washington, DC: U.S. Environmental Protection Agency, 1989), pp. 24–25.

50. Chilton, *Talking Trash,* pp. 19–20.

51. Ibid., p. 20.

52. Ibid., p. 19. See also William D. Ruckelshaus, "The Politics of Waste Disposal," *Wall Street Journal,* September 5, 1989, p. A-16.

53. Samuel Epstein, et al., *Hazardous Wastes in America,* p. 303.

54. Miller, *Living in the Environment,* pp. 474–475.

55. Office of Research and Development, *Controlling Hazardous Waste Research Summary* (Washington, DC: Environmental Protection Agency, 1980), p. 4.

56. *The Resource Conservation and Recovery Act: What It Is: How It Works,* SW-967 (Washington, DC: Environmental Protection Agency, 1983), p. 3.

57. Benjamin A. Goldman, James A. Hulme, and Cameron Johnson, *Hazardous Waste Management: Reducing the Risk* (Washington, DC: Island Press, 1986), p. 20.

58. Ibid.

59. U.S. Council on Environmental Quality, *Environmental Quality 1979* (Washington, DC: U.S. Government Printing Office, 1979), p. 177.

60. Ibid., pp. 176–177.

61. Ibid., p. 177.

62. Andy Pasztor, "U.S. Report That Love Canal Is Habitable Stirs Widely Conflicting Official Reaction," *Wall Street Journal,* July 15, 1982, p. 1.

63. "Occidental Settles Most Injury Claims in Love Canal Case," *Wall Street Journal,* October 11, 1983, p. 3.

64. EPA, *Environmental Progress and Challenges,* p. 80.

65. Barry Meier, "Dirty Job: Against Heavy Odds, EPA Tries to Convict Polluters and Dumpers," *Wall Street Journal,* January 7, 1985, p. 1.

66. See Alix M. Freedman, "Firms Curb Hazardous Waste to Avoid Expensive Disposal," *Wall Street Journal,* May 31, 1985, p. 19.

67. Ronald J. Penoyer, *Reforming Regulation of Hazardous Waste* (St. Louis, MO: Washington University Center for the Study of American Business, 1985), p. 1.

68. Environmental Protection Agency, *1978 Report: Health and Regulatory Reform,* (Washington, DC: Author, 1979), p. 16.

69. *The Resource Conservation and Recovery Act,* SW-967, p. 5; *The New RCRA: A Fact Book* (Washington, DC: Environmental Protection Agency, 1985), p. 4.

70. The New RCRA, pp. 1–2.

71. EPA, *Environmental Progress and Challenges,* pp. 88–89.

72. Penoyer, *Reforming Regulation of Hazardous Waste,* p. 17.

73. Ibid.

74. EPA, *Meeting the Environmental Challenge,* p. 15.

75. "A Problem That Cannot Be Buried," *Time,* October 14, 1985, p 76.

76. Robert E. Taylor, "EPA Says Cleanup of Sites Will Cost $11.7 Billion More," *Wall Street Journal,* December 13, 1984, p. 38.

77. "Everybody Will Probably Pay to Clean Up Toxic Waste," *Business Week,* November 4, 1985, p. 30.

78. "Superfund Cleanup: What Price Delay?" *Business Week,* February 10, 1986, pp. 29–30.

79. Alexander & Alexander Government and Industry Affairs Office, *Washington News,* Vol. 4, No. 11 (October 31, 1986), pp. 1–2. See also Superfund Amendments of 1986, P.L. 99–499.

80. EPA, *Meeting the Environmental Challenge,* p. 15.

81. Ibid.

82. Amal Kumar Naj, "How to Clean Up Superfund's Act," *Wall Street Journal,* September 15, 1988, p. 26. See also Christopher Elias, "Waste Site Cleanup Liability May Be Hazardous to Lenders," *Insight,* November 13, 1989, pp. 42–44.

83. Eric Felter, "Toxic Risks Keep Buyers Guessing," *Insight,* August 13, 1990, p. 41.

84. Dennis R. Connolly, "Superfund Whacks the Banks," *Wall Street Journal,* August 28, 1990, p. A-10. See also Christopher Elias, "Waste Site Cleanup Liability May Be Hazardous to Lenders," *Insight,* November 13, 1989, pp. 42–44.

85. Amal Kumar Naj, "See No Evil: Can $100 Billion Have No Material Effect On Balance Sheets?" *Wall Street Journal,* May 11, 1988, p. 1.

86. Miller, *Living in the Environment,* p. 475.

87. Ibid., pp. 475–476.

88. Ibid., p. 475.

89. Ibid.

90. Robert D. Hof, "The Tiniest Toxic Avengers," *Business Week,* June 4, 1990, pp. 96–98. See also Susan Chollar, "The Poison Eaters," *Discover,* April 1990, pp. 76–78; Richard Lipkin, "Biological Warfare on Toxic Waste," *Insight,* June 19, 1989, pp. 50–51.

91. Miller, *Living in the Environment,* p. 477.

92. Ibid., p. 478.

93. Ibid.

94. Todd Lewan, "Officials: Waste Producers Dump on Latin America," *Times Picayune,* December 11, 1990, p. A-17.

95. Miller, *Living in the Environment,* p. 478.

SUGGESTED READINGS

Block, Alan A. *Poisoning for Profit: The Mafia and Toxic Waste in America.* New York: Morrow, 1985.

Chilton, Kenneth. *Talking Trash: Municipal Solid Waste Mismanagement.* St. Louis, MO: Washington University Center for the Study of American Business, 1990.

EPA Municipal Solid Waste Task Force. *The Solid Waste Dilemma: An Agenda for Action.* Washington, DC: U.S. Environmental Protection Agency, 1989.

Epstein, Samuel, et al. *Hazardous Wastes In America.* San Francisco: Sierra, 1982.

Erwin, Lewis, and L. Hall Healey, Jr. *Packaging and Solid Waste: Management Strategies.* New York: AMACOM, 1990.

Fawcett, Howard H. *Hazardous and Toxic Materials: Safe Handling and Disposal.* Somerset, NJ: Wiley, 1984.

Fortuna, Richard, and David J. Lennett. *Hazardous Waste Regulation: The New Era.* New York: McGraw-Hill, 1987.

Gibbs, Lois. *The Love Canal: My Story.* Albany: State University of New York Press, 1982.

Goldman, Benjamin A., James A. Hulme, and Cameron Johnson. *Hazardous Waste Management: Reducing the Risk.* Washington, DC: Island Press, 1986.

Morell, David, and Christopher Magorian. *Siting Hazardous Waste Facilities: Local Opposition and the Myth of Preemption.* Cambridge, MA: Ballinger, 1982.

Muir, Warren, and Joanna Underwood. *Promoting Hazardous Waste Reduction.* New York: INFORM, 1987.

Office of Technology Assessment. *From Pollution to Prevention: A Progress Report on Waste Reduction.* Washington, DC: U.S. Government Printing Office, 1987.

Peck, Dennis L., ed. *Psychosocial Effects of Hazardous Toxic Waste Disposal on Communities.* Springfield, IL: Thomas, 1989.

Penoyer, Ronald J. *Reforming Regulation of Hazardous Waste.* St. Louis, MO: Washington University Center for the Study of American Business, 1985.

United States Environmental Protection Agency. *The New RCRA: A Fact Book.* Washington, DC 1985.

```
PPL V:    597   WAVE: 001           PICK CTL #: 02602093
INL:  P9224600024S5   TYPE: FPK     CHECK DGT: A7
PARCEL #: 02014700   CARTON TYPE: ENU

LOCATION      QTY    ISBN        TITLE                           ED Fr
FFK            1     013720S414  PRINCIPLE ENURNMNTL MGM
```

SENT WITH THE COMPLIMENTS OF YOUR PH REPRESENTATIVE
JUDITH SAWICKI
                                PO BOX 140669
                                GAINESVILLE   FL 32614

TELEPHONE (904) 336-9180

— CHAPTER 10 —

DEFORESTATION AND
SPECIES DECIMATION

The sustainable management of forest resources and the plant and animal species they contain is one of the most pressing resource management problems facing the world today. While potentially a renewable resource, forests are being mismanaged all over the world and are threatened by human activities related to harvesting the wood resources forests provide or cutting them down in the interests of agricultural or urban development. The destruction of these forests also destroys the habitats of thousands of wildlife species, which are then threatened with extinction. The world simply must come to grips with what is happening to these forests and begin to develop a sustainable approach to forest management that will preserve these resources for present as well as for future generations.

Forests offer humans many useful resources. They supply us with lumber for construction, fuelwood, pulpwood for making paper, medicines that can cure diseases, and many other products worth over $150 billion a year worldwide. Many forests also provide locales for mining, livestock, grazing, and recreation. Worldwide, about half the timber cut each year is used as fuel for heating and cooking, especially in developing nations; one-third is converted into lumber and other wood products used in building; and one-sixth is used as pulp in making a variety of paper products.[1]

But forests also have vital ecological functions, which make them vulnerable. Many forests are watersheds which absorb, hold, and gradually release water that recharges springs, streams, and aquifers. Thus forests regulate the flow of water from mountains that receive a great deal of snowfall to croplands and urban areas, and help control soil erosion, the severity of flooding, and amount of sediment washing into rivers, lakes, and

311

reservoirs. Forests also provide habitats for a larger number of wildlife species than any other part of the natural world, making them the world's major reservoir of biological diversity. They also absorb the noise associated with an urban world and thus provide solitude, and in some cases even absorb air pollutants.[2]

Forests also play a vital role in global carbon and oxygen cycles through photosynthesis in which trees cleanse the air by removing carbon dioxide and adding oxygen to the world's air supply. When trees are harvested and burned, as they are in the Amazon rain forest, the carbon they contain is released into the atmosphere as carbon dioxide, and the destruction of tree cover also leads to the release of some of the carbon stored in the exposed soil in which the trees grow. Thus deforestation creates a double adverse effect in increasing carbon dioxide levels worldwide by removing some carbon dioxide absorbing capacity and adding to carbon dioxide levels at the same time. Large-scale deforestation thus contributes to global warming which, as we described in an earlier chapter, may alter global climate, food production, and sea levels all over the world.[3]

TROPICAL RAIN FORESTS

There are different kinds of forests throughout the world that call for different kinds of management practices. Tropical rain forests are scattered in an uneven green belt that lies roughly between the Tropic of Cancer and the Tropic of Capricorn.[4]

Tropical rainforests are broad-leafed woodlands that have at least 100 inches of rain each year, making them very wet and humid places. There are two types of tropical rain forests. The first is the closed forest where trees and undergrowth combine to cover the ground, making the terrain very difficult to traverse. Closed humid forests are located in high rainfall regions of the Amazon Basin in Brazil and on the islands of Southeast Asia. Open forests, on the other hand, are formations with continued grass cover, such as the savannah woodlands of Africa.[5]

Rain forests once covered 5 billion acres of land in the tropics, but only half of the original rain forests exist today, and even these are rapidly disappearing. It is now estimated that tropical rain forests cover 2,320 billion hectares of the earth's surface (a hectare is approximately equivalent to 3 acres of land surface). These forests cover about 5 to 7 percent of the earth's surface, which is a land area about three-quarters the size of the lower United States. Surveys made by remote-sensing satellites show that an area about the size of West Virginia is completely cleared each year, and another 155,000 square kilometers of tropical forest degraded each year through selective cutting. This destruction is taking place at the rate of close to 40 hectares (100 acres) per minute. If deforestation continues at this rate, almost all tropical forests will be gone or severely depleted in just 30 years.[6]

These rain forests are located in three main geographic areas: Asia, Latin America, and Africa. Asia has 16 tropical countries that cover 336.5 million hectares, and tropical forests cover 305.5 million of these hectares. Some 1.82 million hectares of these forests are being cleared each year. There are 23 tropical countries in South and Central America with a total land mass of 895.7 billion hectares, including 678.7 million hectares of tropical rain forest. These forests are being destroyed at the rate of 4.12 million hectares each year. Finally Africa has 37 tropical countries covering 703.1 million hectares. Forests cover 216.6 million hectares with 1.33 million hectares being cleared annually.[7]

Tropical rain forests are home to from 5 to 10 million species of plants and animals. At least 50 percent, and perhaps even as high as 90 percent, of all plant and animal species exist in tropical rain forests, yet these rain forests cover only a small percentage of the earth's surface. They thus contain the richest diversity of life that can be found anywhere on earth. It is estimated that two-thirds of the plant and animal species in a tropical rain forest are in the canopy, or tops of trees, and when all the trees are removed destroying the canopy, the habitat of these plants and animals is also destroyed.[8]

A report issued by the U.S. National Academy of Sciences in 1982 claimed that a typical 4-square-mile patch of rain forest may contain 750 species of trees, 125 kinds of mammals, 400 types of birds, 100 of reptiles, and 60 of amphibians. Each type of tree in the rain forest may support more than 400 insect species. Actually the number of insects are so great that they can only be guessed at, but one hectare may contain as many as 42,000 species. Some of these species are of such huge size as to stagger the imagination. It has been claimed that some lily pads are 3 feet or more across, some butterflies have 8-inch wing spans, and some fish can grow to more than 7 feet long.[9] Tropical forests represent the most biologically diverse communities and the most complex systems known in the universe.

> No other habitat on earth contains such a profusion or weight of plant life per hectare. Under the tropical sun, moreover, everything grows at astonishing speed. The rainforest produces new vegetable tissues faster than any other community on land. But death, too, is ever-present. A smell of decay hangs in the air and underfoot is a thin layer of debris. The forest's dynamism is fuelled by the speed of decay in the hot, damp, atmosphere, which acts as an incubator for scavenging and digesting organisms, and by the powerful flow of nutrient-carrying water from the ground to the canopy, drawn by the suction of evaporation from its myriad leaves. The rainforest is thus in dynamic balance, at a hectic rate of turnover.[10]

Only 1 percent of plants in the tropical rain forests have been analyzed for their potential use in curing diseases. Yet these plants are the source of one-fourth of all prescription and nonprescription drugs on the market today.[11] Many drugs that are now prescribed in developed countries owe at least part of their potency to chemicals from wild plants in the rain forests. Aspirin is made according to a chemical "blueprint" supplied by a compound extracted from the leaves of tropical willow trees. Quinine, which is used to combat malaria, comes from the bark of a tree in South America. The rosy periwinkle, which has been used by tribal healers for generations, supplies vital materials for drugs effective against Hodgkin's disease, leukemia, and several other cancers. Sales are greater than $100 billion per year for these medical compounds. The U.S. National Cancer Institute has identified more than 1,400 tropical forest plants with the potential to fight cancer.[12]

These forests thus provide a habitat that encourages and supports a biological diversity found nowhere else on earth. As such, they provide a genetic resource of untold value. Tropical rain forests are also a source of food and industrial wood products. They supply half the world's annual harvest of hardwoods and other nonwood products such as rubber, gums, resins, fibers, and nuts. Energy is also provided by the wood in these rain forests and they protect land and water resources by controlling flooding and decreasing wind erosion.

Although the tropical rain forests are thus rich in resources, they are also very fragile and have great difficulty recovering from severe or repeated human disturbances. This fragility is due not only to the scattered distribution of most species and their ecological requirements, but also to their interdependencies. The soil in most tropical forests is poor and easily eroded when the forest cover is removed. One billion people worldwide are affected by floods, fuelwood shortages, and soil degradation caused by tropical deforestation. Many of these people will starve to death during the next 30 years if deforestation of the rain forest continues.[13]

The land beneath the forest is usually poor and yields crops for only two or three seasons. Nutrients in the soil are eroded by rain, and when the land is depleted, the farmers clear more land by burning rain forests. The sun bakes the exposed soil, clouds stop forming over the barren land, and rain patterns change. If the entire forest were destroyed, the land would die, and a reforested Amazon is highly unlikely to rise from the ashes. Temperatures would rise and precipitation levels would fall, severely hindering the growth of new rain forest. There would be a decrease in local evaporation, which provides one-half the water in the Amazon Basin. Eventually, these changes can convert a diverse tropical forest into a sparse grassland or even desert.[14]

> The entire rainforest community, which supports so much life, is held in a fine and delicate balance. As each component dies, its nutrients are recycled by a whole community of decomposing organisms and are then reabsorbed by the plants to provide a new life for the forest. In the rainforests, this system of recycling has evolved over millions of years to become supremely efficient; it is only this which enables their poor soils to support a paradoxically luxuriant growth. The rich vegetation therefore gives a false impression of the soil's potential; for once the trees have gone, the land quickly becomes unproductive. Agriculturalists and cattle ranchers learn this to their cost, as the land they use gradually deteriorates. In the search for new, more fertile soils, they clear ever more forest land, contributing to the destruction already wreaked by development schemes and exploitation for timber and minerals.[15]

It is now being discovered that the rain forest is an incredibly efficient ecosystem that wastes little energy or matter essential to its survival. Because the soil is poor, the forest functions like a delicately balanced organism that recycles most of its nutrients and much of its moisture. Water evaporates from the upper leaves of trees, cooling them in the process as they collect the intense sunlight. This evaporated moisture is gathered into clouds that return the moisture to the system in torrential rainfall. Dead animals and plants decay quickly, returning essential nutrients from the soil back to growing plants. Virtually no decaying matter seeps into the region's rivers because of efficient recycling.[16]

Deforestation

Deforestation is the total conversion of rain forest to other uses in which no forest remains. This practice must be distinguished from *depletion,* which is caused by logging or local usage and removal of some trees, where the forest in some sense is left standing. Each year, 7.5 million hectares of closed tropical forests and 3.5 million hectares of open tropical forests are cleared.[17] The fundamental causes of this deforestation are poverty, overpopulation, insecure land tenure, misguided government policies, inequitable distribution of land and wealth, and the need to put land to more intensive uses. More proximate causes are said to be agriculture, cattle ranching, mining, building of hydroelectric dams with resultant flooding, encroachment, and logging.[18]

The International Hardwood Products Association in Alexandria, Virginia, claims that subsistence farmers in developing countries are responsible for 80 percent of tropical deforestation.[19] However, the Food and Agricultural Organization of the United Nations estimates that half the forest cleared in the tropics each year is for shifting cultivation by landless farmers. As the number of subsistence farmers grows, more land is cleared, thus making a vicious circle. Clearing forest land for permanent agriculture is the most important cause of deforestation.[20]

Rapid population growth and poverty push landless people to clear and cultivate forestland to grow crops and to cut trees for fuelwood. In some countries, wealthy landowners influence the government to encourage landless peasants to clear tropical forests for cultivation because this helps defuse political pressures for equitable land distribution. Thus the government has built roads and other projects to open up these lands to settlement. When they arrive in the rain forest, settlers clear patches of forest to grow enough food on which to survive by using slash-and-burn cultivation. Many of the nutrients in the soil come from the trees themselves, and when these nutrients are exhausted, the farmers move on to another patch of rain forest.

Policies of developing nations and international lending aid agencies encourage this kind of deforestation. The mass migration of the urban poor to tropical forests would not be possible without highway, logging, mining, ranching, and dam-building projects that open up these usually inaccessible areas. Many of these projects have been financed by loans from the World Bank and other international lending agencies whose policies are greatly influenced by developing nations. It was not until 1987 that the World Bank set up a department to review the environmental impacts of the projects it was supporting.[21]

Reliance of the rural poor on wood as a source for energy is the second most important cause of tropical rain forest deforestation. More than one-half the inhabitants of developing nations, or 2.5 million people, do not have adequate fuelwood for cooking and heat and must continually destroy rain forests for these purposes. The women in these countries spend much of their time gathering wood, as the poorest people in developing nations depend most directly on the rain forests for fuelwood. Many countries suffering from fuelwood shortages have inadequate forestry policies and budgets, and are planting 10 to 20 times fewer trees than needed to offset forest losses and meet increased demands for fuelwood and other forest products.[22]

Commercial logging for export is not the primary cause of deforestation on a global basis, however, it can be an important problem in certain supplier countries. Nigeria, for example, was a leading exporter of tropical logs in 1960, but by 1985, its forests had been so depleted that it became a net importer of forest products. Malaysia is currently cutting down its forests three or four times faster than they are being replenished, and has lost half of its rain forests in the past 20 years. In some regions with low population density and limited forest conversion, the economic gains from logging encourage land clearing and road construction.[23] Damage to the rain forest during logging may be caused by injuring seedlings and residual trees. Erosion and an increased susceptibility to wildfire can cause further damage to the residual forest. Logging roads may be used by hunters, timber poachers, or farmers who move in and clear the remaining forest.

Governments of developing countries encourage the exploitation of rain forest resources to pay off foreign debts and allow logging without forest management or reforestation. These governments take the long-term bene-fits of their forests for granted, and sell logging rights too cheaply to exploit short-term benefits. Logging concessions are not usually granted on a com-petitive basis and turn over too frequently for the forests to regenerate. Internal political instability and corruption can keep logging concessions from developing programs for reforestation. There are thus many political problems that do not encourage management of rain forests for the long-term benefit of the country as a whole.[24]

But if destruction of the rain forests continues much longer, the damage to this special kind of ecosystem may be irreversible. The impact of deforesta-tion on regional climates could change the character of the rain forests and lead to even greater extinctions of plant and animal species than is taking place at present. The poor of these regions would then have to endure even more misery. The people in the rest of the world also have a stake in what happens to the rain forests. The world needs the rain forests as a functioning system. This is a more important issue than the issue of who owns the rain forests and thus has responsibility for them. In the final analysis, the responsibility for saving the rain forests belongs to everyone rather than just a few nations.[25]

Solutions

Tropical rain forests are a renewable resource if they are managed properly with long-term interests in mind and on a sustainable basis. The concept of sustainable yield management strives to achieve a balance between the harvest and growth of a forest, which can then provide timber products indefinitely. Sustainable harvesting should not diminish the benefits to future generations, and requires the protection of soil, water, wildlife, and timber resources in perpetuity. The mix of benefits and products from rain forests may vary from region to region, but in the aggregate these forests must be as useful to future generations as the primary forests are to current generations.[26] The Smithsonian Institution, in conjunction with the International Hardwood Products Association, has developed a consensus regarding the principles that should govern tropical rain forest management.

- Forests are dynamic. If not utilized, trees are continually dying and being replaced. Sustainable utilization systems can be devised and are viable so long as they mimic natural forest dynamics and work within the nutrient limitations of the ecosystem. The problems arise not so much in devising such management systems, but in making them work under the prevailing socioeconomic conditions.
- Forests provide a wide variety of goods and services. Nontimber products, such as fruits, nuts, rubber, and rattan, often harvested by forest-dwelling people, provide economic benefits that can be more valuable than timber removal. Economic analysis of the value of timber harvesting should take into account the potential threat to other major opportunities if log extraction damages production of these products.
- Timber should realize its true value. Where timber prices do not fully cover the replacement and environmental costs, there is no incentive to restore the forest so that it can be sustained at its original level. Governments commonly collect far too little forest revenue to reinvest in replacement efforts that incorporate all of the affected environmental factors. Where the logger has no incentive to utilize low-grade and waste products, maximum utilization will not occur, and sustainability could be endangered by high-grading and forest fires (fueled by dry matter left behind after logging operations).

- Fiscal and financial incentives for conservation and regeneration must be provided. In the same way that logging should bear its environmental costs, conservation, regeneration, and reforestation should enjoy profits from the environmental benefits they convey to the society at large.
- Reentering a forest to cut (recutting) too frequently is a common problem, which inevitably degrades the forest. Recutting may occur in order to satisfy the annual volume a logger is obliged to cut, or to take advantage of remaining stands of commercial value if the logger's concession is too short to ensure him the access to the next harvest. Recutting often takes place before there had been adequate regrowth. Frequent recutting compounds any damage from the first cut, thereby slowing down regeneration.
- Timber concession agreements are currently much too short in duration. Most are not more than 20 to 30 years. As a result, the concessionaire does not have practical reason to invest in the long-term future of the concession. Concession contracts should extend over at least two cutting cycles, and should be subject to periodic review for compliance with good management practices.[27]

The primary forests, which are those essentially unmodified by recent human intervention, can best be sustained by the preservation in perpetuity of tracts of such forests that are representative of diverse environments. Once sufficient areas of these primary forests are secured, other primary forest areas may be subjected to sustainable utilization practices that preserve the structure and function of the ecosystem. Secondary forests, those left after exploitation of marketable timber and regrowth after deforestation and agricultural abandonment, can be managed with the goal of accelerating the rate of growth to reach maximum sustainable production, but all resource values such as water, soil, and wildlife must be considered in making decisions. An increasing proportion of tropical lands that are now deforested or inadequately stocked must be planted with useful trees to meet future needs for industrial forest products and to reduce the pressure on primary forests. These are called tree plantations and require continuous monitoring and flexible management.[28]

In July 1989, leaders of the United States, Italy, France, West Germany, Great Britain, Canada, and Japan met in Paris for a summit on environmental issues. These countries endorsed the concept of writing off debts of developing countries in return for preservation of vanishing tropical rain forests.[29] Most major banks in the developed world hold large amounts of hard currency debt from many of these developing countries, but it is unlikely that this debt will be paid in full by these countries. If conservation organizations acquire title to this debt, they may be able to negotiate with debtor countries to obtain repayment in local currency and use the proceeds for conservation of the rain forests. This kind of a debt for nature swap is a very complex process, but it is possible.

Some companies have discovered that selling goods with nature in mind can be a sound business practice. They believe that harvesting rain forests for fruits, nuts, essences, and oils, instead of destroying them through slash-and-burn farming and ranching, can provide the incentive to ensure that the forests survive. For example, Ben & Jerry's Rainforest Crunch ice cream has been available since October 1989, and has proved popular with consumers. Community Products Inc. expected to sell $1.5 million of its Brazil nut-and-cashew brittle. This candy is packaged in colorful tins that tout the environmental integrity of its ingredients, and is sold in department stores and by mail order for $12 a pound.[30]

Interest in this idea of sustainable harvesting has grown in recent years, encouraged by studies such as one that appeared in the British journal *Nature*, which reported that a hectare of land harvested in such a fashion could generate an annual income of almost $700; a plantation or cattle ranch on the same parcel of land would yield only $150 over the same time period. To promote the harvesting of these products, Brazil established four large "extractive reserves" in which logging is banned and long-term harvesting rights are given to rubber trappers and gatherers of nuts and fruits. Several more of these kinds of reserves are under consideration.[31]

The largest rain forest in North America, located in Mexico and called Lacandona, has been under threat for the past 30 years. Two-thirds of it has been lost to logging, farming, and cattle raising or looted of its wildlife by illicit activities such as animal smuggling. The government of Mexico, which sponsored some of the most destructive policies in past years, is trying to reverse the damage by passing laws that include a ban on tree cutting, tougher regulations on trafficking in animals, and a requirement that landholders reforest some of their land. The government began large-scale exploitation of this area in the 1960s by opening it to state-owned lumber companies. Cattle ranchers followed in their wake, cutting or burning the remaining vegetation to create pasture. The World Bank made a $350 million development loan for the region conditional in part on strengthened environmental protection.[32]

Controversy in Brazil over the government's efforts to deal with destruction of its rain forest was reported in *Time* as follows.

> For more than a year, the government of President Jose Sarney has been under relentless attack from environmental activists worldwide. They charge that its policies are not only resulting in the wanton destruction of Brazil's forest, its wildlife and its native peoples, but are also endangering the world environment. Scientists say the fires set by ranchers and homesteaders in the Amazon region are spewing into the atmosphere 7% of the carbon dioxide responsible for the global warming process known as the greenhouse effect.

Last week the Brazilian government sought to quell the outcry with an ambitious new environmental program. The plan, titled Our Nature, was announced by Sarney . . . . Among other things, the plan calls for:

- Establishing a five-year $100 million program to zone the Amazon region for agriculture, mining, and other uses. The zoning scheme would be partly financed by the U.N. Food and Agriculture Organization.
- Suspending, temporarily, raw-timber exports and tax incentives long awarded to Amazon cattle ranchers.
- Regulating the production and sale of the toxic chemicals used in mining and agriculture.
- Creating 7 million acres of new national parkland.
- Studying a possible expansion of the areas set aside for the use of Brazil's 220,000 remaining native people.

. . . Sarney framed the issue as a battle between developed and developing nations (. . . and) reiterated his rejection of so-called debt-for-nature swaps, in which foreign debt is forgiven in exchange for conservation efforts, as just one more way for those who covet the Amazon to meddle in Brazil's affairs.

The President's strident nationalism drew a sour reaction from his many critics. "Sarney declared war on the world today," said Fabio Feldman, a Congressman from Sao Paulo who is a vocal environmentalist. . . . Said another leading ecologist: "It is obvious that the intention of the program is not to save the Amazon but to appease foreign criticism." Copyright 1989 The Time Inc. Magazine Company. Reprinted by permission.[33]

Besides these piecemeal efforts, there has been one major attempt to develop a comprehensive plan to save the rain forests on a worldwide basis. A Tropical Forestry Action Plan (TFAP) was prepared over several years with input from governments, forestry agencies, agencies of the United Nations, and nongovernmental organizations to help tropical countries come to grips with deforestation. Each of these nations was to come up with a formal proposal for managing and protecting its forests. With the help of international agencies TFAP would channel $8 billion in aid over a five-year period to implement those programs. The effort was launched with assurances that mistakes of the past, which included duplication of effort, ripoffs by contractors, consultants, and corrupt officials, and a tendency to promote the donor's priorities at the expense of developing countries, would not be repeated.

The specific purposes of the plan, which covers all tropical forests, is to improve the lives of rural people, to increase food production, to improve methods of shifting agriculture, to ensure the sustainable use of forests, to increase supplies of fuelwood and the efficiency of its use, and to expand income and employment opportunities.[34] The plan has five components: forestry in land use, forest-based industrial development, fuelwood and energy, conservation of tropical forest ecosystems, and institutions.[35]

The plan offers an opportunity to improve coordination of aid to developing nations and to stimulate institutional reforms and new initiatives for a global effort to halt deforestation.

The purpose of the forestry in land-use part of the plan is to develop an interface between forestry and agriculture. Rural people of developing nations are shown how to conserve the resource base of rain forests for agricultural purposes and how to integrate forestry into these agricultural systems. Implementation of this part of the plan includes (1) managing forests and plantations for multiple use, (2) introducing trees to farming systems, and (3) regenerating degraded forests, which is achieved by plating trees that will be used for wood and fuel.

Through forest-based industrial development, it is hoped that the promotion of appropriate raw material harvesting and the building and marketing of forestry product industries will help stabilize and improve the forests. Some of the steps taken to develop a forest-based industry include (1) improving forest utilization agreements, (2) expanding and improving industrial plantations and their management, (3) providing special training on road engineering, and involving rural people in forest-based enterprises including local cottage industries, and (4) developing ways to use residues for energy generation.

Providing fuelwood and energy for people in developing countries where there is an energy crisis is an important goal, as two-thirds of the people in developing countries depend on wood for household energy needs. More than 80 percent of the wood harvested in these countries is burned in cooking, heating, and supplying energy to rural industries. Demand for wood is definitely greater than the supply, and two-thirds of the countries have fuelwood shortages. Efforts to improve this situation include the introduction of more efficient stoves, teaching techniques that improve charcoal making and reduce waste, salvaging wood for fuel whenever a forest is harvested or cleared, and managing woodlands for an increase in production of fuelwood and charcoal.

To conserve tropical forest ecosystems, the Tropical Forest Action Plan is promoting the development of national networks of protected areas. The Cuna Indians, for example, living on Caribbean islands off the coast of Panama, have created 60,000 hectares of protected tropical forest. They are developing an environmental education program for their own people and working with researchers. Rwanda, Africa, one of the poorest and most densely populated countries in the tropics, has founded the Parc National Des Volcans, which benefits the people by protecting the country's most important watershed. The park also protects the endangered mountain gorilla and provides employment and income from tourism.

Finally, the plan attempts to get institutions involved in preserving the tropical forests by providing support for institutions in strengthening public forest administration and other government agencies, and in developing professional, technical, and vocational training. One hundred and ninety institutions in Asia, 100 in Latin America, and 90 in Africa are providing forestry training at the technical or university level. In Nepal, for example, extension field staff workers use audiovisual material to promote community forestry and provide technical support. They have helped establish and manage 7,500 hectares of plantation and build 6,000 stoves.

How successful has this plan been in halting deforestation? A report issued in 1991 was not very complimentary about the plan as it had been implemented up to that point. countries have been chosen for aid because of their ability to digest large amounts of money rather than by the size of their uncut tropical forests. Many of the proposed action plans involved opening of previously pristine forests for exploitation. For example, in Cameroon the TFAP proposed construction of a 370-mile road through virgin rain forest to open it up to development. Apparently the plan was also sold in different ways to rich and poor nations. In industrial nations the plan was touted as a way to save the forests; in developing nations, the plan was presented as one more source of funding for traditional forestry projects.[36]

The most serious problem with the plan, however, seemed to be that it was based on a flawed premise, the assumption that tropical forests can be harvested and managed without damaging the ecosystem, although many doubted there was evidence enough to support this assumption. Since we know so little about the intricate codependencies that tie the myriad species of plants, animals, and insects of these forests into a working system, some biologists wonder whether tropical forestry is sustainable at any commercial level. Under threat of a funding cutoff from sponsoring organizations, the UN Food and Agriculture Organization, which was principally responsible for administering the plan, ceded control of the program to an outside governing council and agreed to participate in the program's redesign.[37]

Since the plan was conceived in 1985, an estimated 210 million acres of tropical forests have been burned, cut, or flooded. Without immediate action, by the year 2000 more than half the population of the developing world will either be short of fuelwood or lack it altogether. This will cause a destructive cycle of deforestation, fuelwood scarcity, poverty, and malnutrition. Indigenous peoples who inhabited the forests for thousands of years will be replaced, and in some cases, their cultures will disappear. Already, 10 to 20 percent of the earth's planet and animal life may have become extinct, with a vast loss of genetic resources.

Large quantities of valuable lumber will continue to be destroyed, depriving nations and communities of opportunities to realize the full economic benefit from forest industries development and trade. More watersheds will be degraded. There will be widespread soil erosion, continued siltation of rivers and dams, and further loss of agriculture land causing food shortages. Flooding may result in further unnecessary loss of life in some countries like Bangladesh that have no forests of their own, but suffer because of deforestation that takes place many miles from the country. All of these problems call for further action to protect the rain forests from further needless destruction. (See box.)

Tax Rich Nations, Save the Jungle

Tropical rain forests benefit the entire world; their protection cannot be left solely to the poor countries where they are found

Every minute 25 acres of rain forests in the tropics disappear as people in Third World countries cut and burn, often to feed themselves. But the gains they win are short-term, and the losses long. Many scientists, including Ira Rubinoff, director of the Smithsonian Tropical Research Institute in Panama, argue that the problem is so severe it requires an unprecedented response now. In the following essay, Rubinoff offers some radical ideas on what must be done—and who must pay.

I T's A HISTORIC day in a Third World nation: after years of politicking and painstaking research, a tropical rain forest becomes a national park. Conservationists around the world celebrate their victory in saving a priceless storehouse of plants and animals.

Five years later, poachers take the park's last surviving leopard. Or illegal loggers destroy a unique area of trees with all its associated plants and animals. Or ranchers graze cattle on the anemic soil of burned-over land.

This is the tragedy of the "paper park," caused by a serious flaw in the efforts of conservationists. In creating preserves, they fail to compensate developing nations for losing the use of resources. As a result, a developing nation's rain forests become casualties in a people's battle to improve their lives.

There is only one way out of this dilemma: the developed nations must pay the Third World for the expense of preserving its forests.

The strategy I propose involves taxing people in developed nations from 50 cents to five dollars per person each year, depending on the country's wealth. People in the United States, for example, would pay the maximum amount, contributing about $1 billion per year. This is equivalent to an increase of about 12 percent in U.S. development assistance programs. The fund,

A huge infusion of cash is needed now to save the genetic diversity found in threatened jungles, argues a scientist with a bold but radical funding plan.

which would total more than $3 billion annually, should flow through an independent institution such as the World Bank.

In return, the 48 tropical forest nations in Africa, Asia and the Americas would set up a system of 1,000 reserves averaging 247,000 acres each (their size would vary widely, of course). These nations would act as custodians of the reserves, which would be inspected annually by an international agency. Each host nation would receive an annual payment based on the area under protection—an average of $3 million per reserve. If the country

failed to maintain the reserve, it would lose the money.

That would be the only string attached, however. Each nation would be able to use its funds as it wished, for reserve protection, agricultural intensification or industrial development, for example, so as to decrease the impact of other economic pressure upon the reserves.

To provide even more incentive, selection of the areas to be included in the reserve system would be up to the host country. This would allow governments to choose sites where there are few conflicts over development. Obviously, not all areas with the greatest natural diversity would be chosen; but if we preserved enough land, diversity would take care of itself.

The entire system would preserve about 10 percent of the Earth's remaining tropical rain forest. This does not mean that 10 percent is the ideal amount, and that the other 90 percent can be exploited or destroyed. But the proposed plan would at least establish a safety net, ensuring that a gene pool is preserved. At the same time, by saving the world's plant and animal species—two-thirds of which live in tropical rain forests—the rich nations would also help ensure their own futures; the genetic base preserved would help everyone.

The most serious argument against my plan is that it's impractical. Hard-pressed governments are unlikely to impose yet another tax on their citizens, especially to foster programs in other countries. My only answer is that no other plan has a chance of saving the world's tropical forests. Without short-term economic incentives, deforestation will continue, and we will see a wave of extinctions the likes of which we have never seen before. Yes, it is expensive medicine; but we cannot even fathom the effects of the disease.

—Ira Rubinoff

Source: *International Wildlife* Vol. 18, No. 3 (May-June 1988), p. 24.

OLD-GROWTH FORESTS

Old-growth, or virgin forests are those containing massive trees that are hundreds and thousands of years old, such as the great stands of douglas fir, giant sequoia, and coastal redwoods in the western part of the United States. These forests are thick with trees and vegetation and generally have a greater diversity of plant and animal life than secondary forests. The latter are, as the name secondary implies, stands of trees that have grown up after the virgin forest was cut down, and result from secondary ecological succession. Many forests in the United States and other temperate areas such as Europe are secondary forests that grew after the logging of virgin forests or the abandonment of agricultural lands.[38] Old growth is described by the Wilderness Society as follows:

> Old growth . . . is distinguished from young and mature forest by its vigorous diversity of tree species and sizes, including massive Douglas-firs up to nearly three hundred feet tall and thirty feet or more in circumference at the base. Beneath these spiring giants grow smaller trees — western hemlock, red cedar, bigleaf maple, and other shade-tolerant species. The trees together form a canopy of several layers that diffuses light into an ample soft radiance; here and there shafts of sun penetrate directly to the forest floor. Because shrubs, herbs, and seedling trees are usually sparse and patchy, the forest seems spacious, deep to the eye. Everywhere, more various even than their living progeny, are the generations of trees gone by — the standing dead with dry needles still intact, limbless snags, rotting stubs coated with moss, and downed logs and limbs of all sizes and states of decay.[39]

Logged areas in the Northwest were replanted haphazardly, or not at all, for the first half of this century. Little thought was given to conservation of these resources. During the last 40 years replanting efforts have intensified and sustained yield has at least developed as a goal of forest management. While rotation cycles vary from forest to forest, and even from site to site, planted trees in this area of the country generally require at least 70 years to reach harvestable proportions. As these secondary crops mature on private lands, timber companies are pressing for higher and higher annual cuts on the national forests and other public lands that contain practically all that remains of the old-growth forest in the lower 48 states.[40]

Conservationists and other environmentalists are fighting to save the rapidly disappearing old-growth stands in national and state forests in the Pacific Northwest, and have been embroiled in controversy for several years. Timber companies want to clear-cut these stands and replace them with tree farms. Only 15 percent of the country's old-growth forests are left, according to some estimates, and at present cutting rates most of these irreplaceable forests will be gone within 15 to 20 years. People who want to stop this deforestation believe that the total destruction of these forests will go down in history as one of the great ecological crimes of the century. They also point out that it is hypocritical for the United States to pressure Brazil not to cut down its tropical rain forests, while we continue to cut down our remaining old-growth forests.[41]

The current plight of the old-growth forests had its origins in the late 1940s, when a postwar housing boom resulted in increased cutting of trees on private lands. The logging industry was thus forced to turn to public lands, including the old-growth forests that were prized because of the high quality and quantity of their timber. The National Forest Service and the Bureau of Land Management cooperated in selling rights to new tracts of forest. This policy, when combined with modern logging machinery that makes cutting on mountain slopes easier, has put old-growth forests are risk.[42] Current pressures have increased because of the profitable trade in logs to foreign countries, which take logs from private lands. As log exports have increased, federal forests, from which logs can't be exported, are left as the last remaining large source of wood and wood products for the domestic market.[43]

Although forbidden to do so by the National Forest Management Act of 1976, timber in virtually every national forest in Washington and Oregon is being sold at a level above a sustained yield level, somewhere around 23 percent above, according to Forest Service data for 12 of the forests.[44] Since World War II, these areas have been logged primarily in a dispersed clear-cut system that checkerboards the landscape with 25- to 50-acre clearings, leaving patches of forest of about the same size or somewhat larger. This practice was implemented to minimize damage to the forest, but the result has been to chop it into pieces, which damages its capacity as a wildlife habitat and jeopardizes the remaining trees themselves.[45]

Clear-cutting removes all trees from a given area in a single cutting to establish a new, even-aged stand or tree farm. The clear-cut area may consist of a whole stand of trees, a group, a strip, or a series of patches. After all the trees are cut, the site is either naturally reforested from seed released by the harvest, or is reseeded by foresters with genetically superior seedlings raised in a nursery. Clear-cutting increases the volume of timber harvested per acre, reduces the need for road building, and shortens the time needed to establish a new stand of trees. Timber companies prefer this method of tree harvesting because it requires less skill and planning than other harvesting methods and gives them a greater return.[46]

But clear-cutting can also lead to severe soil erosion if done on steeply sloped land, sediment water pollution, flooding from melting snow and heavy rains, and landslides. It also leaves ugly, unnatural forest openings that take decades to regenerate themselves. The number and types of wildlife habitats are also reduced and thus the biological diversity of the forests is affected. Once a site has been clear-cut, it is hard to break the cycle and wait 100 to 400 years for an uneven-aged stand to regrow through secondary ecological succession. Presently, about two-thirds of the annual U.S. timber production is harvested by clear-cutting.[47]

Selective cutting involves cutting down intermediate-aged or mature trees either singly or in small groups. This practice reduces crowding, encourages the growth of younger trees, and maintains an uneven-aged stand with trees of great variety. Given enough time, the stand will regenerate itself. If done properly, selective cutting helps protect the site from soil erosion. This method is favored by those who wish to use forests for multiple purposes and preserve biological diversity. But selective cutting is also much more costly, and unless the value of the trees is high, is not economically profitable.[48]

Controversy

To stop continued clear-cutting, the case of the northern spotted owl entered the fray when studies indicated that populations of the owl were declining rapidly as logging shrank and fragmented its habitat. In fact, some studies indicated it may be poised on the brink of population collapse. The Forest Service was charged by law with the perpetuation of vertebrate species native to the national forests, and thus had to come up with some kind of plan to preserve the species. It was well aware that if the owl made the endangered species list, it could virtually shut down logging in the Northwest. Thus initially, the Forest Service proposed setting aside 550 spotted owl habitat areas in Oregon and Washington and 200 more in the Douglas fir zone of northwestern California, each area containing 2,200 acres of old-growth forest.[49]

While the controversy centered on the owls, what was really at stake was the health and survival of the entire Douglas fir ecosystem of the Northwest, the natural ecological system on which owls and watersheds as well as the region's human economy all depend. The owls are an indicator of the plight of that entire ecosystem, but it will accomplish little, so said some environmentalists, to set aside preserves for them while the forest all around these areas remains available for harvesting. If the ecosystem at large is destroyed, so will the owls along with many other forms of wildlife. Thus the Forest Service's plan was criticized on the basis that the acreage was too small and the number of areas too few to ensure the owl's survival.[50]

In April 1989, the U.S. Fish and Wildlife Service recommended that the spotted owl be placed on the endangered species list, which would protect it from further logging. Industry officials predicted an economic apocalypse that would cost the region 132,000 jobs and $3 billion in local payroll, not to mention the $1.6 billion the federal government would have received from selling logging rights in national forests. Environmentalists disputed these figures, calling them wild exaggerations and filed three separate lawsuits against the various federal agencies that control forest and wildlife policies in areas that contain old-growth forests. The owl decision was forced by the Sierra Club Legal Defense Fund, which filed suit against the Fish and

Wildlife Service. It alleged that the agency ignored data collected by its own scientists which showed that, without protection, the owl was in danger of extinction.[51]

Then in September of the same year, a federal appeals court struck down an injunction that had barred timber companies from logging in old-growth forests where the owl was threatened. The ruling technically freed the industry to begin acquiring and cutting down about 500 million board feet of redwoods and Douglas firs on federal lands in Oregon's Cascade Mountains, but did not affect injunctions and suits based on other legal challenges in other areas of Washington and Oregon that contained old-growth forests. The court ruled that plans for timber sales through the end of the decade in the area under consideration were finalized in the early 1980s, and thus could not be challenged by information that became available after the plans had been finalized.[52]

A new concern was introduced in 1990, when environmental groups and cancer researchers asked for federal protection for the Pacific yew, a tree with bark that provides a scarce new cancer-fighting drug. Already in 1960, the National Cancer Institute found the first indications that an extract of the yew's bark could be used against cancer. The active chemical compound in this bark was later isolated and named taxol. It is in very short supply, with researchers stating that current supplies are sufficient to treat only 200 to 300 patients. Efforts to synthesize the drug have not worked. The petition filed by these groups asked the Interior Department to list the Pacific yew as threatened under the Endangered Species Act because its habitat is the old-growth forest. The tree is apparently one of the slowest growing species in the world, and thrives in the shady undergrowth of ancient pine trees.[53]

In response to these pressures, the Forest Service unveiled a new master plan that called for a substantial reduction of logging in national forests: from the current average annual cut of 12.2 billion board feet to an average 10.8 billion board feet by 1995. The plan would halve clear-cutting in national forests and put greater emphasis on wildlife protection and recreation. The timber industry quickly predicted a 20 percent increase in the cost of lumber because of this change, and a consequent rise in housing prices putting thousands of people out of the market. "We are squeezing 65,000 families out of affordable housing," said one industry spokesperson, "to provide bird-houses for spotted owls."[54]

Finally, the owl was brought under protection of the Endangered Species Act by being listed in June 1990, along with a comprehensive logging plan announced by the Bush administration. The plan was said to save 450 pairs of owls, which the administration claimed was 125 more than under a plan proposed by an interagency scientific panel in the spring. Logging would be reduced in 1991 to 750 million to 800 million board feet from about 950 billion board feet in 1990. Some 1,000 jobs would be lost under the plan, as compared with 7,600 under the earlier proposal. The administration also proposed setting up an interagency task force to devise a forest management plan for fiscal 1991 that it says will be designed to protect the owl while mitigating economic dislocation.[55]

Sooner or later the timber industry, Forest Service, and the public at large are going to realize that we can't continue to cut more wood than the land is capable of reproducing, or we will exhaust timber resources for future generations. At the present time, according to some experts, too many trees are falling, millworkers are losing their jobs, spotted owls and other animals face possible extinction, and the land itself is slipping away into rivers and streams. Losses are high for all parties concerned. Rapid growth of demand for logs that depletes the forest must give way to slower growth and eventually some kind of equilibrium where the forest's wealth is conserved and carefully recycled. "Each member of the community is supported by what the land in its health allows, a diverse and vigorous commonwealth sustaining itself through time."[56] (See Exhibit 10.1.)

SPECIES DECIMATION

The controversy is much more than just a battle between a particular type of owl and an industry. It is really a conflict between different philosophies regarding the place of nature and the relationship of human beings to their natural environment. Fundamental questions are involved in the debate about the future of the environment and the priorities to be established. Are the old-growth forests, and by extension, nature itself, there for humans to use and exploit, or should they be preserved in their natural state? How much wilderness does the country need, and how is this need to be balanced against the need for lumber to build housing? How much human discomfort in the form of job changes and other dislocations can be justified in the name of conservation or preservation?[57]

The issue of preserving species of plants and animals goes to the heart of our approach to the environment, and raises some fundamental ethical questions. If we believe that the environment has no value apart from its usefulness to human beings, then the conservation approach makes the best sense. Plant and animal resources must be conserved so that they are not decimated more than necessary to serve human needs for this and future generations. Arguments to slow deforestation because species are being destroyed that may prove to have some medical benefit to humans are based on this view of the environment. If, however, we believe that plants and animals deserve to exist in their own right because they are part of nature, then preservation is the right approach, which means preserving old-growth and tropical forests and the habitats of the species in them because they are a part of nature and deserve to be preserved for their own sakes, not for what benefits they may be able to provide human beings.

The loss of biological diversity through species decimation is the most

Exhibit 10.1

What Old-Growth Trees Do for the Ecosystem and for the Economy

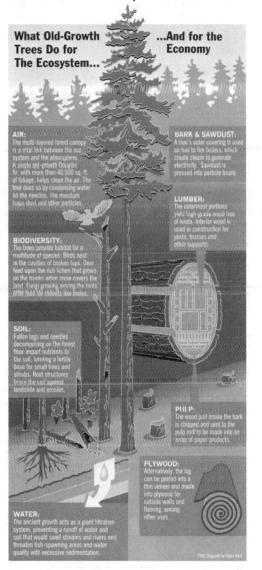

What Old-Growth Trees Do for The Ecosystem...

...And for the Economy

AIR:
The multi-layered forest canopy is a vital link between the ecosystem and the atmosphere. A single old-growth Douglas fir, with more than 40,000 sq. ft. of foliage, helps clean the air. The tree does so by condensing water on the needles. The moisture traps dust and other particles.

BIODIVERSITY:
The trees provide habitat for a multitude of species. Birds nest in the cavities of broken tops. Deer feed upon the rich lichen that grows on the trunks when snow covers the land. Fungi growing among the roots offer food for rodents like moles.

SOIL:
Fallen logs and needles decomposing on the forest floor impart nutrients to the soil, forming a fertile base for small trees and shrubs. Root structures brace the soil against landslide and erosion.

WATER:
The ancient growth acts as a giant filtration system, preventing a runoff of water and soil that would swell streams and rivers and threaten fish-spawning areas and water quality with excessive sedimentation.

BARK & SAWDUST:
A tree's outer covering is used as fuel to fire boilers, which create steam to generate electricity. Sawdust is pressed into particle board.

LUMBER:
The outermost portions yield high-grade wood free of knots. Interior wood is used in construction for joists, trusses and other supports.

PULP:
The wood just inside the bark is chipped and sent to the pulp mill to be made into an array of paper products.

PLYWOOD:
Alternatively, the log can be peeled into a thin veneer and made into plywood for outside walls and flooring, among other uses.

TIME Diagram by Steve Hart

Source: Ted Gup, "Owl vs. Man," *Time,* June 25, 1990, p. 62. Copyright 1990 The Time Inc. Magazine Company. Reprinted by permission.

important process of environmental change, because it is the only process that is wholly irreversible. Once a species is totally eliminated and there are none of that species left, or at least not enough to continue reproduction, that species is gone forever. The chances that the same environmental conditions will ever exist so that the same species will evolve is practically zero. Yet humans take this biological wealth for granted, perhaps because we have always been surrounded by so many plant and animal species that we have not noticed any decimation. Biological wealth is taken less seriously than material or cultural wealth, but biota is part of a country's heritage. Plant and animals are the products of millions of years of evolution centered on that particular place, and hence as much of a reason for national concern as the particularities of language and culture.[58]

Some scientists claim that humans have reduced biological diversity to its lowest level since the end of the Mesozoic era 65 million years ago, when the dinosaurs disappeared. It is the first time in history that plant communities, which anchor ecosystems and maintain the habitability of the earth, will also be devastated. Given the interdependence of human beings and the other species inhabiting the earth, it is remarkable that the task of studying biodiversity is still at an early stage, according to some experts.[59] Some estimates state that the earth is populated with 5 to 30 million different wild species of plants and animals, and that so far scientists have identified only about 1.8 million species, and two-thirds of these are insects.[60] (See Table 10.1.)

Table 10.1
Known and Estimated Diversity of Life on Earth

Form of Life	Known Species	Estimated Total Species
Insects and Other Invertebrates	989,761	30 million insect species, extrapolated from surveys in forest canopy in Panama; most believed unique to tropical forests.
Vascular Plants	248,400	At least 10 to 15 percent of all plants are believed undiscovered.
Fungi and Algae	73,900	Not available.
Microorganisms	36,600	Not available.
Fishes	19,056	21,000, assuming that 10 percent of fish remain undiscovered; the Amazon and Orinoco Rivers alone may account for 2,000 additional species.
Birds	9,040	Known species probably account for 98 percent of all birds.
Reptiles and Amphibians	8,962	Known species of reptiles, amphibians, and
Mammals	4,000	mammals probably constitute over 95 percent of total diversity.
Misc. Chordates[1]	1,273	Not available.
Total	1,390,992	10 million species considered a conservative count; if insect estimates are accurate, the total exceeds 30 million.

[1]Animals with a dorsal nerve chord but lacking a bony spine.

Source: Reprinted from STATE OF THE WORLD, 1988, A Worldwatch Institute Report on Progress Toward a Sustainable Society, Project Director: Lester R. Brown. By permission of W. W. Norton & Company, Inc. Copyright © 1988 by Worldwatch Institute.

These species are like a giant genetic library of successful survival strategies that have developed over billions of years. The biological diversity found in these species is the foundation for the services the ecosystem provides and on which we and other species depend for our existence. They are also the source of future biological evolution and genetic engineering. As more and more species are eliminated, the evolutionary pattern for future species is affected, and biodiversity is reduced for future generations. Thus human beings are destroying the future every time species are eliminated, and reducing the number and kind of plant and animal species that are going to be evolving for future generations.

Whatever the absolute numbers, and the range is as wide as we indicated, there seems to be general agreement among scientists that more than half the species on earth live in moist tropical forests. Some scientists believe that as much as 90 percent of plant and animal species may be found in these forests.[61] There are two species-rich groups: the arthropods (especially insects) and the flowering plants, which are concentrated in these forests as nowhere else on earth. The fragile superstructure of species build up when the environment remains stable enough to support their evolution during long periods of time, but such communities can be easily destroyed by relatively minor disturbances in the physical environment.[62]

The rain forest is an interdependent community where neither animals nor plants can survive without the other, and all are part of an elaborate network of interactions that weaves through every part of the forest. Over time, species adapt to one another with each lineage refining its ecological niche from generation to generation. The requirements of a species for survival become ever more distinct over time, and animals and plants in the forest become increasingly successful survivors, evolving ever more efficient at avoiding exploitation. As species become more specialized, they leave room for others, and so give rise to new species with narrower ecological niches. This makes for an ever increasing biodiversity.[63]

Humans, however, are one predator that can upset the delicate balance of the rain forest and destroy it and all the species it contains. Human activity has already had a devastating effect on species diversity, and the rate of extinctions caused by humans is accelerating. It is estimated the rain forest clearing alone eliminates 2 to 3 percent of all the species in the forest every year. The global loss could be as much as 4,000 to 6,000 species per year. Some experts estimate that this rate is on the order of 10,000 times greater than the naturally occurring background extinction rate that existed prior to the appearance of human beings.[64] Perhaps as much as 25 percent of the earth's species will be lost by 2050, and even this estimate may be conservative. What seems clear is that the earth will witness the extinction of millions of species before the end of the century.[65]

Habitat destruction seems to be the prime mover behind species extinction, as some 67 percent of all endangered, vulnerable, and rare species of vertebrates are threatened by habitat degradation or destruction. If a habitat is reduced 90 percent in an area, roughly one-half of the species in the area will be lost. The big animals and the animals at the top of the food chain go first because it takes a lot of territory to support a meat eater. If the country is carved up with settlements and clear-cutting, the remaining wilderness becomes a series of ecological islands, too small to support the full range of biological diversity that existed previously.[66]

Protecting Species

According to one expert, creating parks and reserves free from human interferences has long been considered the key to conserving plants and animals. Consistent with this strategy, some 425 million hectares of land in some 3,500 areas worldwide enjoy some degree of protection. These areas are set aside to protect an intact example of each of the earth's ecological zones and to reconcile their preservation with the economic needs of surrounding communities. But designating parks, which some think is a static solution to a dynamic problem, is no longer enough to avert a mass extinction of species. According to some estimates, as much as 1.3 billion hectares would have to be set aside to conserve representative samples of all the earth's ecosystems.[67]

Many of these parks and reserves are too small to maintain populations sufficient to ensure species survival. Fragmenting ecosystems, whether done through clear-cutting or cutting roads through rain forest, is destructive of wildlife, which need larger habitats to survive. Many of the parks in the United States, for example, do not encompass an entire ecosystem that is necessary to sustain wildlife. Studies have shown that the smallest parks have lost the greatest share of species, but that even very large parks such as Rocky Mountain and Yosemite have lost between a quarter and a third of the native wildlife. (See Table 10.2.) These parks do not encompass enough area to preserve the habitat of many species that reside in these areas, but extension of the parks to encompass them will meet with severe resistance.

Biologists estimate that as many as 2,000 species of mammals, reptiles, and birds will have to be bred in capacity to escape extinction as natural ecosystems are cleared and fragmented. Zoos have become something of an ark in sustaining animals for which wild habitat is no longer sufficient until such time when human demands on the biosphere stabilize and the animals can be reintroduced into their natural habitat. Zoos are involved in genetic management of increasing numbers of vulnerable species. But zoos are limited by budgets, and probably can afford no more than 900 species — less than half the 2,000 species in these groups that face extinction. And they can do almost nothing for the hundreds of thousands of insects and invertebrates threatened with extinction.[68]

Likewise, botanical gardens could back up ecological restoration by maintaining threatened plant species and restoring them to natural settings

Table 10.2

Habitat Area and Loss of Large Animal Species in North American National Parks, 1986

Park	Area	Original Species Lost
	(square kilometers)	(percentage)
Bryce Canyon	144	36
Lassen Volcano	426	43
Zion	588	36
Crater Lake	641	31
Mount Rainier	976	32
Rocky Mountain	1,049	31
Yosemite	2,083	25
Sequoia-Kings Canyon	3,389	23
Glacier-Waterton	4,627	7
Grand Teton-Yellowstone	10,328	4
Kootenay-Banff-Jasper-Yoho	20,736	0

Source: Reprinted from STATE OF THE WORLD, 1988, A World-watch Institute Report on Progress Toward a Sustainable Society, Project Director: Lester R. Brown. By permission of W. W. Norton & Company, Inc. Copyright © 1988 by Worldwatch Institute.

when appropriate. But conserving the full genetic range of threatened plant species in these gardens alone is unattainable. The Office of Technology Assessment warns that cultivating sufficient populations of plants to maintain diversity is unrealistic, even though it may be theoretically possible for the botanic gardens of the world to grow the estimated 25,000 to 40,000 flowering plants that are threatened. Protecting a diversity of plant life, the agency states, will depend on maintaining them in their natural state.[69]

Another way to protect species, which was the method used by environmentalists in the old-growth controversy, is to protect them more directly through legislation. The real issue in the old-growth controversy, according to most people, was the protection of the trees, but because trees do not have standing before the law, the owl was used as a surrogate. It was considered to be an endangered species, and thus protected by law, giving the environmentalists a way to stop the logging of old-growth forests. Because its habitat was essential to its survival, the owl became a reason to stop the logging of these forests. In order for the owl to survive, its habitat had to be protected.

An endangered species is one having so few individual survivors that the species could soon become extinct over all or most of its natural range. Species that meet this definition are given protection by the Office of Endangered Species of the U.S. Department of the Interior's Fish and Wildlife Service. This office had listed 1,046 species as endangered or threatened by June 1989, with 539 of these species found only in the United States. About 3,000 of the 25,000 plant species in the United States have been identified as endangered by scientists, but only 204 of these plants are under federal protection. It was predicted that by 2000, up to 700 native plant species may become extinct in the country.[70]

The Endangered Species Act of 1973 was enacted to "provide for the conservation, protection, and propagation of species and subspecies of fish and wildlife that are presently threatened with extinction or likely within the foreseeable future to become threatened with extinction." The act makes it illegal for the United States to import or to carry on trade in any product made from an endangered species unless it is used for an approved scientific purpose or to enhance the survival of the species. The law also provides protection for endangered and threatened species in the United States and abroad by making it illegal to in any way affect the life and health of species that are considered to be endangered.

The law gives authorization to the National Marine Fisheries Service of the Department of Commerce to identify and list endangered and threatened marine species. The Fish and Wildlife Service in the Department of the Interior identifies and lists all other endangered and threatened species in the country. When listed as endangered, a species cannot be hunted, killed, collected, or injured in the United States. It is unlawful for any person to take any endangered species, where taking is defined to include "any action to harass, harm, pursue, hunt, wound . . . or attempt to engage in such conduct."[71] Any decision to add or remove a species from the list must be based on biological considerations rather than economic considerations.

Once a species is listed as endangered or threatened, a plan is supposed to be developed for its recovery. The law requires the appropriate agencies to employ all methods and procedures needed to return the listed species to a point where they no longer need protection. It is not enough for agencies to simply avoid activities that impact negatively on the endangered or threatened species, but they must also be responsible to "continuously develop programs which positively affect rare plants and animals and which will bring them to the point where they can be taken off the list of threatened and endangered species."[72] Because of budgetary considerations, however, many of these plans are not developed, and only a few species have recovered sufficiently to be removed from protection.[73]

Inadequate funding and staffing, which reflects political priorities, have resulted in a hopeless backlog of work for those agencies responsible for implementing the legislation.[74] Because of delays, some plant and animal species become extinct before they can be listed.[75] The lack of vigorous enforcement reflects uncertainty about how much of the natural world we really want to preserve. While the law is the most powerful tool for preserving biological diversity, it is not enough according to some critics. If we are

Facts About Endangered Species

- Of the 500 animal species known to have become extinct in the United States since the Pilgrims landed, more than 350 have vanished since 1966, the year the precursor of the Endangered Species Preservation Act was passed by Congress.
- By October 1975, less than two years after the act was passed, the FWS had received petitions to list as endangered 23,962 species.
- Only 1,100 species have been listed as legally endangered or threatened worldwide since 1967.
- As of May 1988, of the 495 species listed as endangered or threatened in the United States, only 229 (57 percent) have even had recovery plans approved.
- Only about 16 of those 495 listed species are actually recovering. Another 18 of those species are already possibly extinct.
- In the past 15 years, only 15 species had been "delisted"—determined to no longer be endangered or threatened. Six of those species were delisted because they became extinct while waiting to be protected.

Source: M. John Fayhee, "A Hard Act to Follow," *Backpacker,* October 1990, p. 89. Reprinted by permission. *Backpacker* magazine, Copyright Rodale Press, Inc., all rights reserved.

serious about sharing the earth with other biological life-forms, "we need to elaborate on the original articulation of the right of other forms of life to exist, and take our commitment to preserving sustainable ecosystems more seriously."[76]

There are said to be serious procedural problems with the way the act works. If anything is done at all, it is after a species may have reached the point of no return. The chances of successfully restoring a species are reduced if we wait until a species is almost gone before taking action. The minimum size required for a species to exist indefinitely without active help by humans is considerably larger than that needed for mere survival over a few generations. We need to be thinking more proactively, according to some experts, about the preservation of entire systems rather than just individual species. What is really needed is a better understanding of ecosystem dynamics and the role certain species play in the whole system.[77]

It is recommended that a strategy encompassing both preservation and active ecosystem restoration where possible is needed to minimize the global extinction crisis. Severely degraded tropical land need not be written off as a total biological loss. Some biologists believe that nearly all the land deforested so far in the Amazon has the capacity to regenerate. This potential for regeneration is based on studies of how natural ecosystems repair themselves. Such restoration aims to reestablish viable native communities of plants and animals, but this restoration cannot be done haphazardly. Advocates of restoration maintain that the successful conservation of biological diversity depends less on keeping humans out of fragile ecosystems than on making sure they do the right things when they are there.[78]

Every species distinction diminishes humanity because every organism contains on the order of 1 to 10 million bits of information in its genetic code. This code has been hammered into existence by an astronomical number of mutations and episodes of natural selection that has taken place over the course of thousands or even millions of years of evolution. For most people, the power of evolution by natural selection may be too great to conceive, let alone duplicate. Species diversity, the world's available gene pool, is one of our planet's most important and irreplaceable resources. Each species represents a unique combination of traits, each one of which is an evolutionary solution to biological problems.[79]

> The loss of biological diversity does not mean the disappearance of a few familiar "showcase" species, but rather the loss of complex interwoven systems of plants and animals that make up the Earth's ecosystems. The loss of biological diversity represents a moral and ethical catastrophe of unprecedented proportions involving natural wonders which have evolved over hundreds of millions of years, and which constitute a priceless resource largely untapped and little understood by mankind. The extinction crisis should give us a new awareness that the living things with which we share the planet are not only a source of beauty, wonder, and joy, but are integral to our very survival.[80]

As species are decimated largely as a result of habitat destruction, the capacity for natural genetic regeneration is greatly reduced, causing, as one scientist puts it, the death of birth. The science of genetic engineering does not make new genes, but depends on rearrangement of existing genes. From this perspective, the ultimate importance of tropical forests is in their genetic stock, from which incalculable and inconceivable benefits may be derived. With each species lost, the potential growth of the life sciences and certain possibilities for genetic engineering are forever curtailed and impoverished. As one scientist put it, "If we permit the loss of the rainforests, and with them a major portion of biological diversity, it might with justice be viewed as one of the greatest acts of desecration in human history."[81] The same could be said for the loss of species and the destruction of habitats all over the world, including the spotted owl and old-growth forests.

Questions for Discussion

1. What resources do forests provide for human purposes? What ecological functions do they also perform? Is there a conflict between these roles? How can this conflict, if it exists, be mitigated? What role do forests play in the global carbon and oxygen cycles of the world?

2. What is a tropical rain forest? Where are they located? How much land did they once cover compared to what they cover today? How many species do they contain?

3. Is the soil that supports the rain forest rich in nutrients? How is the rain forest able to sustain itself? What keeps it going? What is the rain forest' source of energy?

4. What are the fundamental causes of deforestation? How does government policy encourage such practices? Is deforestation a good practice for these countries? Why or why not?

5. What do you think of the principles stated in the chapter regarding rain forest management? Do you think they are feasible from an economic standpoint? Do they recognize the ecological functions of the rain forest?

6. What have some companies done to promote rain forest preservation? Do you think these strategies will have much of an impact? What else can American companies do to deal with the problem?

7. Study the Tropical Forestry Action Plan in detail. What are its major provisions? How successful has this plan been in halting deforestation? What can be done to improve it and make it more effective?

8. What are old-growth forests? Where are they located? What pressures are being put on them? Is it important to preserve them for their ecological functions? Do they have intrinsic value?

9. What role did the northern spotted owl play in the controversy over old-growth forests? What is at stake in this controversy? What is the owl's current status? What is the current state of affairs with respect to old-growth forests?

10. What is different about species decimation versus other forms of ecological destruction? How much biological diversity presently exists when compared with other historical time periods? Does this concern you personally?

11. Where do most of the world's species live? Why? How many are being lost every year? What value do these species have for humans? Do they have a right to exist irrespective of their instrumental value?

12. What can be done to protect and preserve species? What is an endangered species? How does this process of protection work? What strategies are most likely to be effective?

NOTES

1. G. Tyler Miller, *Living in the Environment,* 6th ed. (Belmont, CA: Wadsworth, 1990), p. 285.

2. Ibid., p. 286–287.

3. Ibid., p. 285.

4. Peter H. Raven, "Endangered Realm," in *The Emerald Realm: Earth's Precious Rain Forests,* Martha E. Christian, ed. (Washington, DC: National Geographic Society, 1990), p. 10.

5. Miller, *Living in the Environment,* p. 284.

6. Ibid., p. 287.

7. World Wildlife Fund, Position Paper No. 3, *Tropical Forest Conservation,* August 1989.

8. Tom Lovejoy, "Infinite Variety — A Rich Diversity of Life," *The Rainforests: A Celebration,* Lisa Silcock, ed. (San Francisco: Chronicle Books, 1990), p. 36.

9. Eugene Linden, "Playing with Fire," *Time,* September 18, 1989, p. 77.

10. Julian Caldecott, "The Rainforest — An Overview," in *The Rainforests: A Celebration,* Lisa Silcock, ed. (San Francisco: Chronicle Books, 1990), pp. 14–15.

11. World Wildlife Fund, *Tropical Forest Conservation.*

12. Ibid.

13. Joanne Omang, "In the Tropics, Still Rolling Back the Rain Forest Primeval," *Smithsonian,* Vol. 17, No. 12 (March 1987), pp. 56–67.

14. "Amazon Forest Unlikely to Rise from Ashes," *Science News,* Vol. 137 (March 17, 1990), p. 164.

15. Ghillean T. Prance, "Introduction," in *The Rainforests: A Celebration,* Lisa Silcock, ed. (San Francisco: Chronicle Books, 1990), p. 9.

16. Linden, "Playing with Fire," p. 78.

17. United Nations, Food and Agriculture Organization, *The Tropical Forestry Action Plan.*

18. The Smithsonian Institution and International Hardwood Products Association, *Tropical Forestry Workshop: Consensus Statement on Commercial Forestry Sustained Yield Management and Tropical Forests,* October 1989, p. 2.

19. International Hardwood Products Association, *World's Tropical Forests: A Renewable Resource,* undated, p. 1.

20. *The Tropical Forestry Action Plan.*

21. Miller, *Living in the Environment,* p. 289.

22. Ibid., pp. 291–292.

23. *Tropical Forestry Workshop,* p. 2.

24. Lisa L. Lyles, "A Long and Rocky Road to Reversing Rainforest Destruction," *Nature,* June 9, 1988, p. 491.

25. Linden, "Playing with Fire," p. 85.

26. *Tropical Forestry Workshop,* p. 3.

27. Ibid., pp. 4–5.

28. Ibid., pp. 3–4.

29. Gilbert M. Grosvenor, "Environmental Promises," *The National Geographic Society,* November 1989, p. 536.

30. Susan Dillingham, "From the Rain Forest to the Shelves," *Insight,* June 4, 1990, p. 41.

31. Ibid.
32. John McQuaid, "Mexico Struggles to Exploit, Save Its Rain Forest," *Times-Picayune*, October 17, 1990, p. A-1.
33. Michael S. Serrill, "A Dubious Plan for the Amazon," *Time*, April 17, 1989, p. 67.
34. *The Tropical Forestry Action Plan.*
35. Ibid.
36. Eugene Linden, "Good Intentions, Woeful Results," *Time*, April 1, 1991, pp. 48–49.
37. Ibid., p. 49.
38. Miller, *Living in the Environment*, p. 184.
39. John Daniel, "The Long Dance of the Trees," *Wilderness*, Spring 1988, p. 21.
40. Ibid., p. 23.
41. Miller, *Living in the Environment*, pp. 303–304.
42. Michael D. Lemonick, "Showdown in the Treetops," *Time*, August 28, 1989, pp. 58–59.
43. Charles McCoy, "Spotted Owl's Fate Puts Timber Policy, Northwest Logging Jobs at Loggerheads," *Wall Street Journal*, April 27, 1989, p. A-6.
44. Daniel, "The Long Dance of the Trees," p. 23. Also see Christopher Elias, "Forest Service's Eager Beavers Draw Fire with Timber Sales," *Insight*, October 17, 1988, pp. 38–41.
45. Ibid., p. 27.
46. Miller, *Living in the Environment*, p. 298.
47. Ibid., pp. 298–299.
48. Ibid., pp. 296–297.
49. Daniel, "The Long Dance of the Trees," p. 27.
50. Ibid.
51. McCoy, "Spotted Owl's Fate," p. A-6.
52. Charles McCoy, "Timber Firms Allowed by Court to Fell the Ancient Forests of Western Oregon," *Wall Street Journal*, September 8, 1989, p. B-2.
53. "Cancer Researchers Join Tree Battle," *Times-Picayune*, September 20, 1990, p. A-10.
54. "The Year of the Deal: 23rd Environmental Quality Index," *National Wildlife*, Vol. 29, No. 2 (February-March, 1991), p. 37.
55. Rose Gutfeld, "U.S. Unveils Plan to Save Spotted Owl, But Some See Strategy as Short-Sighted," *Wall Street Journal*, June 27, 1990, p. A-6.
56. Daniel, "The Long Dance of the Trees," p. 33.
57. Ted Gup, "Owl vs. Man," *Time*, June 25, 1990, p. 58.
58. Edward O. Wilson, "Threats to Biodiversity," *Scientific American*, Vol. 261, No. 3 (September 1989), p. 108.
59. Ibid., p. 110.
60. Miller, *Living in the Environment*, p. 318.
61. Lovejoy, "Infinite Variety," p. 36.

62. Wilson, "Threats to Biodiversity," p. 110.
63. Caldecott, "The Rainforest—An Overview," p. 14.
64. Wilson, "Threats to Biodiversity," p. 112.
65. Sierra Club, "The Extinction Crisis," June 1987, p. 1.
66. David Holzman, "Species Extinction Mires Ecosystem," *Insight,* March 26, 1990, p. 52.
67. Edward C. Wolf, "Avoiding a Mass Extinction of Species," *State of the World 1988* (Washington, DC: Worldwatch Institute, 1988), p. 102.
68. Ibid., p. 117.
69. Ibid.
70. Miller, *Living in the Environment,* p. 321.
71. Thomas France and Jack Tuholske, "Stay the Hand: New Directions for the Endangered Species Act," *The Public Land Law Review,* Spring 1986, p. 15.
72. Ibid., p. 4.
73. Miller, *Living in the Environment,* p. 331–332.
74. See John Lancaster, "Endangered Species Act Isn't Working Smoothly," *Times-Picayune,* October 31, 1990, p. C-11.
75. See Cass Peterson and Philip J. Hilts, "Waiting in Line for Protection, Endangered Species Dying," *Houston Chronicle,* September 21, 1987, Section 7, p. 3.
76. Sierra Club, "Endangered But Not Yet Protected," Fall 1986, p. 4.
77. M. John Faybee, "A Hard Act to Follow," *Backpacker,* October 1990, p. 89.
78. Wolf, "Avoiding a Mass Extinction of Species," p. 110.
79. Wilson, "Threats to Biodiversity," p. 114.
80. Sierra Club, "The Extinction Crisis," p. 1.
81. Lovejoy, "Infinite Variety," p. 38.

SUGGESTED READINGS

Anderson, Dennis, and Robert Fishwick. *Fuelwood Consumption and Deforestation in African Countries.* Washington, DC: World Bank, 1985.

Caufield, Catherine. *In the Rainforest.* New York: Knopf, 1985.

Christian, Martha E., ed. *The Emerald Realm: Earth's Precious Rain Forests.* Washington, DC: National Geographic Society, 1990.

Cowell, *The Decade of Destruction: The Crusade to Save the Amazon Rain Forest.* New York: Henry Holt, 1990.

Deacon, Robert T., and M. Bruce Johnson, eds. *Forestlands: Public and Private.* San Francisco: Pacific Institute for Public Policy, 1986.

Erwin, Keith. *Fragile Majesty: The Battle for North America's Last Great Forest.* Seattle: Mountaineer's Books, 1989.

Fritz, Edward. *Sterile Forest: The Case Against Clearcutting.* Austin, TX: Eakin Press, 1983.

Gradwohl, Judith, and Russell Greenberg. *Saving the Tropical Forests.* Washington, DC: Island Press, 1988.

Hazlewood, Peter T. *Cutting Our Losses: Policy Reform to Sustain Tropical Forest Resources.* Washington, DC: World Resources Institute, 1989.

International Hardwood Products Association, *World's Tropical Forests: A Renewable Resource,* undated.

Kelly, David. *Secrets of the Old Growth Forest.* Layton, UT: Gibbs Smith, 1988.

Myers, Norman. *The Primary Source: Tropical Forests and Our Future.* New York: Norton, 1984.

Norse, Elliott. *Ancient Forests of the Pacific Northwest.* Covelo, CA: Island Press, 1989.

Office of Technology Assessment. *Technologies to Sustain Tropical Forest Resources.* Washington, DC. U.S. Government Printing Office, 1984.

Postel, Sandra, and Lori Heise. *Reforesting the Earth.* Washington, DC: Worldwatch Institute, 1988.

Raphael, Ray. *Tree Talk: The People and Politics of Timber.* Covelo, CA: Island Press, 1981.

Reichle, David E., ed. *Analysis of Temperate Forest Ecosystems.* New York: Springer-Verlag, 1970.

Repetto, Robert. *The Forest for the Trees: Government Policies and the Misuse of Forest Resources.* Washington, DC: World Resources Institute, 1989.

Shoumatoff, Alex. *The World Is Burning.* Boston: Little, Brown, 1990.

Silcock, Lisa, ed. *The Rainforests: A Celebration,* San Francisco: Chronicle Books, 1990.

The Smithsonian Institution and International Hardwood Products Association, *Tropical Forestry Workshop: Consensus Statement on Commercial Forestry Sustained Yield Management and Tropical Forests,* October 1989.

Tucker, Richard P., and J. F. Richards. *Global Deforestation and the Nineteenth-Century World Economy.* Durham, NC: Duke University Press, 1983.

Wilderness Society. *Ancient Forests: A Threatened Heritage.* Washington, DC. Wilderness Society, 1989.

Williams, Michael. *Americans and Their Forests.* New York: Cambridge University Press, 1989.

Wolf, Edward C. "Avoiding a Mass Extinction of Species." *State of the World 1988.* Washington, DC: Worldwatch Institute, 1988.

CHAPTER 11

COASTAL EROSION AND WETLANDS PROTECTION

~

The coastlines of the United States protect an ecosystem where plant and animal life is abundant. The coastal zone is the relatively warm, nutrient-rich shallow water that extends from the high-tide mark on land to the edge of the continental shelf. While this area represents only 10 percent of the total ocean, it is home to 90 percent of all ocean plant and animal life and provides resources for most of the major commercial marine fisheries. It is one of the earth's most important ecosystems and thus needs to be protected from environmental degradation.[1]

Several different kinds of habitats are located in the coastal zone, including estuaries, which are coastal areas where fresh water from rivers, streams, and land runoff mixes with salty seawater. Estuaries provide aquatic habitats that have a lower average salinity than the water of the open ocean, making them unique places for the development of aquatic life-forms. Along with inland swamps and marshes and tropical rain forests, estuaries produce more plant biomass per square meter each year than any other ecosystem in the world.[2]

Land that is flooded all or part of the year with fresh or salt water is called a wetland. Those that extend inland from estuaries and are covered all or part of the year with salt water are known as coastal wetlands. These nutrient-rich areas are among the world's most productive ecosystems. Many people view these areas as desolate and worthless wastelands, as sources for mosquitoes, flies, and unpleasant odors. Wetlands are places to be avoided, or better yet, developed. Many people think they should be dredged and filled in to be used for housing or commercial developments or used as depositories for human-generated waste materials.[3]

However, these coastal wetlands provide humans with a remarkable variety of benefits. They serve as a spawning and nursery ground for many species of marine fish and shellfish, thus ultimately providing 70 percent of the country's seafood, including shrimp, salmon, oysters, clams, and haddock. The fishing industry is a $15-billion a year endeavor and provides jobs for millions of people.[4] Wetlands are also breeding grounds and habitats for waterfowl and other kinds of wildlife. Some species spend their entire life in wetlands and other wildlife use them primarily as nesting, feeding, or resting grounds.

Coastal wetlands also dilute and act as filters for large amounts of water-borne pollutants, and thus help to protect the quality of adjacent waters used for swimming, fishing, and habitats for wildlife. Wetlands remove nutrients such as nitrogen and phosphorus and thus help prevent eutrophication of waters. They also filter harmful chemicals such as pesticides and heavy metals, and trap suspended sediments that produce turbidity (cloudiness) in water. Due to their position between upland and deep water, wetlands can also intercept surface-water runoff from large land areas before it reaches open water, and thus filter that water to improve its quality.[5]

Estuaries and coastal wetlands protect population centers in coastal areas by absorbing damaging waves caused by tropical storms and hurricanes, and act as giant sponges to absorb floodwaters. Wetlands vegetation can also reduce shoreline erosion by absorbing and dissipating wave energy and encouraging the deposition of suspended sediments. Plants in wetland areas help prevent erosion because they increase the durability of the sediment by binding soil with their roots. They also dampen wave action in the area and reduce current velocity through friction. Many states are recommending the planting of wetland vegetation to control shoreline erosion in coastal areas.[6]

Inland wetlands are those areas located away from coastal areas that are covered with fresh water all or part of the year. They include bogs, marshes, swamps, and mud flats. Wet tundra, which covers 58 percent of the state of Alaska, is also considered a wetland. Wetlands are most common on floodplains along rivers and streams, in isolated depressions surrounded by dry land, and along the margins of lakes and ponds. Certain wetland types are common in particular regions, such as the pocosins of North Carolina, bogs and fens of the northeastern and north-central states, inland saline and alkaline marshes and riparian wetlands of the arid and semiarid West, prairie potholes of Minnesota and the Dakotas, and the cypress gum swamps of the South.[7] (See Figure 11.1.)

Inland wetlands are also important ecosystems that are rapidly being destroyed and degraded by human activity. They provide habitats for a variety of fish, waterfowl, and other wildlife. Most freshwater fish feed on wetland-produced food and use wetlands as nursery grounds. Most of the

Figure 11.1

Extent of Wetlands in the Lower 48 States

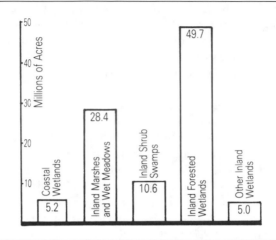

Source: Environmental Protection Agency, *America's Wetlands: Our Vital Link Between Land and Water* (Washington, DC: Office of Wetlands Protection, 1988), p. 6.

important recreational fish spawn in wetlands, and a great variety of birds use the wetlands to raise their young. Wetlands also help reduce the frequency, level, and velocity of floods and riverbank erosion. They act as natural sponges that absorb flooding waters, and help protect adjacent and downstream property from flood damage. Wetlands upstream of urban areas are especially valuable because urban development increases the rate and volume of surface-water runoff, thus greatly increasing the risk of flood damage. Many wetlands also help recharge groundwater aquifers by holding water and allowing it to infiltrate the ground. Wetlands are also vital for growing certain crops such as blueberries, cranberries, and most importantly, rice, which is used to feed half the world's people.[8]

WETLANDS DESTRUCTION

Once there were over 200 million acres of wetlands in the lower 48 states, but by the mid-1970s, only 99 million acres remained. The average rate of wetland loss from 1955 to 1975 was 458,000 acres per year; 440,000 acres of this loss was inland wetlands and 18,000 acres was coastal wetlands. Currently, about 56 percent of the original coastal and inland wetlands areas in the lower 48 states have been destroyed, with about 80 percent of this loss due to draining and clearing of wetlands for agricultural purposes. Agricultural activities have had the greatest impact on forested wetlands, inland marshes, and wet meadows. Urban development was the major cause of coastal wetland losses outside of Louisiana. In addition to direct physical destruction, these habitats are also threatened indirectly by chemical contamination and other pollution.[9] (See Exhibit 11.1)

Nearly half of the estuaries and coastal wetlands in the country have been destroyed or damaged because of these multiple uses that puts these areas under great ecological stress. Most of the damage has been done by dredging and filling operations and contamination by waste material. These wastes contaminate the water and make it unfit for swimming and poison fish and shellfish to the point where they are inedible. About half of the country's estuaries and coastal wetlands remain undeveloped, but with the exception of Alaska, about 70 percent of the country's shoreline is privately owned, and many private owners find it hard to resist lucrative offers from developers. Some of these lands have been purchased by federal and state governments and by private conservation agencies to protect them from development.[10] (See Figure 11.2.)

Exhibit 11.1

Major Causes of Wetland Loss and Degradation

Human Impacts

- Drainage
- Dredging and stream channelization
- Deposition of fill material
- Diking and damming
- Tilling for crop production
- Grazing by domesticated animals
- Discharge of pollutants
- Mining
- Alteration of hydrology

Natural Threats

- Erosion
- Subsidence
- Sea level rise
- Droughts
- Hurricanes and other storms
- Overgrazing by wildlife

Source: Environmental Protection Agency, *America's Wetlands: Our Vital Link Between Land and Water* (Washington, DC: Office of Wetlands Protection, 1988), p. 6.

Figure 11.2

Relative Abundance of United States Wetlands

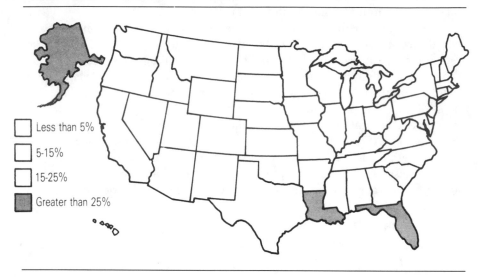

Source: Environmental Protection Agency, *America's Wetlands: Our Vital Link Between Land and Water* (Washington, DC: Office of Wetlands Protection, 1988), p. 6.

Coastal areas of the country are under particular threat because over half of the United States population lives along the coastlines. These coastal areas are also the sites of large numbers of motels, hotels, condominiums, beach cottages, and other real estate developments. Most of the country's rivers have been dammed or diverted to meet energy, irrigation, and flood control needs, and these activities have changed the normal flow of fresh water into coastal wetlands and estuaries and modified their ability to function as a viable ecosystem. A great part of the problem lies in ignorance about the valuable ecological function these areas provide. They are among the most intensely populated and stressed ecosystems because human activities are increasingly impairing or destroying some of their more important services.[11]

Inland wetlands are often dredged or filled in and used as croplands and sites for urban and industrial development. As is the case with coastal wetlands, these areas are often considered wastelands because people do not understand their ecological importance. This destruction has greatly reduced the habitat of birds and other wildlife that live on or near these ecosystems, and has threatened some species with extinction. Better management practices are necessary to prevent further loss of these wetlands and to restore them to their original condition.[12]

EXAMPLES OF WETLAND DEGRADATION

The Everglades is said to be dying because of urban development and pollution. Today the Everglades, or what is left of it, is surrounded by an urban population of 4.5 million people and is polluted by sugarcane farms that have been carved out of its northern reaches. The Everglades were one of the largest wetlands systems in the world, supporting a rich diversity of wildlife. But the population of wading birds has dropped from more than 2.5 million in the 1930s to about 250,000 at present. Some 13 animals in the Everglades are now on the endangered species list. Half of the original Everglades has been lost to development over the past several decades.[13]

The water that naturally replenishes the wetlands once came from Lake Okeechobee in a shallow sheet 50 miles wide, moving slowly south through the Everglades before emptying into the Bay of Florida. But since the mid-1960s, the lake overflow has been channeled through a massive flood control project that directs water to urban centers. This change in water flow patterns has affected the ecology of the Everglades. Runoff from farmlands has also changed the Everglades as high levels of phosphates and nitrates have transformed more than 20,000 acres of grass into cattails. These intruders suck oxygen from the marsh and suffocate aquatic life at the bottom of the food chain. On shallow ponds and canals, algae has grown so thick that the sun is blocked from underwater plants.[14]

Protecting the Everglades is more than just a matter of protecting wildlife and a certain kind of ecosystem. The fate of the cities in south Florida may be closely tied up with what happens in the Everglades. The water supply could dry up if the Everglades becomes a sea of cattails that do not hold and purify water. The Everglades replenishes the aquifer from which the cities of Miami and surrounding areas draw their water supply, and if this aquifer dries up, the sunny subtropical paradise of south Florida could become a barren wasteland. This prophecy became all too true in 1990, as rainfall was less than normal, creating a severe water shortage in south Florida that necessitated drastic water conservation measures.[15]

Extensive losses of wetlands have taken place in Louisiana, Mississippi, Arkansas, North Dakota, South Dakota, Nebraska, Florida, and Texas. The loss of these wetlands has greatly diminished our nation's wetland resources. Water quality has been adversely affected in many parts of the country and damages from floods have increased. In addition, the country has seen a decline in waterfowl populations in recent years, which in part is the result of wetland destruction.[16]

Since the mid-1970s, America's waterfowl population has been in decline. Certain key species among the duck population have been in serious decline for at least a decade. The major problem seems to be the loss of wetlands where waterfowl breed and nest their young. The best nesting grounds in North America, say some wildlife experts, are in a hilly region called the coteau that stretches across parts of South and North Dakota and on into Canada. While this region was once a landscape of wetlands, prairies, and grassy hills, it is now mostly farmland. Thus the loss of habitat in which to breed has resulted in a drop in the number of nests and the number of eggs laid, as well as the number of hatchlings that survive. This loss of habitat is compounded by the increased presence there of contaminants left from the use of agricultural chemicals.[17]

ACTIONS

There are various approaches to wetlands protection that can be taken by governments and private parties. Governments and private conservation organizations can purchase wetlands or easements on wetland areas and establish wildlife refuges, sanctuaries, or conservation areas. This preserves the wetlands in their natural state and protects them from development activities that would destroy their functions. Once these areas have been set aside, they remain in that state and do not become subject to lobbying efforts by private citizens who want to use the wetlands for their own purposes.[18]

Governments can also provide economic incentives to private landowners and industry to promote wetland preservation. For example, landowners who sell or donate wetlands to a government agency or qualified conservation organization can claim the value of the land as a charitable deduction. Governments can also create economic disincentives to wetland destruction, such as the "swampbuster" provisions written into legislation (discussed later). The intent of these disincentives is to discourage the further conversion of wetlands to farmland or other destructive actions.[19]

Regulation of wetlands is also important. Section 404 of the federal Clean Water Act controls activities in wetlands. This law requires a permit from the Army Corps of Engineers in order to discharge dredged or fill material into wetlands. Failure to obtain a permit or to comply with the terms of the permit can result in civil and/or criminal penalties. The corps evaluates permit applications based on (1) regulations developed by the EPA in conjunction with the corps, which set the environmental criteria for permitting projects in wetland areas, and (2) factors that determine if the project is in the public interest. In addition to federal regulations, many states now have laws to manage activities in wetlands.[20]

In 1986, the EPA established an Office of Wetlands Protection, which was charged with providing leadership for a broad-based national effort to protect the nation's wetland resources. In 1989, a Wetlands Action Plan was initiated with a goal of no net loss of wetlands over the short term, and a gain in the quantity and quality of wetlands over the long term. To achieve the no-net-loss goal, the EPA is increasing enforcement of federal restrictions on activities that destroy or degrade wetlands. The EPA is also providing guidance and support to state and local governments for wetlands protection, and working with other federal agencies whose activities have an impact on wetlands, increasing public awareness of the ecological functions of wetlands, and conducting research to fill gaps in science to support wetland decisions.[21]

The EPA is becoming a center of wetlands expertise, according to its 1990 report, by providing more research, training, and communication on wetlands management. It is helping the states build comprehensive wetlands programs that incorporate both regulatory and nonregulatory approaches to wetlands protection. The EPA and other federal agencies involved in wetlands management are also developing better ways to monitor the health and extent of the nation's wetland resources. These agencies want to improve coastal water monitoring and increase the number of estuarine/marine sanctuaries, protected refuges, reserves, and parks to preserve coastal areas and wetlands.[22]

One of the most important concerns is to reduce the pollution of coastal waters. The sources of pollution of these areas is shown in Figure 11.3. Nonpoint sources of pollution are a particular problem, and control programs need to be strengthened in all coastal counties. Controls on point source discharges of toxics, nutrients, and other pollutants also need to be tightened to restore coastal water quality. Raw sewage flows from combined sanitary-storm sewers is an especially severe problem in many older seaboard cities that have combined systems. The EPA is requiring storm-water discharge permits for large cities in all coastal counties and is helping smaller municipalities with storm-water problems.[23]

Other laws, such as the Coastal Barriers Resource Act of 1982, also help to protect coastal zones from further destruction. This act prohibits most new federal expenditures and financial assistance for development of offshore barrier islands, which helps protect their important wetland resources. Of greater significance for inland wetlands is the swampbuster provision of the Food Security Act of 1985, which seeks to discourage the further conversion of wetlands for agricultural purposes by making any person who produces crops on wetlands converted to this purpose after December 23, 1985, ineligible for most federal farm benefits.[24]

There are many private protection strategies in addition to government actions. Because individual landowners and corporations own many of the nation's wetlands, they are in a key position to determine the fate of wetland properties under their control. Whether or not they actually own wetlands, citizens can help protect wetlands by supporting any number of wetland conservation activities. There are many opportunities for private citizens, corporations, and government agencies to work together to slow the rate of wetland loss and improve the quality of our remaining wetlands. Some of these options include the following:

Figure 11.3

Sources of Pollution in Estuaries

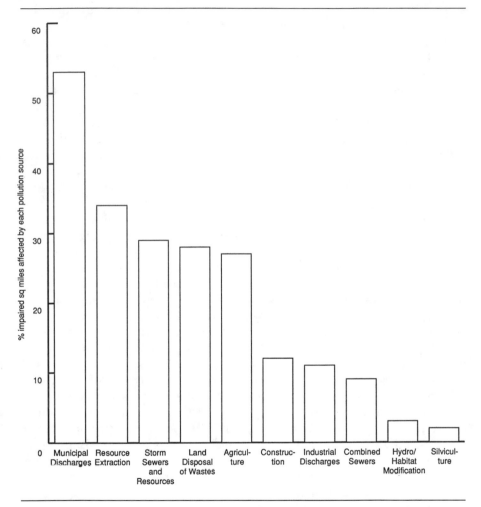

Source: Environmental Protection Agency, *Meeting the Environmental Challenge* (Washington, DC: U.S. Government Printing Office, 1990), p. 5.

- Rather than drain or fill wetlands, seek compatible uses involving minimal wetland alteration, such as waterfowl production, fur harvest, hay and forage, wild rice production, hunting and trapping leases, and selective timber harvest.
- Select upland sites for development projects rather than wetlands, and avoid wetland alteration or degradation during project construction.

- Donate wetlands, or funds for purchasing wetlands, to private or public conservation agencies.
- Maintain wetlands and adjacent buffer strips as open space.
- Construct ponds in uplands and manage for wetland and aquatic species.
- Support various wetland conservation initiatives by public agencies and private organizations.
- Participate in the Clean Water Act Section 404 program by reviewing public notices and, in appropriate cases, commenting on permit applications.[25]

In 1989, President Bush announced a no-net-loss policy with respect to wetland protection. This policy represented Bush's commitment to prevent further destruction of America's wetlands. But the policy never meant protecting wetlands at all costs. In those cases where "unavoidable" damage was not possible to prevent, developers could offset the loss by restoring or creating roughly the same number of wetlands acres somewhere else. There were also several exemptions built into the policy, which critics believed watered down the entire approach. For one thing, mitigation of damage would not be required if the amount of wetlands lost was considered "insignificant," and the mitigation process may not be practicable where there is a high proportion of land that is wetlands. This latter exemption was said to be directed at stripping protection from the arctic tundra areas, which are all wetlands.[26]

These exemptions were seen as huge loopholes through which developers and industry could escape. The words "unavoidable" and "insignificant" could be interpreted in many different ways, and the implementation of these words depended on who was doing the defining in a specific situation. In response to some of these criticisms, federal agencies issued a new definition of wetlands in 1990 that caused further controversy. The definition contained three tests to determine whether a territory qualifies as wetlands and thus comes under the no-net-loss policy. In order to be designated as a wetland, the territory under consideration must have the hydric soil typically found in wet areas, wetlands vegetation, and some wetness, even if the area is saturated for only one week during the growing season.[27]

These characteristics must be present under normal conditions, meaning that if a wetlands area was converted to cropland decades ago, it may still have the potential to revert back to its original wetlands state if left alone. This definition was expected to tighten the 404 program, under which regulation of dredging and filling in wetlands is provided. While the swampbuster bill denied benefits to farmers who drain virgin wetlands, this new definition took aim at already converted cropland. Thus many millions of acres of farmland in some states became wetlands overnight because of this definition.[28]

Farmers were in an uproar. They claimed the new definition is so expansive that vast chunks of farmland will be put under federal regulation for the first time. This definition would affect the cranberry bogs of Massachusetts, the rice paddies of Arkansas, and the sugar fields of Louisiana. Many farmers may need to get a permit from some federal agency before they could work their land. This new definition also discouraged some banks from lending to farmers because of the uncertain designation of their land, which in most cases was used as collateral for the loan. And it was expected to impair farmers' ability to sell excess acreage to developers. The definition thus introduced a new and divisive element into the debate over national wetlands policy and the implementation of the no-net-loss policy.[29]

In any event, protection of wetlands is an important national goal, and more thought must be given to the development of strategies that are fair and just and yet accomplish the goal of saving this essential part of our environment. As with any other part of the environment, once wetlands are lost, it is difficult and expensive to restore them to their original condition, so the best strategy is to take steps to protect what is left and keep them in their original condition. This is essentially the goal behind the no-net-loss wetlands policy, although the question of how this policy is to be implemented is still up for debate. Perhaps the following quote from the EPA sums up the importance of wetlands to the nation and to future generations.

> Wetlands are an important part of our national heritage. Our economic well-being and our quality of life are largely dependent on our nation's wealth of natural resources, and wetlands are the vital link between our land and water resources. As wetlands are lost, the remaining wetlands become even more valuable. We have already lost over half of our nation's wetlands since America was first settled. We must now take positive steps to protect wetlands to ensure that the values they provide will be preserved for future generations.[30]

COASTAL EROSION AND RISING SEA LEVELS

The erosion of coastlines, beaches, and barrier islands has accelerated over the past ten years as a result of rising sea levels. This erosion has become particularly prevalent on the world's sandy coastlines, at least 70 percent of which have retreated during the past few decades.[31] Some 86 percent of California's 1,100 miles of exposed Pacific shoreline is receding at an average rate of between 6 inches and 2 feet per year, and Monterey Bay, south of San Francisco, loses as much as 5 to 15 feet annually. Cape Shoalwater, Washington, which is about 70 miles west of Olympia, has been eroding at the rate of more than 100 feet a year since the turn of the century. In North Carolina, erosion cuts into beachfront property as much as 60 feet in some places, and the Cape Hatteras lighthouse may soon be surrounded by the ocean.[32]

Such coastal erosion is only one of the natural processes that have altered the world's shorelines ever since the oceans were first formed. The scouring action of waves and the pounding of storms, as well as the rise and fall of ocean levels, have changed coastlines over the centuries. These changes threaten developments that have been built on coastal areas as Americans have moved to be closer to the ocean and beaches. Receding coastlines also threaten the survival of shore-dwelling wildlife such as sea turtles that need beaches to lay their eggs.[33]

While sea level fluctuations are part of a natural cycle, over the past 100 years, the ocean has risen more than a foot, a rate faster than at any time in the past millennium. Some scientists believe that these natural changes are magnified by a fundamental change in the world's climate caused by the greenhouse effect. Some projections of sea level rise over the next 40 to 50 years suggest that most recreational beaches in developed areas could be eliminated unless protective measures are taken. Such increased erosion will decrease natural storm barriers, and moderate storms could be turned into catastrophic ones because of the loss of protection. Further sea level rises will also permanently affect freshwater supplies, and large cities around the world could be threatened by saltwater intrusion.[34]

For most of recorded history, the sea level has changed slowly, which has fostered the development of a social order based on its relative constancy. But if global warming is a continuing phenomenon, the earth's temperature will be radically altered, and an accompanying sea level rise would represent an environmental threat of unprecedented proportion. Higher global temperatures can alter sea levels in four ways: (1) decrease of density through the warming and subsequent expansion of seawater, which increases volume, (2) melting of alpine glaciers, (3) net increases in water as the fringes of polar glaciers melt, and (4) discharge of more ice from ice caps into the oceans.[35]

The rate of thermal expansion depends on how quickly ocean volume responds to rising atmospheric temperatures, how fast surface layers warm, and how rapidly the warming reaches deeper water masses. The rate of sea level change expected on a global level in the foreseeable future is unprecedented on a human time scale. With today's level of population and investment in coastal areas, the world has much more to lose from sea level rise than ever before. Only 30 countries in the entire world are completely landlocked, and while only 3 percent of the world's land area is at risk, this area encompasses one-third of global cropland and is home to a billion people. Countless billions of dollars worth of property in coastal towns, cities, and ports will be threatened, and problems will occur with natural and artificial drainage and with saltwater intrusion into rivers and aquifers.[36]

According to estimates by the EPA, erosion, inundation, and saltwater intrusion could reduce the area of present-day coastal wetlands in the United States up to 80 percent if current projections of the global sea level rises are realized. The extent of wetland loss will depend on the degree to which coastal towns and villages seek to protect their shorelines. Some 46 percent of all U.S. wetlands would be lost under a 1-meter rise if shorelines were allowed to retreat naturally. The loss of up to 80 percent of these wetlands is envisioned under a more rapid rate of rise. The economic and ecological cost of such a loss for the United States has not been calculated, let alone for the rest of the world.[37]

Communities have but two choices when faced with such sea level rises. They can either retreat from the shore or fend off the sea by building jetties, seawalls, groins, and bulkheads to hold back the ocean. The price tag attached to some of these options may be higher than even developed nations can afford, especially when the long-term ecological damage these structures themselves can cause is taken into account. Preliminary estimates by the EPA for the cost of holding back the sea from U.S. shores ranges from $32 billion to $309 billion for a 0.5- to 2-meter rise in sea levels. This cost does not include money needed for repairing or replacing infrastructure.[38]

Legal definitions of private property and of who is responsible for compensation in the event of such disasters are already being debated. If the sea level continues to rise, pushing up the cost of adaption, these issues will likely become part of an increasingly acrimonious debate over property rights and individual interests versus those of society at large.[39] In poorer countries, evacuation and abandonment of coastal areas may be the only option, and as millions of people are displaced by rising sea levels and move inland, there will be increased competition with those already living in these areas for scarce food, water, and land. This competition would spur regional clashes and increase international tensions.[40]

There are numerous measures that can be taken by governments and private citizens to deal with this problem. Governments can begin to limit coastal development by ensuring that private owners bear more of the costs of settling in coastal areas. Restricting shoreline development in this country has fallen largely to individual states. Since 1971, 29 of 30 states with coastlines have adopted coastal zone management programs. In North Carolina, for example, developers cannot build large projects any closer than 120 feet from the first line of dunes. The state also outlaws permanent seawalls and human-made barriers. Florida controls seaside construction by requiring approval by the governor and state cabinet for any new building closer than 300 feet to the water's edge. But a major problem with state regulation is the lack of coordination.[41]

The record of the federal government is spotty because there is no single agency responsible for coastal management. The Army Corps of Engineers, for example, has a dual mission of protecting vulnerable wetlands and keeping waterways navigable, goals that are often in conflict. Proposals have been made for wetlands protection, but they have yet to be implemented, raising questions about how well they are going to work in protecting coastal areas and wetlands.

The simplest and most effective response to the problem would be to prevent people from living near oceans. The nonprofit Nature Conservancy encourages this strategy by buying threatened coastal areas and keeping them undeveloped. The organization has made 32 separate purchases in eight states that have sheltered more than 250,000 acres, including 13 barrier islands off the coast of Virginia purchased for $10 million. But this policy is not likely to work on a comprehensive or long-term basis, as the pressures for living close to the ocean are too great for too many people.[42]

THE LOUISIANA STORY

What is happening to wetlands and the coastline in Louisiana is one of the most serious problems regarding coastal erosion and wetlands protection facing the nation. What is done in that region will have a bearing on what happens to this resource across the nation. Louisiana contains 40 percent of the nation's coastal marshes, but even more importantly, some 80 percent of the nation's coastal wetlands loss is taking place there. Each year these coastal marshes produce a commercial fish and shellfish harvest that is worth $680 million and provide 40 percent of the nation's wild fur and hides that have an estimated value of $17 million.[43]

This region contains an ecosystem that supports over 30 percent of the nation's fisheries and 22 percent of its oil and gas production. Coastal marshes also buffer destructive tidal surges caused by hurricanes and tropical storms and reduce flood damage to agricultural areas and population centers. They trap and hold fresh water that is a major source for coastal communities, agriculture, and industry and prevent salt water from intruding into these supplies. The marshlands also provide a feeding, spawning, and nursery ground for a wealth of fish, shellfish, and wildlife.[44]

The wetlands, estuaries, and barrier beaches and islands of coastal Louisiana are at the southern end of the major water flow migration route in the United States. Hunting in this flyway is valued at $58 million annually. Nearly 4 million ducks and geese, which is more than 66 percent of the water fowl that use the flyway, find a winter haven in the coastal wetlands. These coastal marshes are thus ideal for sport fishing, hunting, and water-oriented recreation, and the out-of-pocket expenses of those people who use these areas for recreation exceed $337 million annually.[45]

In past decades, many storms and hurricanes have wreaked their havoc on the Louisiana coast. In the last 40 or 50 years, several hurricanes hit the coast causing more than $2 billion worth of damage. The coastal marshes in Louisiana were very helpful in keeping the losses down, and it has been suggested that had the coastal marshes not offered a buffer to coastal towns and cities the losses would have been at least ten times greater, or some $20 billion in the coastal parishes.[46] If these estimates are true, then the coastal wetlands have at least an $18-billion value as a storm buffer alone. This estimate does not include the value of human lives saved as a result of the buffering effect.

Each year, about 40 to 60 square miles of these coastal wetlands disappear forever. Between 1956 and 1978, about 560,000 acres of this marsh were lost along the coast of Louisiana, mostly by conversion to open water. Another 790,000 acres of wetlands were lost because of conversion to agricultural, urban, and industrial uses. The Corps of Engineers estimates that between the present time and the year 2040, another 1 million acres of wetlands will be lost, which is an area larger than the state of Rhode Island. This means that by 2040, a total of 2.4 million acres of wetlands will have been lost or converted to other uses.[47]

If this rate of loss is not reduced or arrested, the Gulf shoreline will advance inland as much as 33 miles in some parts of the state, jeopardizing federal, state, local, and private investments. Municipal and industrial water supplies will be threatened by saltwater intrusion. Coastal communities and cities such as New Orleans will be more vulnerable to hurricane tidal surges and flooding from tropical storms. Since 60 to 75 percent of the population in Louisiana live within 50 miles of the coast, many of these people may be forced to move inland in the not too distant future. Valuable fish and wildlife and recreational resources will be lost and difficult to restore.[48]

Causes of Destruction

There is no single cause of the wetland loss in Louisiana, but ten major factors have been identified. (See Figure 11.4.) These factors interact with each other, intensifying the impact of each and producing a synergistic effect. Each of these factors accounts for a different percentage of the total loss, but flood protection in the lower Mississippi Valley and economic developments in the Louisiana coastal wetlands have been responsible for a major part of wetland loss and consequent coastal erosion.[49]

The Louisiana coast stretches for thousands of miles of tidal shoreline and involves four different types of marshes: saline, fresh, brackish, and intermediate. Those marshes close to the salty Gulf waters tend to be saline or brackish marshes, and those further inland from the Gulf and nearer to fresh water are the fresh or intermediate marshes.[50] All of these marshes were created over a period of some 7,000 to 10,000 years as the Mississippi River went through its delta switching phases. The river's mouth would switch to and fro like a hose, and in the process create new marshes. During one period, the river would flow in one direction spewing out millions upon millions of gallons of silty water that would settle and form a marsh. Then

Figure 11.4

Major Causes of Wetland Loss

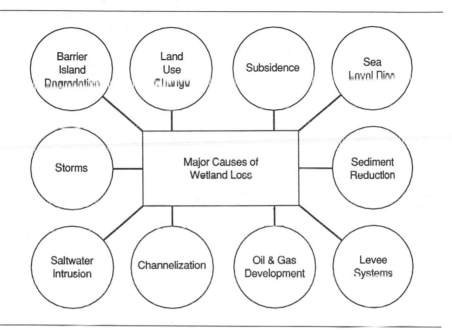

Source: U.S. Army Corp of Engineers in cooperation with the State of Louisiana, *Crisis on Louisiana's Coast: America's Loss,* undated, p. 5.

gradually, the river would switch in another direction to form another marsh.[51]

The Mississippi draws its water supply from springs, lakes, rivers, and ditches of 36 states in the country and from four Canadian provinces.[52] Thus the river covers a huge drainage area whose soil has been deposited along the coast of Louisiana for thousands of years. However, the river has also flooded vast areas of the country, especially in its lower reaches. In 1927, the so-called great flood caused major devastation along the lower reaches of the river. Protecting property along the lower reaches of the Mississippi River and its tributaries from the devastation of flooding has been a national imperative since that time. In order to control this flooding, the nation has invested $5.9 billion in building the world's largest flood control project. This project, called the Mississippi River and Tributaries Project (MR&T), is said to have prevented $111.3 billion of flood damages.[53]

But the flood control project has confined the river between its banks along a good part of its course through southern Louisiana, and thus has changed the natural ecological functions the river performed in replenishing wetlands. The river would overflow its banks every spring, flooding the

adjacent wetlands with nutrient- and sediment-rich water that would build
and sustain the diversity of the marshland. Since the levees were built, about
the only water that flows into the wetlands is rainfall. The Mississippi carries
183 million tons of sediment down to the Gulf of Mexico each year, where it
is dropping off the edge of the continental shelf into deep waters instead of
building new wetlands.[54] (See Figure 11.5.)

Before the levees, the Mississippi River delivered approximately 300
million tons of sediment to coastal Louisiana annually. The amount of
sediment that is not reaching the marshes because of the levee system varies
from .7 to 2.6 tons per day at a flow of 700,000 cubic feet per second (cfs). An
average discharge of 450,000 cfs results in about 1.8 tons being carried for
each unit of discharge. Estimating the rate per day at 810,000 tons and the
weight per cubic yard at 1.5 tons amounts to a loss of about 200 million cubic
yards per year to the ocean where it does not do any good.[55]

With no flood of fresh water each year to push back intruding salt
water, the wetlands which cannot tolerate salt are being killed and replaced
with open water ponds that increase the interface between open water and
wetlands, causing even more erosion of coastal wetlands. Without the annual

Figure 11.5

Mississippi Sediments Discharged into Deep Water

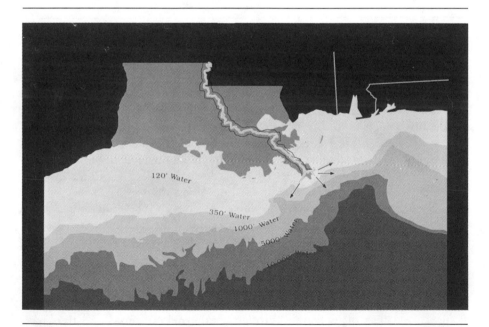

Source: The Louisiana Land and Exploration Company, *Louisiana's National Treasure,* undated,
p. 13.

flow of fresh water containing enriching nutrients and sediment, many of the wetlands along the Gulf of Mexico are sinking out of sight. The river has not been allowed for many decades to do its job of replenishing existing wetlands and building new ones to increase coastal areas.[56]

Economic development activities that have taken place in coastal wetlands interact with and intensify these natural processes. There has been a good deal of leveeing, channelization, oil exploration, and agricultural, urban, and industrial development in these coastal areas to accelerate the rate of loss. The wetlands area is laced with 8,200 miles of navigation, drainage, and petroleum access canals, which interrupt water and sediment flow over the wetlands. These canals segment the wetlands and expose them to further erosion through wave action and other human activities. Salt water also flows into these areas and causes even greater erosion.[57]

Nature is responsible for some of the loss as the long-term influences of subsidence, sea level rise, saltwater intrusion, and erosion have had their effects on the wetlands. There have been significant changes due to natural forces in the relative land and water surface elevations. Subsidence causes the wetlands to sink an estimated 1.8 feet per century, and rising sea levels cover the wetlands with an additional 0.5 foot of water per century. These factors intensify saltwater intrusion and erosion and accelerate the conversion of wetlands to open water. Other minor losses occur as a result of storm-generated waves along the state's 40,000 miles of tidal shoreline and barrier islands.[58]

There are three basic forms of wave erosion that contribute to destruction of the wetlands. The first type is caused by human activities such as jetty construction and sand mining that have contributed to shoreline erosion, which has proceeded at the rate of 33 feet per year along much of the barrier coast. These high rates of erosion threatened established development along the coast and also reduce Louisiana's first line of defense against incoming storm surges. If the beaches and marshes continue to disappear, cities such as New Orleans will be subjected to much higher storm surges and direct wave attack during severe storms.

The second form of wave erosion is lake and bay shore erosion. The physical process where waves erode the shoreline also occurs within estuaries and along the shores of larger lakes and bays. Unlike waves in the Gulf, which originate at some distance from the shore, wave generation within estuaries is localized and is caused primarily by prevailing winds and surface boat traffic. Bay shores facing prevailing winds appear to be the most vulnerable to erosion, but studies claim that the factors causing this erosion vary from location to location.

The third and last type of wave erosion is along canals and bayous. These canals and bayous are natural and human-made waterways that are widening as a result of bank erosion. Wind is less important in this type of erosion; boat wakes and tidal energy seem to be the most important factors.

Several studies have documented canal widening from ship traffic; tidal energy in estuaries has also contributed to barrier island erosion. It is highly likely that boat wake erosion in canals and bayous is more destructive to adjacent marshes than tidal erosion.

Subsidence, or sinking of the wetlands happens when they are no longer replenished by water-borne sediments and become very compacted and sink under the open water. Subsidence is also caused by subsurface withdrawal of oil and gas, as withdrawal from strata less than 10,000 feet below the surface can cause the surface of the land to subside. Dewatering is also a factor in subsidence. When the water table is lowered due to drainage activities, the dewatered upper soils are subject to soil shrinkage, wind erosion, and bio-chemical oxidation. Urban expansion and agricultural drainage and flood control have led to extensive localized surface subsidence.

Because of these factors, the Louisiana coast began to erode, salt water crept further inland, and plant life, unable to live in salty waters, began to die. Waste from drilling operations and chemical runoff from cropland also contributed to this process. As plant life died, so did its rootmat, and as the rootmat died, the soil began to wash away with the waves. Slowly but surely the coastal wetlands began to die and erode. The marshes were no longer populated with dense rushes of alligator weed, water hyacinths, and pickerel-weed. Fresh marshes turned into saline or brackish marshes, and the typical vegetation became oystergrass, saltgrass, and winegrass.[59]

The Impact

Continued loss of the coastal wetlands will threaten most of the investment Louisiana and the nation have made along the coast and will severely diminish related job opportunities. If another 1 million acres of wetlands are lost between now and 2040, commercial fish and wildlife harvests will be down to about 70 percent of the present harvest. This loss will have a national impact, since about 46 percent of the nation's annual shrimp harvest comes from the Gulf waters of Louisiana's coastal marshes. An estimated 155 miles of banks in portions of major waterways built by federal and state governments, including the Gulf Intracoastal Waterway and the Mississippi River-Gulf Outlet, will be affected. The banks of these waterways will be lost to open water requiring increased efforts to maintain.[60]

About 55 miles of hurricane protection levees and floodwalls will have to be shielded from erosion and enlarged to maintain the current level of protection, and in some locations, new projects will have to be mounted to replace the natural protection provided by the coastal wetlands. Nearly 100 miles of federal and state highways, about 27 miles of railroad tracks, 1,570 miles of oil and gas pipelines, and 383 miles of gas, water, electric, power, and telephone lines will have to be relocated. It is estimated that about 1,800 businesses, residences, camps, schools, storage tanks, electric power substations, water control structures, and gasoline pumping stations will have to be protected or relocated. All of this additional protection and relocation because of wetlands loss will cost billions of dollars.[61]

Solutions

For the past several decades, state and federal agencies as well as private business organizations and environmental groups have studied the reasons for the wetlands loss and potential solutions. Each of these efforts has shed more light on the total problem and has confirmed that a piecemeal approach to the problems is not likely to be effective. This research has resulted in a much clearer understanding of the unique dynamics in the coastal area and has identified three approaches to wetland loss in the coastal regions.[62]

The first approach is wetland preservation, through restoring and maintaining the barrier shore and islands off the coast of the state and building freshwater diversion structures in key places along the Mississippi. The former will keep wave action from further eroding the wetlands and help control further saltwater intrusion. The latter goal involves diverting fresh water from the river and allowing controlled flooding in areas where appropriate to enable the river to replenish the wetlands as it naturally did before the levees were built to prevent flooding.[63]

The second approach is to replace lost wetlands by diverting sediment-laden waters through outlets in the riverbanks and disposing sediment dredged from navigation channels into open water areas so new marshland can develop. Throughout the wetlands of coastal Louisiana are 2,800 miles of canals and rivers that are constantly dredged to remain deep enough for navigation. Depositing this sediment back into the wetlands is a common and fruitful practice of the Corps of Engineers. The third approach is to control development in coastal wetlands so that such growth will not further destroy wetlands and add to the problem. Another reason for controlling growth is to reduce the costs associated with relocation should this become necessary.[64]

Since the early 1900s, oil and gas companies have been buying up coastal Louisiana wetlands for exploration. It has been estimated that 1.6 million acres of these wetlands are privately owned, with the oil companies owning a major share. They believe that saving the coastal wetlands is impossible because they see the problem of erosion as one of sediment starvation brought about by the levee system built to control flooding. For this reason they see no reason to prohibit dredging for either a canal or a pipeline. The whole coastal wetland area, according to some companies, will soon be open water anyway. Thus they have fought regulation of their industry.[65]

Gradually, however, a permitting process was established to help mitigate the problem. Once applied for, a permit would have to go through a 30-day public notice period during which time questions could be raised by interested parties, inside or outside of the government. The idea behind this mitigating process was to reduce the damage done to these wetlands. A project that was subject to permitting would have to be evaluated for impacts on soil and water before work could begin. If approved, a permit would then be issued with guidelines established by the EPA and the Corps of Engineers. Companies would then know from the beginning how much restoration would be needed and could determine whether it was economically feasible to continue with the project.[66]

A high priority has been the restoration of Louisiana's barrier islands. These islands are the first line of defense against the sea and storm surges from hurricanes, and efforts have been made to raise the surfaces of these islands and close their beaches. Restoration of these islands will also limit wave erosion of interior marshes and help to prevent increases in the salinity of the bays behind them limiting tidal mixing of the high-salinity waters of the open ocean. The ability of these islands to curtail wetland loss is limited, however, and these islands will not prevent wetlands from being submerged as the sea level rises nor will they prevent marsh erosion along canals and other waterways.

The diversion process plans to redirect water from the Mississippi River at three points in order to retard saltwater intrusion. It is hoped that reducing saltwater intrusion will slow down the loss of marshland and improve fish and wildlife productivity. This diversion plan has been designed by the Corps of Engineers and will be funded by a yearly dedication of at least $5 million from Louisiana's mineral revenues. Louisiana voters overwhelmingly approved establishing a Wetlands Conservation and Restoration Trust Fund, with the amount dedicated each year varying according to the price of oil but not to exceed $25 million. It is hoped that matching funds will be available from the federal government.[67]

Management of the marshes involves a variety of activities including regulation of the flow of water in and out of marsh systems, with the general goal of controlling water levels in the marshes. The size of these operations can vary from several acres to around 5,000 acres, with the larger wetland tracts being partitioned into smaller units. Water flow is usually regulated by a system of dikes or levees and some form of water control structure. Most of these plans incorporate features that prevent inflow of excess salt water and regulate the outputs or inputs of fresh water until a desired water level or salinity is reached. One of the most important advantages to this procedure is that private landowners can implement these measures themselves, and economic incentives are strong for these landowners to manage their marshes in their long-term interests.

All of these approaches are tied together into a master plan which brings together nine projects and plans that were designed by state and federal agencies to implement the three approaches we mentioned. The plan has two phases. The first phase will involve efforts to address restoring the wetlands protection function of the barrier shores and islands and encouraging wetland creation and growth. In the second phase, the focus will be on maintaining projects that were started in the first phase, and implementing the comprehensive coastal plan which is more long term in outlook. This plan will require inputs from many sources and cooperation between public agencies and private interests.[68]

A big job in saving the wetlands is educating the public about the problem and what can be done. Projects involving citizens in cleanup can do a good deal to expose the public to the problem of wetland erosion. In two projects called Coastweeks and Beachsweep, over 3,400 volunteers turned out from across the state to clean 67 miles of coastal beaches. These efforts were sponsored in part by oil companies, state and federal agencies, and environmental groups. Government agencies recognize that a major part of any effort to save the wetlands will involve public understanding and citizen support.[69]

A report compiled by a technical subcommittee of the Gulf of Mexico Program issued at the end of 1990 indicated that between 1955 and 1975, freshwater and saltwater marshes in Louisiana were being converted to open water at the rate of about 50 square miles a year, but since then the rate has slowed considerably to about half that amount. Some experts noted that this reduction of loss corresponded with the reduced rate of dredging that had been allowed and that tighter regulations on this activity were beginning to have an effect. Other argued, however, that the figures merely showed that the more fragile parts of the marshes had already disappeared, and what was left was the tougher interior wetlands that could be expected to erode at a slower rate.[70]

Specifically, the study showed that in 1984, the state of Louisiana lost 26,860 acres of wetlands, but by 1990 that loss had slowed to 15,400 acres. Up to 87 percent of wetlands loss in the southern United States in the 1960s and 1970s was due to conversion of land to agricultural uses, but that much of the wetlands along the Gulf Coast was also giving way to open water. The cost of an acre of wetlands varies. The salt marshes could be replaced at a cost of about $10,000 per acre, but the forested swamp would cost $50,000 an acre or more to restore. The report also indicated that a 1 percent loss of wetlands in the Gulf amounted to a 1 percent loss in the shrimp harvest.[71]

At the end of 1990, a new bill was making its way through the federal government that involved several projects which would be funded by about $35 million a year from the federal gasoline tax. The state would match 25 percent of the federal contribution that would be reduced to 15 percent as soon as the state developed a no-net-loss plan requiring developers to create wetlands to compensate for those they destroy. The first projects financed by the money were likely to be those designed to restore marshland with river bottom material dredged by the Corps of Engineers, with some of the money eventually going to more complex projects such as diverting fresh water from rivers into coastal bays and marshes.[72]

Another bill, however, introduced in 1991, would drastically alter the way permits are issued for wetlands destruction. At the present time, the EPA can veto any permit issued by the Corps of Engineers for development if it determines the environmental damage would be too great. The new bill would eliminate the EPA's authority over wetlands development and would also require the federal government to buy all of the prime wetlands it believes should be protected. The EPA believed the bill would create a system with much more impetus to develop wetlands rather than protect them. This bill was introduced as part of the controversy over the definition of wetlands issued in 1990 that sparked such controversy and caused many in Congress to abandon the existing wetlands regulatory system. All Louisiana congressmen except one supported the bill to limit the EPA's authority.[73]

And so the wetlands controversy continues and is subject to political and economic pressures. Something like sustainable development is probably the most sensible approach to take with respect to the wetlands, for if they continue to erode, there are not going to be enough wetlands left to develop, and those states like Louisiana that have a large proportion of the nation's wetlands will be impoverished. The situation is serious as many people's lives are at stake, and calls for an increased sensitivity of business and government leaders as well as the public to the unique ecology of the region and the importance of wetlands to the life of the region. There are lessons to be learned here that are important for all regions of the country.

Questions for Discussion

1. What are coastal wetlands? What benefits do coastal wetlands provide for humans? What ecological functions do they perform? Why do many people regard these areas as worthless?

2. What are inland wetlands? Give some examples of the different types of inland wetlands around the country. What ecological functions do they perform? Were you aware of these functions before reading this chapter?

3. What are the major causes of wetlands destruction and degradation? What has been the extent of destruction across the country? Why are the wetlands a prime area for development?

4. Describe what is happening to the Everglades. How is the fate of Florida cities like Miami tied up with what happens there? What can be done about the problem?

5. What are the various actions that can be taken to preserve wetlands? What is the government doing? What actions can private parties take to deal with the problem? What actions do you think will be most effective?

6. Describe the controversy over the no-net-loss policy with respect to wetlands. How are wetlands defined? What problems does this definition cause? What is the current status of this controversy? Are wetlands being adequately protected?

7. What is happening to coastlines and sea levels around the country? Why is this happening? What choices do communities near the ocean have if these conditions worsen? What is being done about the problem? What strategies do you recommend?

8. What is happening to coastal wetlands in Louisiana? What services do these wetlands provide for the state and country? How will these functions be affected if coastal erosion continues?

9. What, in your opinion, is the most important cause of wetlands destruction? Are some of these causes a surprise? Do they show what harm can be done through ignorance of ecology?

10. What solutions are being attempted or proposed? Which of these solutions seems to be the most effective? Which are most feasible? What is the current status of the bill mentioned at the end of the chapter? Has it helped or hurt the situation?

NOTES

1. G. Tyler, *Living in the Environment,* 6th ed. (Belmont, CA: Wadsworth, 1990), p. 120.

2. Ibid.

3. United States Environmental Protection Agency, *America's Wetlands: Our Vital Link Between Land and Water* (Washington, DC: Office of Wetlands Protection, 1988), p. 1.

4. Miller, *Living in the Environment,* p. 122.

5. EPA, *America's Wetlands,* p. 4.

6. United States Environmental Protection Agency, *Environmental Progress and Challenges: EPA's Update* (Washington, DC: U.S. Government Printing Office, 1988), p. 60.

7. EPA, *America's Wetlands,* p. 2.

8. Ibid., p. 4.

9. Ibid., p. 6.

10. Miller, *Living in the Environment,* p. 129.

11. Ibid.

12. Ibid., p. 128.

13. James Carney, "Last Gasp for the Everglades," *Time,* September 25, 1989, p. 26.

14. Ibid., pp. 26–27.

15. David Snyder, "Florida Drains Hopes, Aquifers Dry," *Times-Picayune,* March 4, 1990, p. A-1.

16. EPA, *America's Wetlands,* p. 6.

17. Richard Lipkin, "Plans That Are Habit-Forming," *Insight,* November 6, 1989, p. 56.

18. EPA, *America's Wetlands,* p. 8.

19. Ibid.

20. Ibid.

21. United States Environmental Protection Agency, *Meeting the Environmental Challenge* (Washington, DC: U.S. Government Printing Office, 1990), p. 5.

22. Ibid.

23. Ibid.

24. EPA, *Environmental Progress and Challenges,* p. 61.

25. EPA, *America's Wetlands,* pp. 8–9.

26. Bob Marshall, "Bush Lets Industry Shove Wetlands," *Times-Picayune,* February 18, 1990, p. C-16.

27. Rick Raber, "New Definition of Wetlands Bogs Down Some La. Farmers," *Times-Picayune,* April 21, 1990, p. A-1.

28. Ibid.

29. Ibid.

30. EPA, *America's Wetlands,* p. 30.

31. Jodi L. Jacobson, "Holding Back the Sea," *State of the World 1990* (Washington, DC: Worldwatch Institute, 1990), p. 86.

32. Michael D. Lemonick, "Shrinking Shores," *Time,* August 10, 1987, pp. 40–41.

33. Ibid., p. 41.

34. Jacobson, "Holding Back the Sea," pp. 86–87.

35. Ibid., p. 81.

36. Ibid., pp. 83–84.

37. Ibid., p. 85.

38. Ibid., p. 92.

39. Ibid., p. 93.

40. Ibid., p. 95.

41. Lemonick, "Shrinking Shores," p. 47.

42. Ibid.

43. United States Army Corps of Engineers, *Crisis on Louisiana's Coast America's Loss* (New Orleans: New Orleans District, 1989), p. 2.

44. Ibid., p. 1.

45. Ibid., p. 2.

46. Interview with John Wong, Manager, Environmental Division, C.H. Fenstermaker and Associates, Inc., Civil Engineers, Land Surveyors, and Environmental Consultants, New Orleans, Louisiana, as quoted in Stewart T. Gibert, "Management of an Asset: The Louisiana Delta Wetlands," unpublished paper, College of Business Administration, Loyola University, New Orleans, Louisiana, 1990, p. 9.

47. Corps of Engineers, *Crisis on Louisiana's Coast,* p. 4.

48. Ibid.

49. Ibid.

50. Robert Chabrelk and Greg Linscombe, *Vegetative Type Map of the Louisiana Coastal Marshes* (Baton Rouge: Louisiana Department of Wildlife and Fisheries, 1987), pp. 23-24.

51. Coalition to Restore Coastal Louisiana, *Coastal Louisiana: Here Today, Gone Tomorrow?* (Baton Rouge: Author, 1989), pp. 21-22.

52. Paul G. Kemp, Remarks made to a class on Environmental Issues for Management, College of Business Administration, Loyola University, New Orleans, spring semester, 1990.

53. Corps of Engineers, *Crisis on Louisiana's Coast,* p. 6.

54. Ibid., pp. 5-6.

55. United States Army Corps of Engineers, "Atchafalaya Outlet," Mississippi River Commission pamphlet, p. 2.

56. Corps of Engineers, *Crisis on Louisiana's Coast,* p. 6.

57. Ibid., p. 8.

58. Ibid., p. 9.

59. Interview with Mike Windham, a Refuge Project Manager with the Louisiana Wildlife and Fisheries, New Orleans District, as quoted in Stewart T. Gibert, "Management of an Asset: The Louisiana Delta Wetlands," unpublished paper, College of Business Administration, Loyola University, New Orleans, 1990, p. 14.

60. Corps of Engineers, *Crisis on Louisiana's Coast,* p. 9.

61. Ibid.

62. Ibid., p. 10.

63. Ibid.

64. Ibid., p. 11.

65. United States Senate, *The Louisiana Coastal Wetlands Conservation and Restoration Act,* Committee on Environment and Public Works, Subcommittee on Environmental Protection, August 2, 1989, pp. 1-225.

66. Interview with John Wong, as quoted in Gibert, "Management of an Asset," p. 29.

67. Louisiana Department of Natural Resources, Creation of Wetlands Trust Fund Approved, October 1989, p. 3.

68. Corps of Engineers, *Crisis on Louisiana's Coast,* pp. 11-12.

69. Gibert, "Management of an Asset," pp. 45-46.

70. Christopher Cooper, "La. Wetlands Loss Reported Slowing," *Times-Picayune,* December 5, 1990, p. B-3.

71. Ibid.

72. Rick Raber, "Bill May Pave Way for Saving Wetlands," *Times-Picayune,* October 30, 1990, p. B-3.

73. James O'Byrne, "EPA Chief: Bill Will Bog Down Wetlands Work," *Times-Picayune,* April 11, 1991, p. B-3. See also James Gill, "Selling the State Down the River," *Times-Picayune,* April 14, 1991, p. B-7.

~

SUGGESTED READINGS

Bingham, Gail, ed. *Issues in Wetlands Protection*. Washington, DC: Conservation Foundation, 1990.

Burke, David G., et al. *Protecting National Wetlands*. Washington, DC: National Planning Association, 1989.

Coalition to Restore Coastal Louisiana. *Coastal Louisiana: Here Today, Gone Tomorrow?* Baton Rouge: Author, 1989.

Daiber, Franklin C. *Conservation of Tidal Marshes*. New York: Van Nostrand Reinhold, 1986.

Kelley, Joseph T., et al. *Living with the Louisiana Shore*. Durham, NC: Duke University Press, 1984.

Mitsch, William J., and James G. Gosselink. *Wetlands*. New York: Van Nostrand Reinhold, 1986.

National Wildlife Federation. *Status Report of Our Nation's Wetlands*. Washington, DC: Author, 1987.

Office of Technology Assessment. *Wetlands: Their Use and Regulation*. Washington, DC: U.S. Government Printing Office, 1984.

Pilkey, Orin H., Jr., and William J. Neal, eds. *Living with the Shore*. Durham, NC: Duke University Press, 1987.

Simon, Anne W. *The Thin Edge: Coast and Man in Crisis*. New York: Harper & Row, 1978.

Tiner, Ralph W., Jr. *Wetlands of the United States: Current Status and Recent Changes*. Washington, DC: U.S. Government Printing Office, 1984.

United States Army Corps of Engineers. *Crisis on Louisiana's Coast America's Loss*. New Orleans: New Orleans District, 1989.

United States Environmental Protection Agency. *America's Wetlands: Our Vital Link Between Land and Water*. Washington, DC: Office of Wetlands Protection, 1988.

Van Beek, Johannes L., and K. J. Meyer-Arendt. *Louisiana's Eroding Coastline: Recommendations for Protection*. Baton Rouge: Louisiana Department of Natural Resources, 1982.

CHAPTER 12

STRATEGIES FOR BUSINESS

~

The environmental issues we have discussed have had a profound impact on business organizations with both short and long-run implications. In the short run, business organizations face a host of costly regulations that complicate management and require new procedures and techniques that enable business to comply in a cost-effective manner. Business also must cope with a litigious environment and thus must adopt new ways of protecting itself, for example, by performing environmental audits or investigating potential environmental liability when buying land for expansion or considering a merger with another company. A whole new set of considerations has become important to management that must be factored into the decision-making process.

In the long run, business must consider new forms of organizational structures and processes that will enable it to respond to a changing environment in an evermore responsible fashion. There is no turning back to a simpler world where environmental impacts were limited to a few considerations that were mostly economic in nature. Business must now recognize the environment as a major factor in decision making that has long-run implications for the way it does business and the relationships it develops with its stockholders. Already in many companies, structures have changed to permit environmental input from very high levels of the company, in most cases in the form of a vice president for environmental affairs or a similar title. Manufacturing processes too must change to minimize waste and allow for more recycling as we discuss in greater detail later.

In a nutshell, business as well as society as a whole must take responsibility for the environment and manage its environmental responsibilities

369

the way it manages other parts of the business. Managers must learn how to take into account the impacts of their operations on ecosystems and habitats in order to promote sustainable operations that do not undermine the possibilities of economic growth for future generations. Business operations are at the heart of sustainable development because no other organization in our society has such an impact on the environment. Consequently, no other organization has the possibility of making such a positive contribution to sustainable development.

Such changes, however, call for new kinds of thinking and new strategies regarding the environment. While new technologies and products introduced by business have greatly enhanced living standards in many parts of the world, many adverse effects on the environment have also been created. Some of these adverse effects have been brought under some degree of control, but as populations around the world increase and people strive for a higher and higher standard of living, some of the old solutions to industrial pollution and the disposal of industrial wastes are no longer workable. New strategies have to be developed that are responsive to a changing environment.

Some experts claim that by 2030 there will be 10 billion people on this planet, all of whom would like to enjoy a living standard that is roughly equivalent to the advanced industrial democracies. But if all these people were to consume critical natural resources such as copper, cobalt, petroleum, and nickel at current U.S. rates, and if new resources are not discovered or substitutes developed, such living standards could be supported by existing resources for only a decade or less. On the other side of the ledger regarding waste disposal, at current U.S. rates, 10 billion people would generate 400 billion tons of solid waste every year, which is enough to bury greater Los Angeles under 100 meters of such waste material.[1]

Clearly, such growth is not possible. And yet, no one has really come to grips with this kind of reality. Changes are taking place in the world that have profound implications for manufacturing as we have known it in the past. The citizens of Eastern Europe, who have recently freed themselves from decades of communist rule, are attempting to establish democracies and some kind of market system to provide more goods and services for their people. Changes in this part of the world alone have profound implications for resource usage and waste disposal. And none of this says anything about Third World nations and their aspirations for a better life for their citizens.

STRATEGIES FOR MANUFACTURING

It should be clear to even the most casual observer that the present system of manufacturing has to be radically changed to even begin to provide for the needs of all the world's people for higher living standards. The traditional model of industrial activity is one in which raw materials are used by manufacturing processes to produce products to be sold to enhance people's standard of living, and waste material is generated to be disposed of in some fashion. This kind of industrial process exists in market economies as well as centrally planned ones. The major difference is that centrally planned economies are not as efficient or as productive as market economies, and thus do not produce as high a standard of living, nor do they, as we are now learning, mitigate their environmental problems as successfully as market economies.

But while market economies may be able to generate a higher standard of living for those people served by such economies, the industrial system that is at the heart of these economies must be changed. What some experts advocate is an industrial system that is more integrated, an industrial ecosystem if you will, where consumption of energy and raw materials is optimized, waste generation is minimized, and the effluents of one process serve as the raw material for another process. There must be more incentive for recycling, conservation, and a switch to alternative materials than the present system contains, and these incentives must lead to a different kind of manufacturing system than we know at present.[2]

It is recommended that we think of the industrial system as an analogue of biological ecosystems, where conservation and recycling are readily apparent. There is much that we could learn, for example, from the way the rain forests operate and the efficient manner in which nutrients are recycled and a rich growth is supported even though the soil underneath is poor in nutrients. While such an ideal manufacturing ecosystem may never be attained in practice, it can serve as a model on which to base our strategies for the future. Manufacturers and consumers must change their habits to approach this ideal more closely, it is said, if the industrialized world is to maintain its present standard of living and if developing nations are to raise theirs to a similar level without seriously degrading the environment to a point where living standards of the kind we now enjoy are simply no longer sustainable.[3]

If changes of this sort are embraced by industrialized and developing nations, it may be possible to develop a more closed industrial ecosystem that is more sustainable in light of decreasing supplies of raw materials and increasing problems with pollution and waste disposal. While industrial nations will have to make many changes in their current manufacturing practices, some of which will be major in nature, developing nations will have to leapfrog older technologies that are less ecologically sound and adopt new industrial methods which are more compatible with the ecosystem approach and more environmentally sustainable.[4]

Manufacturing processes simply transform stocks of materials from one shape to another. The circulating stock decreases when some material is unavoidably lost as waste material, and the stock increases to meet the needs of a growing population. An industrial ecosystem based on recycling and waste minimization still requires the use of energy and will still generate some waste material and harmful by-products, but at much lower and sustainable levels than are typical with today's system. Industrial processes are required that minimize the generation of unrecyclable wastes and minimize the permanent consumption of scarce material and energy resources. But industrial processes cannot be considered in isolation. They must be linked together and considered as part of a whole system.[5]

The incentives for such changes are already beginning to appear. Waste minimization activities have been aided by regulations to control both solid and hazardous waste disposal. These regulations reflecting long-term environmental costs have increased disposal costs to the point where alternatives to disposal are economically feasible. Many companies are finding it profitable to sell their wastes as raw materials. Other companies are finding it profitable to reuse their own wastes by designing recycling loops in their own manufacturing processes and saving a great deal of money by minimizing the amount of final waste product they create.[6]

The manufacturing process represents only the supply side of the industrial ecosystem where harmful by-products and effluents are created that have to be disposed of in some fashion. The consumer who buys products and throws things away is the demand side of the equation. Materials that are discarded by consumers are the raw materials for the next cycle of production. Changes in manufacturing must be matched by changes in demand patterns if the industrial ecosystem approach is to be fully implemented, and by changes in the treatment of materials once they have reached the end of their useful life. An effective infrastructure for the collection and segregation of various types of wastes can dramatically improve the efficiency of the industrial ecosystem. Since landfills for municipal wastes are becoming harder to find, consumers also face incentives for waste reduction.[7]

Creation of a sustainable industrial ecosystem is highly desirable from an environmental perspective and can also be profitable for companies and consumers. But corporate and public attitudes must change to favor this approach and government regulations must become more flexible so as to encourage recycling and strategies for waste minimization. Regulations, according to some experts, sometimes make waste minimization more difficult than waste disposal. Buying of hazardous wastes, for example, even where they could be used as raw materials, is difficult because of strict requirements for handling and documenting of these wastes, to say nothing of the potential liability the company may face if an accident happens. These regulations discourage innovative treatment of wastes, and many companies choose to avoid these risks and buy their materials through conventional channels.[8]

Regulations typically focus on end-of pipe disposal practices, and provide no advantages for manufacturers who capture and treat low-level effluents or who shift to production processes with more benign by-products. Thus companies have to meet regulatory requirements, but have no incentive to develop more innovative practices that will reduce their waste material. Instead of rules regarding waste disposal, some economists advocate financial incentives to reduce pollution in the form of fees or taxes imposed on manufacturers according to the amount and nature of the hazardous materials they produce. These fees and taxes would give them an incentive to change their manufacturing processes to reduce hazardous waste production, and would make environmental costs internal so they can be taken into account when making production decisions.[9]

Such techniques might make it more feasible to solve environmental problems at the source where they are created in the first place, rather than to focus on destroying or disposing of effluents once they have been created. Manufacturers would be able to share in the overall economic savings that accrued from reduced levels of hazardous materials, and would harness strong economic incentives to reduce costs and gain competitive advantages in the marketplace. Manufacturers that ignore these incentives do not stay in business, and allocating the social costs of pollution would assure that only those manufacturers who were environmentally sensitive would stay in business.[10]

But such economic incentives may not be enough. Some kind of holistic approach will be required if a proper balance is to be maintained between narrowly defined economic benefits and environmental needs consistent with a sustainable society. The concepts of industrial ecology and system optimization must be taught more widely in engineering and business schools and must be recognized and valued by public officials and industrial leaders. Such values and approaches must be instilled into the society and reflected in the policies and procedures adopted by government and industry.[11]

Regulation must avoid counterproductive control measures such as appears to be the case with Superfund regulations. But a regulatory framework that is rational and efficient will be impossible to construct unless government, industry, and environmental groups learn to overcome their current adversarial relationships and work together to solve shared problems. This will only come about if there are shared values with respect to the environment, and shared agreement on strategies relative to what needs to be done to create a sustainable society. Education about ecology and environmental issues can help to create these common values and agreement on what strategies will work to the advantage of the entire society.[12]

Creation of an ideal industrial ecosystem, where use of energy and materials is optimized, wastes and pollution are minimized, and where there is an economically viable role for every product of a manufacturing process, will not be easy to attain. But the incentives are beginning to change and point in this direction. Companies will be able to minimize costs and stay competitive through adhering to an ecological approach to manufacturing where ecological costs and benefits are taken into account. It is also becoming clear that societies will only have a chance to raise their living standards if they take environmental sustainability into account in the policies and consumption patterns they adopt. Coming to recognize that people and their technologies are a part of the natural world may make it possible to imitate the best workings of biological ecosystems and construct artificial ones that are sustainable.[13]

WASTE MINIMIZATION PROGRAMS

One of the key issues concerning our present system of industrial manufacturing is what to do with all the waste generated, particularly that which is considered to be hazardous. Even if business is able to comply with the latest waste disposal regulations, and even if existing dumpsites that pose a threat to human health and the environment are "cleaned up" using the best technology available, this waste material has to go somewhere. Who is to say that our present methods of waste disposal won't also cause problems for future generations? In some sense, we may be just moving the problem around by cleaning up existing dumpsites and disposing of the waste in a so-called more appropriate manner.

In some sense, the disposal of waste has become more of a political than a technical problem. The driving force behind the cleanup of hazardous waste dumps and proper disposal of newly generated waste is public concern. The public is afraid of dumpsites and wants them cleaned up as soon as possible. The public agenda in these situations is often set by the news media. Politicians then start to take notice and bills are passed that create new programs to deal with the problem. Agencies that implement these programs see an opportunity for more money and public visibility by keeping the issue in the headlines. While industry might like to keep a low profile and get the situation corrected without a great deal of media exposure, they are often unable to do this as the issue is played out in the public arena. Industry is assigned responsibility as well as blame for the problem, and ends up footing most of the bill for the cleanup.

Existing sites are obviously not getting cleaned up as rapidly and effectively as possible, given the time and resources that are being devoted to the effort. One way to understand the problem is to look at the incentive mechanisms that exist for some of the players in the game of cleanup. If there are disputes involving liability for the cleanup, law firms stand to benefit, and they will benefit more the longer the dispute continues. Engineering consultants benefit from investigations, not from compromise, and if the state and potentially responsible parties are in some kind of battle, they stand to benefit more from duplication of studies. Public agencies will decide based on the political benefits to themselves, and this may not be consistent with public benefits. If they can convince the public that corporations are bad guys and can't be trusted, they can then find justification to direct the effort themselves and ask for more money to expand their department in order to get the job done.

Companies themselves have an incentive to clean up existing dumpsites where they are potentially responsible parties as quickly and efficiently as possible. In most, if not all cases, they want to get these messy situations behind them and get on with the job of producing goods and services. Yet companies are often not in control of cleanup situations when they become highly politicized. They are at a disadvantage in relation to a state or federal agency that is in a better position to play political gamesmanship. Companies often have very little control over a situation that may require them to spend millions of dollars.

The average cost of cleaning up a site is about $25 million, and many companies face liabilities in 40 to 100 sites. Since the Superfund Act seems to encourage litigation more than anything else, some way must be found to provide more incentives to develop new technologies for effective and permanent disposal. The EPA currently controls the selection of technology for treatment and the cleanup standards to be attained. Where states are involved, the state itself may control these aspects of the situation.

The ultimate solution to this waste disposal problem, if there is one, seems to be one of not producing so much waste in the first place. This approach has been called waste minimization, and involves a new way of thinking about the generation of waste material. This concept typically involves four stages: (1) prevention of waste generation at the source through redesign of products, (2) recycling or reuse of waste material to recover useful products, (3) treatment of wastes such as incineration to reduce toxicity, and (4) disposal of remaining waste material in an appropriate manner. Many companies are focusing their efforts on the first two stages where the benefits can be substantial. The 3M Company has a waste reduction program called "Pollution Prevention Pays" and Dow Chemical has one called "Waste Reduction Always Pays" that are good examples of waste minimization programs.

Pollution Prevention Pays

In 1975, 3M Corporation unveiled its "Pollution Prevention Pays" program (the 3Ps Program). Its goal was to eliminate or reduce sources of pollution in 3M products and processes, in other words, to stop creating pollution in the first place. The 3Ps Program was born out of the environmental awareness of the early 1970s. New federal and state environmental laws and regulations emerged in abundance, restricting pollutant releases and tightening requirements for pollution monitoring and reporting. Companies like 3M took the necessary steps to comply, usually by installing conventional end-of-line controls. The advantage of these "add-ons" was time, as in most cases, standard control equipment could be installed to achieve the desired reductions in a short time period. Regulations often encouraged this approach by specifying a type of technology or equipment that should be installed in order to comply with regulations, rather than specifying a general compliance standard. In other words, government agencies specified how a goal should be accomplished rather than indicating what should be accomplished and letting industry find ways of getting there.[14]

At 3M, the chairman and CEO at the time, Raymond H. Herzog, responded to stricter regulation with a firm position, indicating that the company would comply with existing regulations. Nevertheless, he understood the potentially high cost of end-of-line control and recognized a developing corporate problem in the strong negative reactions of plant and operating division managers to increasing pollution control regulations. While these people agreed with the general intent of the regulations, they were quite concerned about investments with no return and encroachment on their management responsibilities.[15]

Multimillion-dollar capital expenditures add to production costs over the short and long term, harming the competitive position of products and the company as a whole. Thus Herzog was motivated to find a way to meet environmental requirements and keep 3M's products cost competitive. In response to the CEO's request, the corporate environmental staff developed a positive, voluntary employee recognition program optimistically entitled "Pollution Prevention Pays." Recognition was given to projects that (1) prevented pollution, (2) had a return consistent with corporate expectations, and (3) had some innovative content. The program emphasized prevention of pollution rather than control after it was generated.[16] Under the 3Ps Program, technical innovation to prevent pollution and generation of waste at the source is encouraged through the following:

- *Product reformulation:* the development of nonpolluting or less polluting products or processes by using different raw materials or feedstocks.
- *Process modification:* changing manufacturing processes to control by-product formation or to incorporate nonpolluting or less polluting raw materials or feedstocks.
- *Equipment redesign:* modifying equipment to perform better under specific operating conditions or to make use of available resources (such as by-product steam from another process).
- *Resource recovery:* recycling by-products (for sale or for use in other 3M products or processes).[17]

These concepts, of course, were not new at the time they were implemented, but the 3Ps Programs did represent the first organized application of pollution prevention principles throughout one company worldwide. The program has worked because technical employees at every level have become aware that pollution prevention is an important part of their jobs. Further, many engineers and scientists at 3M have a personal interest in environmental protection and conservation. The 3P Program is their opportunity to act on personal concerns while helping their careers, their professions, and their company. Engineering, manufacturing, and laboratory employees have an additional investment in 3P because the selection process is in their hands.[18]

The 3P selection process has a number of stages. Any technical employee or group of employees can nominate a project for 3P by filling out a standard evaluation sheet. Each application is reviewed by a coordinating committee made up of representatives from all the technical groups. This committee meets quarterly to discuss the entries from all 3M locations. On awards day, plaques and official recognition go to individual technical people; managers and supervisors are recognized only if they have made a hands-on contribution. In practice, the 3P program is a composite of individual environmental audits, mini-audits performed every day by individuals looking for a better way to reduce pollution and generation of waste material at the source.[19]

With the program in place for several years, 3M claims it is now seeing a significant environmental payoff, as worldwide annual releases of air, water, sludge, and solid waste pollutants for 3M facilities have been reduced by nearly 450,000 tons. The product and process changes made to achieve these reductions have yielded a secondary benefit in the form of substantial operating savings of $420 million. These numbers are said to be conservative, considering that they are based on first-year-only results — how production costs (operating and maintenance costs, feedstock and raw material costs, and equipment costs) were affected in the first year of project operation.[20] From its beginning in 1975, the company expected four payoffs from the 3Ps Program:

- Improved environment
- Conserved resources
- Improved technologies
- Reduced costs

These benefits are the same criteria by which 3P projects have been judged. That is, projects have been evaluated by the coordinating committee for their success in reducing pollution, saving resources and money, and advancing technology and/or engineering practice. Over the years the program has been in place, 2,261 projects have been recognized for accomplishing these objectives. Worldwide the company has realized the following totals for pollution prevented annually (totals for U.S. operations in parentheses):[21]

- Air pollutants   121,072 tons (110,260 tons)
- Water pollutants   14,550 tons (13,450 tons)
- Sludge and solid waste   314,000 tons (303,000 tons)
- Wastewater   1,602 billion gallons (1 billion gallons)

These results amounted to a reduction of waste streams to all media (the program was multimedia) that are roughly one-half the size today they would have been without these projects. The program moved 3M up the waste management hierarchy, and it helped fit environmental protection more neatly into the overall corporate strategy. And while many projects were not initiated because of their effect on waste streams, the fact that they did have an effect was not lost on the employees. After a time, they began looking for waste streams to reduce profitably.[22]

Projects that have been implemented ranged from improved control of process coating weight at a plant in Wales, to recovery of waste ammonium sulfate from a 3M factory in Minnesota, to better tank cleaning at an Illinois plant that makes adhesives, resins, and polymers. In most cases, the savings and efficiencies have resulted not from the use of new or unusual technology but from the creative application of familiar materials, processes, and technologies.[23]

Through some 3P changes, the company claims to have garnered benefits beyond those originally identified. Various projects have improved employee safety and comfort, reduced equipment downtime, and increased productivity. Relationships with regulators have benefited, too, from a new spirit of industry-government cooperation. Industry awareness has also been heightened about the possibilities and rewards of prevention. 3M's contribution to the latter was recognized in 1985 when the company received the first Award for International Corporate Environmental Achievement from the World Environment Center.[24]

What the 3P Program did not do was totally eliminate the company's waste streams. The best light we can put on the program is that the company reports its waste streams today are growing at a lesser rate than their manufacturing output. This is not an accomplishment that is satisfactory in today's climate. The corporation has realized this and initiated a global program to control voluntarily all major air emission sources by 1993, a program that will have two effects.[25]

First, it will reduce 3M's air emission waste streams to a level compatible with corporate desires for responsible environmental protection. This short-term program will complete with available technology what the 3P Program started but could not accomplish. Second, the controls chosen are mostly treatment options. They will be expensive to operate, maintain, and replace. This will add more economic justification to longer term 3P Programs aimed at reducing or eliminating those air emission waste streams. A similar program is being considered for Resource Conservation and Recovery Act waste streams.

In summary, the 3P Program broke some new ground, substantially reduced the company's reliance on pollution controls, but was not a panacea for eliminating the continuing need for treatment and disposal. Substantial further waste reduction will require longer term research projects and more economic justification. In 1988, 3M initiated a new short-time phase of 3P to reduce their annual hydrocarbon emissions by more than 00,000 tons over and above reductions already achieved. Called 3P + , the program calls for a $150 million investment in air pollution control equipment that is entirely voluntary and will reduce emissions beyond the level necessary to comply with state and federal environmental regulations.[26]

Waste Reduction Always Pays

In 1986, the management of Dow Chemical U.S.A. decided to streamline and formalize its waste reduction efforts under a single program called "Waste Reduction Always Pays" (WRAP). Under this program, the company proposed to take a comprehensive approach to reducing the amount of waste material it dumped into the air, water, and land with the overall goal of reducing the amount of wastes produced by all its facilities. Waste reduction pays long-term dividends in two ways from the company's point of view: (1) when emissions are reduced, the company is making an investment in a clean and safe environment, and (2) waste reduction makes good sense from a business standpoint as where there is waste there is inefficiency, and where there is inefficiency, there is an opportunity to reduce costs.[27]

The company believes that by actively pursuing waste reduction opportunities, it can reduce its waste management costs, improve the productivity of its operations, demonstrate to the public its commitment to environmental protection, and perhaps most importantly, show that a voluntary program of waste reduction can work without government regulation. The program has the following objectives: (1) reduction of waste and emissions to the environment, (2) provision of incentives for waste reduction projects, (3) provision recognition for those who excel in waste reduction, and (4) reemphasis of the need for continuous improvement by recognizing opportunities in waste reduction.[28]

The reduction of waste and emissions to the environment involves elimination, reclamation, treatment and destruction, and the development of secure landfills. The first effort is to avoid producing waste in the first place. Through research and development efforts, Dow strives to utilize production and operating processes that have the highest efficiencies and minimize waste. When the generation of some waste is unavoidable, it is recycled back into the production process or used as a raw material for another process wherever possible. When reclamation is not possible, the waste is treated or destroyed by means of water treatment and/or incineration to eliminate it from the environment. If neither treatment or destruction are possible, the wastes are buried in a secure landfill.[29]

Providing incentives is based on the recognition that economic incentives are needed to cultivate a waste reduction mentality throughout the company. The WRAP Capital Projects Contest was started in 1988, and because of the company's decentralized approach to managing its production facilities, each division has a slightly different version of this program. In some divisions, for example, plants submit projects demonstrating waste reduction or yield improvement that contains a certain return on investment (ROI). Any project that demonstrates an improvement in waste reduction or yield improvement as measured by the ROI receives capital dollars.

In some cases, environmental expenses are charged back to the generator of the waste material, giving the plant manager a strong incentive to minimize wastes. Under this system, plant managers are charged for every pound of waste generated at their plant, with no discount for volume that requires incineration, treatment, and/or landfill. By charging these costs back to the plants, Dow focuses the issue of waste reduction back to the production process itself, prompting chemists and engineers to further improve on the production process.

One of the keys to the WRAP program is recognizing employees who do a good job in waste reduction. In the Louisiana Division, for example, the company publishes descriptions of all contest projects each year, including the names of the winners and the plants in which they work. More important is the awards presentation, which the company calls its version of the Academy Awards, where the vice president of operations presents each winner with an engraved plaque. In 1989, representatives from winning projects nationwide were brought to Washington, D.C., where Dow was conducting a waste reduction seminar, to have the awards presented by each winner's U.S. congressional representative.[30]

Finally, a Continuous Improvement Process (CIP) has been implemented to provide a constant reminder that it is always possible to improve on the present system. The program in some sense stems from a quote attributed to the founder of the company, "If you can't do it better, why do it?" The goal is to provide incentives for continual reduction of wastes until zero emissions are reached. The CIP program also provides incentives for Dow's Technology Centers to constantly improve on the process of waste reduction.[31]

The major responsibility for implementation of WRAP resides with the waste reduction coordinators located in each major plant division in the United States. Coordinating the work of these division people is a U.S. area coordinator who has no line responsibility at the division level but is responsible for overall direction of the WRAP program. The U.S. area coordinator is connected with Dow's executive management and acts as a conduit through which various policies in the waste reduction area are initiated. The WRAP coordinators in each division are responsible for communicating ideas and innovations in waste reduction to other divisions, and are in charge of generating support for the program by encouraging waste reduction ideas at the plant level.[32]

The final organizational component of the WRAP program is the waste reduction issue management team, which is a cross-functional group that works alongside the WRAP coordinators to encourage, reward, and recognize environmental waste reduction throughout the company. This team meets quarterly to discuss current environmental issues and develop strategies on how Dow can better communicate its story about waste reduction. The team also listens to outside groups in order to better understand the issue as it is perceived by people outside the company. Thus such groups as the Sierra Club, the National Wildlife Federation, and the Environmental Protection Agency are invited to meet with the team on occasion.[33]

In implementing the program, each facility has to provide a database for tracking purposes and provide a compendium of proposed or implemented projects that reduce waste. The development of a database requires that each plant develop an inventory of all its process losses to the environment, including losses to the air, water, and solids. This inventory is both quantitative and qualitative and specific as to source. These losses are expressed as a ratio of production rates to account for production variances and allow for the calculation of a weighted average for each facility. This waste index can then be tracked and evaluated by each site at some frequency. Projects that then qualify for consideration under the WRAP program must have a measurable reduction of this waste to the environment. They can be capital projects, maintenance or operational/administrative changes, and while the company would like these projects to save money, some of them may not have a return on investment that can be quantified.[34]

Each facility is also required to develop an action plan that includes the following elements: (1) an inventory of all process losses to air, water, and land, (2) identification of sources, establishment of priorities, and quantification of losses and ratio to production, (3) evaluation of environmental impact and risk, (4) setting of action priorities, (5) determination of cost-effective action, (6) setting of reduction goals, (7) determination of the resources necessary to accomplish goals, and (8) tracking and communication of performance and plans for future reductions.[35]

In 1988 and 1989, the company committed nearly $6 million to underwrite 42 projects aimed at reducing waste as part of the WRAP Capital Projects Contest. It estimates that these capital projects alone reduced waste streams by 88 million pounds annually. These capital funds were only a small part of overall waste reduction spending.[36] Such waste reduction is the cornerstone of Dow's waste management policy and plays a crucial role in environmental protection and the long-term growth of the business. While waste is an inevitable part of the manufacturing process and can never be reduced entirely, making continued compliance with state and federal laws a top priority, continuous improvement in the reduction of waste can be accomplished.[37]

Regarding the future of the program, the following challenges were stated by Dow management: (1) how to build on the initial success of the WRAP program, (2) how to extend WRAP to Dow's growing international operations, and (3) how to respond to continued pressure from environmental advocacy groups on numerous other issues. In response to the first challenge, Dow's environmental staff is considering the establishment of specific reduction goals to further institutionalize the Continuous Improvement Process in waste reduction. These goals may be difficult to implement given Dow's decentralized structure. With regard to the second challenge, Dow recognizes that it will have to work very hard to export a waste reduction mentality, particularly since significant regulatory pressures do not exist in many countries. The final challenge relates to the way in which Dow sees its role in the public policy process. The company takes a long-range approach to public policy by working closely with other groups on the issues, which often leads to a healthy debate over implementation strategies.[38]

RECYCLING

Where waste material cannot be reduced through changes in product or process design, the next strategy companies can develop is to recycle the product either back into their own production process or to make it available for some other company. Recycling means that waste materials have to be separated and collected so that they can be converted into final products that can be marketed and reused. This process involves a reorientation or rethinking of waste that stresses the importance of treating waste materials as resources. It has been suggested that waste material be thought of as resources that are out of place rather than as pollutants which have to be disposed of in some fashion.[39] Recycling is defined by the Recycling Advisory Council as follows:

> Recycling is the diversion of materials from the waste stream and their beneficial use. Recycling is the result of a series of activities by which material that would become or otherwise remain waste are diverted from the waste stream for collection, separation, and processing, and are used as raw materials or feedstocks in lieu of or in addition to virgin materials in the manufacture of goods or distributed in commerce or the reuse of such materials as substitutes for goods made from virgin materials.[40]

Most of the effort made thus far in recycling efforts has been in the area of solid waste. Many cities have developed curbside pickup systems for separated waste and have developed incentives for consumers to separate their waste, making it possible to recycle. Companies have developed office recycling systems to separate the solid waste they generate and make it more feasible to recycle, and have developed policies to use recycled materials wherever possible in order to encourage more recycling efforts. As far as manufacturing is concerned, much of the effort will focus on recycling of hazardous waste, as well as thinking about ways that recycling of solid waste can be made easier and possible with respect to the products that are produced.

The most difficult problem faced by recycling efforts has to do with the creation and maintenance of markets for recycled materials. When recycling of newspaper began to take hold in the 1980s, there was such a glut of recycled newspaper materials on the market that prices dropped significantly. Some business organizations could not sell their supply of recycled collectables because of this glut and were forced to pay for their removal.[41] As recycling programs begin to bring in unexpected amounts of collectables, fluctuations in price can be expected. In other cases, companies wanting to use more recycled material in their products cannot sometimes find enough collectables on the market. When Coca-Cola wished to implement a plan that used as much as 25 percent of recycled plastic in each new bottle, it was unable to locate enough sources of scrap material.[42]

The development of markets depends on sales of goods manufactured from recycled materials. The Coca-Cola case is unusual, because as a general rule, recycling is limited by demand and not by supply. Growth in the number of recycled goods has not matched growth of recyclers.[43] One reason that markets for recycled goods have been slow to develop is because there is a bias against products made from recycled content in favor of those made only from virgin material.[44] Americans are not easily persuaded to use recycled paper, which tends to be of a grayer hue. They prefer white paper made from virgin materials.

There is thus room for a great deal of entrepreneurship in developing products and markets for recycled materials. Companies, both large and small, have opportunities to make profits from products that are made from recycled material and sell them to environmentally conscious consumers. Surveys show that more and more people are concerned about the environment and want to buy products that promote environmental protection and enhancement and conserve resources. By the late 1980s, consumer polls showed that the environmental movement significantly affected the purchasing decisions of consumers, and by 1990, according to *U.S. News and World Report*, 73 percent of Americans saw themselves as environmentalists.[45] Some of the products that have been made to take advantage of this change in perceptions include the following:

- Reusable cotton string shopping bags. In the first six months of business, New York City–based Eco-Bags sold 60,000 bags.

- The Deja Shoe. These shoes are made in Lake Oswego, Oregon, from recycled polypropylene, paper bags, coffee filters, reclaimed scrap tires, foam rubber, and recycled metals.
- Plastic lumber, made from materials in curbside recycling programs and comparable to number 2 southern pine. Trimax of Ronkonkoma, New York, the lumber's creator, recently received a $75,000 grant from the Florida Department of Environmental Regulation to develop mooring poles.
- Reclaimed cleaning solvents. Safety-Kleen Corporation, which began this program in 1968 and earned $50,000 that first year, currently has annual revenues of $500 million.[46]

Large companies can also create markets for recycled products in their purchasing decisions. McDonald's Corporation, working with the Environmental Defense Fund, launched a major waste reduction effort in 1991 that will affect its suppliers, workers, and even customers. The company and the advocacy group announced a series of 42 initiatives aimed at cutting the waste stream by more than 80 percent at McDonald's 11,000 restaurants within a few years. Many of McDonald's 600 suppliers will have to adapt their products and packaging in order to keep doing business with the company. By December 1991, for example, all its suppliers must use corrugated boxes that contain at least 35 percent recycled content, and they will be asked to make regular reports to the company that measure their progress in reaching these waste reduction goals.[47]

Since McDonald's has annual sales of $18 billion, it has tremendous clout as a purchaser. While the potential costs for suppliers are unclear, many purchasers say they are willing to risk the expenditures if they are confident that a broader demand will develop for their recycled products. They can push ahead with efforts to use more recycled materials in their products if they are confident they have a market such as McDonald's can assure.[48] Large companies, then, can have a major impact on the market for recycled products through the purchasing decisions they make and the kind of criteria they establish for these decisions. Markets can be created overnight for recycled products in this fashion.

Plastics recycling has been a particular problem because plastic materials have a recycling rate that is far below that for glass, paper, and metals. Aluminum has been recycled at a rate above 50 percent for some years, for example, while the rate for plastics has hovered around 1 percent. Plastics are amenable to being melted down and reused the same as metal, but the public has been largely unaware that plastics are recyclable. Many curbside recycling programs have not included plastics. There are also not many companies in the country that are built to handle recycled plastic material and make it available to manufacturers who may want to use recycled plastics in their products.

But some companies are making significant efforts to encourage the recycling of plastics. Du Pont operates reclamation centers around the country that conserve 200 million pounds of plastic waste annually.[49] They also use 1 billion pounds of recycled plastics every year in their own products and plan to build capacity to reprocess 2 billion additional pounds. They also plan to produce highway barriers, signposts, and land markers with the materials.[50] Du Pont announced that they intend to build several facilities across the nation for the remanufacture of polyethylene from soda bottles, milk jugs, and other containers. This effort will be a joint venture with Waste Management, where Waste Management will collect and Du Pont will market an estimated 200 million pounds of the plastic material every year.[51]

Dow Chemical and seven other plastics manufacturers have formed the National Polystyrene Recycling Company (NPRC), whose goal is to recycle 25 percent, or 250 million pounds, of the polystyrene used for food applications in the United States every year. This goal is to be reached by 1995, with the material being recycled into a variety of nonfood packaging applications. The NPRC already recycles plastic waste from 450 McDonald's restaurants at its Boston-area recycling plant, and plans to build additional recycling facilities in San Francisco, Los Angeles, Chicago, and Philadelphia.[52]

Thus the economics of recycling is changing, and plastics recycling is the fastest growing segment of the recycling infrastructure, expected to increase at a rate of 31 percent a year for the next several years. At the present time, more than 20 percent of plastic soft drink bottles in the United States are recovered, removing nearly 175 million pounds from the waste stream. This amount is enough to fill 190,000 average-sized garbage trucks. The plastic will be reused in fibers or detergent bottles. In 1989, nearly 75 million pounds of polyethylene milk bottles became drain pipes, lumber replacements, and recycling containers.[53]

The Plastic Bottle Institute, in cooperation with its member companies, has established a nationally recognized voluntary material identification system to assist separation of plastic bottles and create a higher value for recycled material. This system is beneficial because of the uniformity it offers to bottle manufacturers and recyclers alike. Bottles are coded by the most widely used resins, and at present, applies to plastic bottles of 16-ounce capacity and larger, and to other rigid plastic containers. This system will be phased in gradually, but most bottles were expected to be coded by mid-1991, so that the benefits of the system could start to be realized. The coding system is shown in Exhibit 12.1.

One of the major structural problems with recycling on any material is that recycling benefits tend to be long term to preserve the environment for future generations. The price system that dictates how we allocate resources fails to take into account the environmental degradation that takes place and thus distorts the allocation of resources. Society as a whole is asked to bear the costs of environmental degradation and overexploitation of resources

Exhibit 12.1

Plastic Container Code System for Plastic Bottles

Code		Material
1	PETE	Polyethylene terephthalate (PET)[1]
2	HDPE	High-density polyethylene
3	V	Vinyl/polyvinyl chloride (PVC)[1]
4	LDPE	Low-density polyethylene
5	PP	Polypropylene
6	PS	Polystyrene
7	Other	All other resins and layered multimaterial

[1]Stand alone bottle code is different from standard industry identification to avoid confusion with registered trademarks.

Source: "On Earth Day, Get Involved in Plastics Recycling," published by Edgell Plastics Publications, undated.

through a dimunition of services the environment provides. This situation can be corrected by pricing raw materials in such a way so as to reflect the environmental costs of extracting them from the ground, taxing the use of virgin materials to make them more expensive, or creating markets for recycled materials to make them more cost competitive with virgin materials. All of these efforts are probably necessary to some degree to encourage more recycling of materials and to change attitudes to see waste as a resource.

DESIGN FOR DISASSEMBLY

Consistent with this emphasis on recycling and, in some sense, a strategy that is necessary for recycling to take place on the scale that may be necessary to control our waste stream, is a new concept called design for disassembly. This concept generally means the simplification of parts and materials to make them easy and inexpensive to snap apart, sort, and recycle. Taking something apart may rapidly become as important as putting something together, and design for disassembly (DFD) focuses on taking things apart easily so that the various components of a product can be used again to make other products.[54]

Several companies such as Whirlpool, Digital Equipment, 3M, and General Electric are beginning to incorporate DFD thinking in their products in order to make recycling cost effective for all kinds of complex products. BMW has a new car called the Z1 which is said to be the first real DFD product that was designed to be disassembled and recycled. The car has an all-plastic skin that can be disassembled from its metal chassis in 20 minutes, and has doors, bumpers, and front, rear, and side panels made of recyclable thermoplastic. BMW also has a pilot disassembly plant where it chops apart five cars a day to learn new things about DFD, such as the use of pop-in, pop-out two-way fasteners facilitates disassembly whereas glue and screws are to be avoided.[55]

Composites, which combine glass, metals, plastics, and other fibers, make coding and separation of materials nearly impossible and are enemies of recycling. A good example of a composite product that made the news is the palm-sized juice boxes that have become so popular in recent years. These boxes are safe to use and provide good nutrition, but are impossible to recycle. The box is made of five layers of paper and plastic, and a sixth layer of aluminum foil that prevents light and oxygen from entering and spoiling the food. It is said that milk can be safely kept in these packages for five months without refrigeration.[56]

These ultraslim layers, however, make the box difficult to recycle. The layers would have to be separated, making recycling impossible to justify on a cost-effective basis. Because of this difficulty, the state of Maine banned use of the juice boxes in order to prevent them from crowding the state's landfills. Other states were considering similar bans, causing the makers of the boxes to launch a $3 million lobbying campaign. They claimed that their boxes used less packaging material than larger sized glass and metal containers, and that they could be recycled without separating all the layers of material. In order to prove this latter claim, one of the manufacturers was financing a $1.6 million operation to recycle used plastics into wood substitutes.[57]

Another example of a product designed along DFD principles is an electric kettle that can boil water faster than a stove and is made of easily disassembled parts that facilitate recycling. The kettle was made by snapping parts together and took several trials before it was acceptable as a consumer product, but it finally began to be sold in upscale stores across the country. The manufacturer of the product, an organization called Polymer Solutions, plans to produce other products utilizing DFD concepts, including items for the computer, communications, banking, and vending-machine industries. This concept may catch on in many other companies and enable recycling to be done on an even larger scale in the future.[58]

MARKETING STRATEGIES

The success of many of these manufacturing strategies, particularly recycling, depends on consumer demand for recycled and easily disposable products that do not add to the waste disposal problem. Thus the birth of so-called green marketing, which is a response companies have made to an increasing demand for environmentally sensitive products. The products in the green market include biodegradable products, recycled products, and more fuel-efficient cars and appliances. Consumers are increasingly becoming concerned about the environment, and this concern is showing up in the marketplace in the kind of products these consumers are willing to buy.

Wal-Mart was the first retailer to publicly call for more environmentally friendly products from vendors and tag shelves to highlight environmental improvements in products and packaging. The tag does not say a product is safe for the environment, but only that improvements have been made in the product to minimize its environmental impact. The retailer works with vendors and typically asks them what improvements have been made in their product to make it more environmentally friendly. In a more recent effort, the company has also set up recycling centers in the parking lots of its 1,511 stores and is encouraging recycling in TV commercials.[59]

Many companies, like Procter & Gamble, have begun to advertise the environmentally sensitive features of their products. When first introduced in the 1960s, disposable diapers like the Pampers produced by P&G were hailed by many to be the product breakthrough of the decade. They were consistent with the throwaway society mentality of that era, and facilitated care of babies by parents who wanted to save time and effort. These diapers, however, became the focus of public concern about garbage, and even though they constituted only 1 to 2 percent of the total solid waste stream, they were singled out as representative of the problem with the throwaway society.[60]

The issue heated up in February 1989, when the National Association of Diaper Services and Environmental Action, which was a consumer activist group, announced a $100,000 nationwide public education campaign to tell the country about the environmental cost of using disposable diapers. Disposable diapers were called "ecological booby traps that stuff the nation's landfills with an unhealthy legacy of virtually indestructible paper and plastic time capsules." The use of reusable cloth diapers was advocated as the solution to the problem, and would reduce the more than 18 billion diapers that have to be landfilled each year, according to the organization.[61]

In response, P&G discovered that some 80 percent of the diapers could be successfully composted, and is working to increase this percentage by replacing the plastic backsheet liner, waistband, and tape tabs with other material. The biggest problem, however, is that most communities do not have composting facilities, so the company created a $20 million solid waste composting fund to help communities analyze solid waste problems and fund composting research. These composting initiatives are hoped to protect its leadership in the $3.5 billion disposable diaper industry, and counter claims other companies are making about the biodegradability of their products. The company believes that biodegradable diapers are not a solution to the problem because of the difficulty of any product to biodegrade in a landfill.[62]

The biodegradability issue surfaced as many companies began to advertise these features of their products in order to appeal to the emerging green consumer market. Most of these claims were false, as they failed to inform the consumer that biodegradable products need sunlight to decompose, and when buried under tons of other trash and dirt do not receive sunlight under normal conditions. Thus the consumer was being misled. Mobil Corporation was caught in this controversy when it launched its line of biodegradable Hefty trash bags to counter the competition which had beaten it to the market with biodegradable products. Soon after this introduction, biodegradability became a dirty word and Mobil became caught in the middle with six separate state lawsuits that could take years to resolve.[63]

About five years ago, Mobil began to feel the pressure from environmentalists as one of the largest producers of all-plastic packaging. Degradability was then viewed as the ecological cure for the plastics industry by consumer and environmental groups, and marketers began making a push to make degradability a theme in their advertising and promotion campaigns. Mobil reformulated its Hefty line of bags by using an additive that hastened degradation by 25 to 40 percent under the right conditions, and introduced this reformulated product in June 1989 in order to survive in the marketplace. While Mobil didn't extensively advertise this feature of its bags partly because it didn't want to hype degradability as a solution to the solid waste problem, the biodegradability feature was prominently displayed on the package along with a disclaimer that degradability was activated by exposure to the elements.[64]

Mobil had earlier concluded that biodegradable plastics will not help solve the solid waste problem, but believed it had to introduce such a product in order to meet competitive pressures. The company favored source reduction, recycling, incineration, and selective landfilling, but recognized that there were some short-term gains to be made in switching to a biodegradable product, and the public relations value of this move had to be considered as opposed to real solutions to the problem. This position came back to haunt the company when state attorneys general began investigating green claims. While its market share did not change either before or after the product was introduced, the company believed that sales of the Hefty line would have suffered because it would have lost shelf space to its competitors.[65]

The problem is that after the reformulated Hefty line was introduced, the public did a 180-degree turn on its thinking about degradability, and environmental groups, like the Environmental Defense Fund, called for a consumer boycott of many products that carried such claims. People began to realize that most garbage is sent to covered landfills where the degradation process is limited at best, or at worst, does not take place at all because of burial. What Mobil believed was a marketing response turned out to be a marketing nightmare, as the Federal Trade Commission and state agencies began investigating Mobil and other companies for their degradability claims. By March 1990, the pressures were so great from the other direction that Mobil announced it would voluntarily remove degradability claims for all Hefty packaging.[66]

This action, however, didn't protect Mobil from further controversy. In June 1990, seven state attorneys general, from California, Massachusetts, New York, Texas, Minnesota, Washington, and Wisconsin, sued Mobil in seven separate lawsuits. These suits charged Mobil with deceptive advertising and consumer fraud for its degradability claims. The attorney general of Minnesota, for example, stated that "Mobil's advertising claims break down faster than their garbage bags." Officials said that Mobil was targeted partly because of its public position against degradability benefits, which made it look like it was simply trying to profit from consumer trends rather than be environmentally responsible. This incident has taught the company that green marketing can be extremely changeable, and that consumer education is needed on a larger scale.[67]

Green marketing, while initially appearing to be a new area for marketers to rush into in a competitive race, quickly became more complicated. Consumers wanted to express their concerns about the environment through marketplace behavior, but in the absence of knowledge about the environment, were easily exploitable and were left without any means to evaluate environmental claims being made by companies. The federal government and the states became increasingly concerned about these claims, and began to investigate the advertising and promotional campaigns of several companies in order to prevent the process from getting out of hand. The attorney general of Minnesota sounded the alarm when he stated, "The selling of the environment could make the oat-bran craze look like a Sunday school picnic."[68]

Eventually, the environmental theme hit a sour note, as consumers became more wary about environmental claims and companies began to discard their environmental messages.[69] In late 1990, two reports were issued that indicated environmental claims made by manufacturers were confusing rather than helpful to consumers, and called for the development of national standards. One report urged business to adopt specific and substantive environmental claims backed up by reliable evidence. The report suggested that companies avoid vague phrases such as "environmentally friendly" and clarify whether environmental claims are being made for the package or the product. The term recycling also needed to be clarified, as any claims about recyclability were meaningless unless people have access to recycling facilities.[70]

A survey conducted in 1990 showed that most people had little confidence in green advertising claims and had more confidence in green seals and label claims. When asked to rate their confidence that product advertising provides accurate information about impacts on the environment, only 8 percent of the respondents said they were very confident, 43 percent said they were somewhat confident, and 47 percent said they were not confident. When asked to rate their confidence that product labeling provides accurate information about the environment, 12 percent said they were very confident, 51 percent said they were somewhat confident, and only 35 percent said they were not confident. This antiad bias also showed up when respondents were asked to rate green advertising with other influences on purchasing decisions.[71]

The lack of industry-wide norms for green marketing has led both industry groups and consumer groups to lobby Congress for federal standards. But thus far there has been little progress regarding the development of such standards, partly because of discord between environmental groups and producers about the extensiveness of such standards and the accuracy of the underlying science. There is also controversy between manufacturers, as some stand to lose from industrywide standards. There is a belief that far-reaching standards formulated by the federal government might be unacceptable to a congressional majority.

Companies fear that unless the federal government acts soon, state regulators will fill the regulatory void. Thus it was hoped that agencies might act where Congress will not, but so far, the Federal Trade Commission appears unwilling to take part in any multiagency attempt to define environmental terms that are used in marketing. The EPA intends to develop voluntary national guidelines for "recycled" and "recyclable," but draft guidelines were not drafted until the end of 1991, too slow for many marketers. To speed the process, an industry coalition has been formed that plans to ask the FTC to approve its version of voluntary guidelines that would provide marketers with uniform environmental marketing standards.[72]

State legislation is beginning to appear, and several states have already enacted legislation that governs the use of environmental terms. State attorneys general have circulated final recommendations for "responsible environmental advertising" in a separate effort. But their efforts are geared at least in part to prod the federal government into action, as they would like to see the FTC or the EPA develop national green marketing standards. These standards are necessary, it is claimed, so that consumers will have the information they need to make purchasing decisions based on environmental considerations.[73] The multistate task force formed in late 1989 by the attorneys general suggested four points to be followed in developing environmental advertising:

- Claims should be as specific as possible, not general, vague, incomplete, or overly broad.
- Claims should reflect current disposal options — green claims relating to disposability shouldn't be made unless the advertised disposal option is currently available to consumers in the area in which the product is sold and the product complies with the requirements of the relevant waste disposal programs.
- Claims should be substantive.
- Claims should be supported by competent and reliable scientific evidence.[74]

In the meantime, two private services have been developed to evaluate environmental claims and help consumers sort through all the hype by offering environmental seals of approval for products. The Green Cross Certification Company was founded in April 1990 to address the growing confusion over environmental advertising claims in the marketplace. Green Cross certification means that specific environmental claims made about products have been thoroughly checked out, and that these claims meet high standards of performance.[75]

Two levels of certification are awarded. The first level is awarded to a product that meets state-of-the-art performance standards in one or more single claim categories. Claims such as "recycled content" (paper, glass, steel, plastic products), "biodegradable" (cleaning products), and "energy efficient" (light bulbs) are among those being evaluated. The Green Cross certification is accompanied by a specific statement of the achievement that has been documented. (See emblem.)

Courtesy of Green Cross Certification Company. Reprinted with permission.

Courtesy of Green Cross Certification
Company. Reprinted with permission.

In addition, Green Cross will be awarding an Environmental Seal of Achievement (see emblem) to a product that undergoes a full "life-cycle" assessment, and is shown to possess several significant environmental advantages over other products in its category. A life-cycle assessment involves an examination of the resources used, energy consumed, wastes produced, and emissions released as a result of the manufacture, distribution, use, and disposal of a product. To help consumers make the best informed decisions, documented advantages will always be presented in detail along with each Seal of Achievement.

The Green Seal program is led by Earth Day organizer Dennis Hayes, and is still seeking comment from advertisers, consumers, and environmentalists to establish criteria for guidelines for the first five product categories it will approve. These categories include facial tissues, toilet paper, light bulbs, house paint, and laundry detergent. The first seal has not yet been issued because of delays in securing funding from philanthropic foundations. The program intends to use a "modified" life-cycle assessment process that measures a product's environmental acceptability from manufacture through disposal.[76]

Courtesy of Green Seal, Inc.

There are differences between the two programs, which makes for some confusion and draws negative comments from some companies. They have been criticized as being too narrowly focused and shortcutting consumer education. Some critics state that in the absence of nationally accepted definitions for such terms as "recycled" or "recyclable" products cannot be compared with each other in a meaningful manner, especially when two different programs are involved.[77]

The debate on national green marketing standards is thus just beginning. Until definitions and other aspects of the situation are settled, marketers face the challenge of making truthful environmental claims for their own products while wondering if other companies will do the same or engage in questionable advertising practices to gain market share. This is an age-old problem for marketing that appears in all markets, but especially in newly developing ones like environmental marketing or the controversy over health claims that surfaced several years ago. Yet marketing offers great potential to deal with environmental problems through the market mechanism without resorting to further government regulation. But the consumer needs further education and companies need uniform guidelines so that they are all playing on a level playing field. There is much work to be done in this area, and companies are probably best advised to approach this strategy with great caution until standards are developed.

~

Questions for Discussion

1. What impacts has the environment made on business? How is business responding to these impacts? What more will it have to do in the future to respond to people's material needs and at the same time be environmentally sensitive?

2. What new kinds of thinking and strategies seem to be necessary? How should the industrial system be redesigned to meet the needs of the future? How could such redesign take place? What changes will consumers have to make in their practices?

3. What are some of the problems with the current system of regulatory controls? What changes need to be made to enable corporations to restructure their operations? What incentives need to be changed to enable corporations to be more environmentally sensitive?

4. What does waste minimization mean in theory and practice? What problems exist with trying to clean up existing waste dumps? Is it possible to cut down on the amount of waste generated to avoid cleanups in the future? How can this be done? Give some examples.

5. What problems exist with recycling as a solution to the waste problem? What is being done about these problems? How is plastics recycling being promoted? What role does the consumer play in this strategy?

6. Describe the design for disassembly concept. How does this concept relate to recycling? What are some companies doing to promote this concept? Do you believe it will catch hold in more companies?

7. Where do marketing strategies fit into the environmental picture? What is currently being done by some companies in this regard? What pitfalls exist with respect to so-called green marketing strategies?

8. Is the development of federal standards with respect to green products the answer? What problems are these standards likely to cause? Will the Green Cross and Green Seal programs work very well in dealing with this problem? What is the answer?

NOTES

1. Robert A. Forsch and Nicholas E. Gallopoulos, "Strategies for Manufacturing," *Scientific American,* Vol. 261, No. 3 (September 1990), p. 144.

2. Ibid.

3. Ibid.

4. Ibid., pp. 144–145.

5. Ibid., pp. 146, 149.

6. Ibid., p. 150.

7. Ibid., p. 151.

8. Ibid.

9. Ibid., p. 152.

10. Ibid.

11. Ibid.

12. Ibid.

13. Ibid.

14. Robert P. Bringer, "Pollution Prevention Plus," *Pollution Engineering,* Vol. XX, No. 10 (October 1988), pp. 84–89.

15. Robert P. Bringer, "The Prevention of Hazardous Waste Generation: An Idea Whose Time Has Come," *International Environment Reporter,* Vol. 11, No. 8 (August 10, 1988), pp. 452–454.

16. Ibid.

17. Bringer, "Pollution Prevention Plus," pp. 84–85.

18. Ibid., p. 85.

19. Ibid.

20. Ibid.

21. Ibid., p. 86.

22. Bringer, "The Prevention of Hazardous Waste Generation," p. 452.

23. Bringer, "Pollution Prevention Plus," p. 87.

24. Ibid., p. 85.

25. Bringer, "The Prevention of Hazardous Waste Generation," p. 453.

26. Bringer, "Pollution Prevention Plus," p. 84.

27. Dow Chemical Company, "Waste Reduction Always Pays," undated, pp. 1–2.

28. "Dow Chemical: Managing Environmental Issues," pp. 9–10.

29. Ibid., p. 10.

30. Ibid., p. 12.

31. Ibid., p. 13.

32. Ibid.

33. Ibid., p. 14.

34. Dow, "Waste Reduction Always Pays," pp. 4–5.

35. Ibid., p. 5.

36. Ibid., p. 2.

37. Ibid., p. 5.

38. "Dow Chemical: Managing Environmental Issues," p. 15.

39. Council on Environmental Quality, "Municipal Solid Waste," Annual Report 1987–1988 (Washington, DC: U.S. Government Printing Office, 1988), p. 3.

40. *The Philadelphia Recycling Manual for Managers of Apartments and Condominiums,* January 1990, p. 3.

41. "Trash Can Realities," *Audubon: Speaking for Nature,* March 1990, p. 91.

42. Ibid.

43. Ibid. See also Bill Paul, "For Recyclers, the News Is Looking Bad," *Wall Street Journal,* August 31, 1989, p. B-1.

44. "Is Recycling the Answer," *American City and County,* May 1990, p. 40.

45. Philip E. Barnes, "Business' Hottest Niche Market: The Environment," *B&E Review,* April-June 1991, p. 9.

46. Ibid., pp. 7–8.

47. Frank Edward Allen, "McDonald's Launches Plan to Cut Waste," *Wall Street Journal,* April 17, 1991, p. B-1.

48. Ibid.

49. Joani Nelson-Hrochler, "Old Packages Never Die," *Industry Week,* September 4, 1989, pp. 88–89.

50. Vickey Cahan, "Waste Not, Want Not? Not Necessarily," *Business Week,* July 17, 1989, p. 117.

51. Randolph B. Smith, "Pressure for Plastic Recycling Prompts a Mix of Tough Laws and Cooperation," *Wall Street Journal,* February 2, 1990, p. B-2.

52. Dow Chemical Company, "Recycling Plastics: Great Things Are Worth Repeating," *Special Reprint from 1989 Annual Report,* 1990, p. 9.

53. Ibid.

54. Bruce Nussbaum, "Built to Last—Until It's Time to Take It Apart," *Business Week,* September 17, 1990, p. 102.

55. Ibid.

56. Gary McWilliams, "The Big Brouhaha over the Little Juice Box," *Business Week,* September 17, 1990, p. 36.

57. Ibid.

58. Nussbaum, "Built to Last," pp. 105–106.

59. "Trimming Wal-Mart's Green Policy," *Advertising Age,* January 29, 1991, p. 20.

60. Laurie Freeman, "Procter & Gamble," *Advertising Age,* January 29, 1991, p. 16.

61. Ibid.

62. Ibid., pp. 16, 34.

63. Jennifer Lawrence, "Mobil," *Advertising Age,* January 29, 1991, p. 12.

64. Ibid., pp. 12–13.

65. Ibid.

66. Ibid., p. 13.

67. Ibid.

68. Randolph B. Smith, "Environmentalists, State Officers See Red as Firms Rush to Market Green Products," *Wall Street Journal,* March 13, 1990, p. B-1.

69. Randolph B. Smith, "Plastic Bag Makers Discarding Environmental Claims," *Wall Street Journal,* March 30, 1990, p. B-1.

70. Joann S. Lubin, "Environment Claims Are Sowing More Confusion, 2 Reports Say," *Wall Street Journal,* November 8, 1990, p. B-8.

71. Dennis Chase, "P&G Gets Top Marks in AA Survey," *Advertising Age,* January 29, 1991, p. 10.

72. Jennifer Lawrence and Steven W. Colford, "Green Guidelines Are the Next Step," *Advertising Age,* January 29, 1991, p. 28.

73. Ibid.

74. Ibid.

75. Letter to the author from Mitchell Friedman, Public Relations Manager, Green Cross Certification Company, September 30, 1991.

76. Laurie Freeman, "Ecology Seals Vie for Approval," *Advertising Age,* January 29, 1991, p. 30.

77. Ibid.

Suggested Readings

Akinsanya, Adeoye A. *Multinationals in a Changing Environment.* New York: Praeger, 1984.

Dominguez, George S. *Marketing in a Regulated Environment.* New York: Wiley, 1978.

Dow Chemical Company, "Recycling Plastics: Great Things Are Worth Repeating," *Special Reprint From 1989 Annual Report,* 1990.

Forsch, Robert A., and Nicholas E. Gallopoulos. "Strategies for Manufacturing," *Scientific American.* Vol. 261, No. 3 (September 1990).

Friedman, Frank B. *Practical Guide to Environmental Management.* Washington, DC: Environmental Law Institute, 1988.

International Labor Conference. *Environment and the World of Work.* Geneva: International Labor Organization, 1990.

Petulla, Joseph M. *Environmental Protection in the United States: Industry, Agencies, Environmentalists.* San Francisco: San Francisco Study Center, 1987.

Tokar, Michael. *The Green Alternative: Creating an Alternative Future.* San Pedro, CA: R. & E. Miles, 1988.

Winter, Georg. *Business and the Environment.* New York: McGraw-Hill, 1988.

Yandle, Bruce. *The Political Limits of Environmental Regulation.* Westport, CT: Quorum Books, 1989.

CHAPTER 13

STRATEGIES FOR A
SUSTAINABLE SOCIETY

~

There are numerous strategies that business can adopt to be more environmentally sensitive (see Chapter 12). Most of these strategies have to do with reducing waste and in the process using resources more efficiently by recycling them or by adopting conservation measures designed to reduce energy and resource usage. Dealing at the firm level is something of a micro approach to environmental problems in analyzing what corporations either individually or as a group can do to make themselves more sustainable. This chapter deals with a more macro level. It discusses what society as a whole needs to do to become more sustainable.

A sustainable society is able to satisfy its economic and social needs without jeopardizing the prospects of future generations. Many experts believe that our present industrial societies use too many virgin resources and degrade the environment in too many ways, and that such practices cannot continue much longer. If people all over the world want to increase their standard of living on a par with advanced industrial nations like the United States, resources will be used even faster and environmental degradation will increase. The world simply cannot sustain such activities, it is believed, and aspirations of this sort will exceed the earth's carrying capacity with respect to resources and all aspects of the environment.

Some experts claim that if we have not attained sustainability within the next 40 years, environmental deterioration and economic decline are likely to be feeding on each other, pulling us into a downward spiral of social and economic disintegration.[1] The foundations for further economic growth will be eroded and social upheaval will take place throughout the world on an unprecedented scale. Sustainable development raises questions about intergenerational equity as well as equity among the peoples of the world as developing nations strive to better themselves with shrinking resources. Progress toward sustainability hinges on a collective sense of responsibility for the earth and to future generations. There are difficult questions regarding national sovereignty and individual rights and responsibilities that need to be considered. The capacity of national leaders and of international institutions will be severely tested in the effort to put the world on a firm ecological and economic footing.[2]

According to some estimates, since 1900, the number of people inhabiting the earth has multiplied more than three times, and the world economy has expanded more than 20 times during the same time period. The consumption of fossil fuels has grown by a factor of 30, and industrial production has increased by a factor of 50, with four-fifths of that increase occurring since 1950 alone. While there have been great gains in human welfare because of these developments and the potential for future gains is even more promising, development at this pace has also produced environmental destruction on a scale never before imagined and is undermining prospects for future economic development as well as threatening the very survival of the earth's inhabitants.[3]

The question being asked ever more frequently by commissions and policymakers all over the world is, "Can growth on the scale projected over the next one to five decades be managed on a basis that is sustainable, both economically and ecologically?" The answer to this question is not evident to some experts, as the obstacles to sustainability are mainly social, institutional, and political. It is believed that economic and ecological sustainability are usually dealt with as two separate questions by all governments and international organizations when they are, in fact, interrelated. Economic growth cannot continue if such growth undermines the ecological conditions that support continued growth.[4]

A five- to tenfold increase in economic activity translates into a greatly increased burden on the ecosphere. Such an increase is not unrealistic as it represents annual growth rates of only between 3.2 and 4.7 percent, well within the aspiration levels of many countries of the world. Such growth has severe implications for investment in housing, transportation, agriculture, and industry. Energy use would have to increase by a factor of five just to bring developing countries, given their present populations, up to the levels of consumption now existing in the industrialized world. Similar increases could be projected for food, water, shelter, and other essentials to human existence.[5]

Sustainable growth has implications for the distribution of economic wealth and income throughout the world. It would require a minimum of 3 percent annual growth in per capita income in developing countries, and the need for policies to achieve greater equity within these countries. Greater equity must also be achieved between the industrialized world and developing countries, as the latter consume about 80 percent of the world's goods and have only one-quarter of the world's population. With three-quarters of the world's population, developing countries command less than one-quarter of the world's wealth. This imbalance is getting worse, and cannot be continued if sustainable growth is to become a reality.[6]

Many developing countries, as well as large parts of many developed countries, are resource based. Their economic capital largely consists of stocks of environmental resources such as soil, forests, fisheries, and other such natural resources, and their continued development depends on maintaining, and perhaps increasing, these stocks of resources to support agriculture, fishing, and mining for local use and for export purposes. But during the past two decades, the poorer countries of the developing world have experienced a massive depletion of this capital. Environmental and renewable resources are being used up faster than they can be restored or replaced, and some developing countries have depleted virtually all their ecological capital and are on the brink of environmental bankruptcy.[7]

According to the World Commission of Environment and Development, sustainable growth is based on forms and processes of development that do not undermine the integrity of the environment on which they depend. But modern civilizations have been characterized by unsustainable development utilizing forms of decision making that do not take the future into account. They have ignored the long-term ecological costs of development and these costs are now coming due in economies all over the world. Yet many governments refuse to change their policies to correspond with an emerging reality and continue to act as if environmental conditions can be ignored and that nature will take care of itself.[8]

Conditions that are necessary to make development sustainable include (1) reviving growth particularly in developing nations, (2) addressing equity issues between generations and between countries of the world, (3) meeting the essential needs and aspirations of people all over the world, (4) reducing rates of population growth, recognizing that development is the best means of population control, (5) adopting policies that do not deplete the basic stock of ecological capital over time, (6) making a significant and rapid reduction in the energy and raw material content of every unit of production, and (7) merging environmental and economic concerns into decision-making processes in both the public and private sectors.[9]

The latter condition, according to Jim McNeill, secretary general of the World Commission on Environment and Development, is the most important condition for sustainable development. While economic and ecological systems have become totally interlocked in the real world, they remain almost totally divorced in our institutions. Environmental protection agencies have been set up by governments around the world, but they have been hamstrung by limited mandates and budgets. Meanwhile, agencies created to promote economic development have not been made to take responsibility for the environmental implications of their policies and expenditures. The resulting imbalance results in promotion of economic growth at the expense of the environment.[10]

> Environmental agencies must be given more capacity and more power to cope with the effects of unsustainable development policies. More important, governments must make their central economic, trade and sectoral agencies directly responsible and accountable for formulating policies and budgets to encourage development that is sustainable. Only then will the ecological dimensions of policy be considered at the same time as the economic, trade, energy, agricultural and other dimensions — on the same agendas and in the same national and international institutions.[11]

The market is one area where the merging of environmental considerations with economic decision making could have a major impact. The market is the most powerful instrument for driving development that societies have available, but whether or not the market supports sustainable or unsustainable forms of development is largely a function of public policy on the part of government structures. The market does not take into account the external environmental costs associated with producing, consuming, and disposing of goods and services. But policymakers rarely take these external costs into account when considering fiscal and monetary policies or trade policies, all of which have environmental implications. When these externals are taken into account, the assumption is often made that resources are inexhaustible or that substitutes will be found before we run out of some resources, or that the environment should subsidize the market. Many policymakers also believe that the environment can take care of itself and no one needs to worry about its condition.[12]

Ignoring the environmental implications of policy means that the costs of environmental degradation are borne by the larger community in the form of air, water, land, and noise pollution and of resource depletion. Or these costs are transferred to future generations who are stuck with a degraded environment that will no longer support growth rates that have been attained in the past. Internalizing these costs requires government intervention, but this is one way of trying to represent the real costs of development in economic decision making. Another way would be to integrate resource accounts in national economic systems, so policymakers would have a more accurate picture of the way certain economic policies are affecting ecological systems and stocks of resources.[13]

> With the gradual integration of the environment in economic decision making, budgets for energy, agriculture and other sectors should begin to include funds to cover the environmental costs of their respective activities. Eventually, the burden of financing sustainable development should be assumed by such budgets. In the interim, sustainable development will demand large sources of new funding.[14]

The annual budget developed by nations around the world establishes the framework of economic incentives that shape the behavior of people and institutions in that society. As such, the budget is perhaps the most important environmental policy statement that any government makes each year, because in the aggregate the budget and the way it is implemented serves to enhance or degrade the external environment and increase or reduce its stocks of ecological capital. Budgets that levy taxes on excessive energy usage, tax the use of virgin resources, and tax the production of pollution or generation of waste can have a significant effect on the consumption patterns of consumers and the cost structure of industry, and can promote the transition to a sustainable society.[15]

ENERGY STRATEGIES

Human beings around the world expend in one year a quantity of fossil fuels that it took nature roughly a million years to create. Oil alone accounts for 38 percent of commercial energy consumption, and the OPEC nations control three-fourths of proved crude oil reserves, including all recent additions. The United States imported $40 billion worth of oil in 1987, an amount equal to one-third of the country's trade deficit, and during the same year, spent $15 billion to protect oil supplies. Natural gas provides a fifth of all commercial energy, and many electric utilities consider natural gas to be the best short-term substitute for oil as a fuel for some power plants. But the Middle East and ex-Soviet republics hold nearly 70 percent of natural gas reserves. Reserves of coal could last 275 years at current production rates, and the United States and the former Soviet Union each control a quarter of global coal reserves.[16]

Environmental, geopolitical, and economic pressures on continued reliance on fossil fuels as the backbone of our energy supply are prompting a search for energy alternatives. The world economy of the future is not likely to be powered by fossil fuels, and continued reliance on these fuels will cause catastrophic changes in climate if there is anything to the theory of global warming. But even in the absence of such effects, fossil fuels are an ever-increasing problem because of the pollution they cause and the fact that they are a nonrenewable resource. Sooner or later, the world is going to run out of coal, oil, and natural gas, and it is going to be more and more difficult to find new sources of supply. The technology involved in developing new sources is becoming more and more expensive, and on a net energy basis, may become counterproductive at some point. In other words, more energy is used to find and produce new sources of supply than the energy they contain.

Nuclear power is controversial at best, as questions have been raised about reliance on this source in the future. One problem with nuclear power is that over the past 40 years it has absorbed the preponderance of government energy investments and has diverted attention from more attractive options. Nuclear power has become increasingly more expensive and accident prone in the last decade, and the critical problem of disposing of radioactive wastes has yet to be solved. Even on a limited scale, nuclear power requires vast financial resources and technical skills, curtailing the development of other options.[17]

It is predicted that before fossil fuels are exhausted, energy systems all over the world will be run by solar resources that are replenished daily by incoming sunlight and geothermal energy. As solar energy is by nature diverse, the mix of energy sources in any particular region will reflect the climate and natural resources of that region. Due to the abundance of sunlight, the direct conversion of solar energy will be the cornerstone of a sustainable world energy system. Sunshine is available in great quantities, and is more widely distributed than any other energy source.[18] Solar power will thus be the basis of world energy production, with a mix of other sources as becomes necessary and feasible in certain regions of the world.

Photovoltaics offer advantages for small applications. They convert sunlight directly into electricity without using the mechanical processes involved in solar thermal conversion. They are versatile and can be used by homeowners throughout the world for various applications. Wind power is an indirect form of solar energy because it is generated by the sun's differential heating of the earth's atmosphere. By the year 2030, it is estimated that the United States could be producing 10 to 20 percent of its electricity from wind power. Hydropower now supplies one-fifth of the world's electricity, but its expansion in developed countries is unlikely because of public opposition to new dams and water power projects. But prospects for future growth of this source are promising in the Third World where the undeveloped potential is still large.[19]

The use of biomass, or using living green plants as a source of energy, is another means of capturing solar power. Through photosynthesis, these plants convert sunlight into biomass that can be burned as a source of energy. The use of bioenergy will expand during the next several decades, but its growth will be constrained because of costs and availability. Geothermal power is another possibility, but these resources must be tapped slowly enough so as not to deplete accessible reservoirs of heat and maintain their renewability. Such resources can become nonrenewable if used too rapidly.[20] Thus there are a variety of renewable resources that can be used to replace fossil fuels and some mixture of these can be part of an energy strategy that is sustainable into the future.

Whatever mix is developed, land-use practices are expected to be shaped by the development of economic and social systems that are based on renewable energy supplies. In both industrial and developing nations, energy production will inevitably be much more decentralized, leading to the breakup of huge utility companies that have been a dominant part of the economic scene in the late twentieth century. Decentralization of energy production will make our energy supplies less vulnerable to disruption and more conducive to market principles and democratic political systems.[21]

Some studies show that one-fifth of the world's population consumes more than 70 percent of the world's commercial energy. The amount of energy used to produce a unit of gross national product, however, also fell by one-fifth between 1973 and 1985, providing a rough measure of improvements in efficiency. The most rapid growth in energy consumption now occurs in developing countries, but even so, these countries still consume four to seven times less energy per person than the industrialized countries. Developed countries have captured the power of fossil fuels, but the penalty is the loss of personal and environmental health. Efficiency is said to be the best hope, and investments in energy efficiency can help to reduce fossil fuel demand without sacrificing economic growth.[22]

A sustainable society will have to become much more efficient in the use of resources. Some experts have concluded that the simultaneous pursuit of renewable sources and greater efficiency while abandoning the nuclear option is the only safe and cost-effective way to provide for our energy needs in the future. But renewable sources of energy do not have nearly as large a potential to displace fossil fuels in the short run as energy efficiency improvements. The potential for renewable energy will grow as new technologies are developed and improved; however, improved energy efficiency must become the cornerstone of national energy policies in the immediate future.[23]

RECYCLING AND REUSE

Consistent with what we discussed in Chapter 12, society as a whole will have to think in terms of recycling and reuse of materials. The present society, which is rooted in the concept of planned obsolescence and convenience, will be seen as an aberration. Waste reduction and recycling industries will largely replace the garbage collection and disposal companies of today. Society will become dramatically less energy intensive and less polluting if the throwaway mentality is replaced by a recycling ethic. Recycling is also a key to controlling land, air, and water pollution and getting such pollution down to acceptable levels.[24]

In a sustainable economy, the principal source of materials for industry will be recycled goods, and industrial companies will feed largely on what is already in the system, turning to virgin raw materials only to replace any losses in use and recycling. A hierarchy of options will most likely guide a materials policy: (1) avoid using any nonessential item, (2) directly reuse a product, (3) recycle the material to form a new product, (4) burn material to extract whatever energy it contains, and finally, (5) dispose of it in a landfill. Sustainability over the long term, however, depends more on eliminating waste flows than on any other single element. Companies must reduce the volume of waste generated in industry by restructuring manufacturing processes.[25]

A sustainable society also involves recycling nutrients. The nutrients in human waste, for example, can be reused safely as long as the process includes measures to prevent the spread of disease. Some cities will probably find that it is more efficient to use treated human sewage to fertilize aquacultural operations than to use commercial products. This will save a good deal of money as well as protect the environment from fertilizer runoff. Households will begin to compost more yard wastes and find this material a rich source of humus for gardening. In this way, each household can reduce the amount of waste it produces as well as reduce the need for fertilizer.[26]

By using resources more efficiently, and by systematically reducing the flow of waste and recycling or reusing most remaining materials, the basic needs of the planet's growing number of human residents have a chance of being satisfied without destroying the very life support systems on which we all depend. The creation of a sustainable society involves the development of a more livable environment with less air and water pollution, and less waste to dispose of that can pose a threat to human health and the environment. Such a society will be a more pleasant place in which to live because unsightly litter that blights the landscape will have been reduced.[27]

POPULATION AND FOOD SUPPLIES

The population problem is most difficult because it touches on individual rights and religious beliefs, areas that spark a good deal of controversy. Yet many experts think that population stabilization is the only acceptable goal in a world where growth in human numbers is leading to a life-threatening deterioration of the environment. Future food security may also lie more in the hands of family planners than farmers. Some arguments are made that it is more humane and ethical to encourage planning with respect to population growth than to let the forces of nature reduce population through starvation and the ravages of disease. The earth has a certain carrying capacity, and when that capacity is exceeded, natural forces are set in motion to reduce the level of people on earth and bring it into some kind of equilibrium. To wait for natural constraints to limit population size, however, is to accept famine, low living standards, unemployment, political instability, and ecological destruction.

With respect to food supplies, there is little opportunity for expanding cultivated areas around the world. Irrigated areas around the world, while growing slowly, are declining in some key countries. For farmers in advanced countries, there are few new technologies to draw on to increase yields, as returns on the use of additional fertilizer are diminishing, to say nothing about the environmental effects of increased fertilizer usage. There is thus little chance to increase the supply of food to meet a growing population, where the annual increment in world population is projected to climb to record highs in the years immediately ahead. Achieving a satisfactory balance between food and people is becoming ever more difficult and may not be possible without dramatically lowering birthrates in countries where population is still growing rapidly.[28]

Drought-damaged harvests in several key producing countries in 1987 and 1988 brought world grain stocks to one of their lowest levels in decades. If there were no additional investments in agriculture or technological progress, it has been estimated that the world grain harvest would fall 14 million tons annually, which is nearly 1 percent a year, as a result of environmental degradation. This decline is indicative of a general downward spiral in food production throughout the world, and should set off alarm bells for policymakers in countries that are vulnerable to such a decline.[29]

The growth in world food output is being slowed by (1) environmental degradation, (2) a worldwide scarcity of cropland and irrigation water, and (3) a diminishing response to the use of additional chemical fertilizer. Soil erosion is slowly undermining the productivity of an estimated one-third of the world's cropland, as each of the world's farmers lose an estimated 24 billion tons of topsoil from their croplands in excess of new soil formation.[30] Expansion in the world's irrigated area is estimated to be slowing as gains from new capacity are offset by losses from waterlogging and salinity, falling water tables, and the silting of existing reservoirs. The irrigated land area per person shrunk by close to 8 percent over the last decade. And finally, many developing countries as well as developed countries are beginning to experience a diminishing response of crops to the use of additional fertilizer.[31]

Protection of the existing cropland is one of the keys to raising output of food on anything approaching a sustainable basis in order to feed current populations. Security of food supplies for the future depends on safeguarding existing cropland from both conversion to nonfarm uses and from the erosion that reduces its inherent productivity. Much cropland, particularly in developed countries, is lost each year to expanding urban developments that take more and more good farmland out of production. The rise in the price of land that is useful for development purposes provides a dynamic that makes this conversion process move forward. Erosion of soil is particularly acute in developing countries where flooding is still a problem and where wind and other kinds of erosion lead to soil degradation.

Countries that have made the shift to smaller families have four things in common according to some experts: (1) an active national population education program, (2) widely available family planning services, (3) incentives for small families, and (4) widespread improvements in economic and social conditions. The latter is perhaps a most critical element and has implications for the distribution of wealth and income among countries of the world. Studies consistently show that fertility declines as economic and social conditions improve. As incomes rise and employment opportunities for women expand, couples choose to have fewer children. Rather than implement family planning programs that interfere with individual rights, perhaps the best approach is to better the economic and social conditions in those countries where population is still growing rapidly.[32]

POVERTY

Any attempt to create a sustainable society on a worldwide basis must take into account the inequities that presently exist between countries. The poor people of the world not only suffer disproportionately from environmental damage caused by the industrial nations that are better off economically, they have become a major cause of ecological decline themselves as they have been pushed onto marginal land by population growth and inequitable land development patterns. Economic deprivation and environmental degradation reinforce one another to form a downward spiral that is difficult to arrest, much less turn around. But poverty must be dealt with in order for a sustainable world to be developed.[33]

Absolute poverty signifies the lack of sufficient income in cash or kind to meet the most basic of human needs for food, clothing, and shelter. Such deprived conditions spread into all aspects of a person's life: susceptibility to disease, limited access to most types of services and information, lack of control over resources, subordination to higher social and economic classes, insecurity in the face of changing circumstances, and erosion of human dignity and self-respect. The threshold for absolute poverty varies widely from $50 to $500 per year, according to one source, depending on such factors as prices, access to subsistence resources, and availability of public services.[34]

Since mid-century, the wealthy nations have almost tripled their per capita income, but in the poorest countries that figure has remained effectively level. Worldwide, the average income per person has doubled since 1950, growing to a level of $3,300 in real terms, but the fruits of this growth have almost all gone to those in fortunate circumstances. This average disguises the gross disparities in income distribution that characterize the majority of countries. In most countries of the world, 60 to 70 percent of the people earn less than the national average income, and almost nowhere do the poorest fifth of households earn even 10 percent of national income while the richest fifth commonly receive half of such income.[35]

According to some experts, the world as a whole is probably less equitable than any nation taken individually. The upper fifth of humans living in the richest countries have average incomes that are 15 times greater than the fifth living in the poorest countries. The gap between rich and poor nations has grown since 1950 because the rich have gotten richer, and since 1980, at least, the poor in many developing countries have been getting poorer. In 1989, approximately 1.2 billion people lived in absolute poverty around the world, which was a larger figure than ever before. These figures reflect a rate of 23.4 percent, which was an increase from 22.3 percent in 1980, showing that during the 1980s, the global poverty rate rose despite substantial reduction in the number of impoverished people in some countries. Two thirds of these ~~people are under the age of 15, and the prospects for~~ these young people to better themselves are even worse than for their parents.[36]

Such stark poverty drives ecological deterioration when people in desperate situations overexploit their resource base and sacrifice the future to salvage what they can out of the present. Ecological decline, in turn, perpetuates poverty, as degraded ecosystems offer diminishing yields to their inhabitants, thus setting into motion a downward spiral of economic deprivation and ecological degradation. This poverty trap appears on every continent and the net effect is universal. The poor are usually concentrated in fragile regions where the land is least productive and tenure least secure. This geographic concentration of poverty is driven in part by heightened population growth rates that poverty itself brings.[37]

Where poverty is not a cause of environmental decline, it often results in environmental abuses caused by other groups in society. Three-fourths of hazardous waste landfills in the southeastern part of the United States are in low-income black neighborhoods. More than half of all blacks and Hispanics in the country live in communities with at least one toxic waste site in their midst. The storms, floods, droughts, famines, and social upheavals that may result from global climate change are exactly the kind of events that make poor people poorer. Climate change would further direct resources away from the poor into erection of seawalls to protect property, new irrigation systems, flood protection, and countless other projects designed to protect the investments of the wealthier classes of society. Such actions would condemn half of humanity to absolute poverty.[38]

In order for development activities to help the poor and reverse the downward spiral, they must be empowered rather than just cared for by increasing welfare support. The poor must not only be seen as beneficiaries of welfare programs, but as active participants, advisers, and leaders, as true development does not simply provide resources for the needy, but enables them to provide for themselves. Poor people must be encouraged to organize themselves to fight poverty and environmental decline, and must be provided the resources that will empower them to mount this effort. The ingredients for success include literacy, secure land rights, local control over common resources, credit, clean drinking water and primary health care, and family planning. Failure to launch an assault on poverty that includes these elements will guarantee the continued destruction of much of our shared biosphere. While environmental damage penalizes the poor more severely than the wealthy, eventually the circle becomes complete and affects people in any status or country.[39]

ACCOUNTING SYSTEMS

Creation of a sustainable society involves changing national accounting systems to reflect the impact of economic growth on the environment. The economic indicators used by most countries do not distinguish between resource uses that sustain progress and those that undermine progress. Economic indicators of developed countries show that during the past several decades, world trade has increased, gross national product or its equivalent has grown, millions of new jobs have been created, and that in general, economies in the developed part of the world have continued to progress. But these indicators say nothing about the environmental degradation that has resulted from this increased economic activity.

The gross national product, for example, includes all the goods and services produced by a nation over some period of time. It is the most basic indicator to show whether the economy is progressing and thus the country is healthy, or whether a recession is occurring that bodes ill for most people in the country. While most measures of GNP include depreciation of plant and equipment, they do not take into account the depreciation of natural capital including nonrenewable resources such as oil and coal and renewable resources such as forests. This shortcoming can lead to a serious overstatement of national economic and social well-being.[40]

To take just one example out of many that could be mentioned, Lester Brown points out that countries which overcut forests actually do better in the short run than those that manage their forests on a sustained yield basis. Conventional measures treat the trees cut down as income to the country and as an addition to gross national product. But no subtraction is made to account for the depletion of a natural asset that may not be able to be replaced fast enough to compensate for the depletion. This advantage is short-lived, however, as overcutting eventually destroys the resource base entirely, leading to a complete collapse of the forest products industry in that country.[41]

Another example could be taken from the food-producing sector of a nation. Much grain is currently produced by cultivating highly erodible land that will eventually become wasteland or by intensifying farming in ways that lead to excessive soil erosion and loss of cropland. In addition, much grain-producing land is irrigated by drawing down water tables that will eventually be exhausted. According to one expert, if adjustment were made for all grain produced with the unsustainable use of land and water worldwide, it would show a grain output well below current consumption and give a much bleaker sense of global food security. Current accounting systems reward short-run practices that undermine long-run food security and create an illusion of progress.[42]

Governments must begin thinking of developing national accounting systems that reflect more accurately real changes in output. Something like an ecological deflator must be applied to measure real progress. The environmental degradation that is caused by economic growth must be subtracted out to show the real progress that has been made by a society. Or some way must be found to treat natural resources as capital assets that are depreciated as they are used up just like industrial capital is depreciated and reflected in national accounts. At the present time, countries all over the world are living off nature, assuming that resources are inexhaustible and that the environment is indestructible. No effort is made to account for resource usage and environmental degradation. Thus nations have no idea of how sustainable the growth they experience at present is as far as the future is concerned.

A NEW CONSCIOUSNESS

Creating a sustainable society calls for major shifts on several fronts simultaneously to restore some kind of equilibrium that will continue to make the planet hospitable. There needs to be a global balance between births and deaths, carbon emissions and carbon fixation, soil erosion and soil formation, and tree cutting and tree planting. The people of the earth will either mobilize to reestablish a stable relationship with the earth's natural support systems or continue down the path of environmental deterioration. At some point, experts say that a continuing preoccupation with the unstable present will begin to obliterate hopes for reclaiming the future. Environmental deterioration is gradual and difficult to arrest, let alone turn around, once it has reached a certain point. The adjustments needed in economic and social systems around the world are permanent for they are the prerequisites for long-term survival.[43]

1. Shifts in employment will be among the most visible changes as the transition to a sustainable society gets under way. Many people will find their skills are valued in new or expanded lines of work.

2. The trend toward ever larger cities and an increasing ratio of urban to rural dwellers is likely to reverse itself. The increasing energy intensity of food production and distribution cannot continue indefinitely. Smaller human settlements will also be favored by the shift to renewable energy sources which will support decentralization of human activities.

3. Sustainability will gradually eclipse growth as the focus of economic policy-making, as gross national product will be seen as a bankrupt indicator. This measure undervalues qualities a sustainable society

strives for, such as durability and resource protection, and overvalues many it does not, such as planned obsolescence and waste. In future decades, policymakers will measure economic and social advances by sustainability criteria rather than simply by growth in short-term output.

4. Global military expenditures will be cut heavily as countries recognize that environmental threats to security have supplanted the traditional military threats. Sustainability cannot be achieved without a massive shift of resources from military endeavors into energy efficiency, soil conservation, tree planting, family planning, and other needed development activities.

5. Materialism cannot survive the transition to a sustainable world. Personal self-worth is now measured by possessions just as social progress is measured by gross national product. Societies must unleash the tremendous quantities of energy that are associated with consumption activities (designing, producing, advertising, buying, consuming, and discarding of material goods), and form richer human relationships, stronger communities, and greater cultural diversity.

6. As the amassing of personal and national wealth becomes less of a goal, the gap between haves and have-nots will gradually close, eliminating many societal tensions. The idea of waging war could become an anachronism as world leaders realize the kind of cooperative effort it will take to repair the earth and create sustainable societies.[44]

Some commentators see the move toward sustainable development as comparable to two other major changes in societies in past centuries, the agricultural revolution and the industrial revolution. Such a change will have far-reaching implications for societies all over the world, as they begin to see that environmental protection and economic development are complementary rather than antagonistic processes. The old notion of trade-offs between economic growth and economic development is no longer viable. Economic growth and development must take place and be maintained over time within the limits set by ecology—by the interrelations of human beings and their works, the biosphere, and the physical and chemical laws that govern our world.[45]

The earth and its creatures are considered the property of humankind, to be dominated, manipulated, and controlled for purposes of enhancing the welfare of humans. But humans believe they somehow stand outside of nature and are not subject to the laws of ecology. Advanced technology gives impetus to the basic assumption that there is essentially no limit to the power humans have over nature. These unconscious assumptions give rise to unsustainable practices. In the developing world, it takes the form of development at any cost, even if it means the wholesale destruction of forests and the creation of industrial centers that are sources of severe environmental pollution. In the developed world, unsustainable development has generated wealth and comfort for about one-fifth of humankind, and while environmental protection activities have developed in these countries, they have been ameliorative and corrective, not a force for serious restructuring. These activities have been encompassed within the consciousness of unsustainability.[46] Creation of a sustainability consciousness would include the following elements:

1. The human species is part of nature. Its existence depends on its ability to draw sustenance from a finite natural world; its continuance depends on its ability to abstain from destroying the natural systems that regenerate this world.
2. Economic activity must account for the environmental costs of production.
3. The maintenance of a livable global environment depends on the sustainable development of the entire human family.[47]

According to William Ruckelshaus, this change in consciousness will come about when it is in the interests of individuals and organizations to change, either because they benefit from changing or because they incur severe sanctions if they do not change. Changing interests with regard to the environment require three things: (1) a clear set of values consistent with the consciousness of sustainability must be articulated by leaders in both the public and the private sector, (2) motivations need to be established that will support the values, and (3) institutions must be developed that will effectively apply the motivations.[48]

The first of these things has happened as leaders around the world have enunciated sustainable development as a desirable goal for their countries. The second and third steps are more difficult because the appropriate motivations and institutional structures are inadequate to the task or nonexistent. The difficulty of moving from stated values to actual practice stems from certain basic characteristics of modern industrialized nations. The first problem is the economic one of externalities, that the environmental cost of producing a good or a service is not accounted for in its price, thereby producing the tragedy of the commons mentioned by Garret Hardin in Chapter 1. Industrialized societies refuse to treat environmental resources as capital and spend them as income, which leads to overspending. All of nature's systems are closed loops, while economic activities are linear and assume inexhaustible resources or bottomless sinks in which to dispose of our waste materials.[49]

The second problem is the political one of motivating people to act in a democracy. Modifying the market to reflect environmental costs is by necessity a function of government, and those who are adversely affected by such changes often have disproportionate influence on public policy to prevent such modifications from taking place or mitigating their effects. The critical question for industrial democracies is whether they will be able to overcome political constraints on shaping the market system to promote long-term sustainability. Over the long term, it is likely, according to Ruckelshaus, that some form of emissions trading system will be necessary on a much larger scale than has been tried in order to deal with pollution. This system will provide the necessary motivation to deal with pollution.[50]

Well-designed incentive programs are cost effective and can work to reward people for implementing ecologically sound practices. Incentives could be provided for efficiency improvements for utilities and other companies, as well as consumers. The tax base could be restructured to favor environmentally friendly investments, and because taxes adjust prices, they can be used to help meet many environmental goals such as reducing the possibility of global warming and promoting the use of recycled materials. Fees could be set on carbon emissions from the burning of fossil fuels and thereby slow global warming, and on the use of virgin materials thus encouraging recycling and reuse. Determining tax levels that reduce harm to human health and the environment without damaging the environment is a complicated task, but it could be done if the political will was available.[51]

Such green taxes could also be used to raise funds for global initiatives that require transfers from rich countries to poorer ones in order to provide incentives for them to develop environmentally sound technologies. Such transfers would serve as partial payment for the ecological debt industrial countries have incurred by causing most of the damage to the global environment. An example of such an effort is provided by the establishment of an environmental fund in 1989 to be managed by the World Bank in cooperation with the United Nations Environmental Program. It is hoped that more than $1 billion will be raised in the first three years to help developing countries with the energy, forestry, family planning, and other investments that will be needed to move the global economy onto a sustainable track.[52]

The important international institutions in today's world are those concerned with money, trade, and national defense. If concern for the environment becomes as pressing as these issues were in past years, then comparable institutions will be developed. To further this goal of institution building, money, information, and integration will be needed. Institutions such as the United Nations Environment Program (UNEP) need more money to do the job they have been assigned. Strong international institutions are also needed to collect, analyze, and report on environmental trends and risks, and make this information available to all countries of the world. Regarding integration, the world cannot afford duplication of effort to solve common problems. Coordinating institutions need to be developed and strengthened to combine the separate strengths of nongovernmental organizations, international bodies, and industrial groups in order to focus their efforts on specific problems.[53]

The world is now facing a crisis of governance resulting from the mismatch between the international and sometimes global environmental consequences of domestic economic policies and the national interests that shape these policies. The link between cause and effect has been severed by the nature of today's international political system. Unless this can be remedied by creating new international institutions or by expanding the authority of existing ones, no mechanism will exist to promote responsible behavior. To leave processes that will directly influence the future habitability of the planet to chance is risky beyond reason.[54]

Senator Albert Gore, Jr., recommends the creation of a Strategic Environmental Initiative (SEI), which is the environmental counterpart to the Strategic Defense Initiative started during the Reagan administration. Such an initiative would be a global effort to develop and share with all nations new technologies that allow sustainable development. The SEI would identify new technologies that appeared to be effective and then spread them throughout the world. In the United States, for example, SEI could mean more fuel-efficient cars and energy-efficient appliances, manufacturing that relies on recycled materials, and a second green revolution that requires fewer fertilizers and pesticides. Training centers would need to be established around the world to create a core of environmentally educated planners and technicians to develop environmentally attractive technologies and practices.[55]

Another institution that Gore recommends is an Environmental Security Trust Fund that would be built on a simple principle: Consumers will pay into it for actions that harm the global environment and get money back for actions that make good environmental sense. This fund would give consumers market incentives to protect and restore the environment through a series of fees and rebates. The fund, for example, would establish mechanisms for assessing fees on products that are energy intensive; energy-conserving alternatives would receive rebates. Technologies that rely on ozone-depleting chemicals would have fees associated with them while ozone-safe chemicals would earn rebates. The fees would be levied at the time of purchase and the rebates would be applied after the purchase.[56]

There are thus many institutional proposals to promote sustainable development, some of which may be difficult to implement but deserve consideration. Sustainable development requires a multifaceted approach, as there may be as many responses as there are ecological circumstances, economic factors, and cultural constraints. There is no single cookbook-style recipe for sustainable development, and no manual can ever set out the principles and practices of such a broad concept.[57] It is as much a state of mind as anything else, a new kind of consciousness that looks at economic growth in a different perspective. It involves a redefinition of what is politically and economically possible and what has to be done to sustain growth into the future.

Finally, in creating the consciousness of advanced sustainability, we shall have to redefine our concepts of political and economic feasibility. These concepts are, after all, simply human constructs; they were different in the past, and they will surely change in the future. But the earth is real, and we are obliged by the fact of our utter dependence on it to listen more closely than we have to its messages.[58]

To help create this consciousness on a worldwide level, the United Nations Environmental Program (UNEP) was formed in 1972 to act as a catalyst to influence the world community to preserve the atmosphere, fresh water, the oceans and seashores, the soil, and precious biological diversity, and to protect our environment against the insults of hazardous wastes and toxic chemicals. The group provided leadership in the negotiation of key international agreements on protection of the ozone layer and transboundary shipments of hazardous waste. Its environmental assessment programs provide an international database which is useful for addressing regional and global environmental management problems including global climate change, ozone depletion, and coastal marine pollution. There are thus some international institutions already functioning that are addressing global environmental concerns.[59]

NEW DIRECTIONS

Regarding environmental developments in the United States, the new Clean Air Act contains a market-oriented strategy with respect to control of sulfur dioxide emissions to attack the acid rain problem. The trading of pollution rights is the centerpiece of the plan, which is something of an experiment that will be watched with great interest. Under the plan, the government will set a national limit on emissions of sulfur dioxide, but instead of dictating how the target will be met, the marketplace will be allowed to determine the cheapest, most efficient way to meet the target. The government will not dictate the technology to be used nor fine companies for not meeting standards, as they do in traditional command-and-control type of regulation.

Each company will be allocated an acceptable level of sulfur dioxide production, which will amount to its fair share of the national limit. If a company manages to produce less than its share, it will receive permits that represent the shortfall, which it can sell to firms that do not meet the target and yet stay in operation. Companies thus have an incentive to cut their emissions so they can profit from selling their surplus permits. At first, these pollution credits will be bought and sold on a statewide basis, but eventually the market will be expanded to cover the entire country. This experiment will be watched with great interest, because theoretically, such a trading system could be set up with just about any kind of pollutant. It is thought that global warming, for example, could be dealt with by an international system of permit trading with regard to carbon dioxide and other greenhouse gases.

There are three approaches to pollution control that involve different administrative and compliance costs. These are command-and-control type of regulations, which are most widely used at present, setting emission fees, and the use of performance standards. Command-and-control regulations allow no flexibility on the part of companies to search out and implement the most cost-effective type of control from a technological and management standpoint. For that reason, this approach to regulation is the most costly option when measured in terms of pollution reduction per dollar spent. But it is the least-cost option for the regulators who will administer the program. They can simply state what must be done by companies and follow up to see that it is done through enforcement activities. This approach emphasizes inputs rather than outputs.[60]

After many failures with this type of regulation, there is a need to experiment with other forms of pollution control that may be more effective. Emission fees are more complex for all parties and are difficult to design and operate. Appropriate fees have to be determined, pollution has to be measured regularly so that charges can be levied, and environmental quality has to be monitored to determine the results obtained from the fee schedule. When conditions change, the fees would have to be altered to reflect these changed conditions. However, such fees would induce cost-effective behavior on the part of polluters and also provide additional revenue to the government that could be used for public purposes.[61]

Performance-based standards, which are being implemented in the new Clean Air Act, involve stating goals for major sources of pollution based on value judgments regarding the protection of human health and the environment, and letting polluters have complete flexibility to choose how to reduce pollution. When coupled with a market mechanism to reward cuts below the standard, a powerful incentive is created to motivate polluter behavior. Progress will have to be monitored to make sure companies are reporting their emissions accurately, but there will be no fines or other enforcement measures imposed on the system. Such standards should be cost effective, as companies will be motivated to use the most effective means to meet the goals that have been set by the government.[62]

In addition to experimenting with different methods of pollution control, the EPA has been admonished for paying too little attention to natural ecosystems over its 20-year history. The agency has considered the protection of public health as its primary mission and has been less concerned about risks posed to ecosystems. This lack of concern reflects society's views as expressed in legislation. Ecological degradation is viewed as a less serious problem because it is subtle, long term, and cumulative. But natural ecosystems such as forests, wetlands, and oceans are extremely valuable, and the EPA was thus asked to correct this imbalance that currently exists in national environmental policy.[63]

Responding to human health risks and largely ignoring risks to ecosystems is inappropriate because in the real world there is little distinction between them, and there is no doubt that over time the quality of human life declines as the quality of natural ecosystems declines. Ecological degradation either directly or indirectly degrades human health as well as the economy. As the extent and quality of saltwater estuaries decline, both human health and local economies are adversely affected. As soils erode, forests, farmlands, and waterways can become less productive. And while the loss of species may not be noticed immediately, over time the decline in genetic diversity has implications for the future health of the human race as a whole.[64]

Human health and welfare in the final analysis rest on the life support systems and natural resources provided by healthy ecosystems. Human beings are part of an interconnected and interdependent global ecosystem, and change in one part of the system affects other parts, often in an unexpected manner. Thus it has been recommended that when the EPA compares the risks posed by different environmental problems in order to set priorities for action, the risks posed to ecological systems must be an important part of the consideration. The EPA's priorities for action should reflect an appropriate balance between ecological, human health, and welfare concerns, and the agency should communicate to the public that it considers ecological risks to be just as serious as risks to human health and welfare, because of the inherent value of ecological systems and their links to human health and welfare.[65]

The EPA is thus being asked to take a more eco-centered approach, and find value in ecosystems as such, rather than simply focusing on human health and welfare. Such a suggestion is consistent with shifting the ethical focus of environmental concerns from a human-centered approach to more of an ecological approach, and attaining a balance between the two approaches. Ecosystems need to be protected for their own sakes, but ecosystems have a direct connection with human well-being, as human life cannot flourish in a degraded environment that is not capable of providing the services necessary for human life to be sustained. It is well to remember that such connections exist in nature, and policy mechanisms and outcomes should reflect this fundamental nature of reality.

~

Questions for Discussion

1. What is a sustainable society? In your opinion, is this a feasible option for industrial societies? Is it necessary? What path is sustainable growth most likely to take in Third World countries?

2. What is intergenerational and intragenerational equity? Does sustainable growth require that these issues be addressed? Why or why not?

What implications does sustainable growth have for the distribution of income and wealth throughout the world?

3. What conditions are necessary to promote sustainable development? How can these conditions be created? What changes would have to be made in governmental policies to bring these conditions about? What changes are necessary in the industrial system?

4. What issues have to be addressed in a sustainable society? Discuss each of these issues and think of policies that could be justified on sustainable grounds. Are these policies realistic for industrial countries? Third World countries?

5. How do we account for progress? What measures are used? Do these measures say anything about resource usage and environmental degradation? What changes would you recommend to reflect reality more accurately?

6. Is a new consciousness necessary for the future? What elements will this new consciousness include? Do you see these elements emerging? What can be done to hasten this development?

7. What institutional changes are necessary to promote sustainability? Are these changes taking place? What kind of systems are most effective for motivating people to respond to environmental problems? Are these in evidence in our society?

8. What new directions are being advocated in our society to deal more effectively with environmental problems? Are these directions consistent with your value system? What else would you recommend?

~

NOTES

1. Lester R. Brown, Christopher Flavin, and Sandra Postel, "Picturing a Sustainable Society," *State of the World 1990* (New York: Norton, 1990), pp. 173–174.
2. Lester R. Brown, Christopher Flavin, and Sandra Postel, "Outlining a Global Action Plan," *State of the World 1989* (New York: Norton, 1989), pp. 174–175.
3. Jim McNeill, "Strategies for Sustainable Economic Development," *Scientific American,* Vol. 261, No. 3 (September 1989), p. 155.
4. Ibid., pp. 155–156.
5. Ibid., p. 156.
6. Ibid.
7. Ibid., p. 157.
8. Ibid.
9. Ibid., pp. 158–163.

10. Ibid., pp. 162–163.

11. Ibid., p. 163.

12. Ibid.

13. Ibid., pp. 163–164.

14. Ibid., p. 164.

15. Ibid., p. 163.

16. John H. Gibbons, Peter D. Blair, and Holly L. Gwin, "Strategies for Energy Use," *Scientific American,* Vol. 261, No. 3 (September 1989), pp. 136–138.

17. Brown, Flavin, and Postel, "Outlining a Global Action Plan," p. 176.

18. Brown, Flavin, and Postel, "Picturing a Sustainable Society," pp. 175–176.

19. Ibid., pp. 177–178.

20. Ibid.

21. Ibid., p. 179.

22. Gibbons, Blair, and Gwin, "Strategies for Energy Use," p. 136.

23. Brown, Flavin, and Postel, "Outlining a Global Action Plan," p. 177.

24. Brown, Flavin, and Postel, "Picturing a Sustainable Society," pp. 181–182.

25. Ibid., pp. 182–183.

26. Ibid., p. 184.

27. Ibid.

28. Brown, Flavin, and Postel, "Outlining a Global Action Plan," pp. 184–185.

29. Lester R. Brown and John E. Young, "Feeding the World in the Nineties," *State of the World 1990* (New York: Norton, 1990), pp. 64–65.

30. Ibid., pp. 60–61.

31. Ibid., pp. 65–68.

32. Brown, Flavin, and Postel, "Outlining a Global Action Plan," pp. 190–191.

33. Alan B. During, "Ending Poverty," *State of the World 1990* (New York: Norton, 1990), pp. 135–136.

34. Ibid., p. 136.

35. Ibid.

36. Ibid., p. 139.

37. Ibid., p. 146.

38. Ibid., p. 148.

39. Ibid., p. 152.

40. Lester R. Brown, "The Illusion of Progress," *State of the World 1990* (New York: Norton, 1990), p. 8. See also Sandra Postel, "Toward a New Eco-nomics," *Worldwatch,* September-October 1990, pp. 20–28.

41. Ibid.

42. Ibid., p. 9.

43. Brown, Flavin, and Postel, "Outlining a Global Action Plan," pp. 192–193.

44. Brown, Flavin, and Postel, "Picturing a Sustainable Society," pp. 188–190.

45. William D. Ruckelhaus, "Toward a Sustainable World," *Scientific American,* Vol. 261, No. 3 (September 1989), p. 167.

46. Ibid., p. 168.

47. Ibid.

48. Ibid., pp. 168–169.

49. Ibid., p. 169.

50. Ibid., pp. 169–172.

51. Sandra Postel, "Accounting for Nature," *Worldwatch,* Vol. 4, No. 2 (March-April 1991), pp. 30 33.

52. Ibid., p. 33.

53. Ruckelshaus, "Toward a Sustainable World," p. 174.

54. Ibid., p. 187.

55. Senator Albert Gore, Jr., "Seizing the International Environmental Initiative," *Harvard International Review,* Vol. XII, No. 4 (Summer 1990), pp. 26–27.

56. Ibid., p. 27.

57. Norman Myers, "Making the World Work for People," *International Wildlife,* Vol. 19, No. 6 (November-December, 1989), p. 14.

58. Ruckelshaus, "Toward a Sustainable World," p. 174.

59. Frederick M. Bernthal, "Recognizing the Global Nature of Environmental Problems," statement before the 15th session of the Governing Council of the United Nations Environment Program, Geneva, Switzerland, May 16, 1988, pp. 1–2.

60. Bruce Yandle, *Why Environmentalists Should Be Efficiency Lovers* (St. Louis: Washington University Center for the Study of American Business, 1991), p. 14.

61. Ibid.

62. Ibid., p. 17.

63. United States Environmental Protection Agency, *Reducing Risk: Setting Priorities and Strategies for Environmental Protection* (Washington, DC: U.S. Government Printing Office, 1990), p. 9.

64. Ibid.

65. Ibid., p. 17.

SUGGESTED READINGS

Berger, John J. Restoring the Earth: *How Americans Are Working to Renew Our Damaged Environment.* New York: Knopf, 1985.

Borelli, Peter, ed. *Crossroads: Environmental Priorities for the Future.* Covelo, CA: Island Press, 1988.

Brown, Lester R., Christopher Flavin, and Sandra Postel. "Outlining a Global Action Plan." *State of the World 1989.* New York: Norton, 1989, pp. 174–175.

Brown, Lester R., Christopher Flavin, and Sandra Postel. "Picturing a Sustainable Society." *State of the World 1990.* New York: Norton, 1990, pp. 173–174.

Clark, W. C. *Sustainable Development of the Biosphere*. New York: Cambridge University Press, 1986.

Collard, David, et al. *Economics, Growth, and Sustainable Environments*. New York: St. Martin's Press, 1988.

Daly, Herman E., and Clifford W. Cobb. *For the Common Good: Redirecting the Economy Toward Community*. Boston: Beacon Press, 1989.

Geller, E. Scott, et al. *Preserving the Environment: New Strategies for Behavior Change*. New York: Pergamon Press, 1982.

Hamrin, Robert D. *A Renewable Resource Economy*. New York: Praeger, 1983.

Henning, Daniel H., and William R. Manguin. *Managing the Environmental Crisis*. Durham, NC: Duke University Press, 1989.

Kristensen, Thorkil, and Johan Peter Paludan. *The Earth's Fragile Systems: Perspectives on Global Change*. Boulder, CO: Westview Press, 1988.

McNeill, Jim. "Strategies for Sustainable Economic Development." *Scientific American*, Vol. 261, No. 3 (September 1989), p. 155.

Pearce, David W., et al. *Sustainable Development: Economics and Environment in the Third World*. Brookfield, VT: Gower, 1990.

Postel, Sandra. "Accounting for Nature." *Worldwatch*. Vol. 4, No. 2 (March-April 1991), pp. 30–32.

Redclift, Michael. *Sustainable Development: Exploring the Contradictions*. New York: Routledge, 1989.

Ruckelshaus, William D. "Toward a Sustainable World." *Scientific American*, Vol. 261, No. 3 (September 1989), p. 167.

Stivers, Robert L. *The Sustainable Society: Ethics and Economic Growth*. Philadelphia: Westminister Press, 1976.

Timberlake, Lloyd. *Only One Earth: Living for the Future*. New York: Sterling, 1987.

United States Environmental Protection Agency. *Reducing Risk: Setting Priorities and Strategies for Environmental Protection*. Washington, DC: U.S. Government Printing Office, 1990.

Uusitalo, Lisa, ed. *Consumer Behavior and Environmental Quality: Trends and Prospects in the Ways of Life*. New York: St. Martin's Press, 1983.

INDEX